[Archigram]

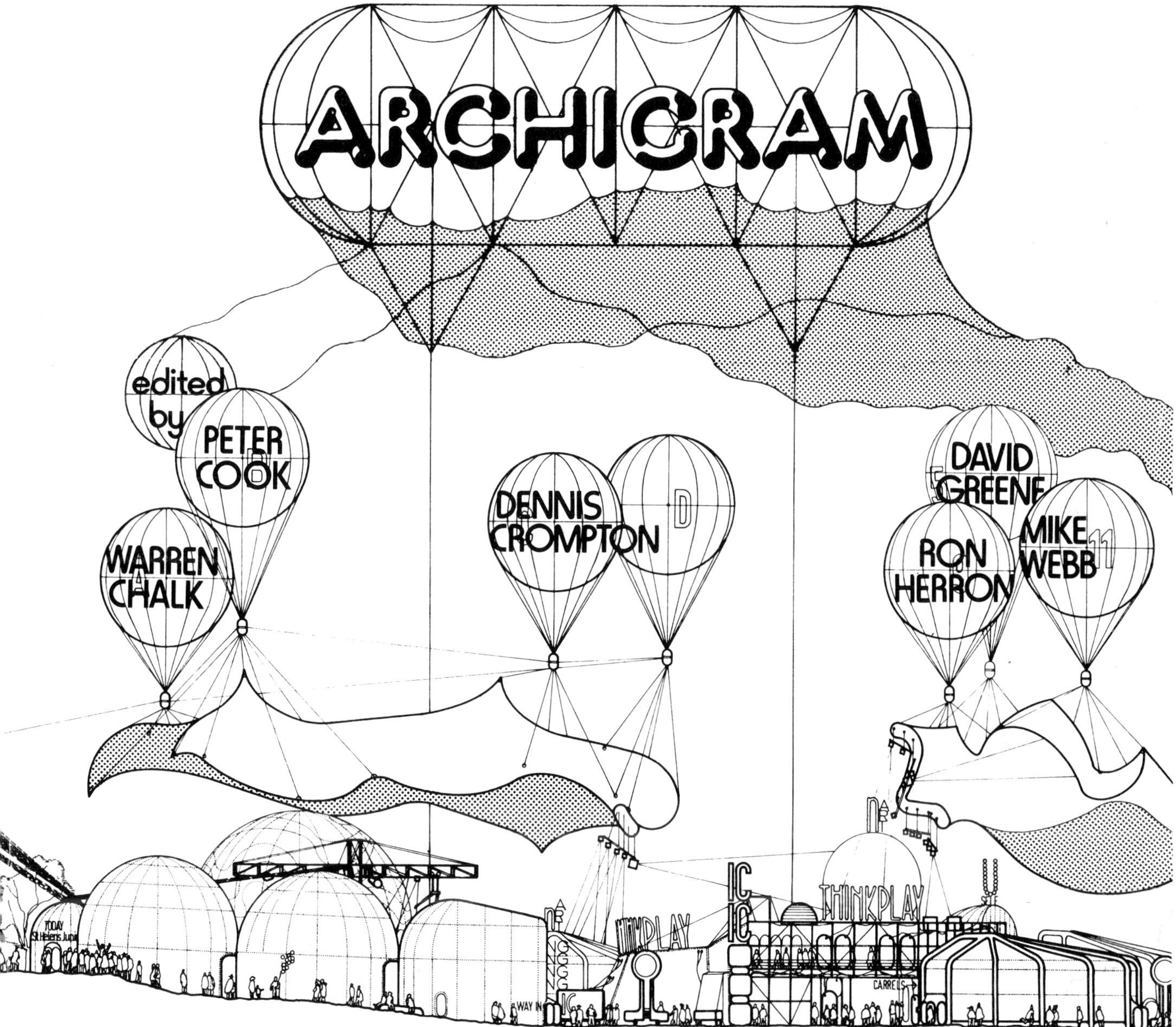

PRAEGER PUBLISHERS
New York · Washington

Notes on the making of the book

Originally we started to collect the material of the earlier issues of *Archigram* magazine so that it could be reprinted in one volume. Soon, though, we began to feel the limitations of this. We could tell that our efforts had progressively shifted outwards, and that the magazine – the thing which had originally brought the Archigram *group* together – had become but one of a series of vehicles for our ideas.

Primarily we are concerned with the development of ideas, by way of *design* as the mode of experiment. Somehow, a reciprocity sets up between objective notions and specific designs. There seems to be no describable structure to the way in which these refine, except that among the group there is from time to time an intense welling-up of enthusiasm for a group of ideas and (perhaps much later) we realize that we have set for ourselves a *Gestalt*.

It then seems that cheerfully, and without perversion, we disintegrate the structure of our work from within – almost as soon as it can be defined. This is consistent with our attitude towards change, and our mistrust of 'definitive' architecture. It is therefore a natural consequence that the notion of metamorphosis should recur so often, particularly in our more recent work. This book has itself metamorphosed from a reprint job to a chronicle and (a little) from a chronicle to an attempt to summarize certain phases or syndromes. This accounts for some jumps and shifts within an otherwise sequential presentation.

Wherever possible we have attempted to present a project in the way in which it was illustrated at the time of its design. The text has been written by us all in part – so the writing style is probably patchy. We hope that it is understandable.

Peter Cook

BOOKS THAT MATTER

Published in the United States of America in 1973
by Praeger Publishers, Inc., 111 Fourth Avenue,
New York, N.Y. 10003

Library of Congress Catalog Card Number: 72–92494

Printed in Great Britain

Contents

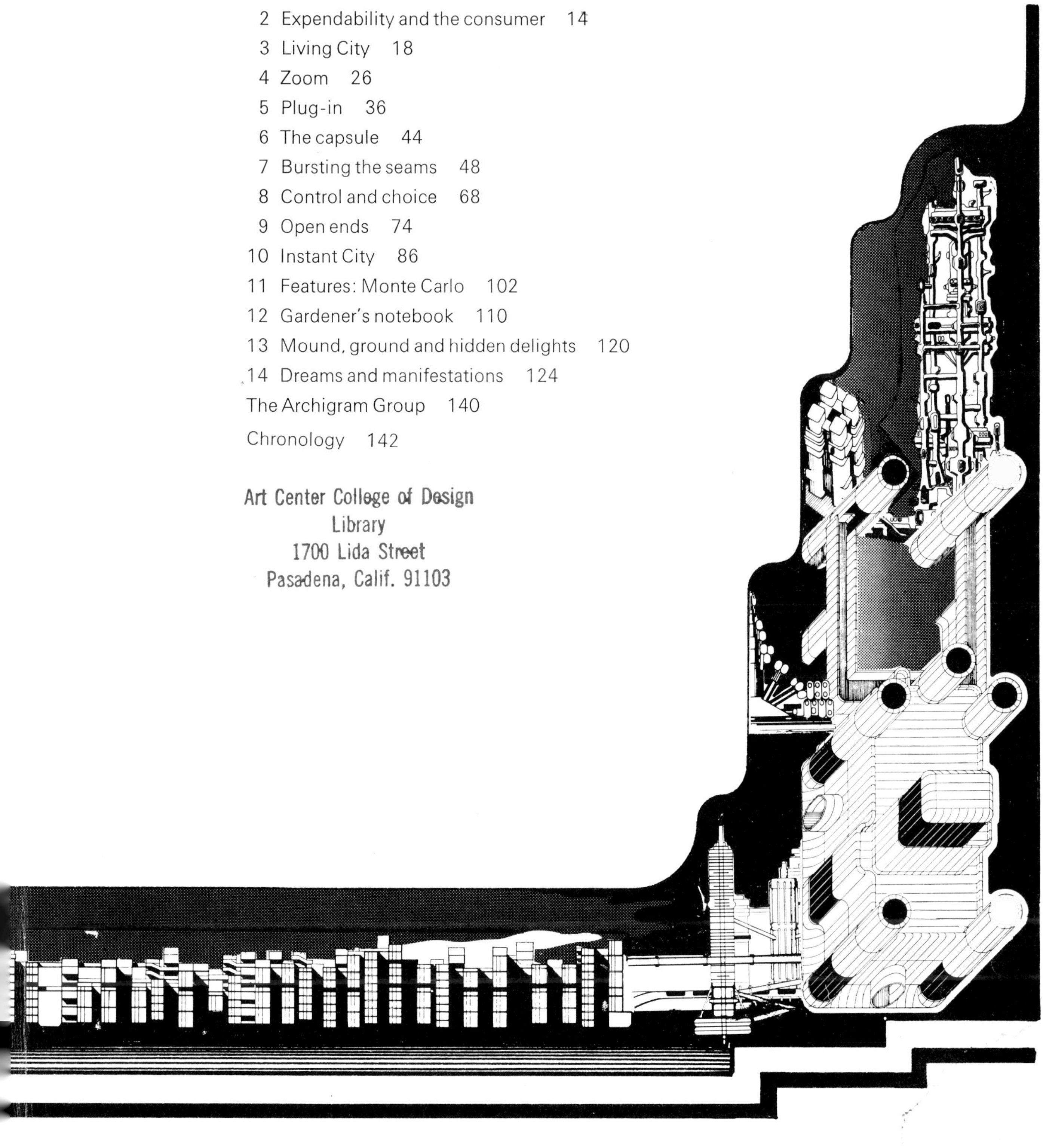

A comment from Arata Isozaki

It was during the mid-1960s. Living in this confused, swelling city of the Far East, I was struck by a series of extraordinary and not undisturbing shock waves emanating from London. I did not resist them, and they lulled me into a pleasant intoxication. There was Pinter's drama, the pop music of the Beatles and Pink Floyd, and the miniskirts of Carnaby Street. But above all there was the enormous destructive power carried to me on the wings of an underground magazine called *Archigram*.

Like artistic movements of the past, these shock waves of the 60s were characterized by their imprecations against the means and ends of the Establishment, but unlike past movements this one had no manifesto. Nor does it seem possible that the Establishment, with the heart of the data-manipulating mechanism of our age resting firmly in its grip, might be shaken by the static act of manifesto manufacture. No, the Establishment is clever: it is a master of disguise, pervading every corner of our daily lives, at times even posing as ourselves. No direct blow, however fierce, can disturb this situation. What is necessary is to exchange our old methods and material for pulses capable of beaming complex stimuli to the senses over a prolonged period of time.

In this society, where information is privileged above all else, *Archigram* has created possibly the only style capable of inducinr radical change. To compose a manifes is a relatively easy task. To direct a virtu shower of projects at the entire world ar to maintain that shower over a period (ten years, however, is an achievement ı no such mean dimensions. Behind it lie almost inconceivable effort.

The reason I value *Archigram's* work ove all that which has been performed durin the last ten years to dismantle the apparatus of Modern Architecture is that it has beer consistently counter-cultural in character *Archigram* has not limited its area of planning to architecture alone. At times its work has been graphic. At times it has been plastic. And at times it has taken the form of new technical proposals. In each case, however, the work done has been totally divorced from the patterned logic architecture has created within itself. When all values have thus been turned topsy turvy, *Archigram* has established a ne structure of values, a new syntax, an demonstrated the possibility of an inde pendent subculture. Japan's Metabolisı Group, in contrast to *Archigram*, lacke this perspective on the necessity of dis covering counter-cultural values. As result, it made the easy identification wit the ideas of managerial planning in th rapidly expanding city economy, an ultimately found itself being manipulate in the interests of the government's mere tricious policies.

Archigram's work is being assessed an appreciated anew today because, no merely in architecture, but in a far broad sphere, pre-established systems of ever kind are disintegrating before our eye What *Archigram* has done is to demonstrat clearly one part of this process. It is m hope that with the publication of *Archigram's* work of the last ten years an eve more intense exchange of communicatio will take place, that the malignant cells c the counter culture will be transplanted t every part of the world, to every area o culture, and that the process of disintegration will become increasingly violen and universal.

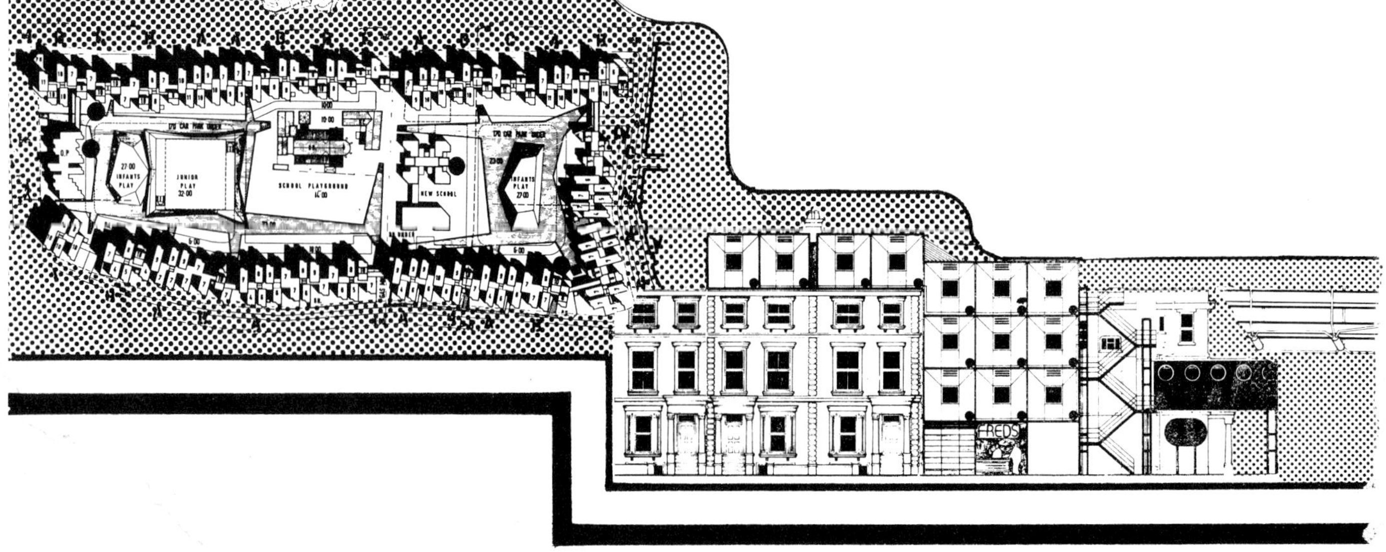

A comment from Peter Reyner Banham

Free inflatable venus de milo offer with every urban rapid transit system purchased (offer terminates shortly before twentieth century).

Annually, around the beginning of August, a big car appears in our road. I know it's coming, because I have seen it an hour, a day, a week earlier in Carnaby Street. It is usually a Mercedes, registered in Amsterdam, Dusseldorf, Brussels, Zurich, Hong Kong, Milan . . . In it are four intense young men in gear and sun glasses appropriate to the mode of the day, and a stunning bird, usually Japanese or Black-is-Beautiful.

The car eases itself to a halt by the kerb alongside me, the driver winds the window down and asks, in English only slightly tinged with his native accent, 'Can you direct us to the bureau of the Archigram organization?' And I look diagonally across Aberdare Gardens from 64 to 59 and say, 'Yes, it's over there, but I wouldn't bother if I were you because I can see the living room window is shut and that means neither Peter nor Hazel is in . . .' Then I take pity on them and explain that the address they all know from the subscription form is just the Cooks' private flat, and that (until the Monaco job) was the entire office space of the Archigram-What Organization-You-Must-Be-Joking-Mate.

Sharing a street in NW6 with Archigram has always been interesting; as a family we had a hand in *Archigram 7* (my son helped pack and fold it) and I had the privilege of taking the first hot-off-the-press copies of *Amazing Zoom Archigram Four* to the US (because I met P. Cook in the street the night before I flew out). It has provided me with the kind of ringside view of a Movement that every critic or historian should experience at least once for the sake of his education. As a result I am one of the few non-members of the group to attempt to lecture on Archigram, which brings me to Baffled Archiquery No. 2.

In its purest form (Rosario, Argentina, July 18, 1968) it reads: 'How are the theoric propositions of Archigram realized in everyday working?' and it is related to Archiquery No. 1 (Can you direct, etc.) by a strong thread of total incredulity, viz., that all the work books, drawings, slide shows, films, happenings, conferences – is done by the six to eight principals who normally comprise the group, with their own fair hands, in their own time and in the privacy of their own homes for the sheer hell of doing it.

'Theoric propositions?' You too must be joking, *caballero*! Archigram is short on theory, long on draughtsmanship and craftsmanship. They're in the image business and they have been blessed with the power to create some of the most compelling images of our time. In Rosario the Fifth Year Studio was lined with megastructures plugged full of capsules. The only thing that wasn't strictly from Aberdare Gardens was the load of Theoric Propositions the Rosarians had draped over them – Urban Identity, Spatial Integrity, Alienation, and all that.

We don't use that kind of language in NW6. Hard as it may be for the average Cand. Phil. from Gothenburg or Lisbon to comprehend, it's all done for the giggle. Like, designing for pleasure, doing your own thing with the conviction that comes from the uninhibited exercise of creative talent braced by ruthless self-criticism. It's rare in any group – having the guts to do what you want, and the guts to say what you think – and because it's so rare it's beyond quibble. You accept Archigram at it's own valuation or not at all, and there's been nothing much like that since Frank Lloyd Wright, Mies and Corb . . . 'Keep together, boys,' said Duke Ellington as the band passed under the busts of Bach and Beethoven in Carnegie Hall, 'we're in fast company!'

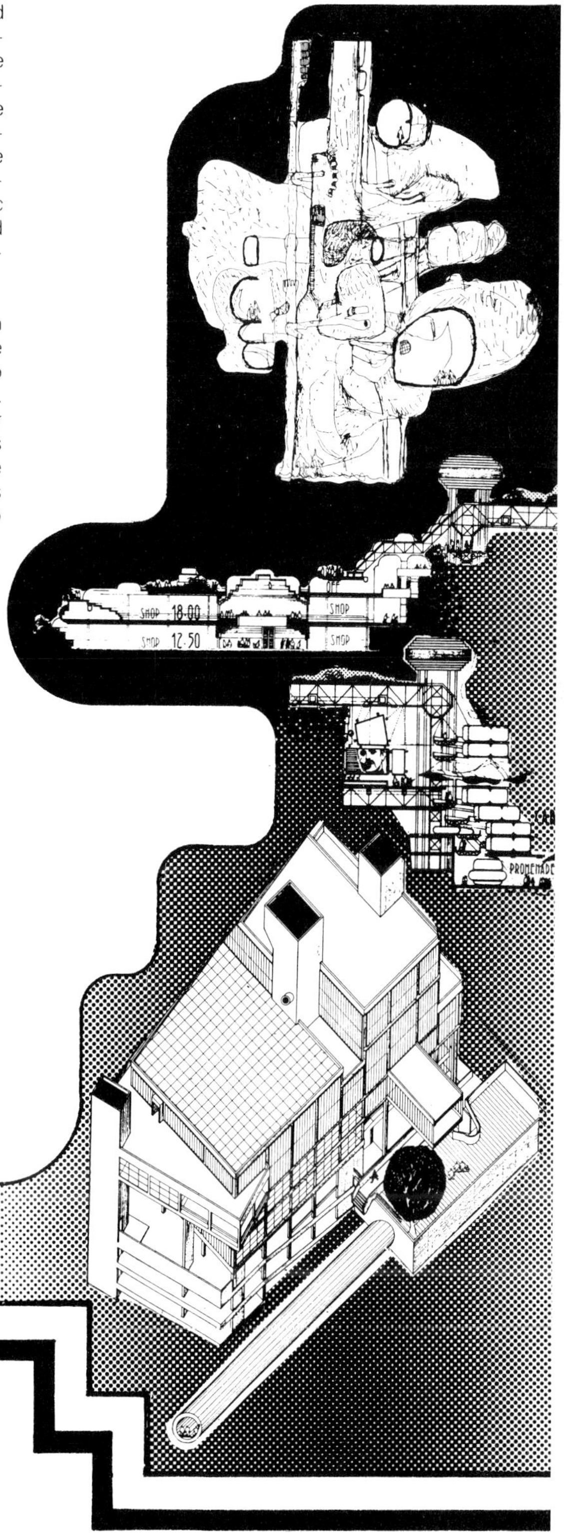

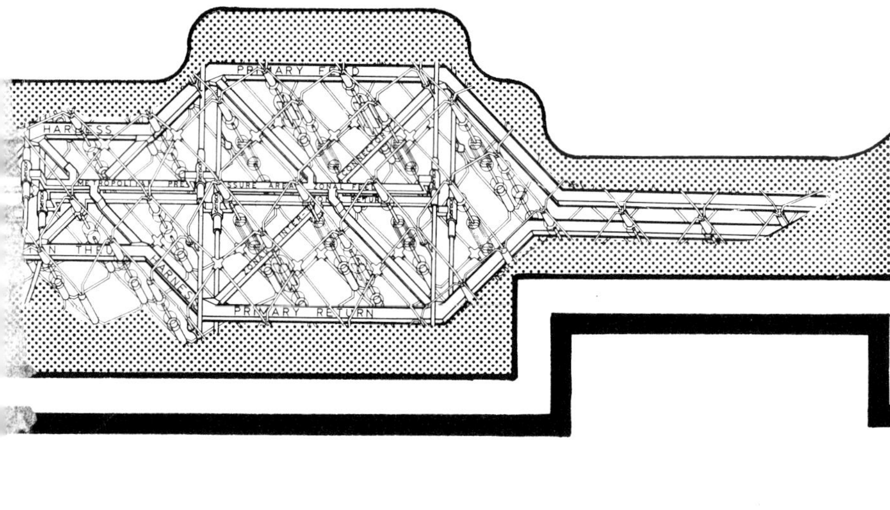

A comment from Hans Hollein

In 1964 Philip Johnson handed me a copy of – some kind of – a magazine with the remark that it carried one of my projects and that he thought I would like it (this strange or funny magazine) and that I could keep it. This was my first encounter with *Archigram*, and from the first moment flipping through it, unfolding cut-out models of cities, meeting those to me so familiar images, magazine-clippings and historical references, I had a sense of kinship, of common endeavour, of parallel efforts and (possibly) goals.

Subsequent contacts revealed that Archigram was not only a magazine title but was also *people* – most important, and later personal meetings, at various places all over the world, showed them further not to be a single-minded body but a many facetted organism, a cluster of very separate individualities, tied together by common background, by common point of 'take off' (often 'zooming' away in very different directions), by common beliefs for new necessities but also as much just by emotion. Also tied together – especially after dispersion – by communication, demonstrating in their own sphere some of the axioms of their philosophy – flexibility, mobility, impermanence, *ad-hoc*. With a number of them I became good friends, the ways, the means how, the reasons why and the places where we met are again proving correct a certain way of thinking, a certain belief.

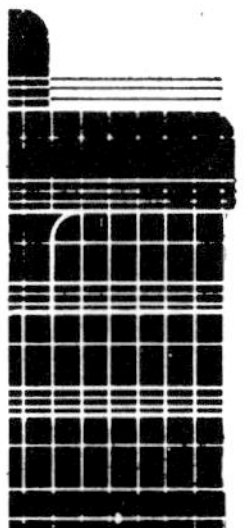

Architecture is a medium of communication. And what attracted me on my first encounter with Archigram (maybe because it seemed so parallel to my own thinking) was their realization of this conception in the widest sense, and with a clear – however intuitively based – strategy.

To clear the ground one had to create a new spirit and a new understanding of architecture, and at a certain point in the development and propagation of this idea certain means and media were almost mandatory to open the debate. The international style and the international scene had stagnated. The great builders had little more to offer. The dogmas had been formulated some time ago (and partly had been *built* in the meantime). One was talking niceties and published a lot of buildings (if possible photographed by Ezra Stoller) and marginal comments centered around the problems of this realization. Hardly ever discussed were new concepts and ideas. These discussions had to be reopened and provoked. A new generation had built little or nothing and thus could not enter the debate with buildings. It questioned whether it should even enter this debate with buildings, more – whether the building was worthwhile discussing. One wanted to discuss subjects instead of objects, *Konzepte* instead of *Rezepte*. One also wanted to discuss 'city' and 'life' in its widest sense.

At this specific time, the late 50s and early 60s, almost simultaneously at various places in the world, be it Japan, England or Austria, this discussion was started. It had to be provoked. To do this, to give this discussion the broadest possible base, certain means and media were developed – independently, but rather similar. I want to label them *evocative images*. Plug-in cities with cranes hovering, walking cities, cities of giant trusses between giant doric columns, aircraft-carrier-city in a landscape. The message these images carried had an immediate impact. Suddenly, the dialogue started and has not stopped yet.

The great importance of Archigram (the people and the magazine) at that initial phase was that both their work and the medium – the magazine – carried this evocative, provocative substance. I do not think Archigram has lost this momentum. They have progressed from the initial stage and ventured into a variety of avenues, at times fascinated by modern technology and space-age gadgets, at times more English, eccentrics in insular isolation, with a stiff upper lip, and a disregard for developments elsewhere. Interestingly, they have always remained architects.

For a while it seemed that their work was lacking in social (and political) conscience, disregarding the single individual in favour of a technological supremacy. I trust this proves incorrect, looking at their work in a long span, with emphasis on different aspects at due times. Their ideas are always for *people*, for a better *life* for people. There may be a lot of exclusions. But then there are so many who can continue and expand their work. Archigram (the people) have also to be understood as teachers, *Archigram* (the magazine) as an educational campaign.

The time of the 'evocative images' is mainly over. It is also no longer the question to stimulate discussion. It is on. Many battles have been won. The Archigram ideas and imagery have been integrated by the students, the establishment and profiteer-architects. This is as comforting – because of the success of an idea – as it is saddening – because the idealists have much success but little possibility to realize their ideas themselves – which would mean best and not perverted. Many thoughts of Archigram seem, after having been formulated, so selfevident, almost so commonplace, that they soon will not be regarded as specific utterances, as individual viewpoints, but as expressions of common, hidden, subconscious longings. They became part of a new architectural vernacular which to an outsider obscures the source. He mistakes the clever implementor for the inventor.

Archigram will be on new tracks. In a world which measures the difference between a world champion and his runner-up is 1/100th of a second, Archigram very often, and especially at some decisive and crucial points in the formulation of new architectural thinking, have been ahead just this decisive 1/100th of a second before many others, 'archizooming' behind them.

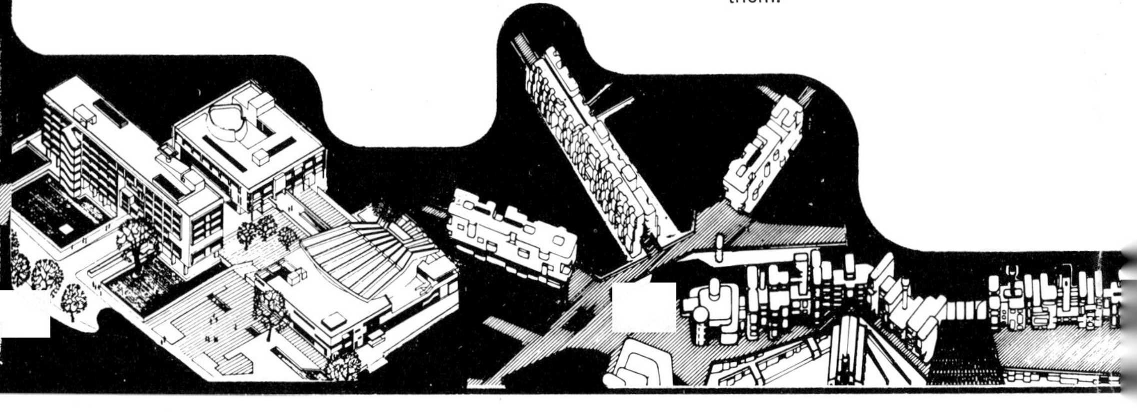

A comment from Peter Blake

I can't think of any one, identifiable event that broadened my own perceptions as drastically as the advent of Archigram. At least in the area of architecture and related matters. Until the day when the first Archigram manifesto appeared on my desk, I had been working and thinking pretty much in the standard, establishment fashion of the 1950s: Great Form Makers, the pure Miesian tradition, everything neat and nice. It is true that I had long been interested in peripheral areas: Charles Eames got me excited over marine hardware, Giedion told me about nineteenth-century Patent Office drawings and models of various kinds of equipment, and Philip Johnson lead me to Machine Art. But, on the whole, architecture and urban design, to my mind, had to do with the Great Form Makers – Wright, Corbu, Mies, Grope, with occasional explorations of De Stijl and Rietveld, of the Russian Constructivists, of the Italian Futurists, and so on.

Then Archigram struck, and my world hasn't been the same since. I took off for Cape Kennedy (and I've gone there several times since) and saw that 'walking buildings' easily the size of Seagram were, in fact, a reality; that plug-in capsules containing highly sophisticated workshops, and unpluggable at any time, were, in fact, a daily reality in the huge gantries that service the Saturn rockets; that megastructures with floors that slide up and down and sideways were not something that Harvard students did when they wanted to cop out, but were, in fact, a stunning reality in the largest building on earth – the Vehicle Assembly Building, a structure so vast that it could have something like eight Seagrams wheeled into it, and plug those Seagrams into capsules and mobile floors and all the rest; a structure so vast that, under certain weather conditions, clouds sometimes form near its ceiling, 500 ft-plus above sea-level; and it sometimes rains inside.

I really would not have known where to look if it hadn't been for *Archigram*. Oh, well, I might have got there sooner or later, but life is short and so I owe Archigram half a dozen years. Everything, absolutely everything, suddenly became architecture: I saw an ad in *Time* magazine, I think, and it showed an aerial view of a completely prefabricated town, with its own roads, heliport, offices, housing, factory, and built-in mobility. It also happened to be afloat about ten miles due South of Shreveport, Louisiana, and it was one of dozens of such science-fiction 'towns' in the Gulf that mined the bottom of the ocean. (That same day somebody announced one of those US 'New Towns' that look like a slicked-up Welwyn Garden City.) It seemed to me that John Johansen would be somebody to commission to write for the *Architectural Forum* about that floating city – and I called him and he flew down there and *his* life was changed a bit, too.

So we all owe something very important to Archigram: the dramatic broadening of our perceptions, our visions. Since Archigram, some of the things that have *really* interested me are, for example, Disney World – an absolutely staggering New Town twice the size of Manhattan, with capsulated hotels traversed by monorail trains, and a navy that ranks ninth in the world, and a submarine fleet that ranks fifth, right after the US, the USSR, Britain and France. It has cost $400 million so far, and that is only 10 per cent of it: when its STOL Port and its jetport and its four additional US-Steel-prefabbed hotels and its satellite EPCOT (Experimental Prototype Community Of Tomorrow) are completed, Walt Disney World will run into the billions – and it will be by far the most ambitious New Town on earth. Before Archigram, I would have sneered – as, indeed, I did at Disneyland, California (Charlie Eames bawled me out for that); since Archigram, and its consciousness-raising manifestoes, I no longer sneer.

When I think about what Archigram did for me and for some of my contemporaries, I am suddenly reminded of Le Corbusier's *Vers Une Architecture* – a pamphlet that, in the early 1920s, spelled out visions of a new world through images of automobiles and ships and planes, and of silos and factories, and of plumbing fixtures. The pamphlet has a quaint look about it now, and it needed up-dating. My friends at Archigram have done that job – and a great deal more. And, because of what they have done, the world of architecture in this century and the next will never again be quite as projected.

P.S. Critics of Archigram, especially after reading the above, are sure to ask: 'What about the human factor?' – or something like that. The answer, I think, is this: Le Corbusier's most widely-quoted dictum was: 'A house is a machine for living in.' And the same question was asked of him. None of his questioners really understood, for Corbu was talking about *French* machines – machines that are ravishingly beautiful, but don't necessarily work terrifically well. Corbu's machines were poetic machines; and Archigram's machines are equally poetic. 'What about the human factor?' Well, I cannot think of a more humanistic language than the language of poetry; and whether they like it or not, the Archigram gang is a gang of wild-eyed poets.

Archigram 1

In late 1960, in various flats in Hampstead, a loose group of people started to meet: to criticize projects, to concoct letters to the press, to combine to make competition projects, and generally prop one another up against the boredom of working in London architectural offices. The inevitable 'grapevine' accounted for the dispersed origins: the 'AA', the Regent Street Polytechnic, Bristol, Nottingham. The instinct was to continue the polemic and enthusiasm of architecture school (all were recent graduates), and it became obvious that some publication would help. The main British magazines did not at that time publish student work, so that *Archigram* was reacting to this as well as the general sterility of the scene. The title came from the notion of a more urgent and simple item than a journal, like a 'telegram' or 'aerogramme', hence 'archi(tecture)-gram'. The large discussion group began to disintegrate with the realization that within it was a wide divergence of outlook. By this time Peter Cook, David Greene and Mike Webb, in making a broadsheet, had started a new Group.

It was as important to break down real and imagined barriers of form and statement on the page as in built form on the ground, as in these poems by David Greene:

The love is gone.
The poetry in bricks is lost.
We want to drag into building some of the poetry of countdown, orbital helmets,
discord of mechanical body transportation methods and leg walking
Love gone.

Lost
our fascinating intricate
movings are trapped in soggen
brown packets all hidden all
art and front, no bone no love.

A new generation of architecture must arise
with forms and spaces which seems to reject
the precepts of 'Modern' yet in fact
retains these precepts. WE HAVE CHOSEN TO
BYPASS THE DECAYING BAUHAUS IMAGE
WHICH IS AN INSULT TO FUNCTIONALISM.

You can roll out steel   any length
You can blow up a balloon   any size
You can mould plastic   any shape
blokes that built the forth bridge
THEY DIDN'T WORRY
You can roll out paper   any length
take Chambers' dictionary THAT'S LONG

You can build concrete   any height
FLOW? water flows or doesn't or does
flow or not flows
YOU CAN WEAVE STRING   any mesh
TAKE THIS TABLE you've got a top there
top and four legs
you can sit IN it you sit ON it, UNDER it or half under

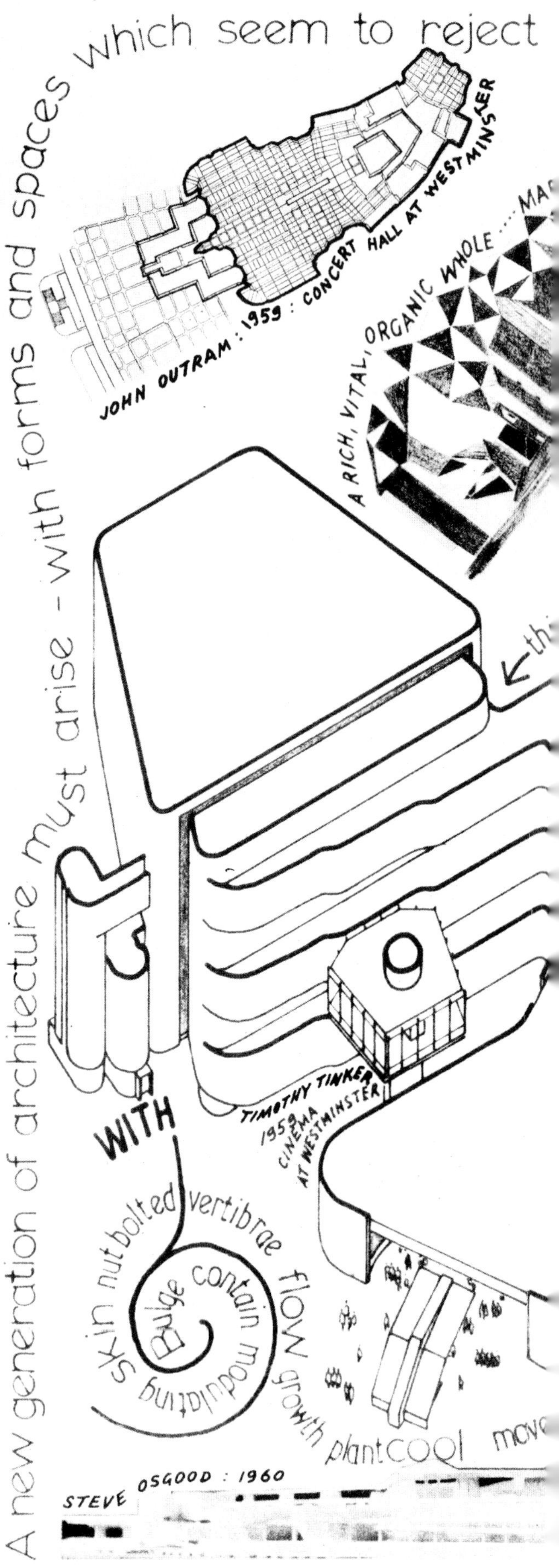

Archigram 1 Published May 1961 Peter Cook and David Greene

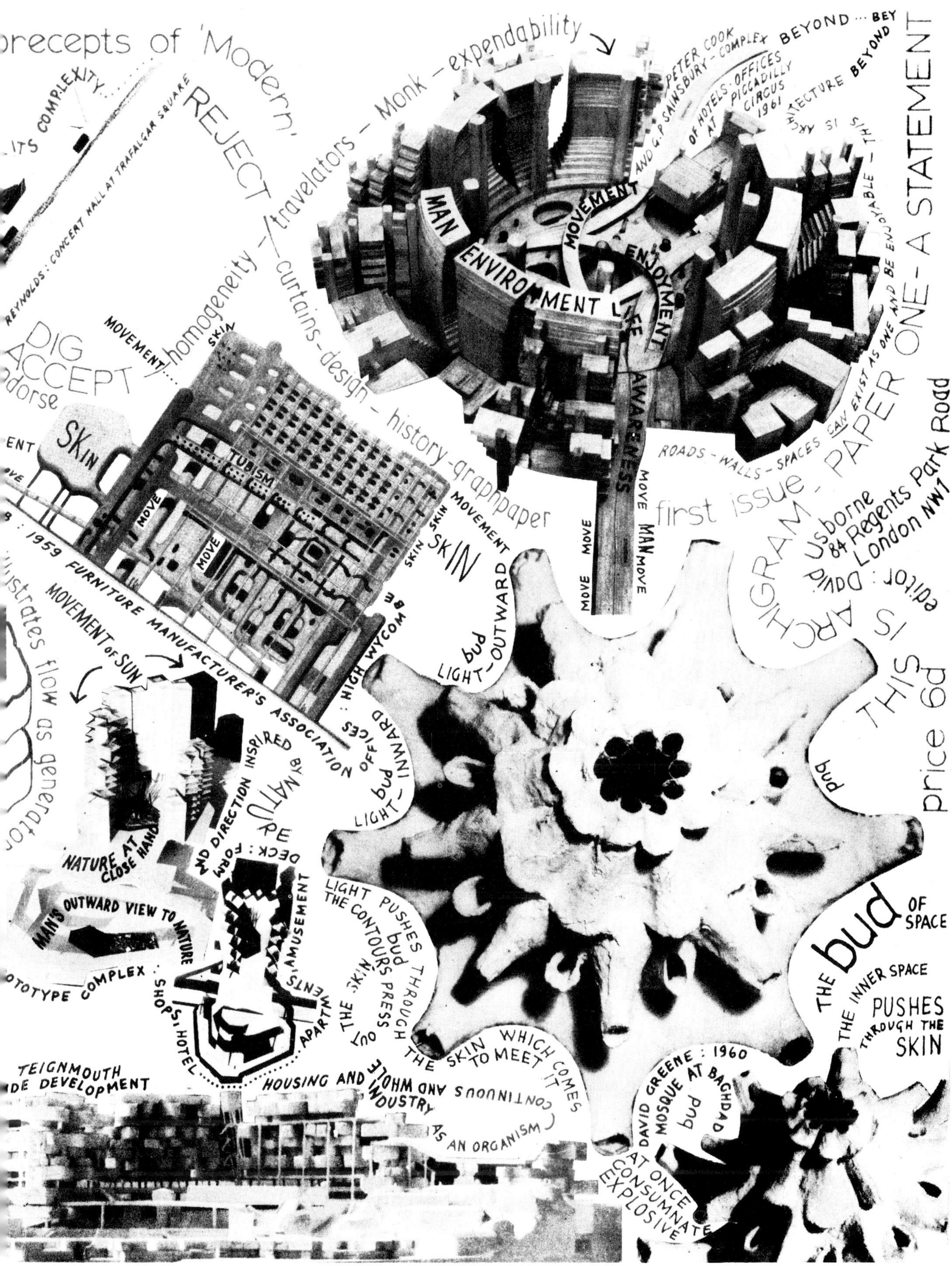

Main page from *Archigram 1*

Mike Webb Furniture Manufacturers Association Building for High Wycombe (Project set to Mike Webb whilst in 4th Year at Regent Street Polytechnic) 1957

top Elevation Furniture Manufacturers Association

centre Plan

below Peter Cook: Metal Cabin Housing: 1962

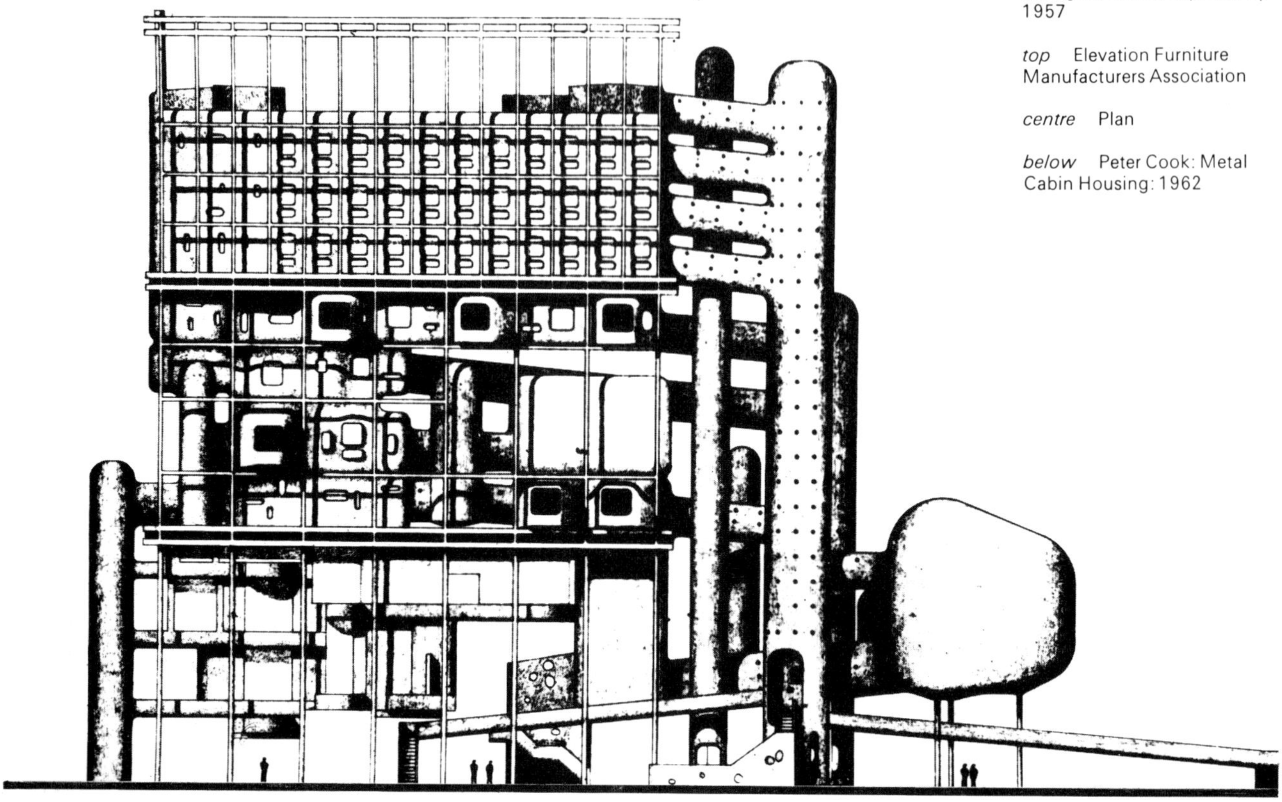

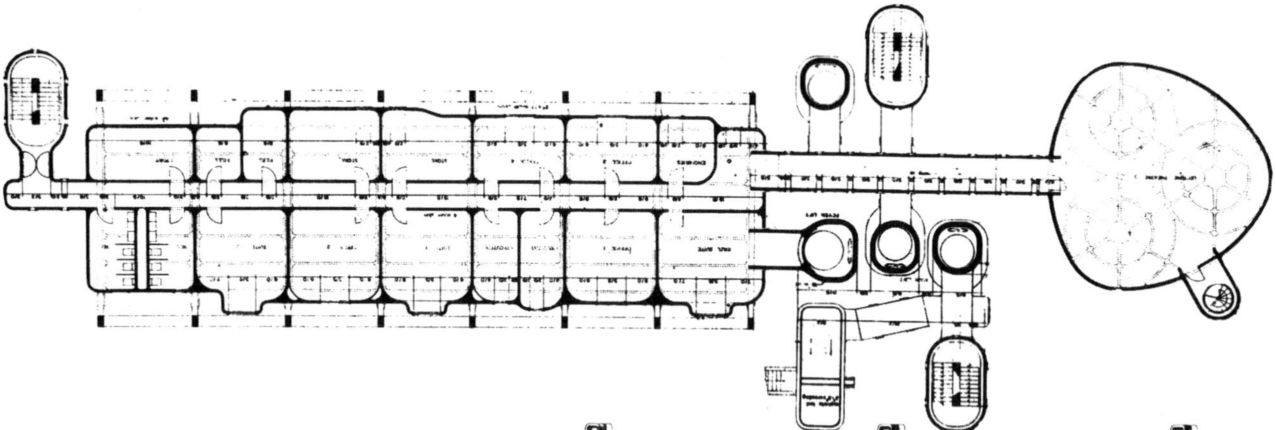

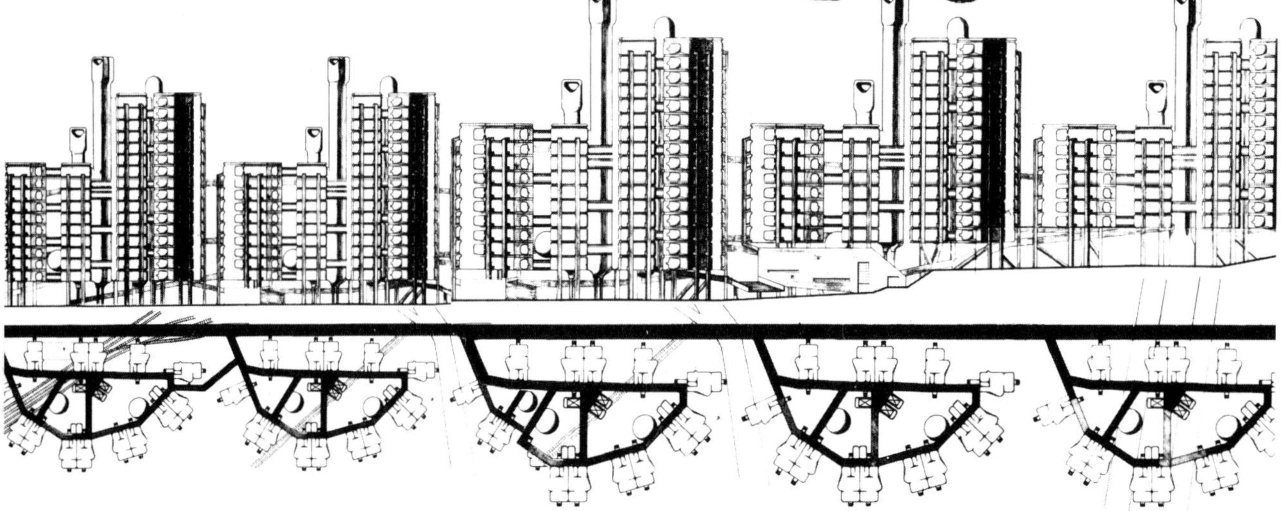

Furniture Manufacturers Association: end elevation

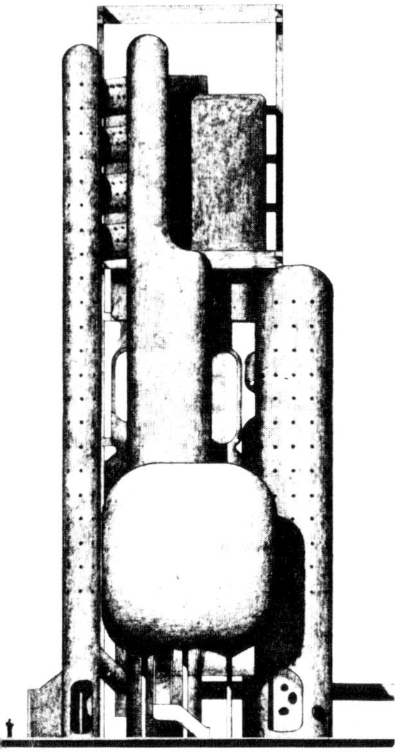

Cliffside Entertainments Stalk: sketch 1961 David Greene

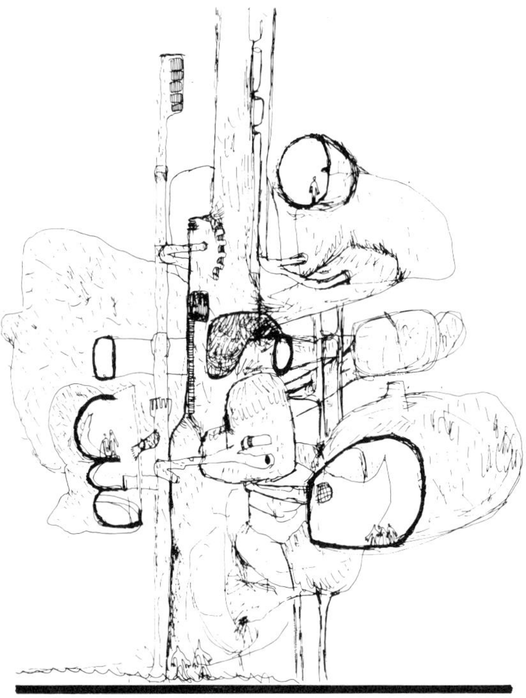

Cliffside Entertainments Stalk: fibreglass model 1961 David Greene

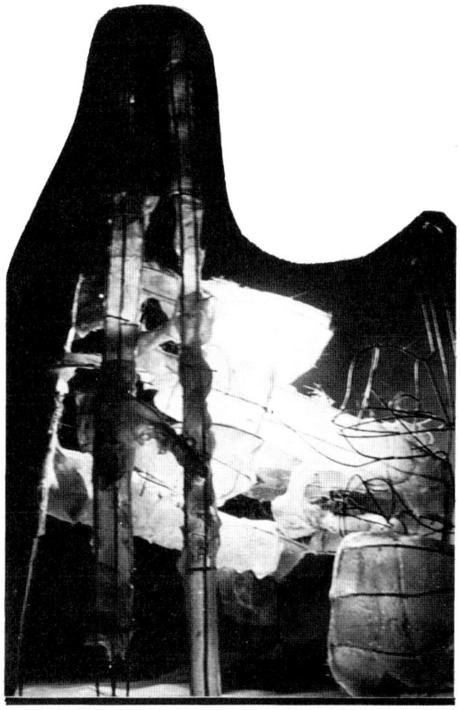

centre Spray Plastic House 1962 David Greene

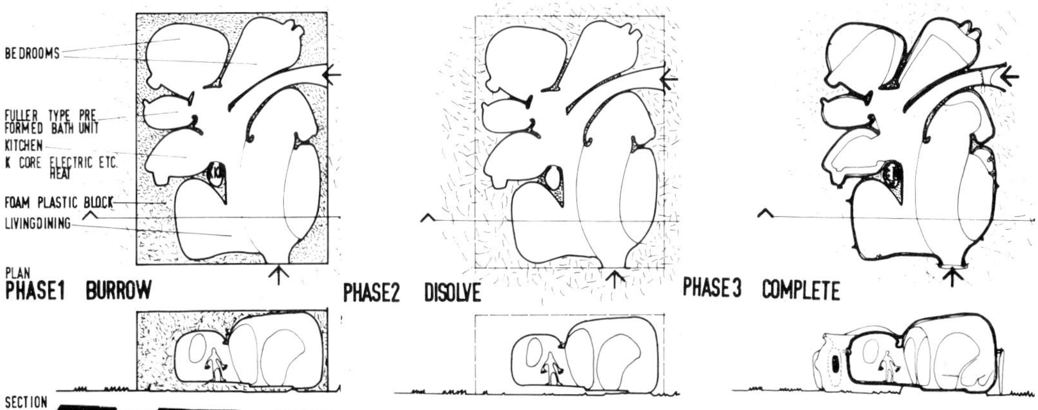

below Elevation and Plan Halesowen Housing Competition 1958 (2nd prize-winning design) Ron Herron and Warren Chalk

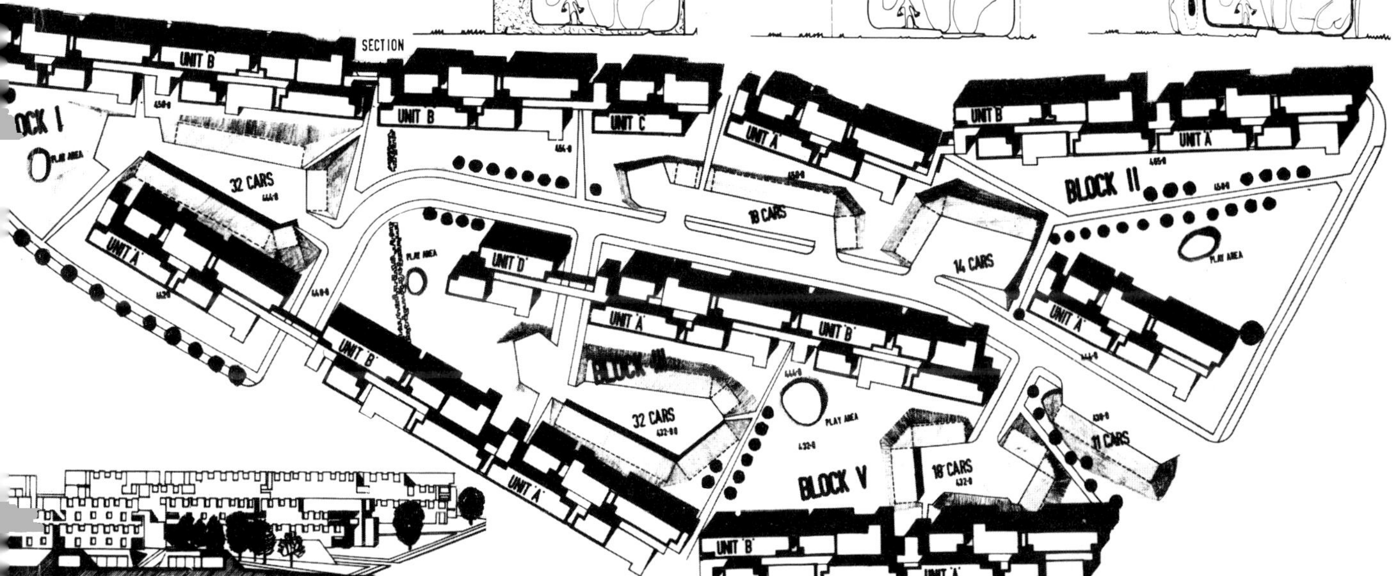

Sin Centre Entertainments Centre for Leicester Square 1959–62 Mike Webb (Thesis project at Regent Street Polytechnic)

Sin Centre

Mike Webb

The scheme is for an entertainments' palace on the site of the Empire Theatre, Leicester Square (that is, close enough to Piccadilly Circus to attract large crowds). A large department store at street level and 10,000 square feet of office space is placed above. The entertainments palace includes a bowling alley, cinema, theatre, dance area, coffee bars, pubs, etc. In a scheme of this nature where large crowds are present the circulatory systems become very important in order to maintain an easy flow through the various spaces. The circulatory systems, vehicular and pedestrian, are specially designed units, the juxtaposition of which generates the overall form of the building. Of the three main types of car parking – customer, attendant and mechanical parking (autosilo) – customer parking was found to be the most suitable for this scheme. The building is conceived as a 'drive-in galleria', that is, an extension of the street inside the building (cf. Kahn's circular parking towers for Philadelphia). After considering many car ramp layouts, a system of two separate ramps was chosen, taking cars up and down respectively. Cross-over ramps enable cars to switch from the up to the down ramp. The total capacity is 350 cars. Pedestrian access to the platforms is by travelators and escalators. There is a visual and structural similarity between these two systems of access, the latter being a rectangular version of the former.

The entertainments palace decks are dependent for their form on the possible permutations arising out of their position in relation to the two fixed circulatory systems (vehicular and pedestrian). The accompanying illustrations show the component basic parts – into which the scheme breaks down. The relationship between the vehicle and pedestrian access systems is fixed; the decks, however, are interchangeable and the formal layout is only one of many possible permutations.

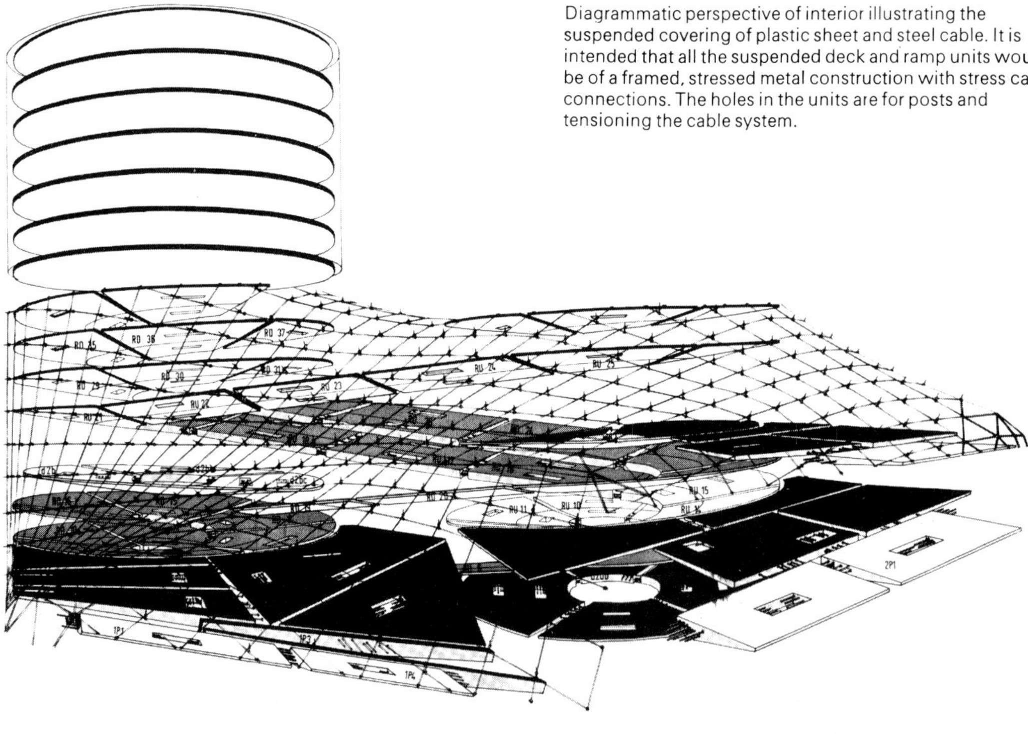

Diagrammatic perspective of interior illustrating the suspended covering of plastic sheet and steel cable. It is intended that all the suspended deck and ramp units would be of a framed, stressed metal construction with stress cable connections. The holes in the units are for posts and tensioning the cable system.

The two access systems are designed to act as vast springs – one circular, the other rectangular – which are prevented from deflection by concentric, strutted transverse springs in the form of escape staircases. The decks are composed of aluminium units prestressed together so that the whole building may become 'live' (i.e. giving an inherent understanding of the forces present in the structure). The unit joints would be covered by the floor finish.

The curved glass roof filled with advertising signs is formed from steel cables anchored to the structure. The cladding is of transparent plastic panels connected to each other with flexible joints. The cable network binds the whole structure together inducing automatic prestressing of the aluminium deck units.

The floors of the circular office block on top of the building are hung by means of tension cables from heavy cantilever beams supported off the top of the staircase towers. The services of the building have been laid out to emphasize the focal points of the structure (i.e. the staircase towers). Thus drawings produced by structural engineers, heating and ventilating engineers, lighting consultants and drainage contractors all have the same points of visual emphasis.

Sin Centre: photograph of model

Sin Centre: section and elements

The symbols and numbers used for these parts are as follows:

RU: Vehicle Ramp Up (i-27)
RD: Vehicle Ramp Down (38-1)
GP: Ground Floor Pedestrian Access (1, 2)
1P: First Floor Pedestrian Access (1-4)
2P: Second Floor Pedestrian Access (1, 2)
3P: Third Floor Pedestrian Access (1, 2)
Vehicle Access System: Blue; Decks: Red

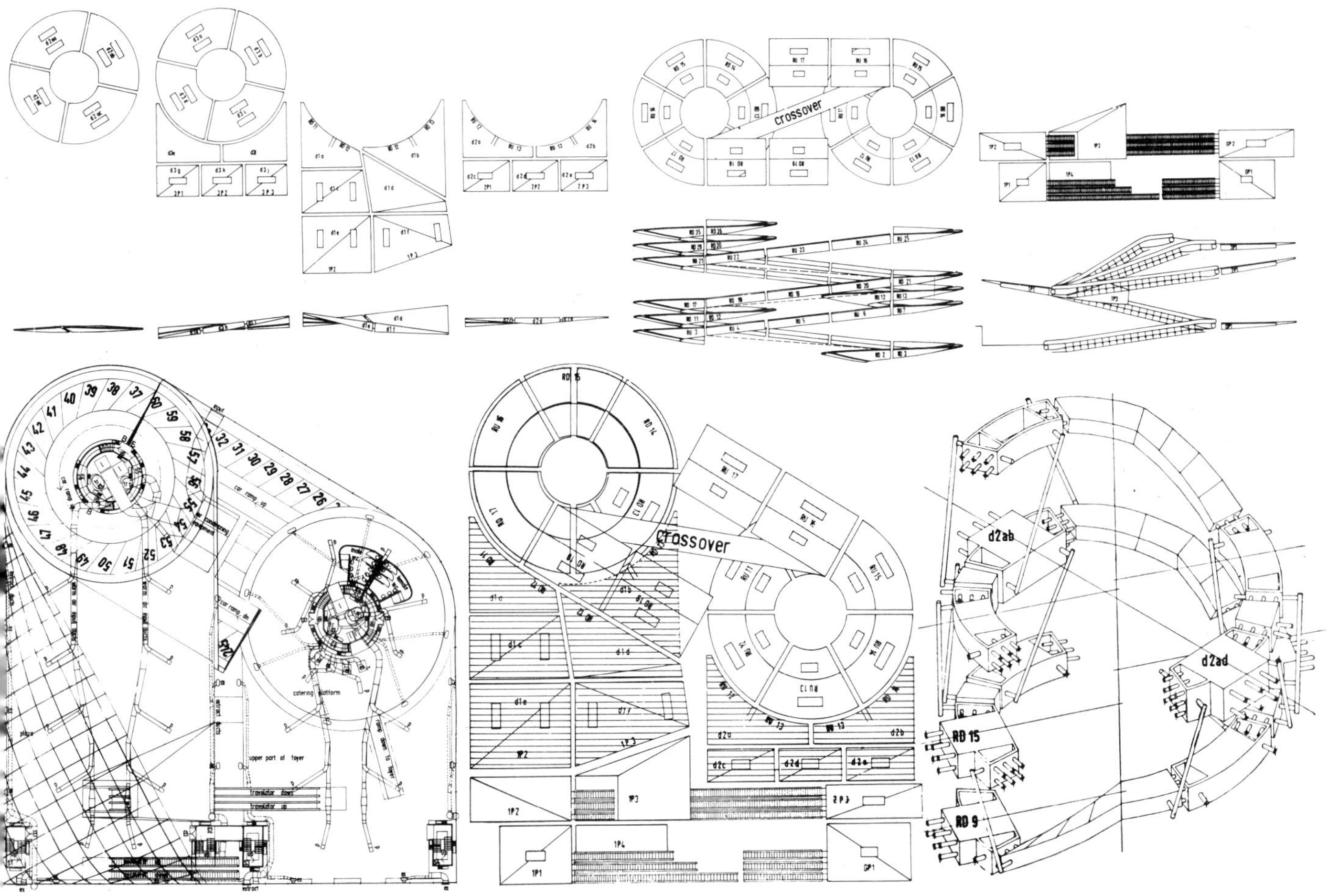

2 Expendability and the consumer

Cover and two typical pages from *Archigram 3* 1963 (collages by Peter Taylor and Peter Cook)

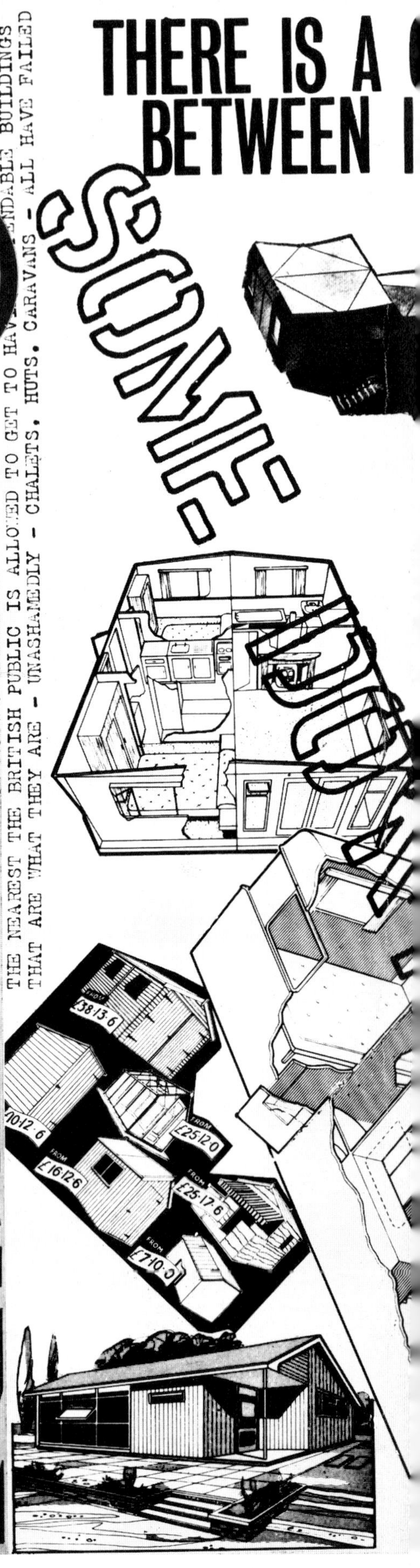

AND IMAGE

left: EXPANDING HOUSE
by CESARE PEA
below: BATHROOM
(patent drawing) by
BUCKMINSTER FULLER

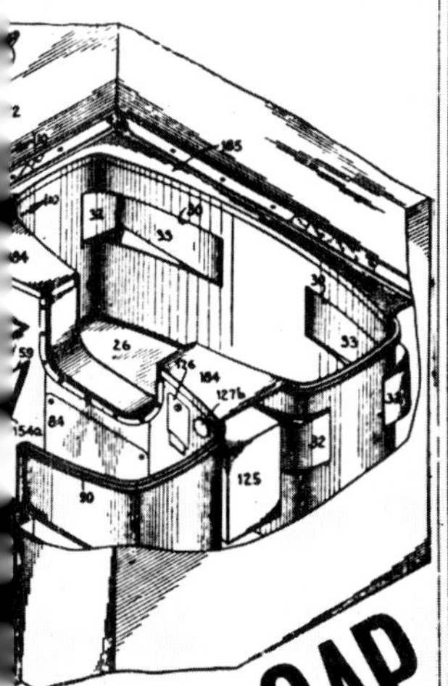

SOME THINGS BRIDGE THE GAP

PROBLEM : IS THIS EXPENDABLE ARCHITECTURE ?

ALL THESE.... (1) ABSTRACTA SYSTEM DOMES, (2).. DYMAXION CAR, (3) LCC TEMPORARY HOUSE, (4) PLASTIC TELEPHONE EXCH., (5) WICHITA HOUSE, (6) PANEL FOR LAB. BUILDING IN PLASTIC FOR THE ANTARCTIC SURVEY; AND THE DISPOSABLE PACKS OF FOOD, RAZOR BLADES, ETC.; ALL SHARE THE DISTINCTION OF a, BEING SERIOUS ATTEMPTS AT DIRECT DESIGN FOR OBVIOUSLY LIMITED LIFE-SPAN OBJECTS; AND b, HAVING ACTUALLY SUCCEEDED IN BEING PRODUCED AS SUCH.

THEY ARE, BY THEIR VERY EXISTENCE, AN ENCOURAGEMENT TO DESIGNERS WHO HAVE TO FOLLOW ON TO PRODUCE THESE SORT OF THINGS IN QUANTITY.

ALSO, THE CONNECTION IS MUCH GREATER BETWEEN THE TRULY DESIGNED EXPENDABLE BUILDING AND THE PACKAGE, THAN BETWEEN IT AND THE 20 YEAR LIFE-SPAN HOUSE WITH THE 80 YEAR LIFE-SPAN LOOK.

This is the significant sameness of all these.

Archigram 3
In one important respect *Archigram 3* was quite different from its predecessors: it was a manifesto with a single idea. All the material was required to support that idea and it mattered slightly less than before that this material was new, theoretical or practical, local or foreign. In fact, it was important to show the anachronisms of reality and theory. It was necessary to accumulate evidence. Sometimes the evidence of the real object made less sense than the architectural gesture, a point being missed by caravans, temporary huts and bungalows. Expendability could be proved as a fundamental aspect of a dynamic, pluralist society, but this had to be transferred into an architectural conversation.

The initial impact of the issue was a hollow reaction to the argument. Students looked at the examples as new objects in themselves. For the first time older architects were being made angry.

Housing as a consumer product 1966 Warren Chalk (previously published in *Arena*, Journal of the Architectural Association)

Editorial from Archigram 3

Peter Cook

More and more

Almost without realizing it, we have absorbed into our lives the first generation of expendables . . . foodbags, paper tissues polythene wrappers, ballpens, E.P.s . . . so many things about which we don't have to think. We throw them away almost as soon as we acquire them.

Also with us are the items that are bigger and last longer, but are nevertheless planned for obsolescence . . . the motor car . . . and its unit-built garage.

Now the second generation is upon us – paper furniture is a reality in the States, paper sheets are a reality in British hospital beds, the Greater London Council is putting up limited-life-span houses.

Through and through

With every level of society and with every level of commodity, the unchanging scene is being replaced by the increase in change of our user-habits – and thereby, eventually, our user-habitats.

We are becoming much more used to the idea of changing a piece of clothing year by year, rather than expecting to hang on to it for several years. Similarly, the idea of keeping a piece of furniture long enough to be able to hand it on to our children is becoming increasingly ridiculous. In this situation we should not be surprised if such articles wear out within their 'welcome-life' span, rather than their traditional life span.

The attitude of mind that accepts such a situation is creeping into our society at about the rate that expendable goods become available. We must recognize this as a healthy and altogether positive sign. It is the product of a sophisticated consumer society, rather than a stagnant (and in the end, declining) society.

Our collective mental blockage occurs between the land of the small-scale consumer-products and the objects which make up our environment. Perhaps it will not be until such things as housing, amenity-place and work-place become recognized as consumer products that can be 'bought off the peg' – with all that this implies in terms of expendability (foremost), industrialization, up-to-date-ness, consumer choice, and basic product-design – that we can begin to make an environment that is really part of a developing human culture.

Why is there an indefinable resistance to planned obsolescence for a kitchen, which in twelve years will be highly inefficient (by the standards of the day) and in twenty years will be intolerable, yet there are no qualms about four-year obsolescence for cars ?

The idea of an expendable environment is stil somehow regarded as akin to anarchy . . . as if in order to make it work, we would bulldoze Westminster Abbey . . .

We shall not bulldoze Westminster Abbey

Added to this, the idea of a non-permanen building has overtones of economy, austerity economy. Architects are the first to deny the great potential of expendability as the buil reflection of the second half of the twentietl century. Most of the buildings that exist tha are technically expendable have the fact skilfully hidden . . . they masquerade as permanen buildings – monuments to the past.

Housing as a consumer product

Warren Chalk

One of the most flagrant misconceptions helc about us is that we are not ultimately concerned with people. This probably arises directly from the type of imagery we use. A section through, say, something like City Interchange, appears to predict some automated wasteland inhabited only by computers and robots. How much this is justifiec is difficult to assess, but if our work is studiec closely there will be found traces of a very rea concern for people and the way in which they might be liberated from the restrictions imposed on them by the existing chaotic situation, in the home, at work and in the tota built environment.

Human situations are as concerned with environmental changes and activity within th city, as with the definition of places. Important in this is the precept of situation as a ideas generator in creating a truly living city Cities should generate, reflect and activat life, their structure organized to precipitat life and movement. Situation, the happening within spaces in the city, the transient throw away world of people, the passing presence o cars, etc., are as important, possibly more important than the built environment, the buil demarcation of space. Situation can b caused by a single individual, by groups or crowd, their particular purpose, occupatior movement and direction.

This is in fact a follow-on from thinking relate to the South Bank scheme where the origina basic concept was to produce an anonymou pile, subservient to a series of pedestria walkways, a sort of Mappin Terrace for peopl instead of goats.

So once again the pedestrian, the gregariou nature of people and their movement is upper most in our minds and the built demarcatio of space used to channel and direct pedestria patterns of movement.

In an attempt to get closer to the genera public, to study their attitudes and behaviou we have extended ourselves beyond th narrow boundaries of conventional architectural thought, causing the misconceptions about what we are trying to do. We must extend the conventional barriers and find people without any formal architectural training, producing concepts showing a marked intuitive grasp of current attitudes related to city images and the rest. In the world of science fiction we dig out prophetic information regarding geodesic nets, pneumatic tubes and plastic domes and bubbles.

If we turn to the back pages of the popular press we find ads for do-it-yourself living-room extensions, or instant garage kits. Let's face it, we can no longer turn away from the hard fact that everyone in the community has latent creative instincts and that our role will eventually be to direct these into some tangible and acceptable form. The present gulf between people, between the community and the designer may well be eventually bridged by the do-it-yourself interchangeable kit of parts.

In a technological society more people will play an active part in determining their own individual environment, in self-determining a way of life. We cannot expect to take this fundamental right out of their hands and go on treating them as cultural and creative morons. We must tackle it from the other end in a positive way. The inherent qualities of mass-production for a consumer orientated society are those of repetition and standardization, but parts can be changeable or interchangeable depending on individual needs and preferences, and, given a world market, could also be economically feasible.

In the States one can select a car consisting of a whole series of interchangeable options, as Reyner Banham has pointed out (in his article on Clip-on Architecture), Chevrolet produce a choice of seventeen bodies and five different engines.

The current success of pop music is to an extent due to the importance of audience participation; the 'Frug' and the 'Jerk' are self-expressive and free-forming. The pop groups themselves are closer in dress and habits, including musical dexterity, to the audience. Despite pop music becoming a vast industry its success depends on its ability to keep up with the pace of its consumer taste.

Of course the idea of mass-produced expendable component dwellings is not new. We are all familiar with Le Corbusier's efforts in collaboration with Prouvé and with Prouvé's own bits and pieces, with Buckminster Fuller's Dymaxion house, the Phelps Dodge Dymaxion bathroom and the Dymaxion deployment unit, Alison and Peter Smithson's House of the Future at the Ideal Home Exhibition of 1955, Ionel Schein's prefabricated hotel units and the Monsanto Plastic House in Disneyland; there has also been work done by the Metabolist Group in Japan and Arthur Quarmby in England.

The Plug-in Capsule Home is an attempt to sustain the idea in the hope that some brave soul might eventually be persuaded to finance research and development.

The techniques of mass-production and automation are a reality, yet we see the research that goes into, and the products that come out of, today's building and are dismayed.

The Plug-in Capsule attempts to set new standards and find an appropriate image for an assembly-line product.

The order of its design criteria are in correct order to consumer requirements. First, a better consumer product, offering something better than, and different from, traditional housing, more closely related to the design of cars and refrigerators, than placing itself in direct competition with tradition.

3 Living City

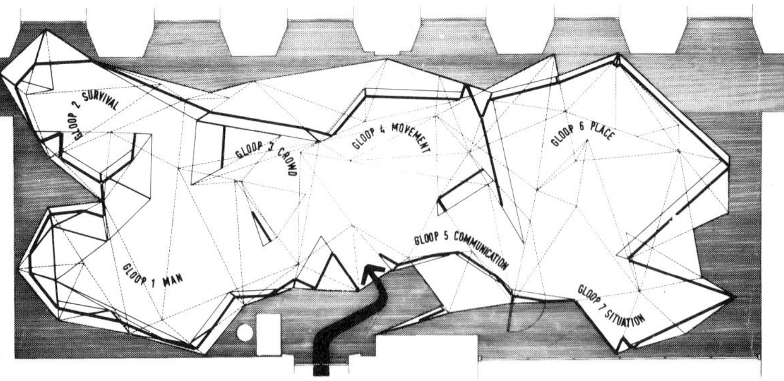

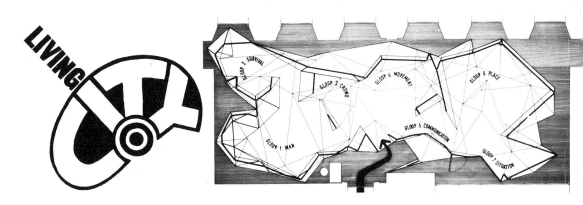

Living City Exhibition Institute of Contemporary Arts, London, Summer 1963 (this was the first group project of the Archigram Group and was made possible on a Gulbenkian Foundation Grant)

far left Living City Exhibition symbol

left Living City Exhibition: plan

below Living City Exhibition: various views and components

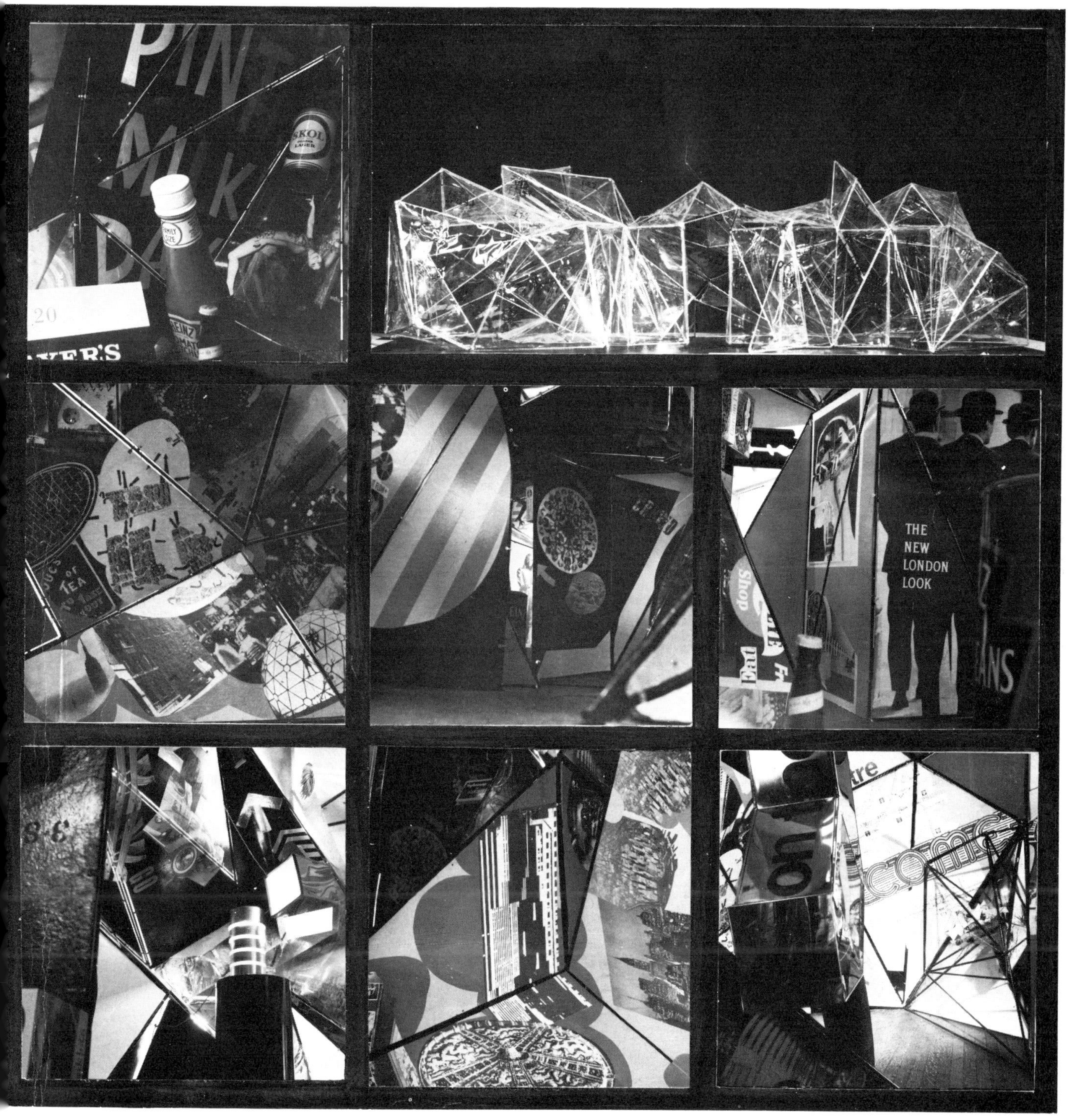

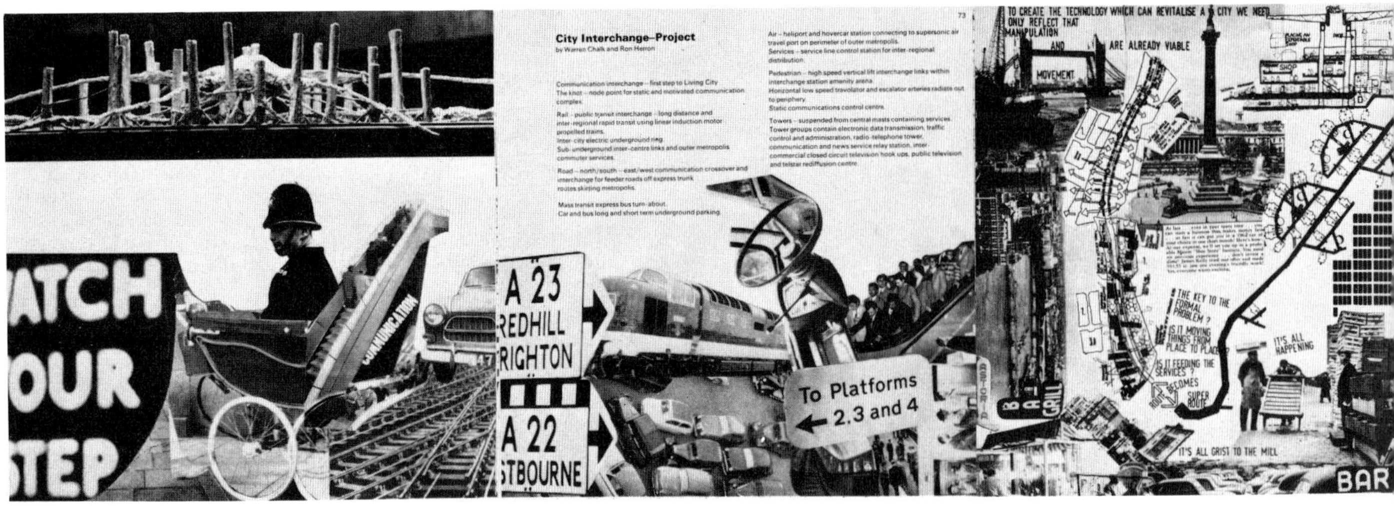

Extracts from Living Arts magazine no. 2, June 1963

The exhibition Living City (held at the Institute of Contemporary Arts in London in June 1963) was the first project to be carried out by the whole Archigram Group. Its brief was to express the vitality of city life, rather than suggest a plan for a new city.

Architecture is only a small part of city environment in terms of real significance; the total environment is what is important, what really matters. The object was to determine the effect total environment has on the human condition, the response it generates – and to capture, to express, the vitality of the city. We must perpetuate this vitality or the city will die at the hands of the hard planners and architect-aesthetes.

The re-creation of environment is too often a jaded process, having to do only with densities, allocations of space, fulfilment of regulations; the spirit of cities lost in the process. The warning has come from William H. Whyte in *The Exploding Metropolis* and Jane Jacobs in *The Death and Life of Great American Cities*. The problem facing our cities is not just that of their regeneration, but of their right to an existence.

In the living city all are important. The triviality of lighting a cigarette, or the hard fact of moving two million commuters a day are both facets of the shared experience of the city. So far, no other form of environment has been devised that produces the same quality of experience shared by so many minds and interests. When it is raining in Oxford Street, the architecture is no more important than the rain, in fact the weather has probably more to do with the pulsation of the living city at a moment in time.

Living City is not a blueprint for a city. Architecture is not in evidence here, our aim is to capture a mood, a climate of opinion, to examine the phenomena of city life, to create an awareness within the spectator of himself, his attitudes, and the significance of the throwaway environment about him.

Living City takes the form of a complete structure, an organism designed to condition the spectator by cutting him off from the everyday situation, where things are seen in predictable and accepted relationships. This city stimulator is a 'conditioning chamber, like the corner of some giant brain or analogic computer, and has compartments we have called 'Gloops'. Each gloop defines an area of basic constant and reasonably predictable fact. Man, Survival, Crowd, Movement, Communication, Place, Situation: all contributing and interacting one on another and sum totalling to Living City.

The term 'Gloop' was coined to define an area of the exhibition; it derived from the idea of a loop-enclosure of a soft profile and was one aspect of the original intention to build the exhibition structures from spray plastic. There are seven gloops.

Survival Gloop – Cities have been used by man since the beginning of time in order that he may survive. Survival in city is big business, conditioning many pays dividends – buy speed, horsepower, happiness. Each man to his own survival kit, the artefacts of adjustment and escape – and it's all throwaway, nothing matters any more than anything else, important shift keys at every step. Man in-city will always have a survival kit – food, drink, sex, drugs, clothes, cars, make-up, money – in order to live, and survival conditions the living city.

Crowd Gloop – An indication of the kaleidoscopic coming together of all manner and types of man and the way in which they interact upon one another in the shared experience of living city.

The cosmopolitan scene, the structure of community, the influence of 'family' and 'togetherness', of commuters and consumers, of man as individual, as groups or as anonymous crowd.

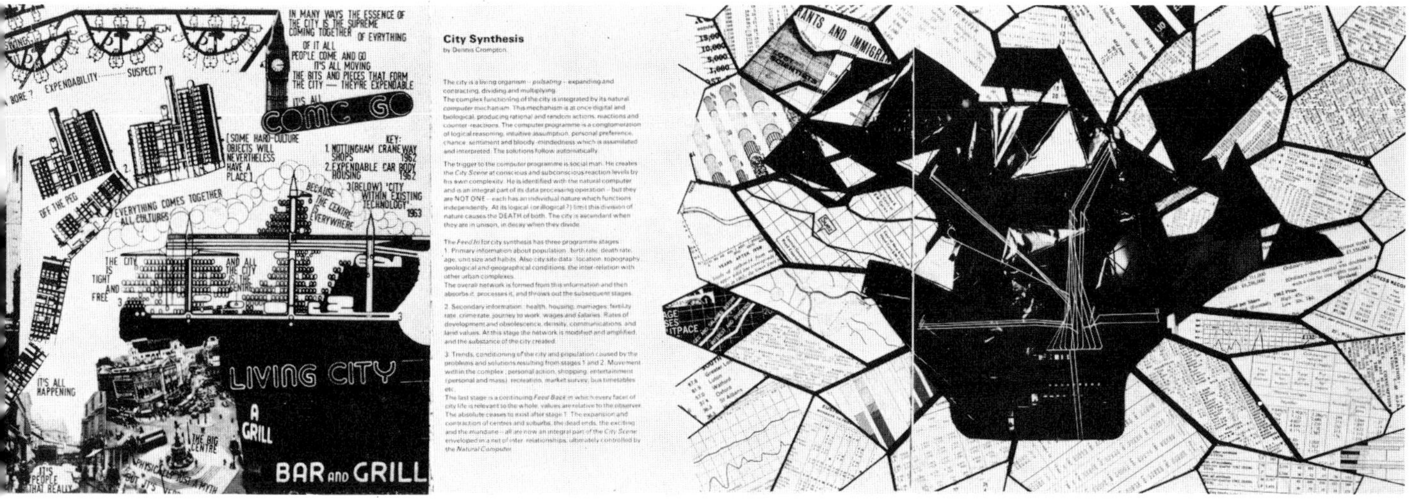

City Synthesis
by Dennis Crompton

The city is a living organism – *pulsating* – expanding and contracting, dividing and multiplying.
The complex functioning of the city is integrated by its natural *computer* mechanism. This mechanism is at once digital and biological, producing rational and random actions, reactions and counter-reactions. The computer programme is a conglomeration of logical reasoning, intuitive assumption, personal preference, chance, sentiment and bloody-mindedness which is assimilated and interpreted. The solutions follow automatically.

The trigger to the computer programme is social man. He creates the *City Scene* at conscious and subconscious reaction levels by his own complexity. He is identified with the natural computer and is an integral part of its data processing operation – but they are NOT ONE – each has an individual nature which functions independently. At its logical (or illogical ?) limit this division of nature causes the DEATH of both. The city is ascendant when they are in unison, in decay when they divide.

The *Feed In* for city synthesis has three programme stages:
1. Primary information about population: birth rate, death rate, age, unit size and habits. Also city site data: location, topography, geological and geographical conditions, the inter-relation with other urban complexes.
The overall network is formed from this information and then absorbs it, processes it, and throws out the subsequent stages.

2. Secondary information: health, housing, marriages, fertility rate, crime rate, journey to work, wages and salaries. Rates of development and obsolescence, density, communications, and land values. At this stage the network is modified and amplified, and the substance of the city created.

3. Trends, conditioning of the city and population caused by the problems and solutions resulting from stages 1 and 2. Movement within the complex, personal action, shopping, entertainment (personal and mass), recreation, market survey, bus timetables etc.
The last stage is a continuing *Feed Back* in which every facet of city life is relevant to the whole, values are relative to the observer. The absolute ceases to exist after stage 1. The expansion and contraction of centres and suburbs, the dead ends, the exciting and the mundane – all are now an integral part of the *City Scene* enveloped in a net of inter-relationships, ultimately controlled by the *Natural Computer*.

Pages from *Living Arts* magazine Issue No. 2 June 1963. This Magazine formed the catalogue to the exhibition

Movement Gloop – Here is an attempt to examine the significance of the conceptual sense of movement in-city, which gives a certain kind of form and value to otherwise vacant and static spaces. Human movement is determined by biological factors and depends on the structure of bones, joints and muscles. An individual's age, sex, height, weight and other constitutional factors determine to a great extent the duration and speed of the movements he can make. Gesture, the free action of walking, running, jumping, climbing, help to determine patterns of action in the city.

Objective movement cycles can be classified; i.e. directed movement, purpose movement, multi-directional movement and psychological movement, etc. These patterns have the effect of splitting and isolating known city environments in loosely defined but distinct areas and movement between is limited or changing. The flow, high speed/medium/slow speed, stop-go movement of traffic is an exciting aspect of the living city, and important in determining its future mood and appropriate form.

Man Gloop – City is an organism housing man, man made, for man. We have tried to determine the characteristics of man in the future. What will his ultimate development be? Presumably he will still be in control to operate the mechanism, to activate the switch; he will still be at the centre of things. The robot figure that opened 'This is Tomorrow' at the Whitechapel Gallery 1956 has been superseded by today's spaceman, the nearest man has yet come to realizing the ideal SUPERMAN dream, the ultimate in physical and mental development.

Communications Gloop – The foreseeable rapid rate of change in transportation method may eventually make invalid the concept of a rigid mobile communications network as the main urban structure. A whole area of study is open for experiment of expendable systems and more flexible technology in terms of communication networks. Static communications are becoming increasingly important in so far as they may be exploited to produce new concepts in city planning. Large organizations will control their own visual communications network, allowing for a city centre control with satellites dispersed in constant touch with the communication centre, no longer dependent on physical communication. This will result in a revaluation of the accepted city-centre format.

Place Gloop – The intelligibility of built environment, the content, use and arrangement of space in the city is the theme of 'Place'. As the city centres tend to become more and more like one another, so their success and identity will be lost. Architecture alone cannot achieve this feeling of 'place'. It alone is not enough to give identity. It is the content and the use that are important.

What we feel and think about city is not new in the sense that it was unthought of before but only in that the idea of Living City has not been acted upon before our generation.

All of us, in varying degrees according to our perceptiveness, find living city in situation. Our interest in this is for the immediate and ultimate future of city, and an awareness of city is necessary before we can move forward.

Situation Gloop – Is concerned with environmental changes and activity within the Living City context, giving characteristics to defined areas. 'Situation' is the happenings within spaces in-city. The transient throw-away objects, the passing presence of cars and people are as important, possibly more important, than the built demarcation of space. Situations can be caused by a single individual, by groups or a crowd, their particular purpose, occupation, movement or direction. Situation can be traffic, its speed, direction, classification. Situation may occur with change of weather, time of day, or night. This time/movement/situation thing is important in determining our whole future attitude to the visualization and realization of city; it can give a clue, key, in our effort to

'Interchange' project 1963 Ron Herron and Warren Chalk. Study of a multi-transport mode-node zone monorails interchange with guided vehicles and tracked railways

Interchange: section

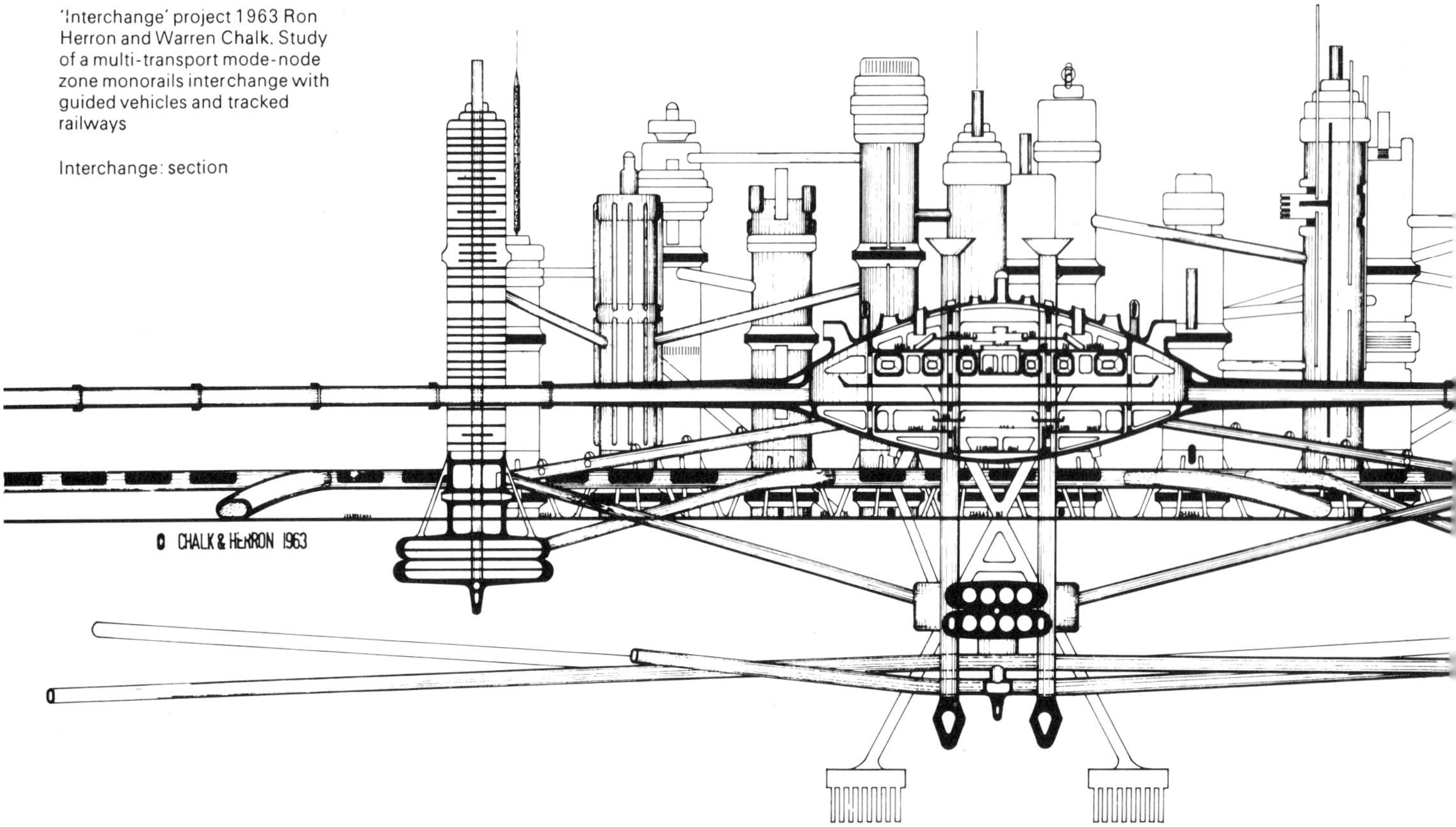

escape the brittle ingratiating world of the architect/aesthete, to break away into the real world and take in the scene.

Man is the ultimate subject and the principal conditioner, so that the exhibition is a mirror of man himself.

What have cities been doing during the few thousand years in which they have existed?

They have provided society with a physical centre – a place where so much is happening that one activity is stimulated by all the rest. Trends originated in cities. The mood of cities is frantic. It is all happening – all the time. However decadent society may be, it is reflected most clearly and demonstrably in the metropolitan way of life.

We are seeking the living city.

'Story of a Thing' 1963 David Greene and Michael Webb. An apocryphal tale

right Interchange: perspective

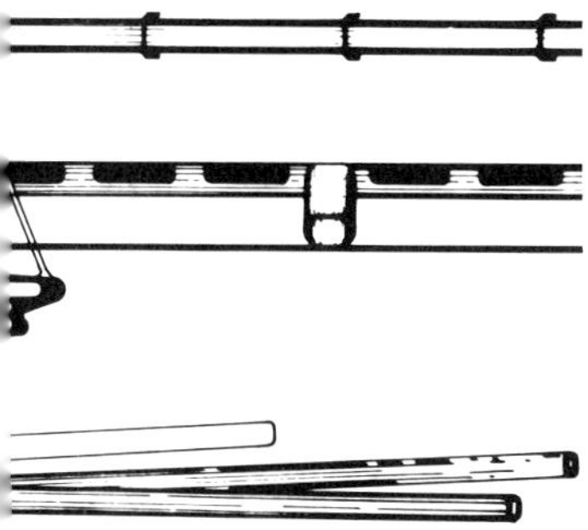

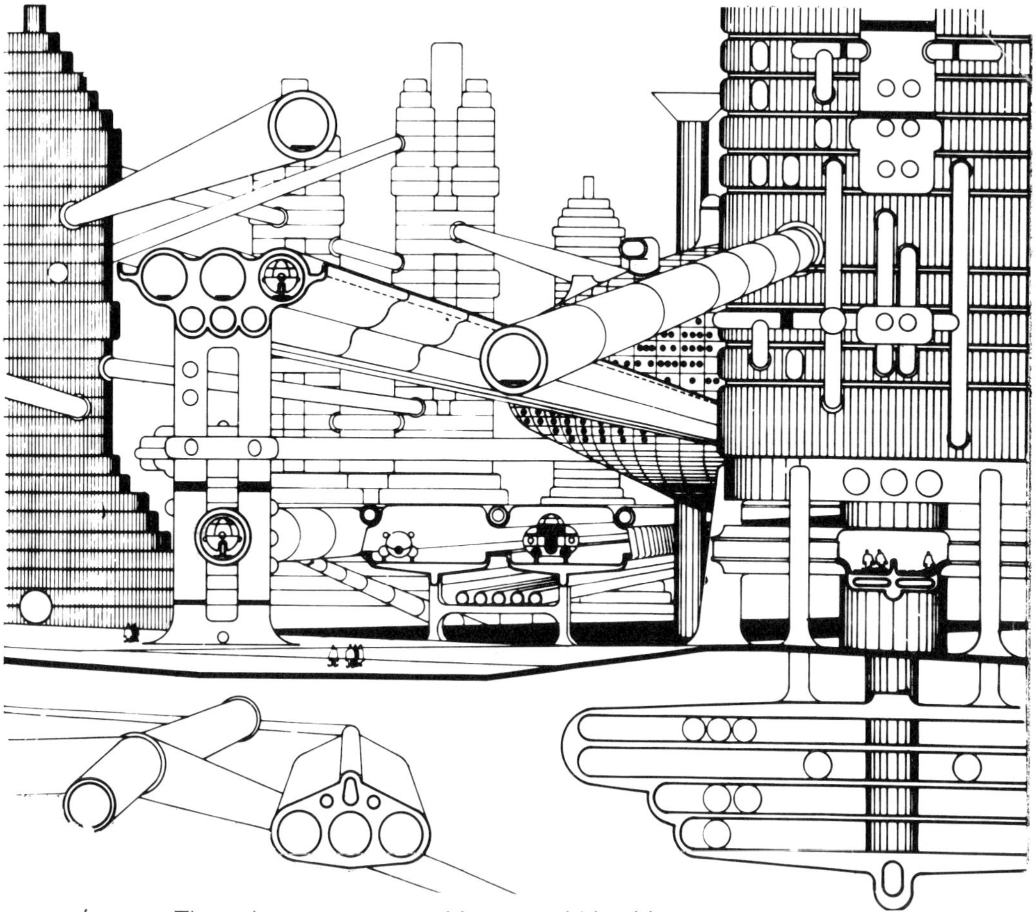

'Fashion' is a dirty word, so is 'temporary', so is 'flashy'. Yet it is the creation of those things that are necessarily fashionable, temporary or flashy that has more to do with the vitality of cities than 'monument buildings'. The pulsation of city life is fast, so why not that of its environment? It reflects rise and fall, coming and going . . . change. So why not build for this?

The only way to create cities – or within cities, is to stop pretending about the significance of 'Architects' Architecture': for by hanging on to the comfort of such a context for re-creating the living city we are opting out of the struggle to maintain it. We shall find instead a vast suburb without any cities, and in it the odd pocket of architects building their own houses – no longer involved.

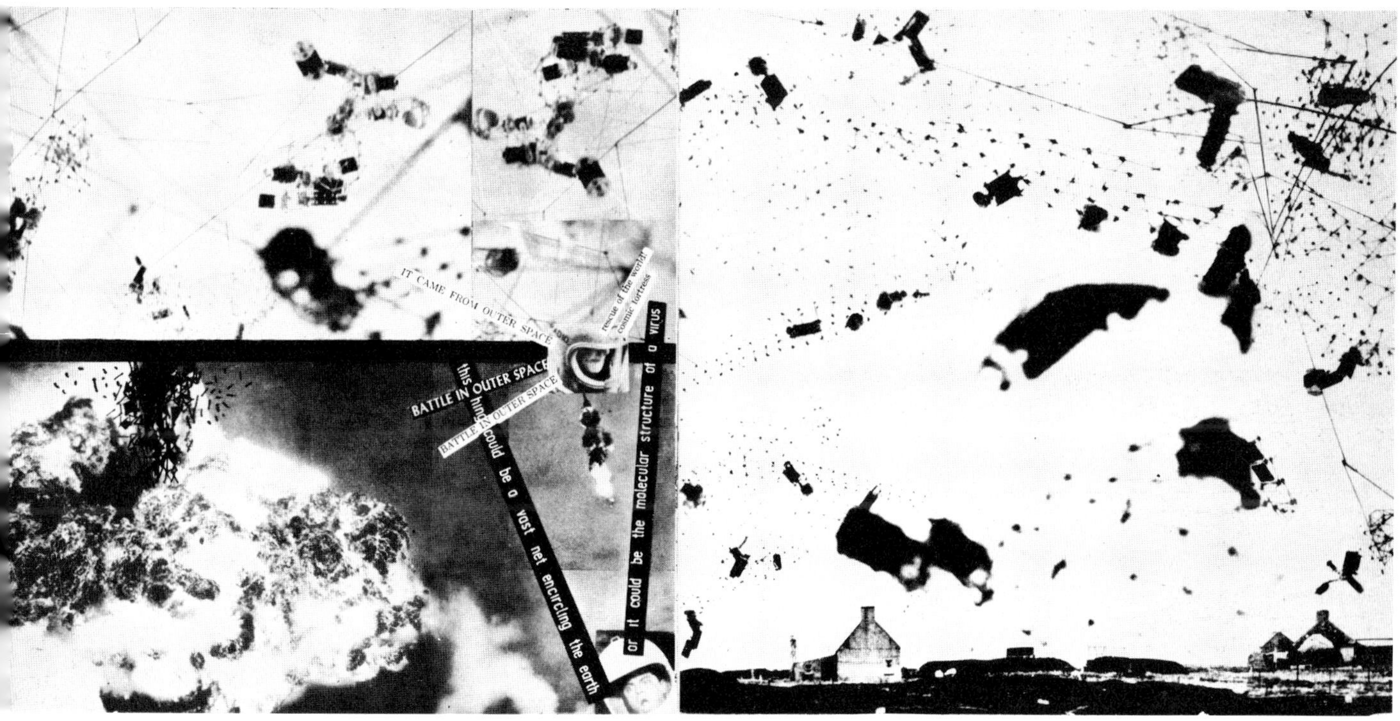

The metropolis

Editorial from *Archigram 5*

(This was the theme of *Archigram 5*, issued in the winter 1964–5)

Outside architecture, the intensity of metropolitan life has been sought and cherished as being somehow more conducive to all the great positives: to creativeness, emancipation, involvement, enlightenment and the rest. Metropolitan architecture has overtones and undertones beyond the satisfaction of a brief by the adaption of a style; a breakaway gesture can be contained within a four-walled context which itself is in quite a normal urban organization. Random situations have also from time to time generated ingenuity that has directly fed the development of architecture. The intellectual wing has always been fond of solving the problem of 'The City', as a vehicle for connecting style with sociology. By establishing a complete environmental

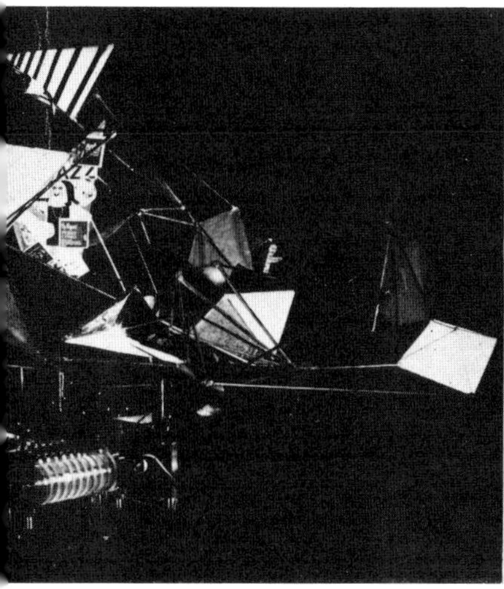

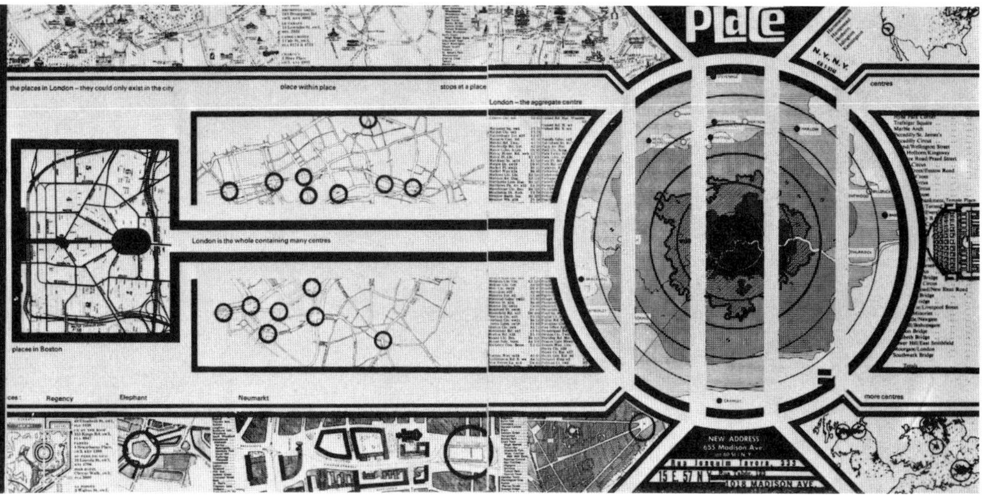

above Illustrations from *Living Arts* magazine, issue No. 2 June 1963

left Collage from *Archigram 5* showing the following projects: *top left:* housing pile by Moshe Safdie; *top right:* Living Pod stack by David Greene; *middle left:* Cluster City by Arata Isozaki; *middle right:* Mole Hill project by Peter Cook; *lower middle right:* Ziggurat by Leopold Gerstel; *bottom left:* Housing Project by Henri Sauvage; *bottom right:* City Structure by Yona Friedman

context they justify their preconceptions *in toto*.

Suddenly all this has been called into question. Are cities still necessary? Do we still need the paraphernalia of a metropolis to house the executive function of a capital city? Do we need the agglomeration of five, ten or twenty million people in order to learn, be entertained, enjoy good food or take part in higher productivity? The idea of cluster, and then of grouping of parts and functions that are so different but sited so close together that elements cease to be defined, is a further sophistication of metropolitan organization. This leads us to the proposition that the whole city might be contained in a single building. The concept of vehicular/pedestrian segregation is now an accepted part of planning theory. But once one accepts this and the idea of multi-level single buildings, it is only logical to conceive of multi-level cities. The organization of, say, New York, which tolerates multi-level components connected by only two horizontal levels (street and subway), and both of those at the base, is archaic. However, a truly multi-level city will demand a connection system and an environment-penetration that is not just vertical or horizontal but also takes advantage of the diagonal.

The crust of the city

The dictionary definition of crust is a 'hard outer layer'. This outer layer is, in our definition, the zone where activity hits the air. In present-day cities this consists of a relatively unsophisticated series of chunks of building riddled by roads. The relationship to the sun, air, sky and distance rarely takes advantage of the potential of different and scattered elements congealing together in a random way.

The molehill

With the Molehill (or 'heaped-up') section the crust surface can take maximum advantage of the air against its balconies as well as against its roof surfaces. It is a natural environment 'heap', with perhaps biological and psychological overtones as well.

Structure, diagonals and connections

Any discussion of the connection between the significant diagonal and a multi-level city eventually separates into those diagonals that occur by necessity (the road filter from Tange's Tokyo Bay plan), those that emerge from the implications of a basic (or heroic) idea, and those that come about through sheer contrivance.

The implications of space-use in a complex organization have been realized by degrees over many years. Piranesi obviously foresaw today's city situation. Much later, in the early 1920s, Neutra devised a first-stage multi-level connection, only involving, for the moment, two connecting levels above ground. Tony Garnier's Cité Industrielle had certainly used connecting fingers at high level but the derivation was strongly associated with real industrial situations, which was a justification of a heroic device. In a direct 'working-part' situation, there is the need to communicate with any part of the machine for maintenance purposes, and the further need for the fluids and solids being processed to flow from one zone to another.

A major problem of the organization (and the imagery-control) of large areas of city is the achievement of a consistency running through parts with widely differing functions and sizes: add to this the problems of absorbing growth and avoiding the piecemeal one-offness of block-to-block relationship. The answer may be found in a large-scale structural idea, which is anyhow a necessity of a product of current engineering experimental consistent building.

The emergence of the diagonal is not only a product of current engineering experimental preference, it also implies a purpose of the structure that is new to buildings: to provide an umbrella within which growth and change (of the smaller, functioning parts) can take place. Nor, despite the prominence of the controlling structure in all these schemes, do they ever become boring.

4 Zoom

ZOOM....INTO A POP-UP WORLD OF TOWERS....PROTOTYPES OF THE CITY OF THE FUTURE .... RINGED BY THE CITY OF ZOOM....HERE ARE FOUR PROJECTS FOR TOWERS FOR AN INTERNATIONAL EXHIBITION....tower(1) is by Warren Chalk, every level revolves, the bubbles which make up the tower shine and are constantly different....the completely chameolonic building.
tower(2) by Ron Herr
a complex of tubes,
and grasping light,
city in the vertical
WHIZZ
BLEEP
POP UP INTO A NEW WORLD
ZOOM
in tower(3) by Frank Linden, the shafts rise clear and metallic above and through the plugged-in entertainments rooms, the cage is diagonal the communication ties are horizontal......
tower(4) by Peter Cook spreads a net of structure and drapes a skin around the tower, the outcrop occurs again at the middle and top of the structure, movement is always on the diagonal......

Pop-up page from *Archigram 4*: a series of Entertainment Tower projects

far right above *Archigram 4* 1964: Cover illustration

far right below Space probe: article from *Archigram 4* assembled by Warren Chalk 1964

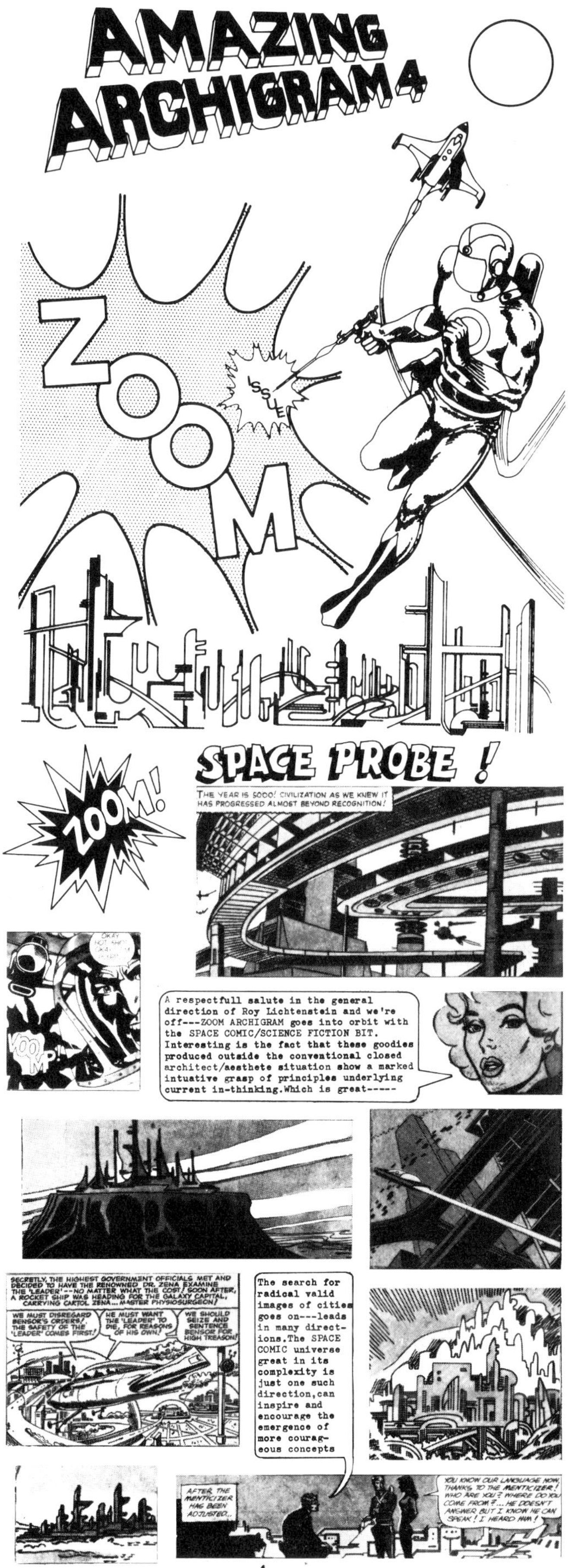

1.

Zoom and 'real' architecture

Editorial from *Archigram 4* Peter Cook

We return to the preoccupation of the first *Archigram* – a search for ways out from the stagnation of the architectural scene, where the continuing *malaise* is not just with the mediocrity of the object, but, more seriously, with the self-satisfaction of the profession backing up such architecture. The line that 'Modern Architecture has arrived' seems more than ever inappropriate.

Certainly it has never been more possible to produce buildings that are at once well-mannered . . . and quite gutless. Great British architecture now has more to do, organically, with the 'line-of-least-resistance' tradition – from Queen Anne's Mansions to the Hilton, through Dolphin Square – than with the New Architecture of the twenties and thirties. Though it would be ridiculous to force an 'heroic' phase in the present decade the cycle has too quickly reached the 'tragic'.

Mainstream-fanciers can currently report further unashamed use by everybody of the 45° corner, stepped section, 3-D precast panel, and the rest – a cosmetic borrowed from the originals' beauty-box to tart up the latest least-line (tradition) scheme.

It would have been too easy to look over one's shoulder and fill *Archigram* with three dozen of the respected goodies of the last fifty years (interesting that so many would be pre-1930), and the comment, 'What have we lost? What are we missing?' Yet set against such a feeling of loss is the continuance of something that has not yet disappeared into historical perspective – a tradition that is still developing, and is still original to many of the basic gestures of modern architecture. It shares much of its expression with those dim, neurotic, enthusiastic days of the Ring, *Der Sturm*, and the Futurist Manifesto – the architectural weirdies of the time feeding the infant Modern Movement. Our document is the Space-Comic; its reality is in the gesture, design and natural styling of hardware new to our decade – the capsule, the rocket, the bathyscope, the Zidpark, the handy-pak.

Is it possible for the space-comic's future to relate once again with buildings-as-built? Can the near-reality of the rocket-object and hovercraft-object, which are virtually ceasing to be cartoons, carry the dynamic (but also non-cartoon) building with them into life as it is? Or shall we be riding in these craft amongst an environment made of CLASP? The ridiculousness of such a situation can be compared with the world of Schinkel seen by the Futurists.

There is the same consistency in an 'Adventure-Comic' city of the 1962–63 period and in Bruno Taut's projects for Alpine Architecture of 1917, the same force of prediction and style. The cross fertilization can come from the

2.

Space probe: article from *Archigram 4* 1964 assembled by Warren Chalk

3.

4.

'design' world, but only – and this is the point – when the idea is big enough – so we frequently find conditioned environments of domes over cities and representations of tensegrity nets in cartoons. The point made in *Edilizia Moderna 80*, where the movement-tube emerged as an essential aspect of the more sophisticated skyscraper city (as opposed to a city which is a collection of skyscrapers – and relative to only one level of horizontal circulation) has long been realized by the comics' skyscraper cities.

One of the greatest weaknesses of our immediate urban architecture is the inability to contain the fast-moving object as part of the total aesthetic – but the comic imagery has always been strongest here. The representation of movement-objects and movement-containers is consistent with the rest, and not only because 'speed' is the main gesture.

The positive quality that the rocket (both actual and represented), the Futurist scribble and the space-city share is their ultimateness – which has most significance as a counterweight to so-called 'real' architecture. We connect this material with serious projects for making living space, entertainment space – and the city, in the context of the near future.

Cedric Price's work has particular relevance to this 'connection' with reality. Price is almost the only architect in England actually building tensegrity structures, pop-up domes and disposable buildings – and therefore coming to grips with the near future. The towers (page 26) are also relevant to this situation in the never-land between gesture and architectural laboratory work.

It is significant that with this material there exists an inspirational bridge, stretching both forty years into the past and perhaps forty years into the future, and perhaps the answer lies neither in heroics nor tragedy, but in a re-emergence of the courage of convictions in architecture.

Space probe sequence continued

left Science fact/Science fiction assemblage from *Archigram 4* 1964 Ron Herron

right 'CSB 63.4' 1964 David Greene A mechanized Pod-House

rocket research
today
brain
space comics
ZOOM!
engineering know-how
WILL BURTIN
science fiction
&ZOOM
tubes
zoom
SCIENCE FACT
SF bubbles
CITY INTERCHANGE
atomium
chalk & herron
steel
zooooom
space probe the search for a valid direction
ZOOM!
SF
wwwooshhh
satellite
tomorrow
orbit
FICTION
SCIENCE

STAGE ONE STATIONARY FIELD
CONTROL UNIT SPECIFICATION
NOTES POPULATION MAX. 8
NO. USE, PERSONAL HABITATI
ON. UNLOADED WT. SEA LEVEL
18 CWT. 3 NO. PNTS. OF PEN
ETRATION. 42 NO. SUSPENSIO
N PNTS. SELECT 3 NO. MIN.
NO COMPRESSION. USABLE VOL.
MAX. 16,000 CU. FT. MIN.
10,000 CU. FT. INSTANTANEOU
S SELECTIVE VOL. CHANGE. OP
ERATIONAL CRITERIA LIMITS:
INTERNAL PRESSURE 29kpsi-31
kpsi TEMP +8=+80 EXTERNAL P
RESSURE 20kpsi-40kpsi TEMP-
30:+90. CONSTANT INTERNAL T
EMP AND PRESSURE MAINTAINED
UP TO LIMIT OF 3deg. PER HR.
& 5kpsi/hr. EXTERNAL FLUCTU
ATION. EQUIPMENT. 3 NO. M
ICROTHERMIC BALANCES & EQUA
LISERS CAPACITY PER ¼deg. 9
7.304G. (PRESET) COUPLINGS:
FEGANE PRESSURE HEAT & GRAV
ITY CORRECTION UNITS ALL AC
CESSABLE FROM COCOONS FIN
ISHES: EXTERNALLY, MECHANIC
AL EQUIPMENT VACUUM SEALED
TRANSPARENT POLYEUROGENE FI
LM. OPAQUE AREAS COLOURS SE
LECTED FROM 10 yr7.5/12,2.5
y5/2,7.5r5/16, 2.5pb3/8. IN
TERNALLY SURFACES SPRAYED T
O CUSTOMERS SPECIFICATION M
AX. FINISH LD. 1 LB. SQ. IN.
COOKING & HYGIENE APPARATUS
ANY CONFORMING TO U.N.B. DI
M. & FIXING STANDARDS. GUA
RENTEE FREE INSPECTION EVER
Y 12000 HRS. COMPONENTS UP
TO 10000HRS. DELIVERY & FIX
ING MAX. 17 HRS. WITHIN 350
0 MILES

C.S.B.63'4.

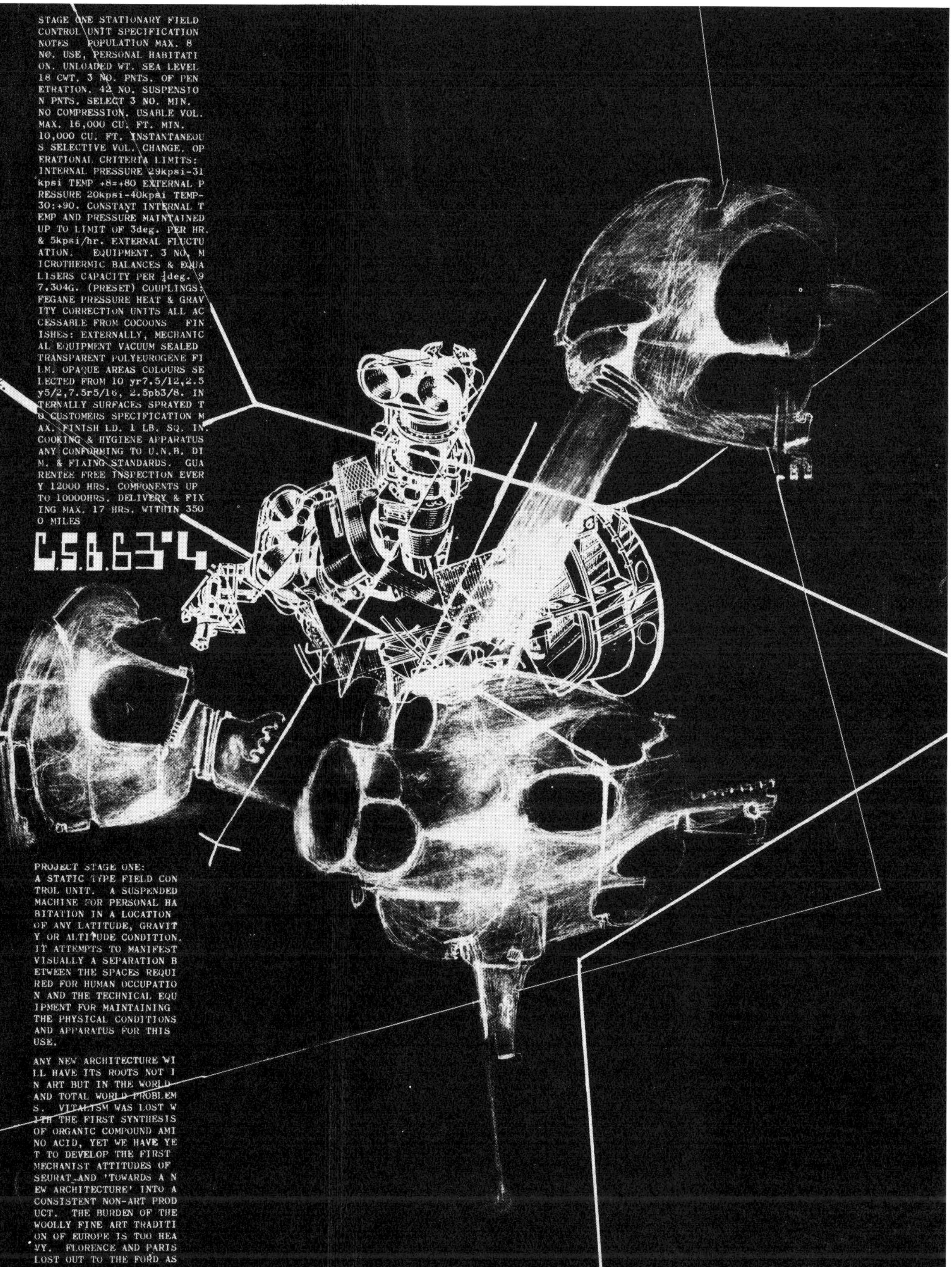

PROJECT STAGE ONE:
A STATIC TYPE FIELD CON
TROL UNIT. A SUSPENDED
MACHINE FOR PERSONAL HA
BITATION IN A LOCATION
OF ANY LATITUDE, GRAVIT
Y OR ALTITUDE CONDITION.
IT ATTEMPTS TO MANIFEST
VISUALLY A SEPARATION B
ETWEEN THE SPACES REQUI
RED FOR HUMAN OCCUPATIO
N AND THE TECHNICAL EQU
IPMENT FOR MAINTAINING
THE PHYSICAL CONDITIONS
AND APPARATUS FOR THIS
USE.

ANY NEW ARCHITECTURE WI
LL HAVE ITS ROOTS NOT I
N ART BUT IN THE WORLD
AND TOTAL WORLD PROBLEM
S. VITALISM WAS LOST W
ITH THE FIRST SYNTHESIS
OF ORGANIC COMPOUND AMI
NO ACID, YET WE HAVE YE
T TO DEVELOP THE FIRST
MECHANIST ATTITUDES OF
SEURAT AND 'TOWARDS A N
EW ARCHITECTURE' INTO A
CONSISTENT NON-ART PROD
UCT. THE BURDEN OF THE
WOOLLY FINE ART TRADITI
ON OF EUROPE IS TOO HEA
VY. FLORENCE AND PARIS
LOST OUT TO THE FORD AS
SEMBLY LINE. RUBENS AN
D POLLOCK LOST OUT TO T
HE AD-MEN AND THE REVEL
ATIONS OF THE ELECTRON
MICROSCOPE. SCULPTURE
LOST OUT TO BIOCHEMICAL
MODELS AND THE GOD-FING
ERS ON THE TEST PADS.

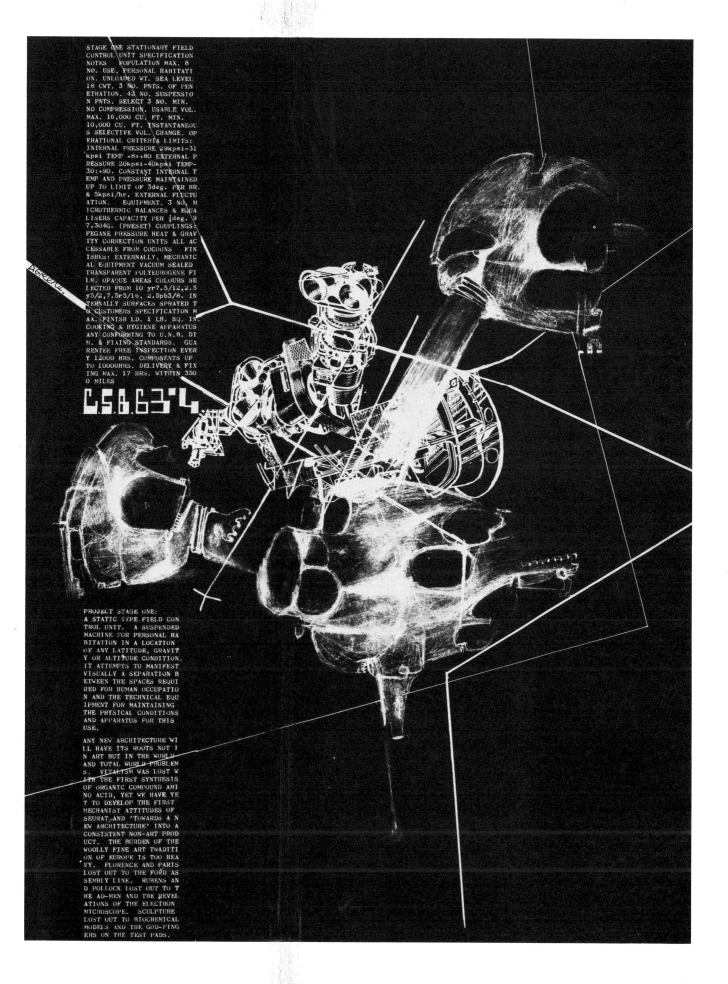

An unaccustomed dream

Warren Chalk

No magic is so strong that it may not be overtaken by a newer brand. Images and iconography are disposable and extravagant homage inevitably arouses suspicion.

Initially associated with the iconography of the space programme and its underwater equivalents (and possibly the only architect member of the British Interplanetary Society), the urgent appeal in the sixties has now cooled for me. Man has leapt up and down on the moon, played a golf-stroke even, and we are not much better for it.

We have plumbed the depths of the ocean and anti-gravitated to another planet, but it is belligerently simple – clearly a military defence operation, and the spin-off back on earth in the final analysis is minimal.

Nevertheless, Archigram in 1964 and long before that, seeking new directions, embraced this technology wholeheartedly and produced underwater cities, living capsules and the rest.

David Greene, Spider Webb and I clamoured ecstatically over the rocket support structures at Cape Kennedy. I visited the NASA control centre at Houston and later witnessed the second Surveyor (manless) moon landing on the monitors at the Jet Propulsion Laboratories in Los Angeles, collecting small fragments of the moon surface. But it was an omen. The technician assigned to me, sitting in front of a bank of 39 close-circuit TV monitors of the lunar operation, was in fact watching the Johnnie Carson Show on the fortieth.

But it is an enigma, transient urges, buried instances of a personal past, still stir the blood; because still no single architect or designer can hold a candle to the particular iconography that happened then.

Not to worry, the artist, designer, architect, may have no relevant role in society in any accepted form, but leaping about stimulates hide-bound mentalities. Cartoons and clowns are more meaningful than the Nixons, Heaths, Germaine Greers or Frosts of this world – hollow pretentiousness for humane humility.

Only more sophisticated humanity, only more sophisticated technology, working together in harmony, will help our children's children's children.

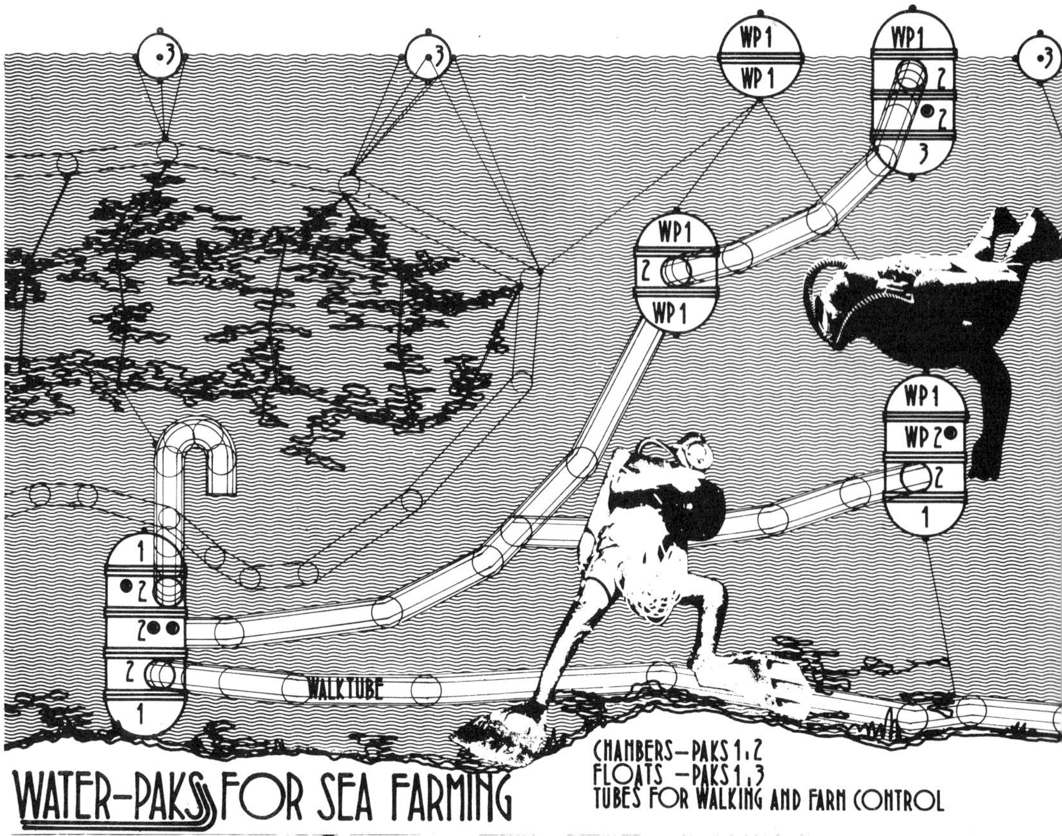

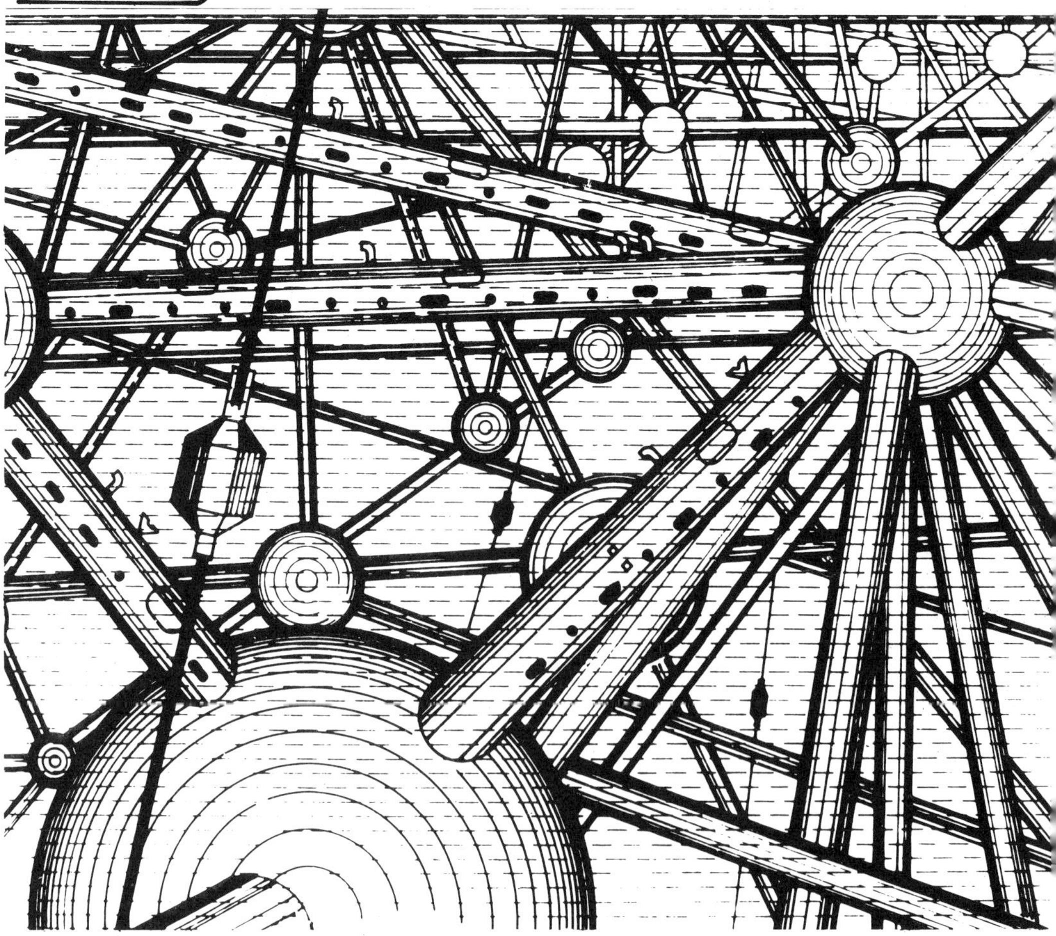

above Peter Cook: Sea Farming: 1968

above right Ron Herron: Walking City on the Ocean: 196

below Warren Chalk: Underwater City: 1964

below right Warren Chalk: Collage from *Archigram 5*: 19

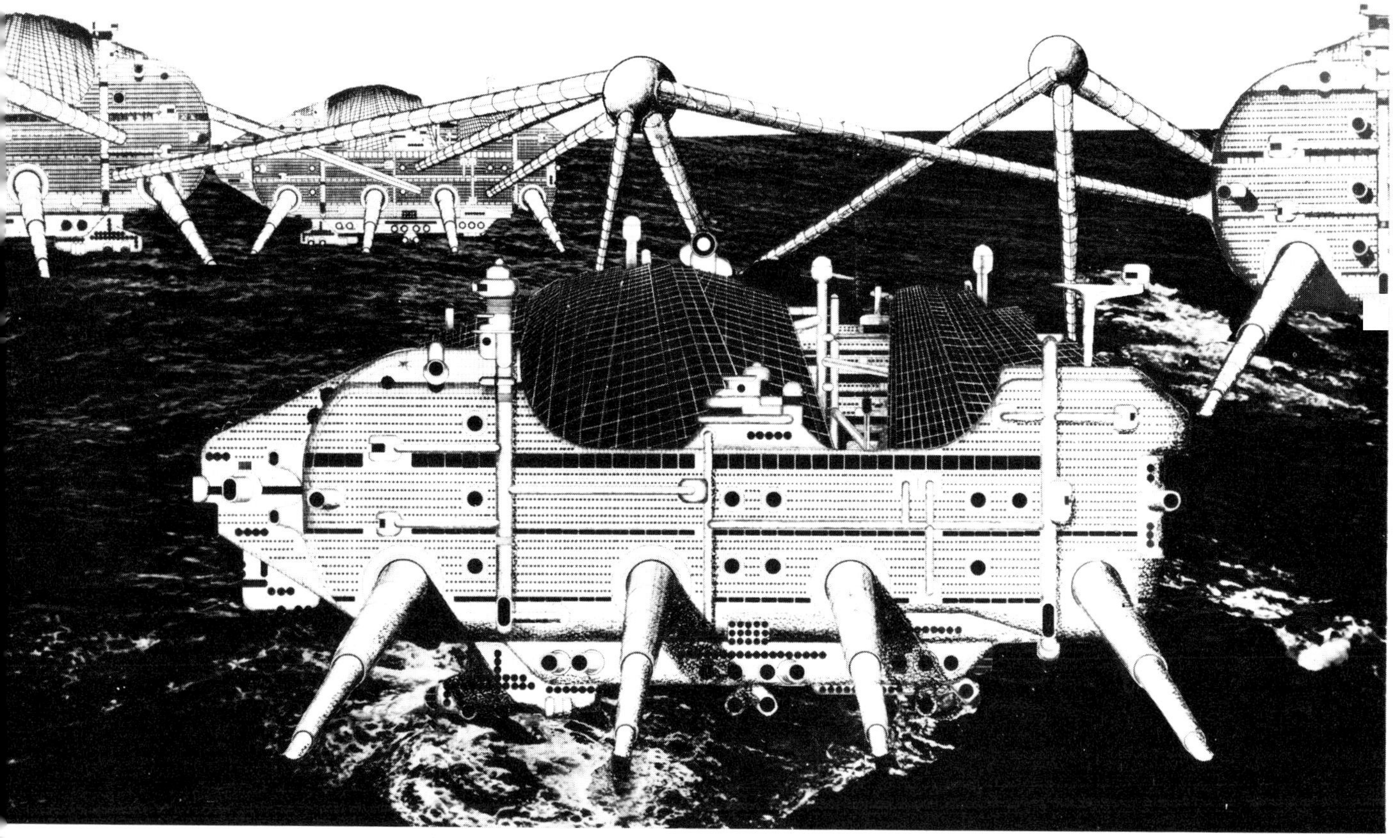

AQUAMAN
HARDWARE
U.S. NAVY
SEALAB I

Montreal Tower
Peter Cook

The Montreal Tower was a project commissioned by Taylor Woodrow and executed at the Euston office. It was presented to the authorities of the (then) forthcoming Montreal Expo as a 'central feature'. It had to incorporate a central concrete tower and provide a wide variety of public entertainment functions. This brief was extended to form a 'skin' and 'guts' proposition: a vertical tree with enormous roots on to which could be hung temporary exhibition elements that would be removed and replaced after the Expo.

In many ways, the project served as a trial run for notions of structural and component replacement that were developed in the Plug-in City. By comparison, the structure of the tower is closer, and the lift tubes – though diagonal – still form a separate structure. A skin wraps around the whole of the temporary infill.

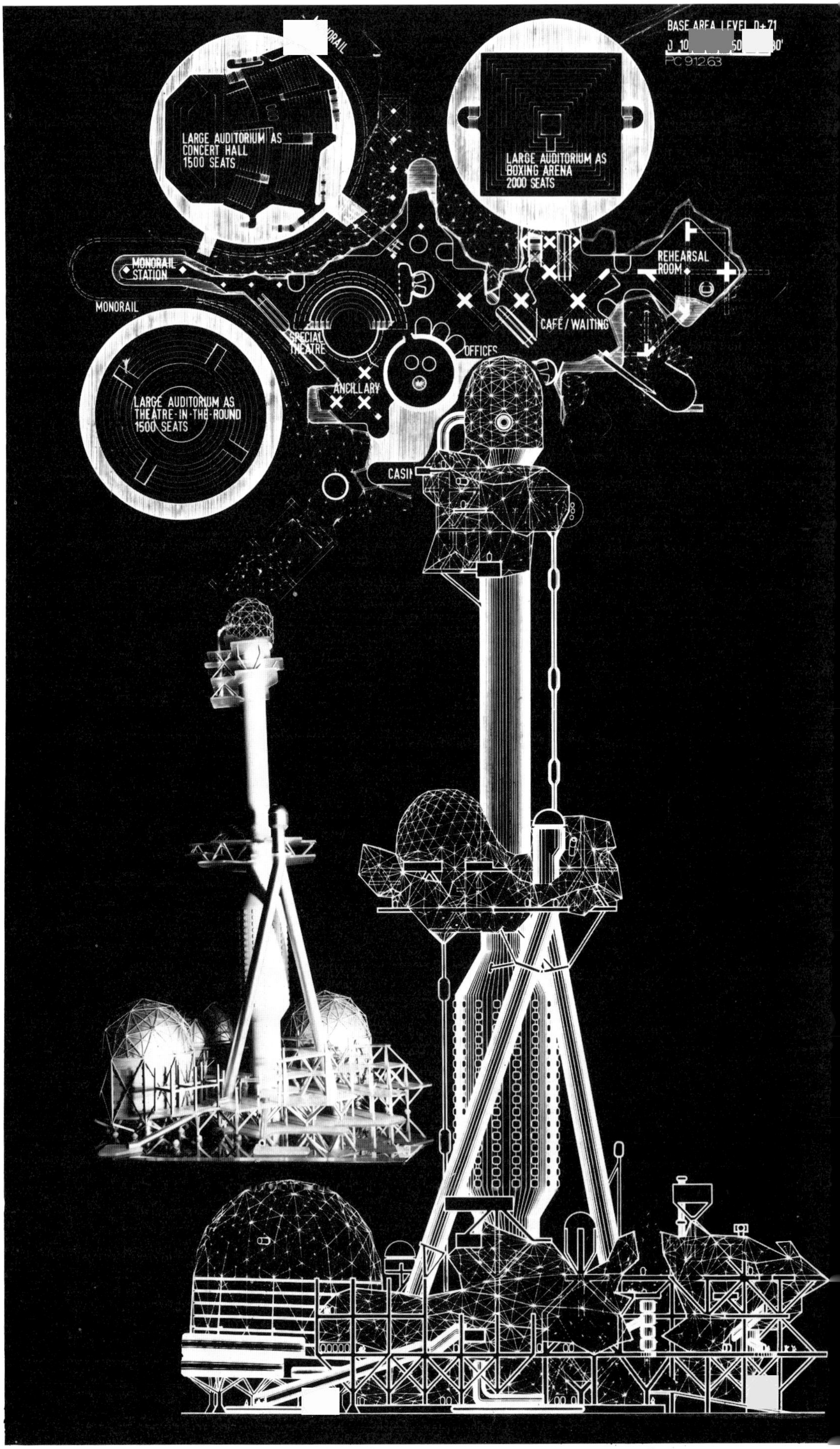

Montreal Tower: plans, elevation and views of model 1963 Peter Cook

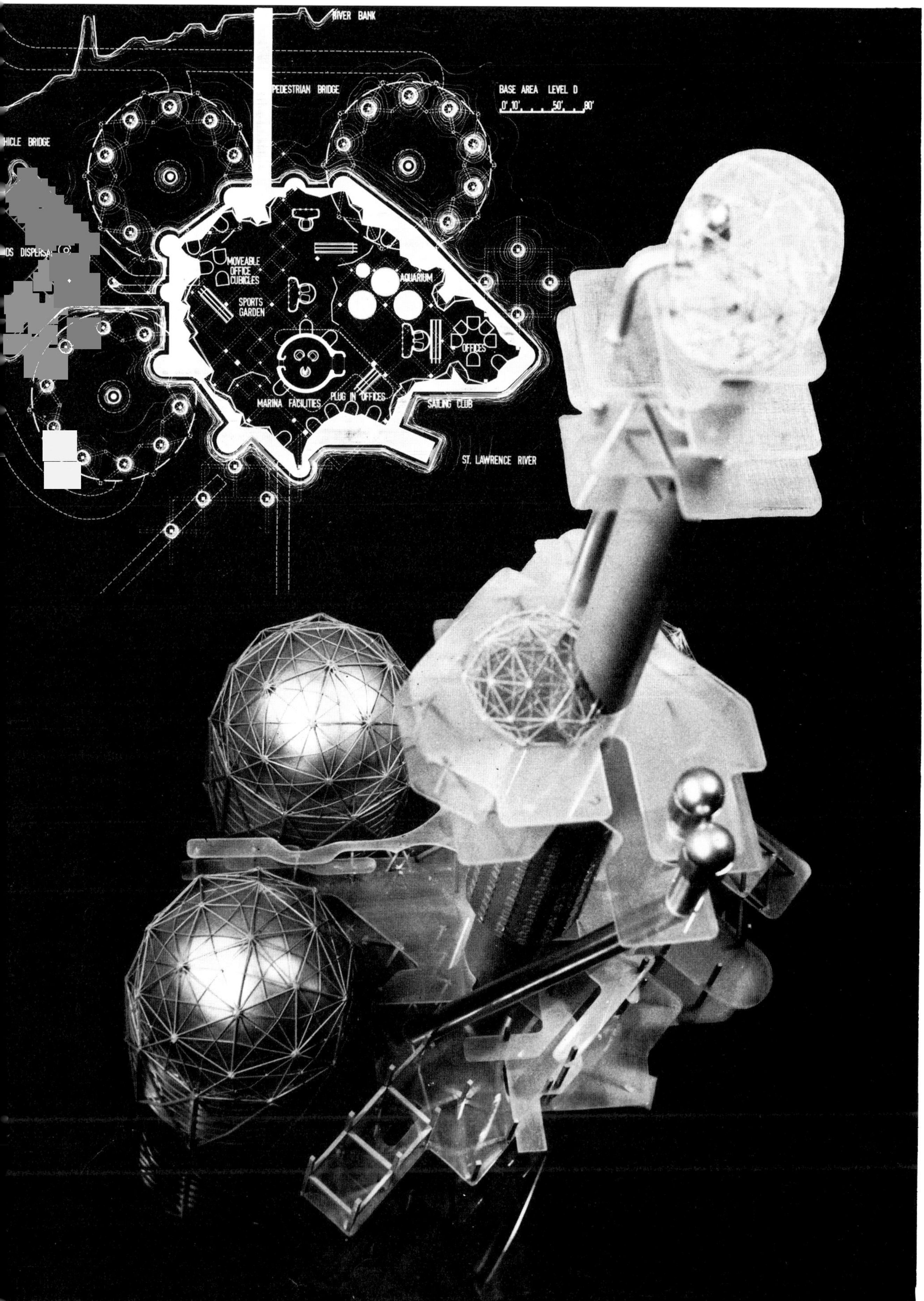
RIVER BANK
PEDESTRIAN BRIDGE
BASE AREA LEVEL D
0' 10' 50' 80'
MOVEABLE OFFICE CUBICLES
SPORTS GARDEN
AQUARIUM
OFFICES
MARINA FACILITIES
PLUG IN OFFICES
SAILING CLUB
ST. LAWRENCE RIVER

5 Plug-in

Plug-in City

Peter Cook

The Plug-in City as a total project was the combination of a series of ideas that were worked upon between 1962 and 1964. The metal cabin housing (page 10) was a prototype in the sense that it placed removable house elements into a 'megastructure' of concrete. The discussions of *Archigram 2* and *3* built up a pressure of argument in favour of expendable buildings: and it was then inevitable that we should investigate what happens if the whole urban environment can be programmed and structured for change.

The 'Living City' exhibition paralleled these material notions with the equally explosive ones regarding the *quality* of city life: its symbolism, its dynamic, its gregariousness, its dependence upon situation as much as established form. As a final preliminary, the Montreal Tower was useful as a model for the structuring of a large 'plug-in' conglomeration, with its large, regular structure and its movement-tubes (which were to be combined in the 'city' megastructure), and its proof that such a conglomeration does not need to have the dreariness that is normally associated with regularized systems.

It is difficult to state which phase of the work on Plug-in City forms the *definitive* project. During the whole period 1962–66 elements were being looked at, and notions amended or extended as necessary: so the drawings inevitably contain many inconsistencies. The term 'city' is used as a collective, the project being a portmanteau for several ideas, and does not necessarily imply a replacement of known cities.

The axonometric (right) is usually assumed to be the definitive image, for obviously classical reasons. It is 'heroic', apparently an alternative to the known city form, containing 'futurist' but recognizable hierarchies and elements. Craggy but directional. Mechanistic but scaleable. It was based upon a drawn plan, which placed a structural grid on a square plan at 45° to a monorail route that was to connect existing cities. Alongside ran a giant routeway for hovercraft (the ultimate in mobile buildings), the notion being that some major functions of the several linked parts could travel between them. The essential physical operations are stressed: the craneways and the bad weather balloons, and the lift overruns are deliberately exaggerated. But overriding all this was the deliberate *varietousness* of each major building outcrop: whatever else it was to be, this city was not going to be a deadly piece of built mathematics.

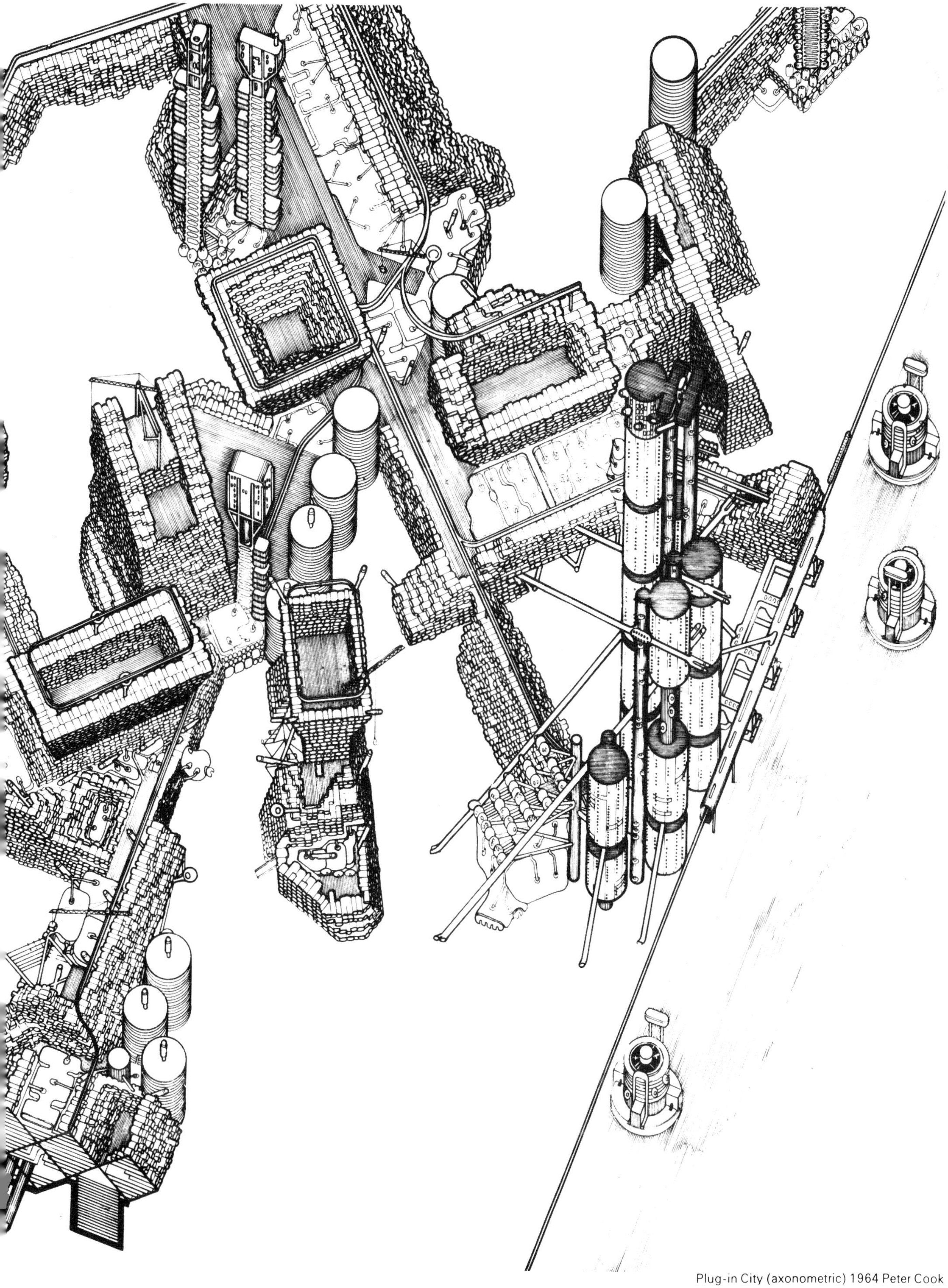

Plug-in City (axonometric) 1964 Peter Cook

In the various studies (right) that built up the total project, one can trace the succession of priorities that are gradually overlaid, and one can see how the sections evolved. The Nottingham project (a) was a proposal for shopping, but the problems of frequent servicing and the breakdown of normal 'department store' or 'lockup' boundaries triggered a notion of a viaduct-like structure against which the shops could lean. The goods servicing and the unit replacement were complementary: and already a major part of the Plug-in proposition existed. With the craneway running along the viaduct and a service tunnel system, it is only a short step to the incorporation of housing elements. In a diagram drawn for the Living City exhibition (b) the business of replacement and transportation are dominant.

We then turned towards a specific application of 'Plug-in' thinking: the rentable office floor. The axonometric (c) shows a pylon that contains lifts and services with a 'tray' hanging off each side. One tray is the 'front' office, the other the 'backroom' office. Each part would be exchangeable. Various ideas about automated shopping and diagonalized movement combine with the Plug-in Office tower in (d) – a hypothetical 'businesstown' along an international route.

In (e) (a preliminary for the Maximum Pressure Section page 40(a)) and (f) housing is the primary element. The problems being worked over were remarkably normal to any high-density housing proposal, namely, stacking, access and illumination. In fact (f) is very much of its period: the 'classic' 'A' frame, with community space in the centre. It is transitional in its architecturalness and neatness: the floors are very regularly infilled, the secondary (suspension) structure neatly indicated with dotted lines, the housing units regularly stacked and identical. That the central *implication* of the Plug-in City is its open-endedness is at this stage belied. If any occurrence can overlay any other, and the boundaries of taste and use are to be eliminated by individual wishes, then any section must not only be capable of extreme limits of absorption, but should try to illustrate them. This, then, is the real development marked by (g). Its basic functions are illustrated by the two 'cartoon' sections (h), (i). In later work, the majority of these components 'melt' – the offices diagonalize in the high intensity areas, the one-storey housing elements become looser 'areas' and the electric city car replaces the monorail. But already the proposition as it stood was throwing back at us confirmation of our hunch: that urban, or architectural, or mechanical or human mechanisms thrive on being stirred together.

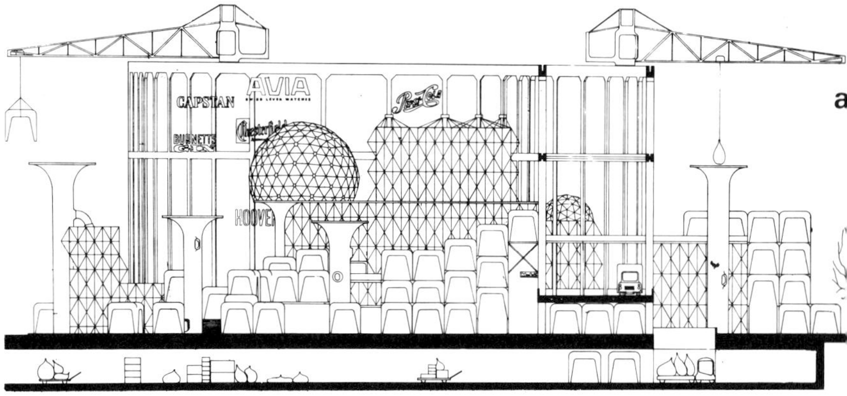

a

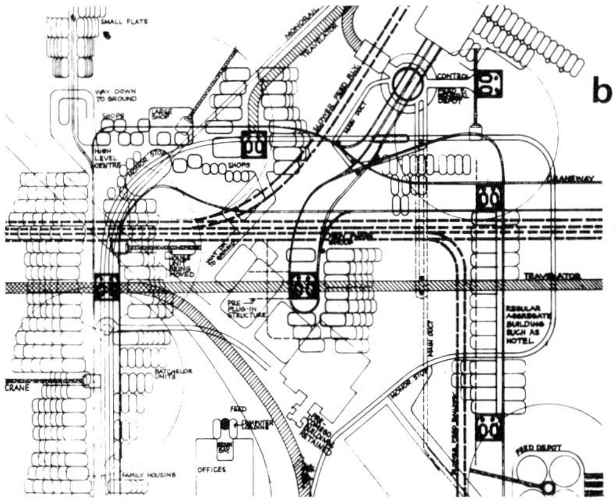
b

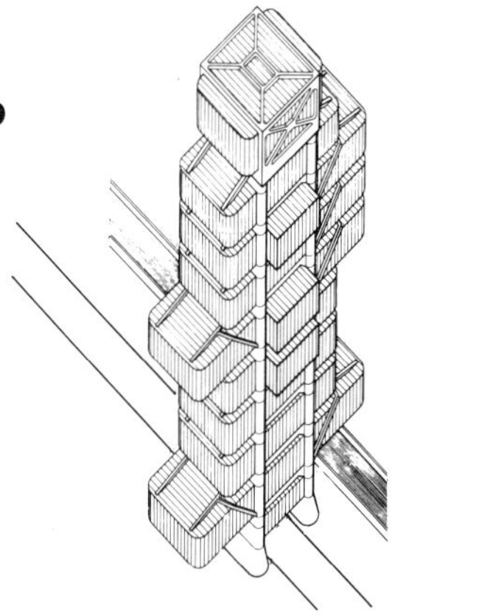
c

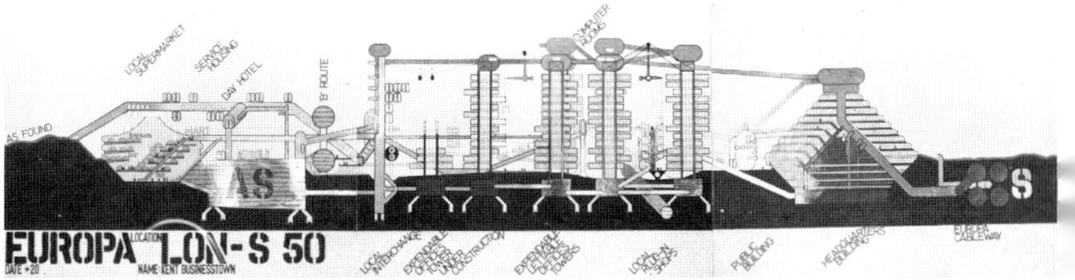

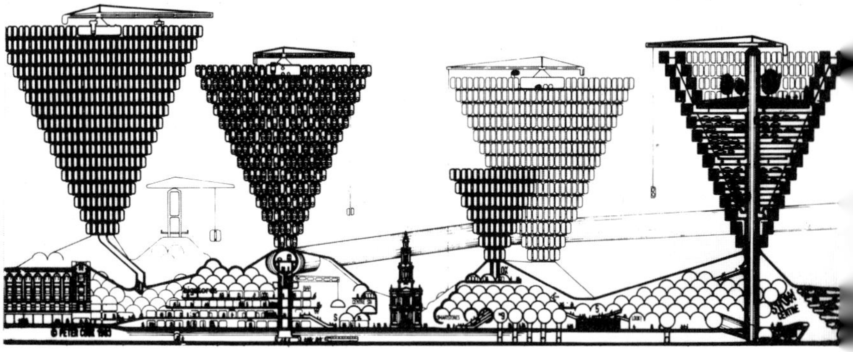

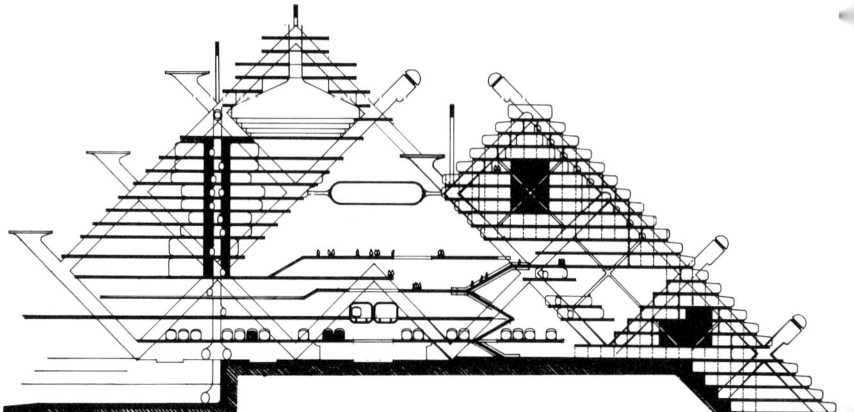

left, top to bottom
Nottingham Shopping Viaduct 1962 Peter Cook and David Greene: section
'City Within Existing Technology' 1963 Peter Cook: Plan
Plug-in Offices 1964 Peter Cook
'Europa' 1963–64 Peter Cook: Section. This incorporates a series of Plug-in Offices Stacks
Housing for Charing Cross Road 1963 Peter Cook
Plug-in City: early section 1964 Peter Cook

g

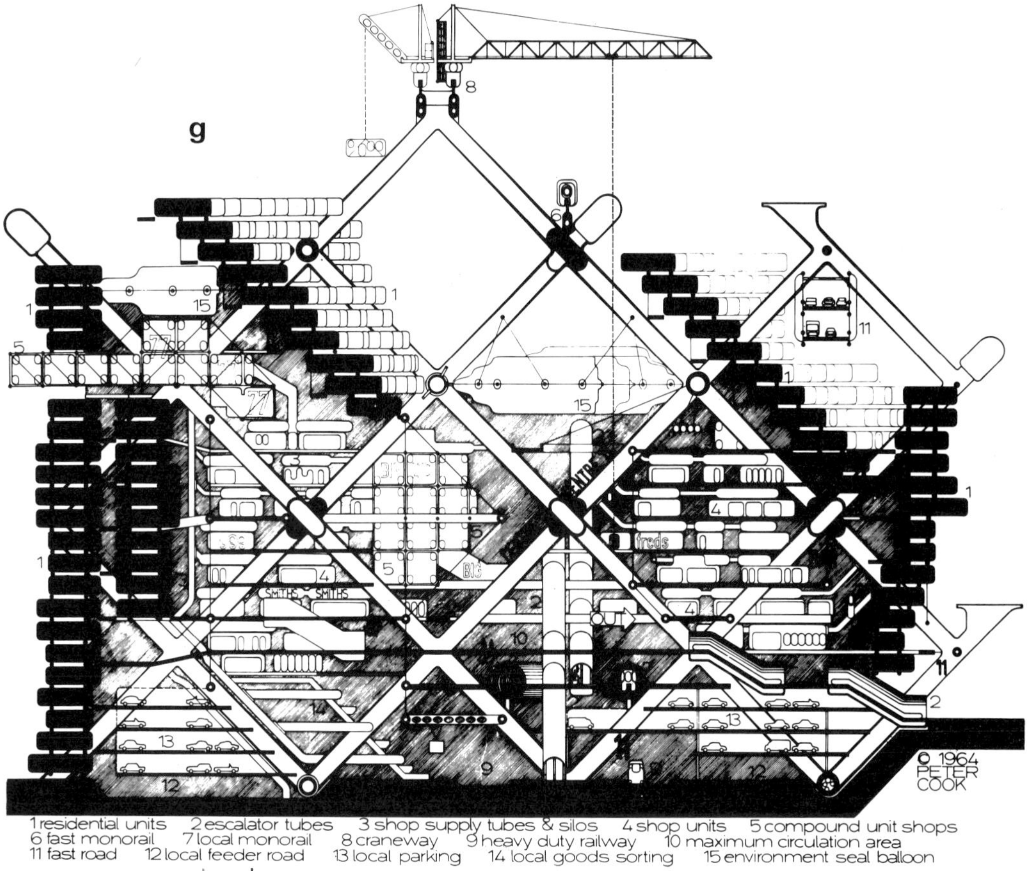

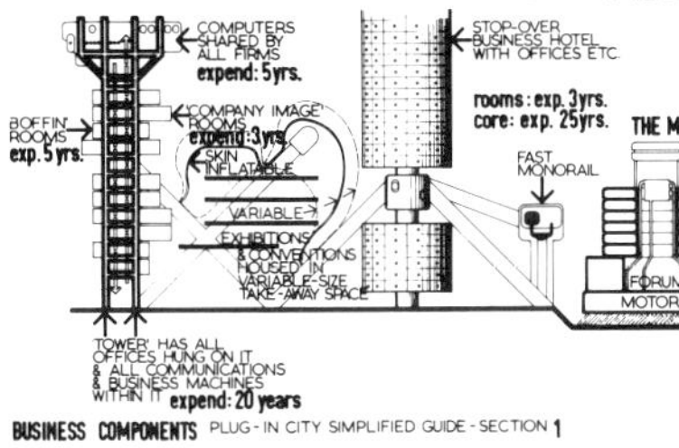

h

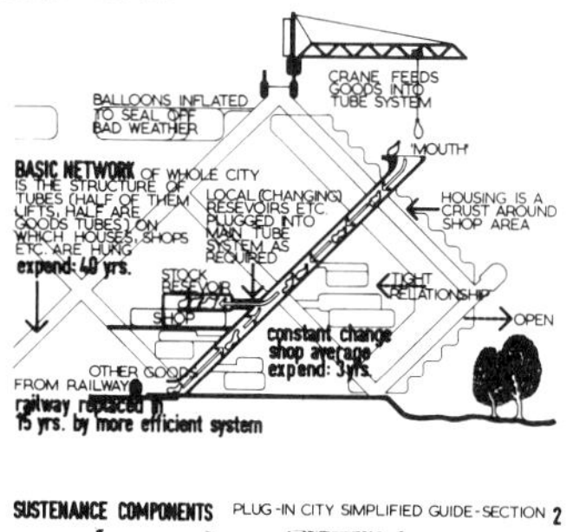

i

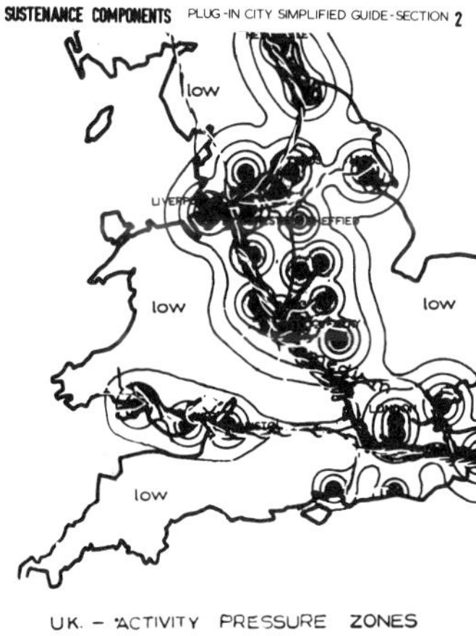

j

Definition: The Plug-in City is set up by applying a large scale network-structure, containing access ways and essential services, to any terrain. Into this network are placed units which cater for all needs. These units are planned for obsolescence. The units are served and manoeuvred by means of cranes operating from a railway at the apex of the structure. The interior contains several electronic and machine installations intended to replace present-day work operations. Typical permanence ratings would be:

Bathroom, kitchen, living room floor: 3-year obsolescence
Living rooms, bedrooms: 5–8-year obsolescence
Location of house unit: 15 years' duration
Immediate-use sales space in shop: 6 months
Shopping location: 3–6 years
Workplaces, computers, etc.: 4 years
Car silos and roads: 20 years
Main megastructure: 40 years

In addition to the main craneway there are smaller craneways and mechanized slipways as well as telescopic handling elements.

The map (j) illustrates the effect of a large infiltration of Plug-in City network upon the field force of Great Britain, linking the existing centres of population and effecting, eventually, a total city of them all.

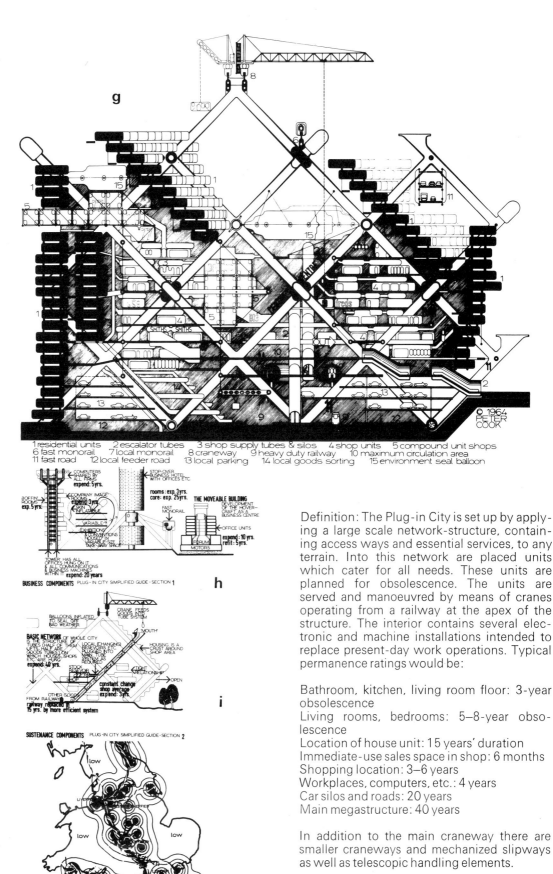

right, top to bottom
Plug-in City: typical section 1964 Peter Cook (This section corresponds with a typical finger on page 37)
Plug-in City: sustenance components
Plug-in City: business components
Plug-in City: national network 1964 Dennis Crompton

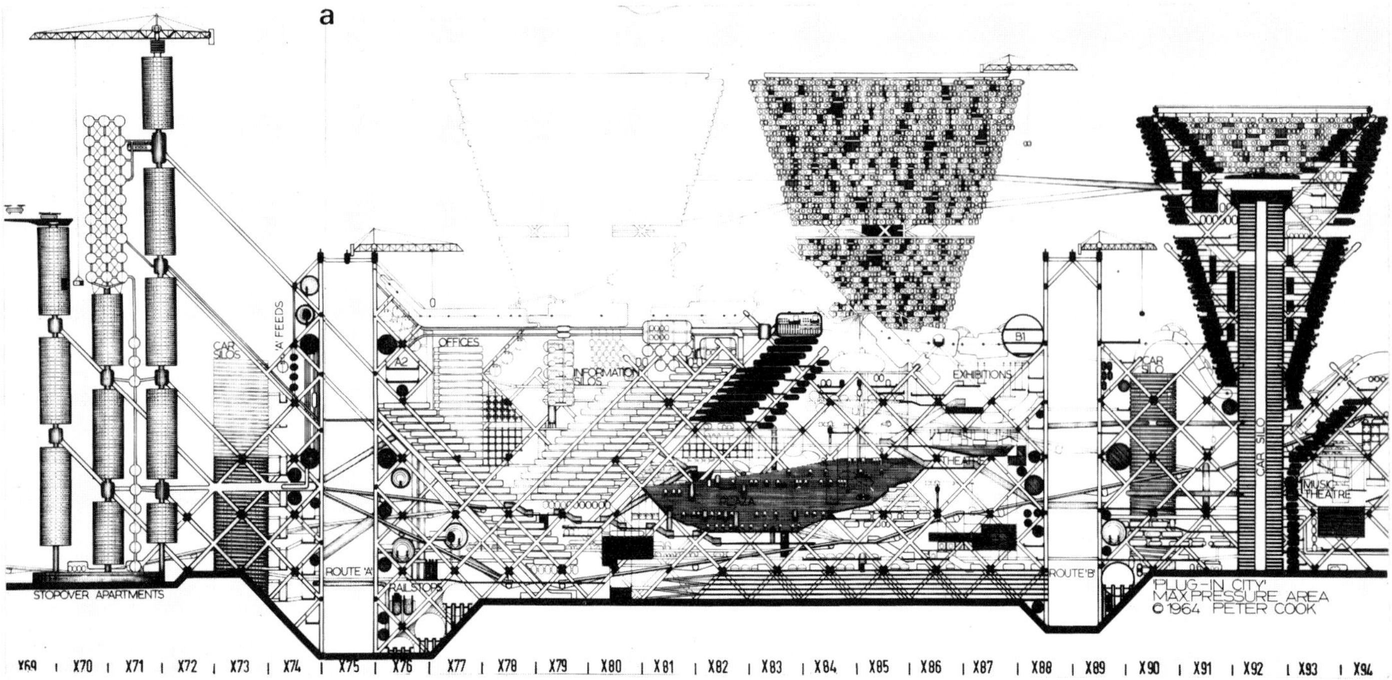

above Plug-in City: maximum pressure area (section) 1964 Peter Cook

left Plug-in City: network over London

far left Plug-in City: network at Paddington

below Computer City 1964 Dennis Crompton

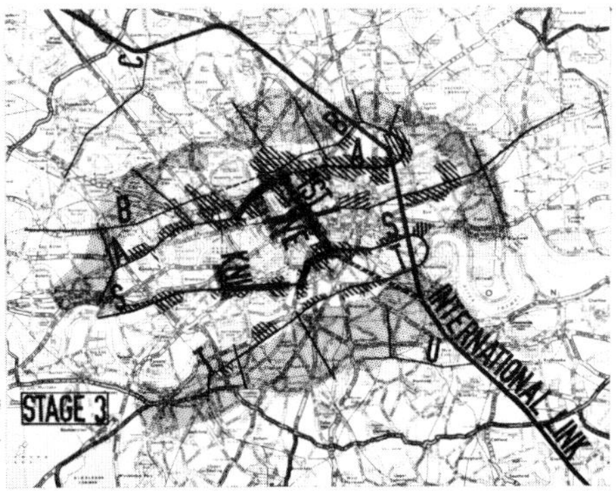

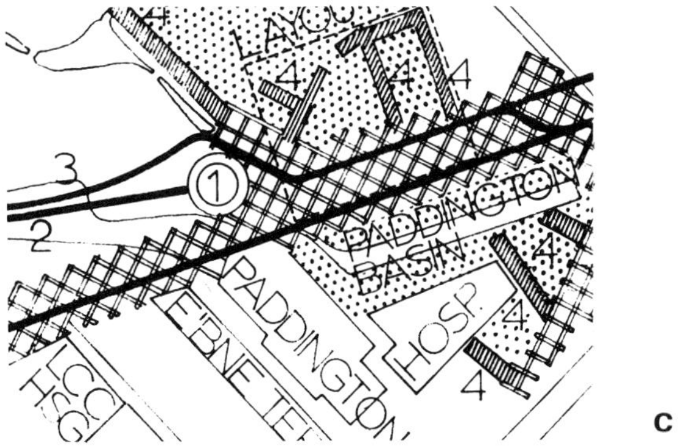

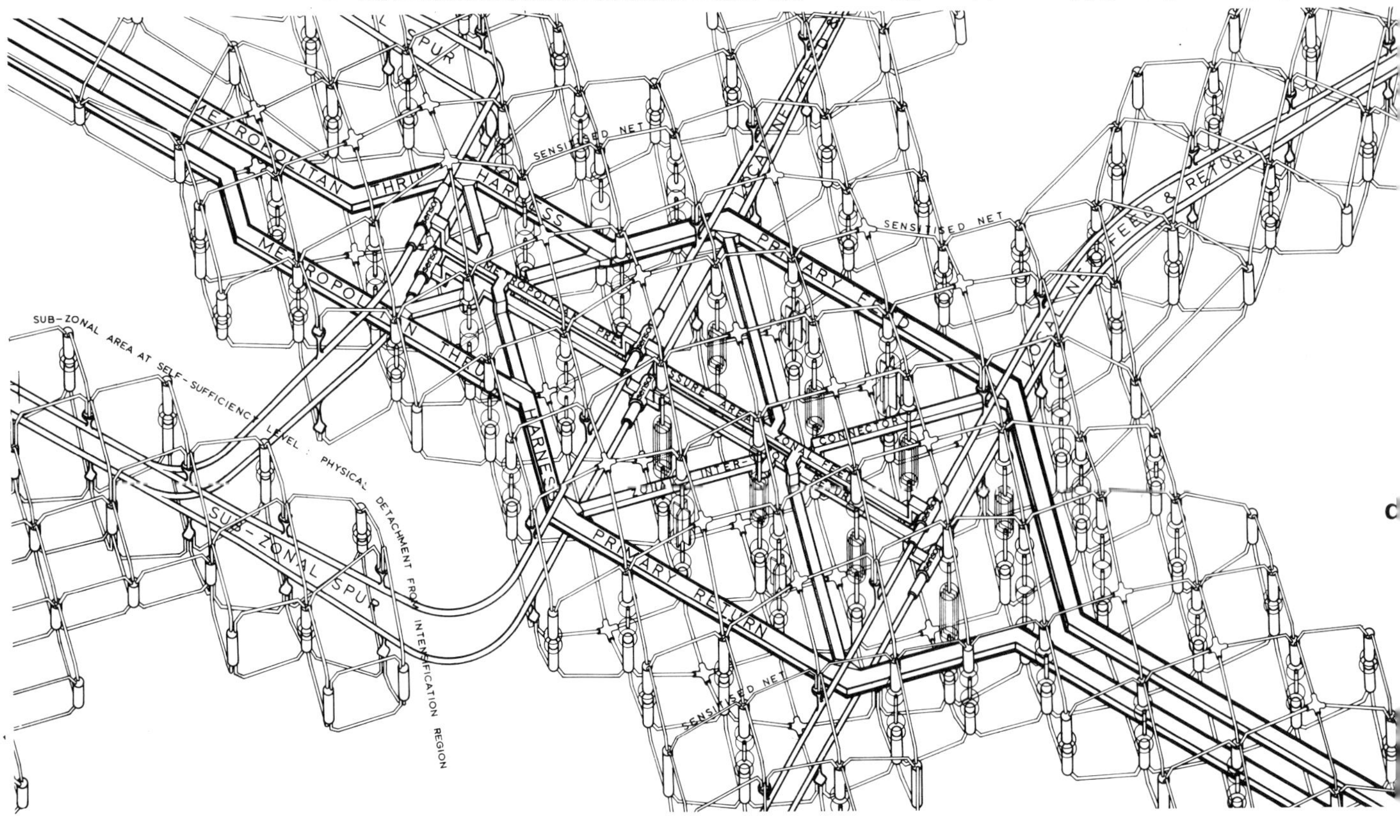

Plug-in City at Paddington: model 1965–6

Plug-in City at Paddington: plan 1965–6

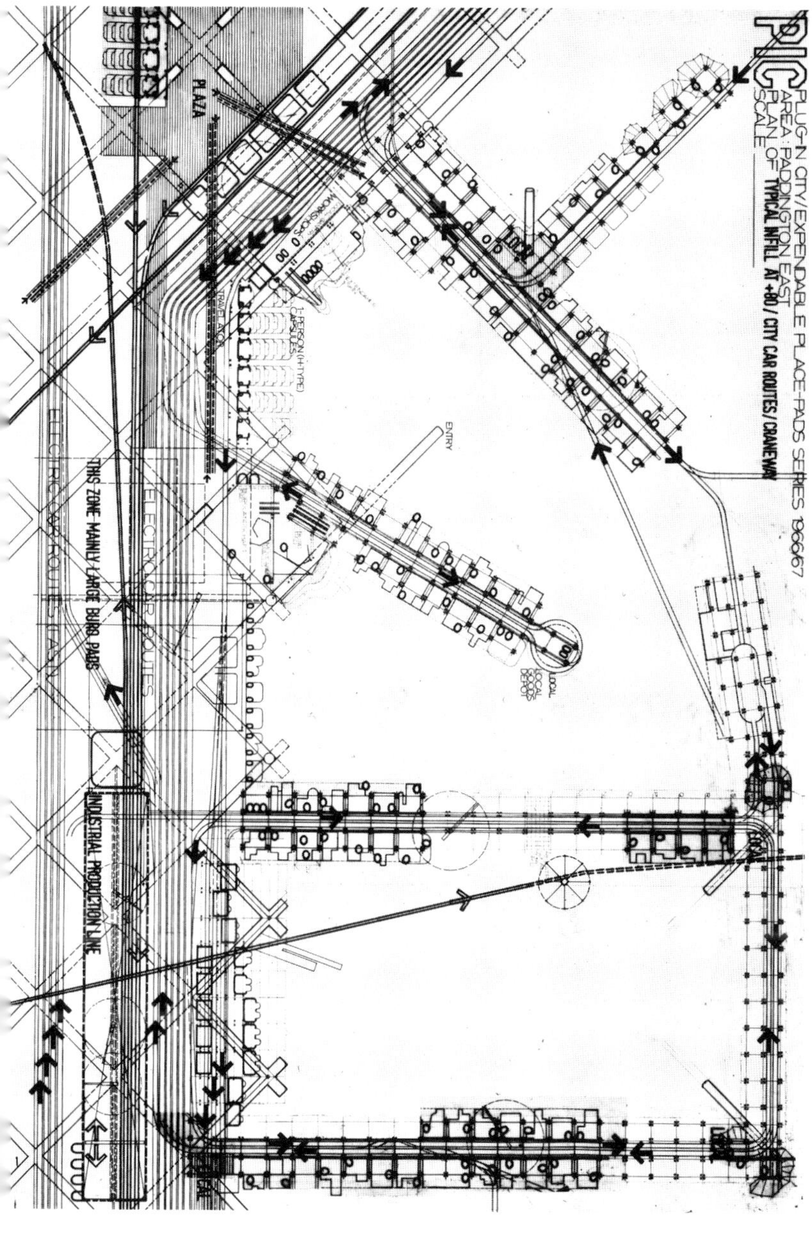

The High Intensity area of the Plug-in City is seen as a typical condition of the overlaying of the system upon London (map (b)). Key routeways run East/West through the old 'twilight' zones. They are tangential to a continuing route running from Central Europe to Scotland. In the Section of the High Intensity area (a) the routes 'A' and 'B' form main cleavages in the structure which provide a complete drop for the cranes. Craneways are multiplied along these routes. Main feeder roads and feeder service-ways are located either side of the routes. Pedestrian ways tend to run at right angles to the routes. They take the form of travelators if spanning from key level to key level, and escalators or stairs in lower key conditions. The section demonstrates several standard features of Plug-in City: the diagonal framework of 9-foot diameter tubes, intersecting at 144-foot intervals in an eight-way joint. One in four of the tubes contains a high-speed lift. One in four contains a slower, local lift. One in four contains an escape tube, and the remaining tube is for goods and servicing. Floor levels are created as necessary within the system, and are usually suspended from a subsidiary structure.

There is a hierarchy of relative permanence (page 39), but there is also an inherent relationship between this scale and those of weight and position related to the general cross-section.

This seems to relate to the speed of operation of elements as well. The longest-lasting elements tend to be at the base of the section. The shortest-lasting elements tend to be towards the top (or the periphery). Hence the heavy railway is at the base, and the environmental seal balloons are at the top. Faster roads and monorails are at the top, parking roads at the base. The lower middle region tends to contain the busy areas of walkabout space. It is here that the plaza is located; it is here also that the main lifts disgorge.

The later application of the project, to the Paddington area of London, incorporates a system of electric city cars, and begins to include a vertical 'cage' structure for dwellings (see page 47(b)). It was the last part of the project, though many of the ideas are continued – with totally different interpretation – in the 'Control and Choice' project of 1967.

The Computer City Project is a parallel study to Plug-in City. It suggests a system of continual sensing of requirements throughout the city and, using the electronic summoning potential, makes the whole thing *responsive* on the day-to-day scale as well as on the year-to-year scale of the city structure.

Plug-in University Node 1965
Peter Cook

University Node: general elevation of one wing

(sequence 1–15) Growth and Change Cycle of University Nod

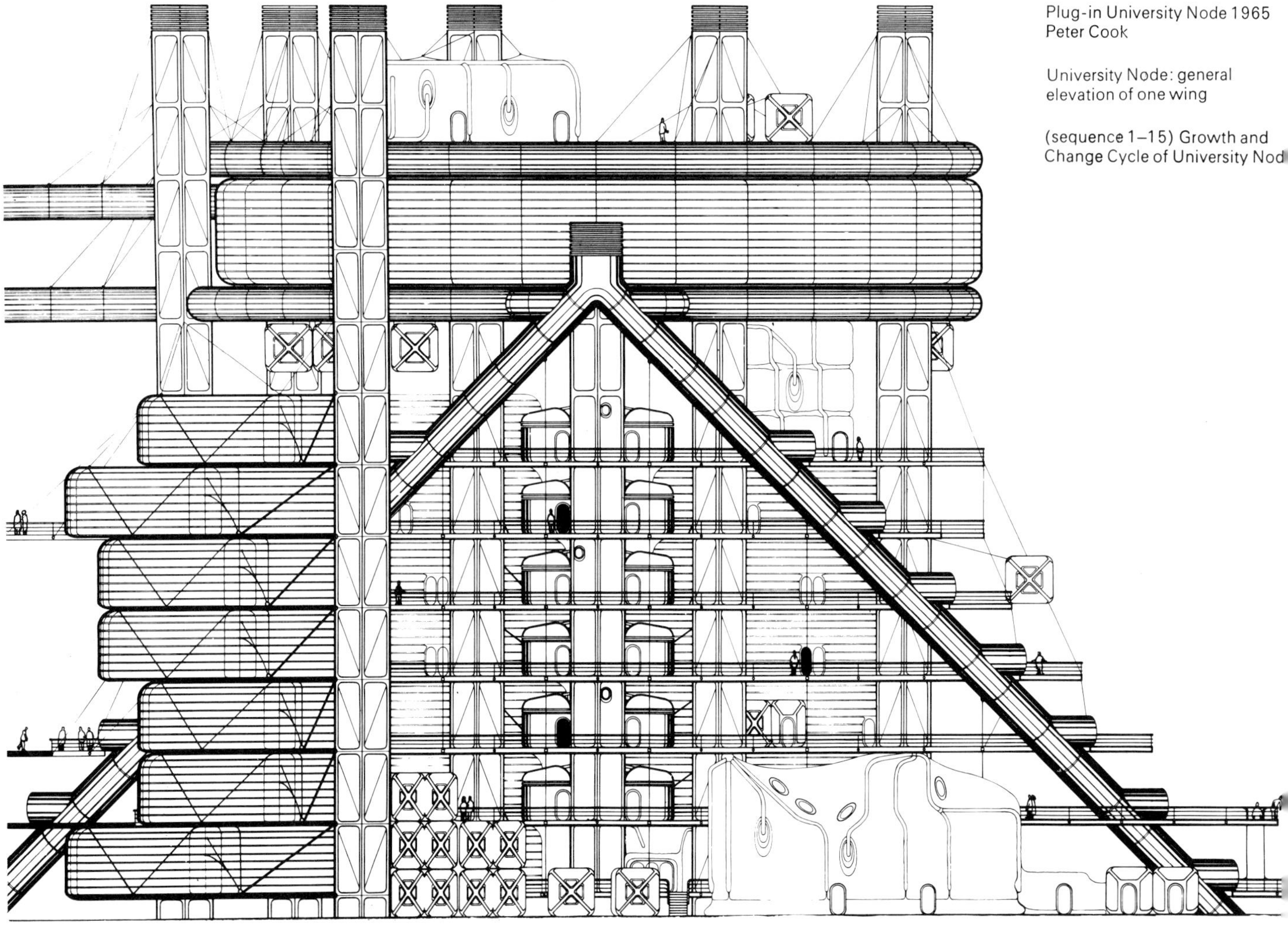

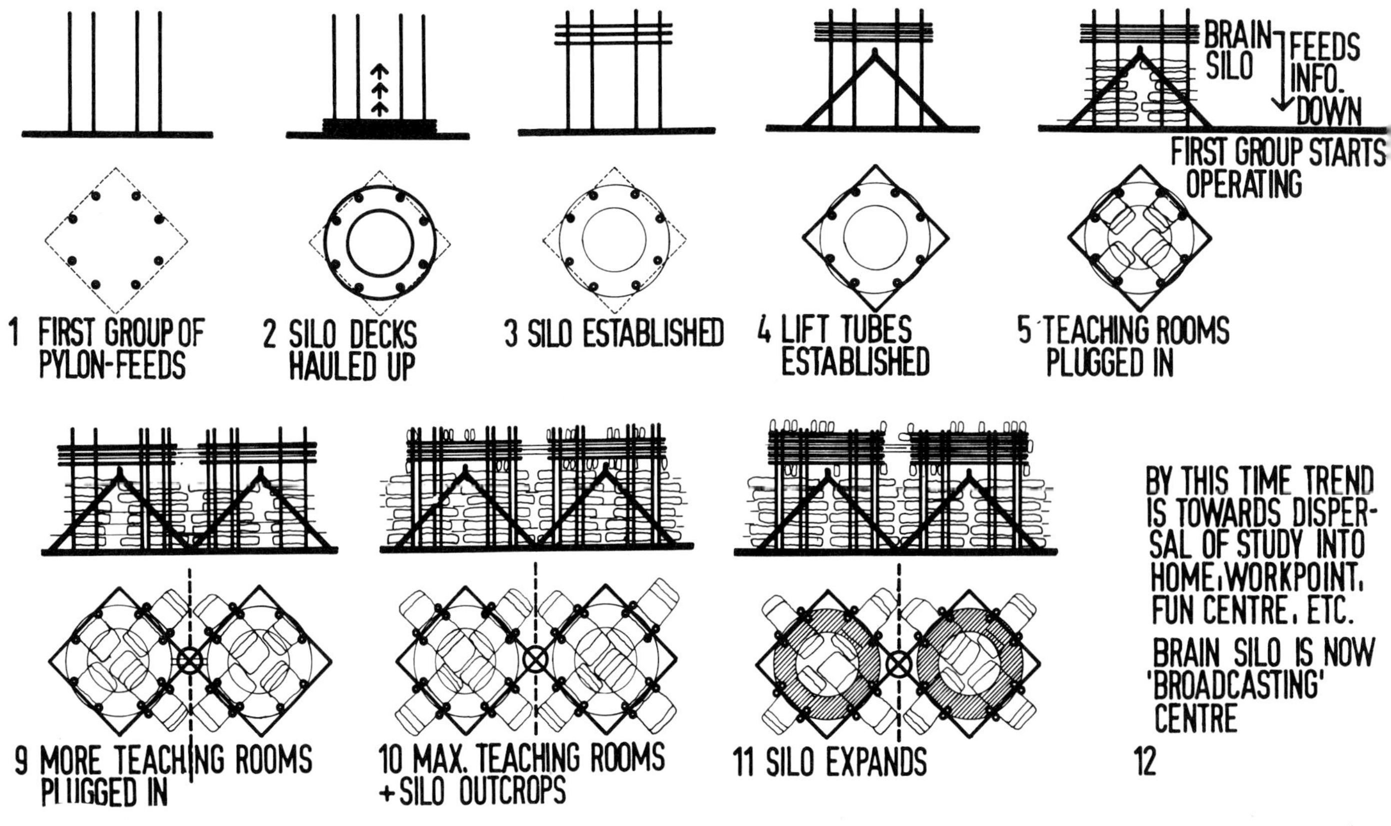

Plug-in University Node 1965

Peter Cook

The University Node was an exercise to discover what happened to the various notions of *gradual* infill, replacement and regeneration of parts on to a Plug in City megastructure: but with a specific kind of activity.

Peter Cook was at this time working with a group of students who were also looking at the future of universities as institutions – and at new ways of teaching. The sequence below anticipates the loosening-up of parts. The 'always - complete - but - never - finished' nature of Archigram projects continues from now (1965) onwards.

The main enclosures are simply tensioned skins slung on trays which collectively create the 'node'. Each student can have a standard metal box and can choose to have it located anywhere on the decking. In a sense, this anticipates the 'nomad' nature of subsequent projects.

The nature of Plug-in City: involving the replacement of one function by another (though occupying the same location) could be demonstrated and a more intense glimpse of the likely detail of rooms, lift-tubes, skins and even hand-rails be disclosed.

University Node: model

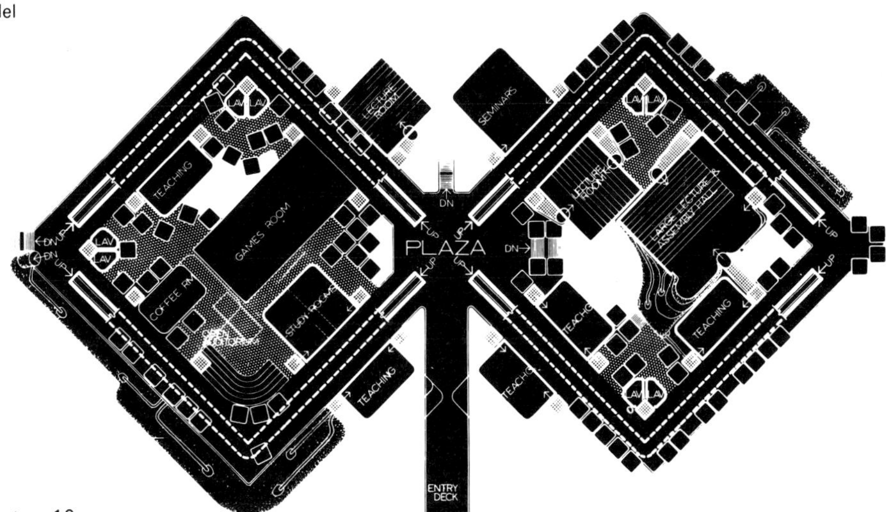

Plan at approximately stage 10

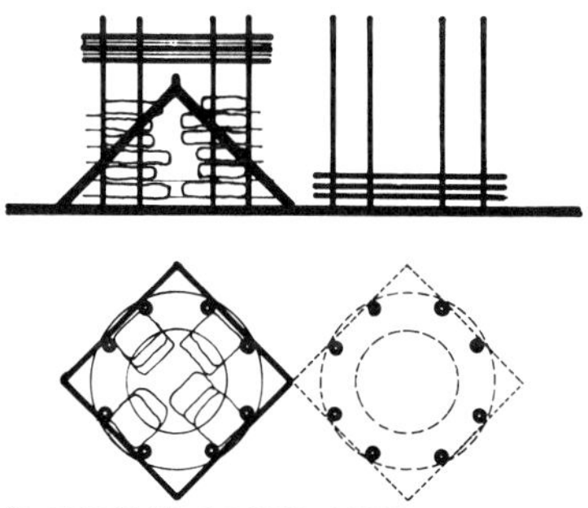

6 SECOND GROUP GETS UNDER WAY

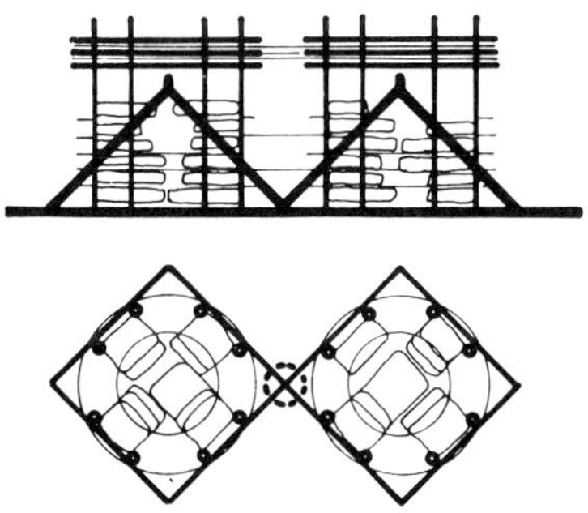

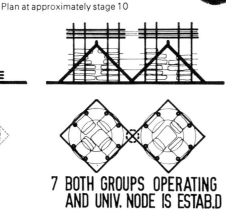

7 BOTH GROUPS OPERATING AND UNIV. NODE IS ESTAB.D

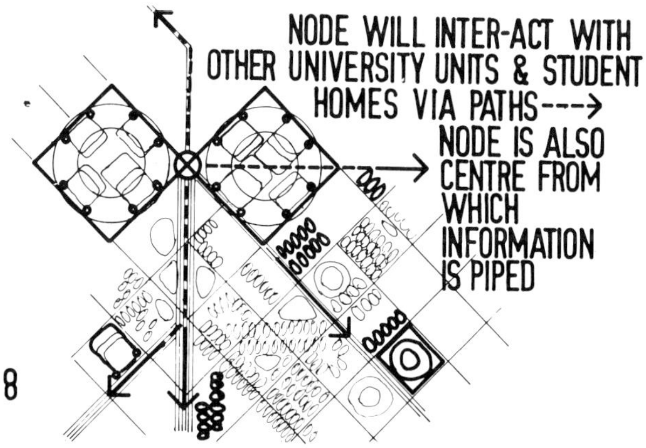

NODE WILL INTER-ACT WITH OTHER UNIVERSITY UNITS & STUDENT HOMES VIA PATHS--->
NODE IS ALSO CENTRE FROM WHICH INFORMATION IS PIPED

8

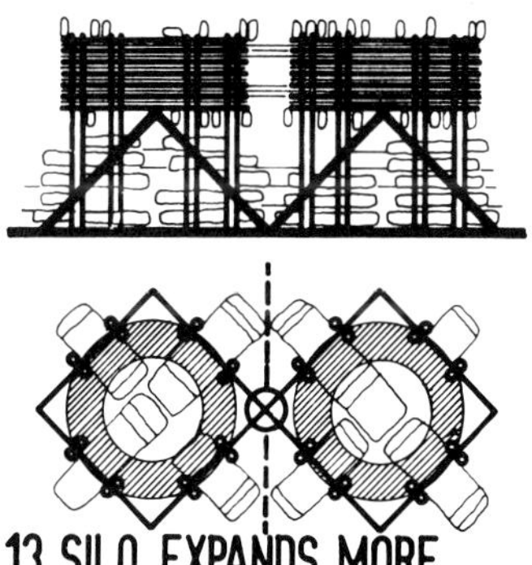

13 SILO EXPANDS MORE TEACHING ROOMS DECREASE

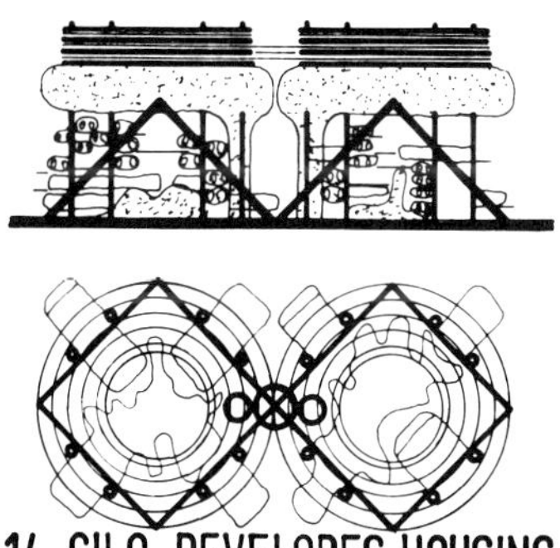

14 SILO DEVELOPES,HOUSING REPLACES TEACHING RMS.

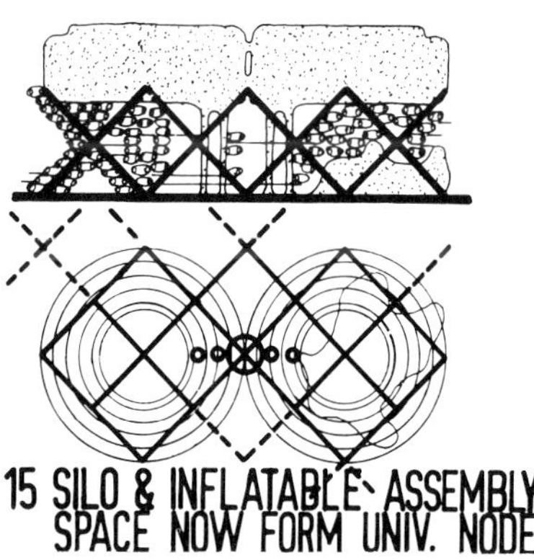

15 SILO & INFLATABLE ASSEMBLY SPACE NOW FORM UNIV. NODE

IDEA OF THE 'UNIVERSITY' AS SUCH MAY GO BUT PLUG-IN SYSTEM ALLOWS FOR PHYSICAL CHANGE

6 The capsule

Warren Chalk started to use the word 'capsule' in 1964. The Archigram Group at that time formed a part of the Taylor Woodrow Design Group, under Theo Crosby, and it was the habit of the company to feed the Group with experimental projects. The notion of a completely new prefabricated dwelling was one of these: the only constraint was that it should stack up into a tower structure.

From every point of view the space capsule was an inspiration: how different in concept and in efficiency from the tradition of buildings! The statement was a capsule *dwelling*, with the ergonomy and the sophistication of a space capsule. The parts would be tailored and able to be updated as technology moved forward, and as the dweller changed his needs. Simultaneously, the Plug-in City was being developed, and whilst both projects remained quite separate it soon became obvious that the capsule dwelling would be a preferred type within a Plug-in City. It also became obvious that the wedge-shaped unit sitting into a tower was a limitation of the concept.

The capsule dwelling was a set of components: whilst snugly and efficiently locked together they were capable of total interchangeability. To use the automobile as an analogy: the Ford floor tray could be traded in for a Chrysler floor tray. There would be a continual exchange taking place, with constantly changing and evolving parts. Perhaps a dream-machine as well as a mere 'house'? The whole tower would be organized to allow the larger elements to be replaced by crane and the smaller elements manoeuvred from within: as a result all parts could be capable of being opened-out or clipped-in. The main parts were conceived as pressed – metal or GRP, though later the possibility of pressed paper started to interest the Group.

Conceptually, the 'capsule' serves to describe an approach to housing by presenting a series of very sophisticated and highly *designed* elements locked together within a 'box' which is itself highly tailored. It is an industrial design approach. It implies a deliberate – even a preferred – lifestyle. It suggests that the city might contain a defined conglomeration of such a lifestyle, rather like a hotel. At the same time it is definitive, and would bypass many of the myths of urban design which depend upon hierarchies of incident and the treatment of housing as a folk art.

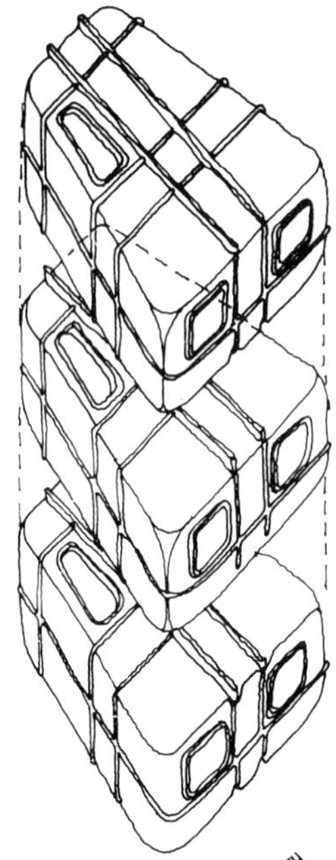

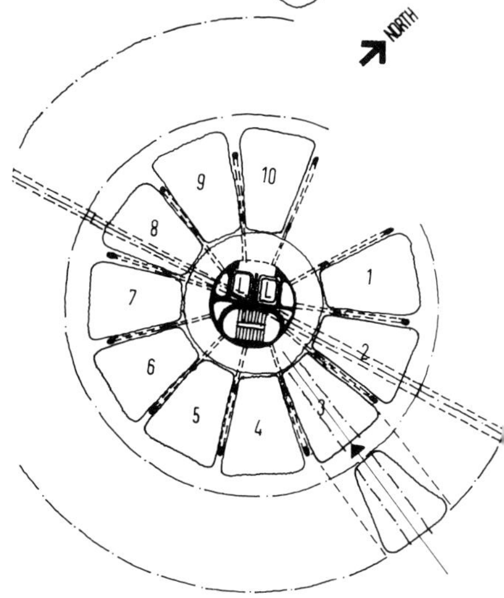

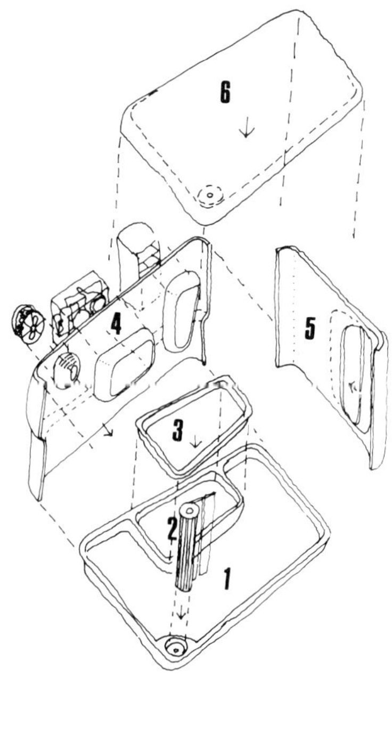

Plug-in Capsule Homes 1964 Warren Chalk

top Capsule Homes: stack-up process

centre Capsule Homes: typical plan

lower Capsule Homes: typical components of one capsule (1) floor tray (2) pull-out screen (3) bed tray (4) audio-visual component (5) inner wall leaf (6) ceiling tray

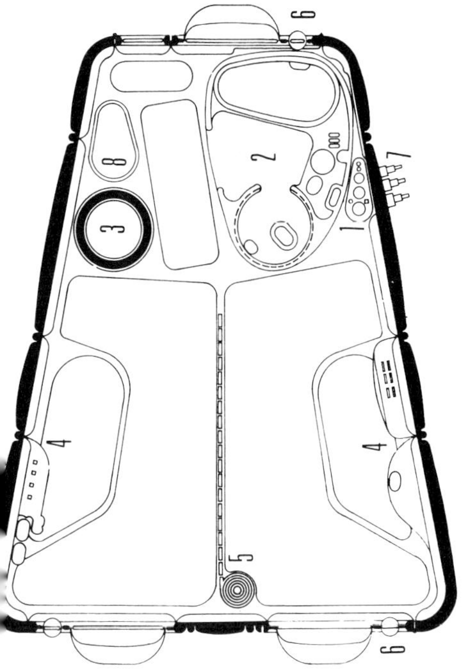

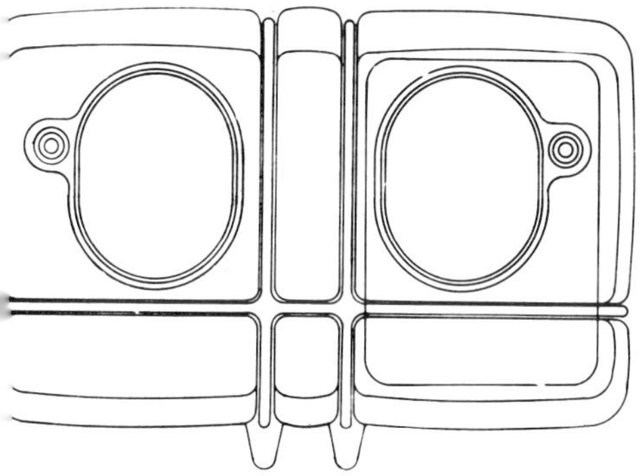

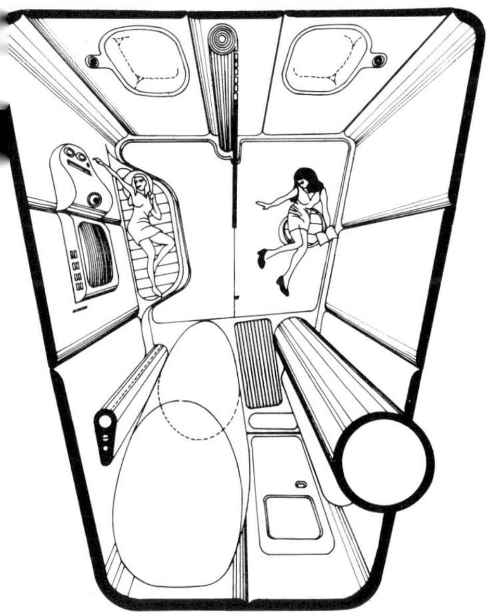

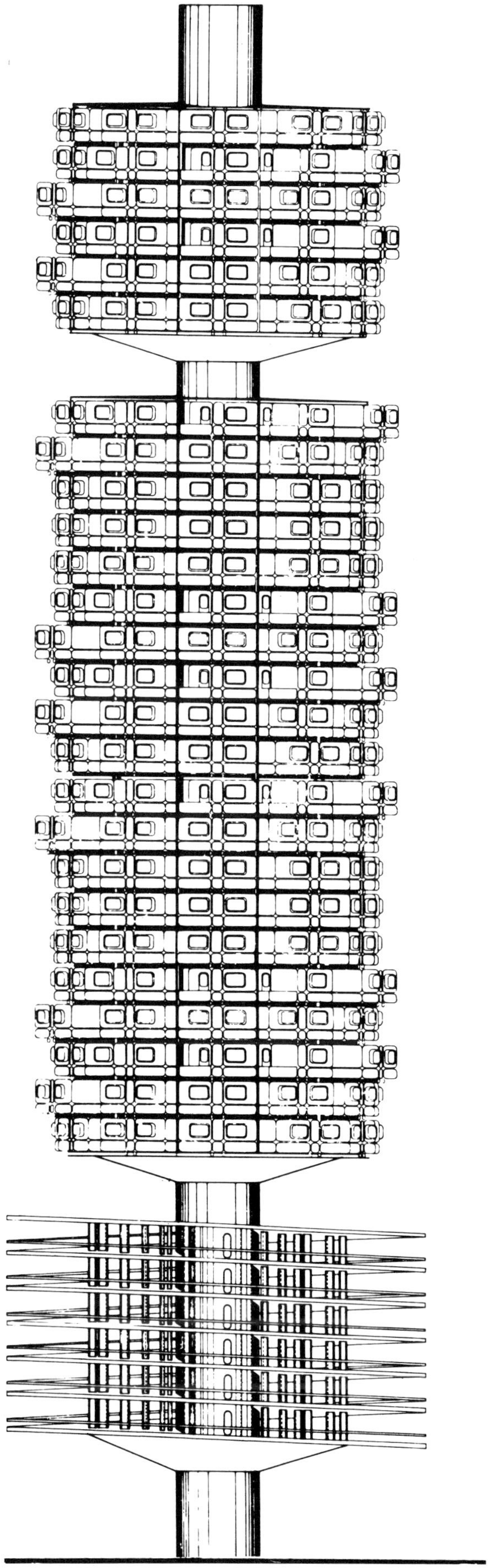

op Capsule Homes: plan of capsule unit (1) service duct
2) bathroom (3) pneumatic lift (4) clip-on appliance wall
5) pull-out screen (6) wide service door (7) services
onnection (8) storage unit

entre Capsule Homes: elevation of one unit

ower View of Typical capsule interior

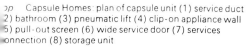

ght Capsule Homes: tower

Gasket homes 1965

Ron Herron, Warren Chalk

The concept stimulated another experiment a year later: the 'Gasket' housing, which, as its name suggests, uses a series of plastic strip profiles of different patterns that can be built up into an almost infinite series of enclosures. Without the restriction of the tower layout these units show a more relaxed attitude towards servicing and enclosure. They are suspended from a megastructure, and are independent of one another. In many ways this project anticipated the Living Pod of 1966 (pp. 52, 53). It too is a 'capsule', but the number of elements that are peripheral to the 'industrial design' part begin to multiply out. We have by this time the instance of the capsule as only *one* of a series of environmental elements that are only *sometimes* interdependent. The Pod and the Auto Environment (p. 56), and in fact all of Archigram's later housing experiments, move away from the 'preferred relationship' concept. But without it, they would have been impossible. In the time between the 1964 capsule and the writing of this book there have been several *built* examples of capsule-like units (particularly in Japan and Germany), but they nearly all miss the point of the essential hybrid quality of the capsule dwelling, the *tautness* – even a delightful artificiality of its intended lifestyle?

During 1967 there was one more sortie into capsule territory, while Peter Cook was working at Hornsey College of Art. There was a brief moment when the possibility of a prototype existed, and the Hornsey Capsule is more simplified as a form than the earlier capsule. It is basically made from three standard elements which combine to give a one or a two-person unit. It was planned to integrate with larger 'Family Cage' dwellings (p. 60) and the capsule concept seems even now to be a logical approach for pre-family dwellings.

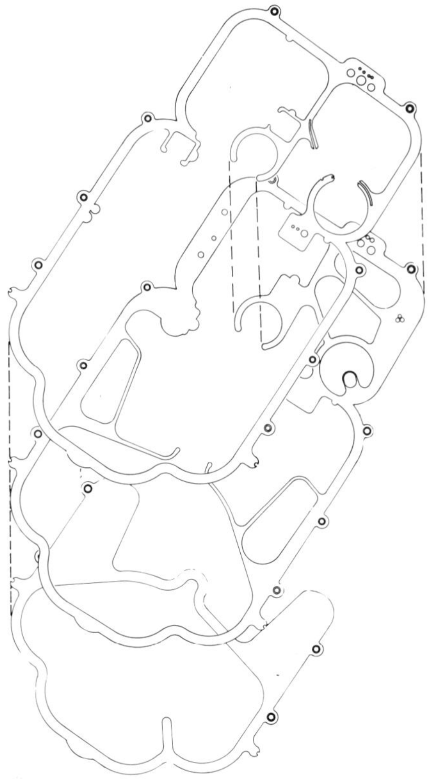

Gasket Homes: 1965 Ron Herron and Warren Chalk

Gasket Homes: superimposition of gaskets

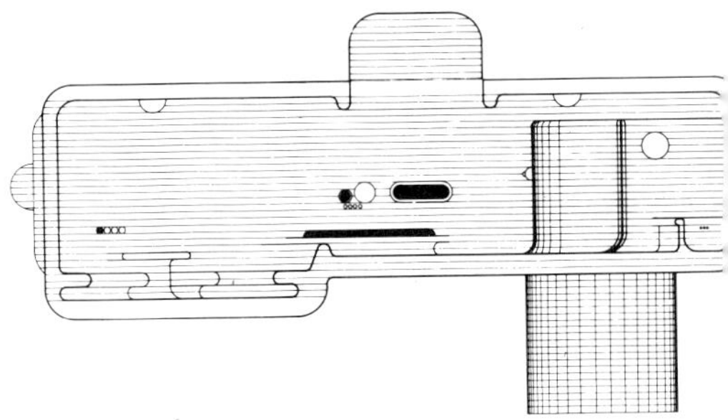

Typical section of one unit

Capsule Pier 1965 Ron Herron

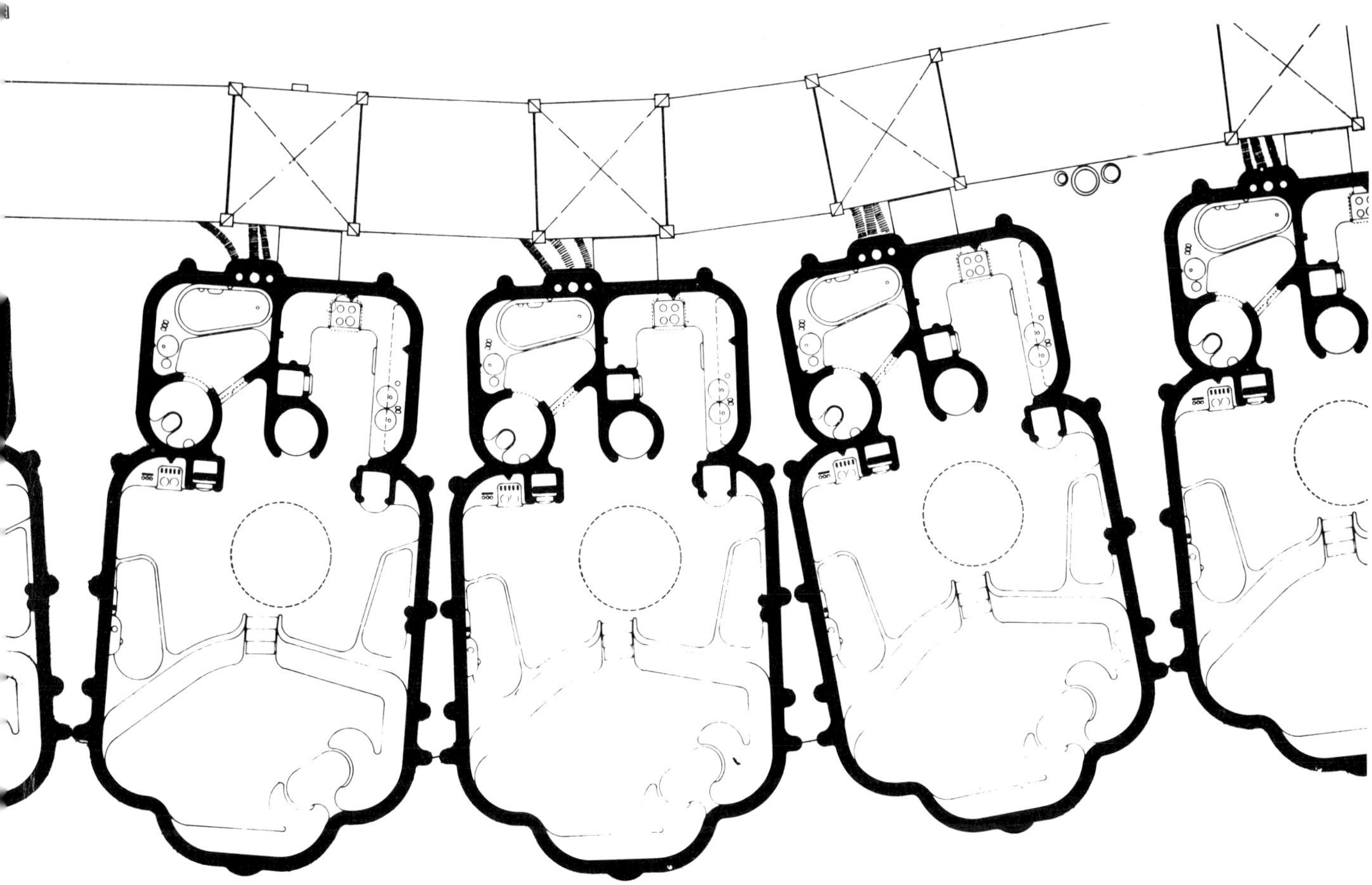

Gasket Homes: plan of series of units

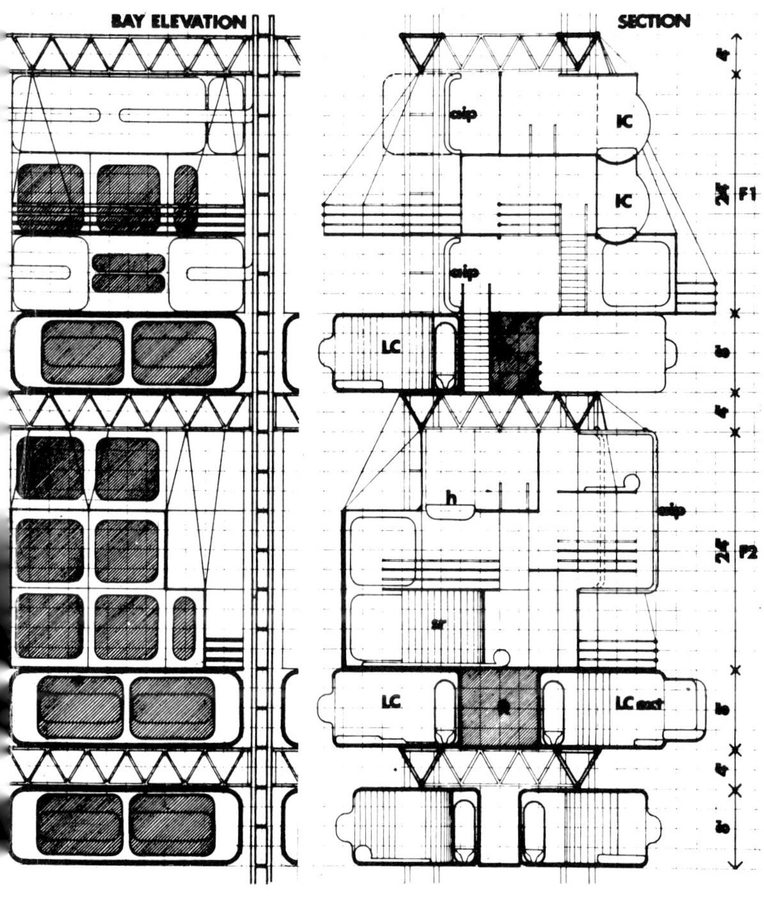

Hornsey Capsules: family cages (elevation and section) 1965–6 Peter Cook

Hornsey Capsule: elevation and plan

C

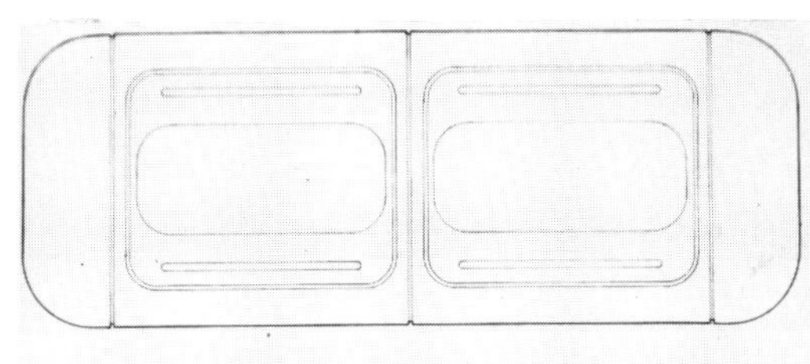

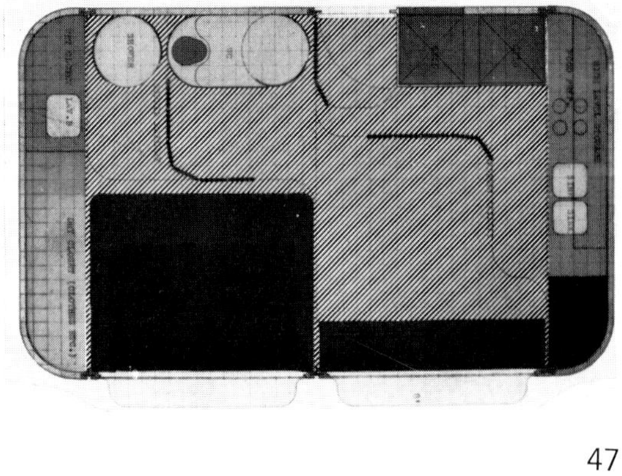

Up to the period of *Archigram 3* (1963) the experiments discussed in the magazine and designed by the group made direct conversation with the tradition of modern architecture. This conversation took the form of either suggesting replacements for earlier models of useful building, or of deliberately flying in the face of a known position by suggesting its inefficiencies. During the period of *Archigram 3* (which was concurrent with the practical effort inside the Taylor Woodrow Construction Company) the range of these conversations widened so that the throwaway architecture and the plug-in kits would be added to the rest of the vocabulary.

Gradually the Archigram partly began to set up its own motion and generated further departures from mainstream vocabulary. What is much more important is the way in which the middle period experiments of the Plug-in City, the capsules and the Walking City created values that replaced almost a total range of modern architecture values. From 1965 onwards, the discussions were sufficiently removed to gain a certain freedom and coolness. It began to be less necessary for the criteria of a project to respond to any architectural morality and the projects themselves began to form a natural generic series.

The Living Pod, the Auto-Environment and various dwelling cases are very much a half-step between the mechanical (problem-solving) assembly and the really free-ranging set of parts that respond to personal needs. The gesture of translating events from a formal limitation to a mechanized liberation began to be symbolic more than directly necessary. Perhaps some necessary conflict between gestures and the great desire to manifest: to build: to experiment.

The experiments were beginning to burst the seams of architectural response but at the same time the examples began to fall into two categories: the ultimate stage and the half-step. In a way it was very useful to play the two against each other, and later we began to find that the continuing process of metamorphosis brings both together again as merely stages in a continually evolving state of parts and functions.

Physically, too, the objects seemed to be bursting their seams. In the Living Pod, what is basically a capsule has satellite parts working inside it, but these themselves can also travel outside. In the Mobile Village, an organism is at once building and vehicle, small and large, tightly-knit and extended. The Auto-Environment develops from an organization of panels and surfaces into a continuous system of parts of very varied kinds, the only link being the intention to widen the performance of the home. The discussion of house and car as interrelated is a necessary response to the planning problem of what to do with cars, but at the same time it questions the need for fixed places at all. And parallel to this burst is all the time a feeling, backed-up by the newspapers and one's own observations, that the world is beginning to evolve quite complex environments without the need for architects or respect for architectural interaction. One feels carried along by history. The various icons themselves begin to be linked by style. The bits and pieces necessary to sustain the experiments from 1965 onwards have less apparent family likeness and begin to need to borrow less from obvious hardware. They begin to be hybrids. With this stage there is a frightening prospect: that the whole thing might become further and further out, deeper and deeper involved in its own introvert discussion of experiment after experiment, and project referring only to previous projects finally losing touch with industry and with people, unless one is careful. Part of the answer to this was a deliberate attempt to deal with living places; the home, communication, the locality. This was partly in direct reaction to the question: the Plug-in City is all very well, but how could you actually realize some of these ideas on a smaller scale? The first response was to look at local infill – a mews conversion, a row of eight houses – and then to develop this outwards again. One Archigram method has been continually to revolve the scale of investigation, from urban to local to home to personal to specific object and then, imperceptibly, back again.

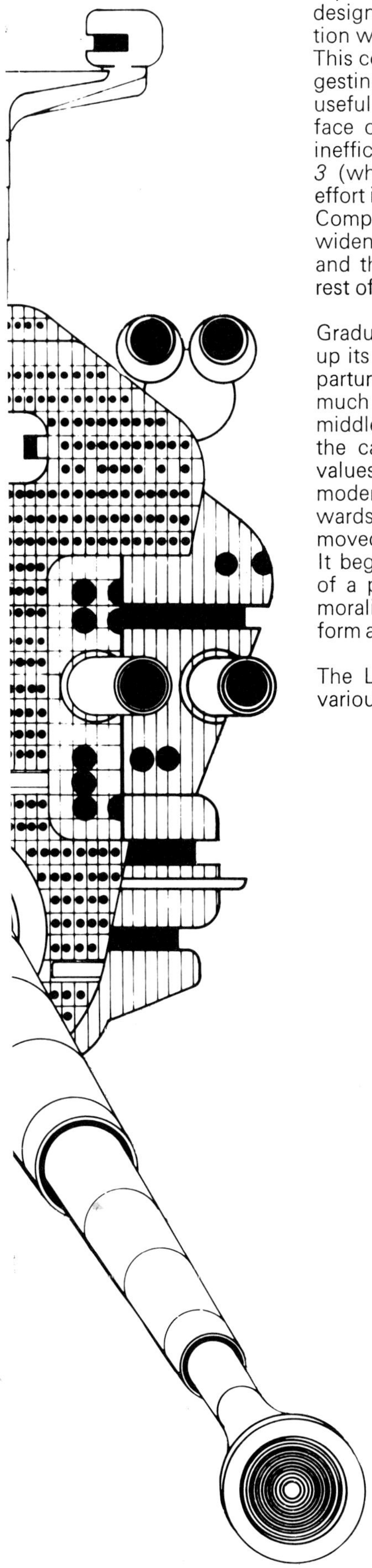

Walking City: detail 1964 Ron Herron

This is the value of the half-step in relation to any near absolute that is being thought of. Once one has an open-ended system with one experiment at one scale and with one degree of technology or organizational anticipation, it can be seen as affecting the whole range of other experiments. The half-step living capsule can be seen as the prototype for a generation of capsules gradually evolving until the term and definition of capsule is irrelevant to the developed hybrid. At the same time this can be seen in relation to an urban philosophy (at a practical, infill level as well as at a problem-solving level) and this urban development is only part of a continuing process in which the urban model itself will disappear into something else.

Perhaps, ultimately, this bursting of the seams (which appears dramatic because we are looking at it only in terms of architecture and a break in architectural tradition) is simply no nore than the playing-out of history as applied to shelter and various aspects of human interface.

The Archigram projects from here onwards share a developing divergence from the com-plete, contained object. They begin to escape rom the need to replace type solutions of the past with updated type solutions. Plug-in City vas still in some respects a replacement 'city', he Capsule houses were still replacement houses'.

A hybrid that is sometimes machine, sometimes rchitecture, sometimes animal-like growth, ometimes electrical circuitry, sometimes part of a mathematical progression and sometimes ompletely random – (this characterizes Archigram work from 1966 onwards). Michael Vebb's Auto-Environment series is probably he first break into this more evolutionary way f structuring a project.

'he seams of 'building type' are at last roken. It means that the following work is ometimes difficult to explain on a compara-ve basis. It means that there is an accelerating istance away from 'buildings as built': yet in ne mind of the designers of these projects this reakaway seems to have brought a new eality, unfettered by the architectural hangup. an assembly can choose its parts or its refer-nces from any set available, there is the hance that the result is *really* appropriate to a articular situation.

his thinking is explored in *Archigram 8* April 1968), the essays of which appear in hapter 8. But it was only towards the end of 967 that the feeling behind the projects ould be expressed verbally in such terms. this way, the Blow-out Village, the 1990 ving System, the Rent-a-Wall and the ushicle must all be seen as increasingly eed from the hierarchies of parts that build-gs with their traditional rules have hitherto stained.

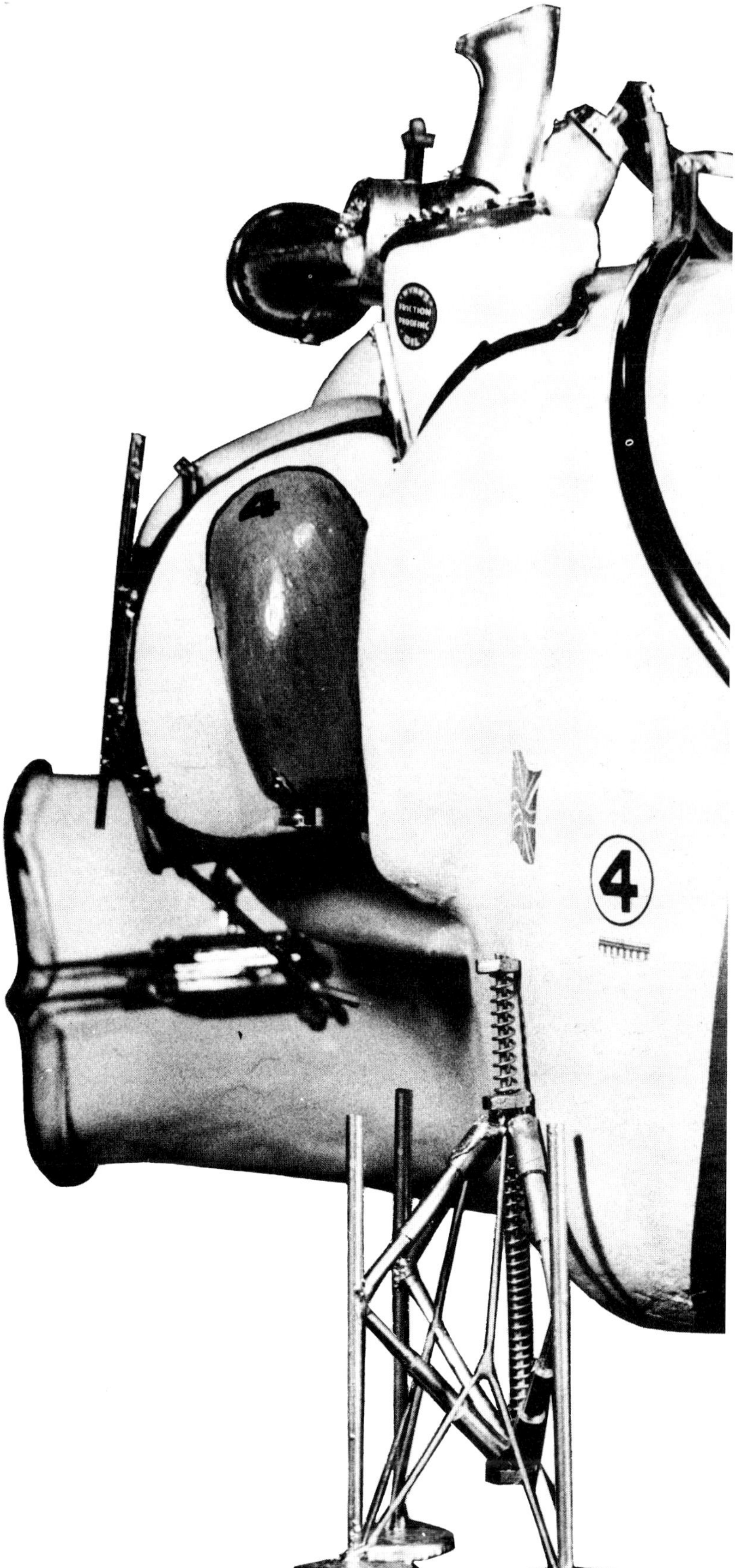

Living Pod: detail 1965 David Greene

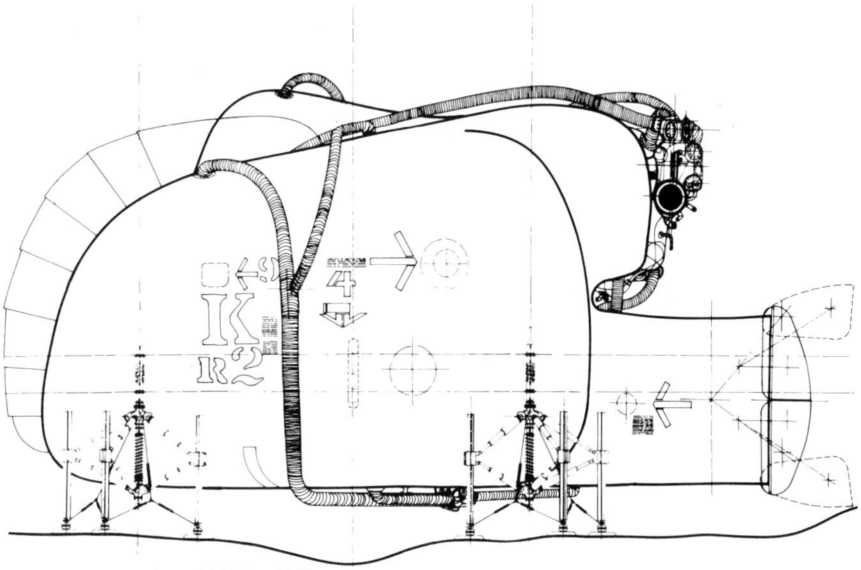

Living Pod project: 1965 David Greene

above Living Pod: elevation

below Living Pod: plan at level of capsules

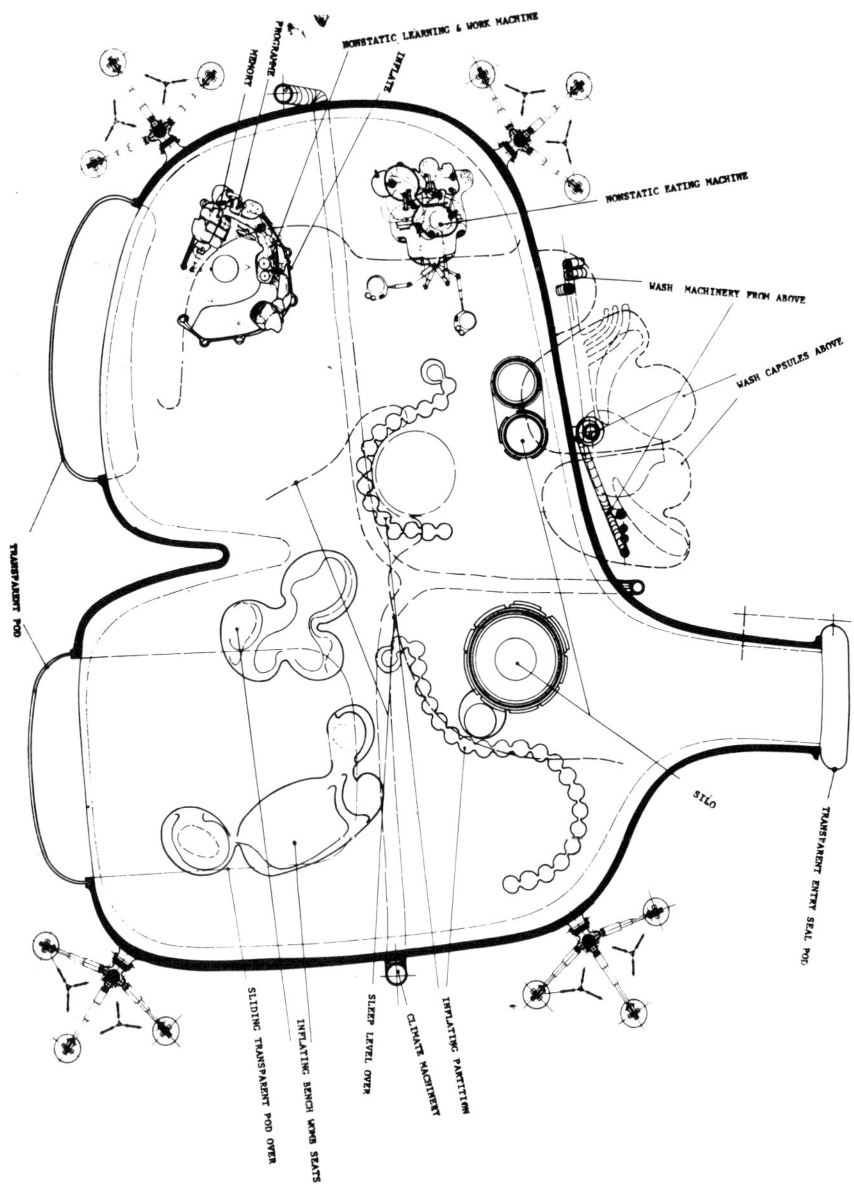

Living-pod David Greene

Paradigms: Trailer homes, 'Prefabs', etc. Development: The 'house' is regarded here as consisting of two major components: a living-pod and attached machines.

Description: Part one, a pod (type KR2) 2-level GRP BS P91304. Colour, bonded white. Twelve support nodes (6 tension, 6 compression). Four apertures (25 per cent surface), 1 access aperture, all with vacuum fixing seals, inner bonded sandwich of insulation and/or finish. Multi-purpose inflating floor 45 per cent area.

Part two: Machinery, 4 automatic self-levelling compression legs for maximum five feet water or 40° slope. Two transparent sectionalized sliding aperture seals with motors. Transparent entry seal with ramp and hydraulics. Two wash capsules with electrostatic disposal, air entry, and total automatic body cleaning equipment. One only with total body water immersion possibility. Two rotating silos for non-disposable clothing, sundry dispensers and silos for disposable toilet and clothing objects, etc. Vertical body hoist. Climate machinery for temperate zone (with connections to inflating sleep mats and warm section of inflating floor). Non-static food dispenser with self-cook modifications. Non-static media, teach and work machine with instant transparent cocoon ring. Inflating screens to sleep mats.

Appraisal: Although this capsule can be hung within a plug-in urban structure or can sit in the open landscape it is still a 'house'. Really one is left with a zoom-land trailer home. Probably a dead end. A basic assumption that must be reassessed in terms of the possibility of increasing personal mobility and technological advance. Anything is probable. The outcome of rejecting permanence and security in a house brief and adding instead curiosity and search could result in a mobile world – like early nomad societies. In relation to the Michael Webb design (p. 64) the suit and cushicle would be the tent and camel equivalent; the node cores an oasis equivalent; the node cluster communities conditioned by varying rates of change. It is likely that under the impact of the second machine age the need for a house (in the form of permanent static container) as part of man's psychological make-up will disappear.

With apologies to the master, the house is an appliance for carrying with you, the city is a machine for plugging into.

opposite Living Pod: Collage including (top to bottom): General section, Food machine section, Food machine plan, model (made by David Greene with Buddy Clarke), teaching machine plan, teaching machine model, general plan

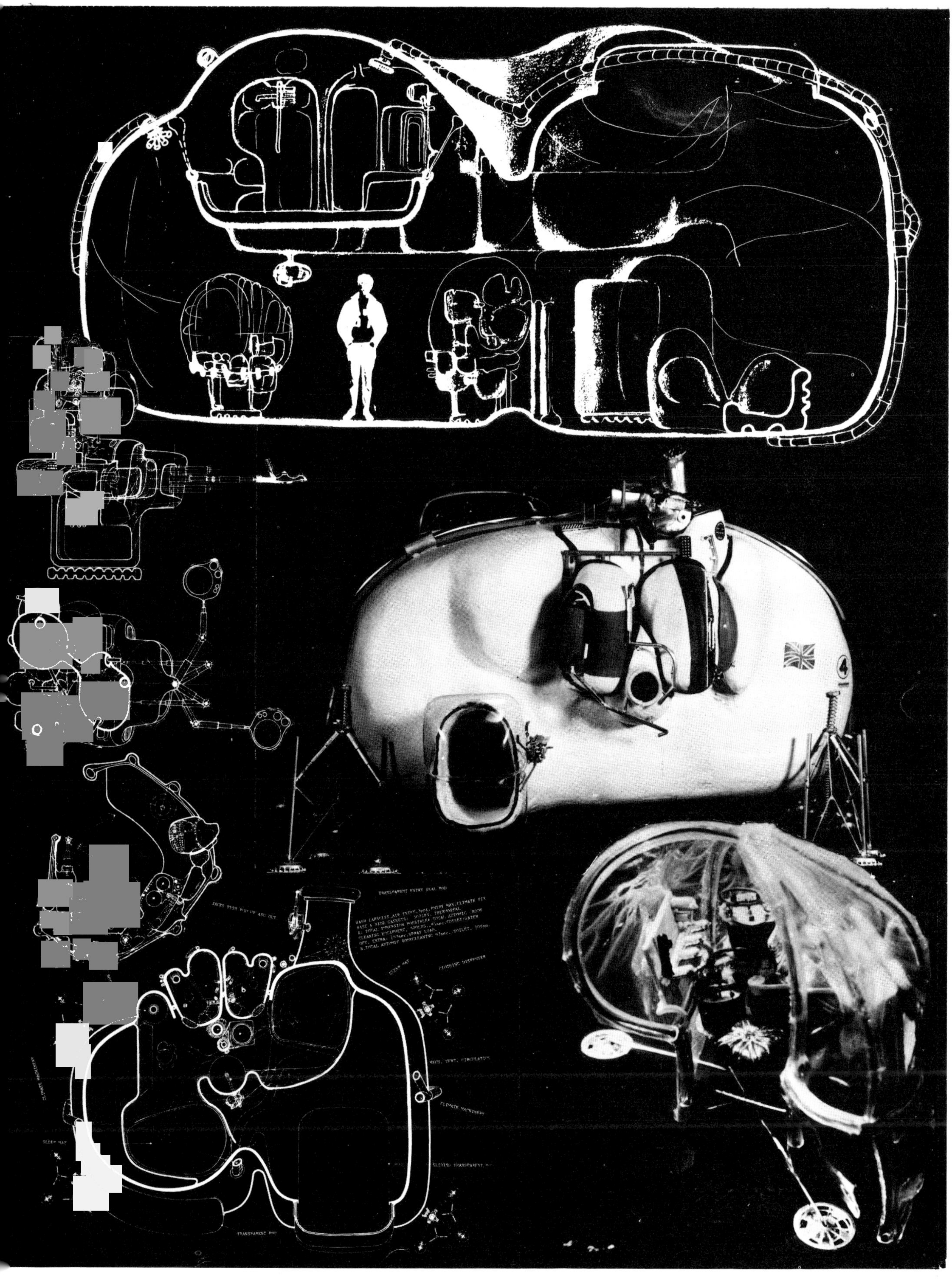
TRANSPARENT ENTRY SEAL POD
JACKS PUSH POD UP AND OUT
SLEEP MAT
CLOTHING DISPENSER
CLIMATE MACHINERY
TRANSPARENT POD

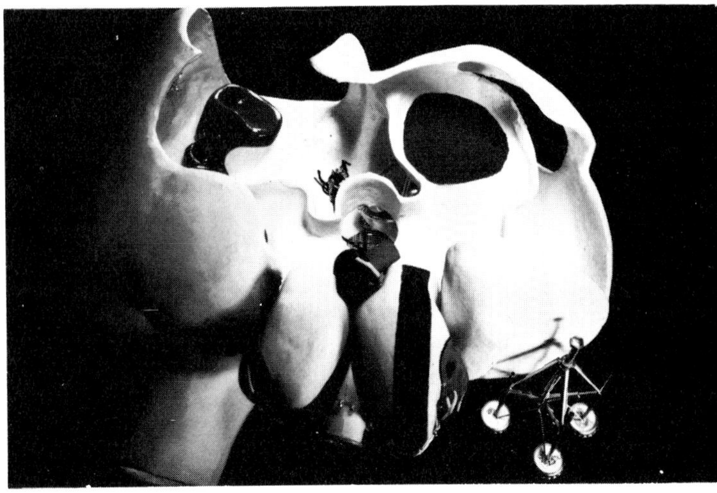

Living Pod: model showing interior

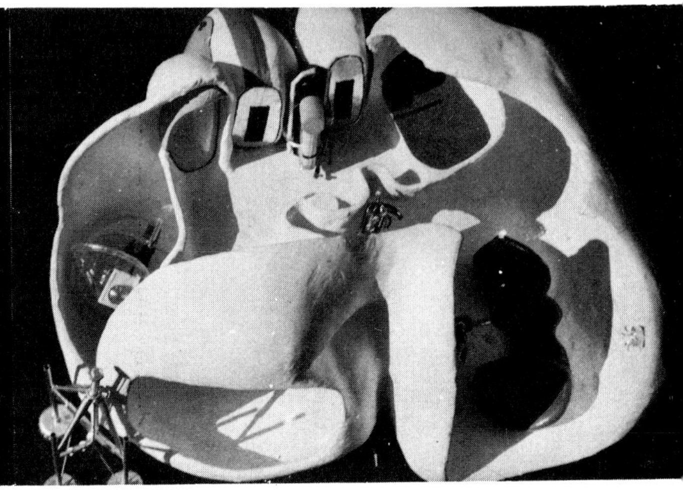

Living Pod: model

Drive-In Housing Diagrams showing the phases of erection

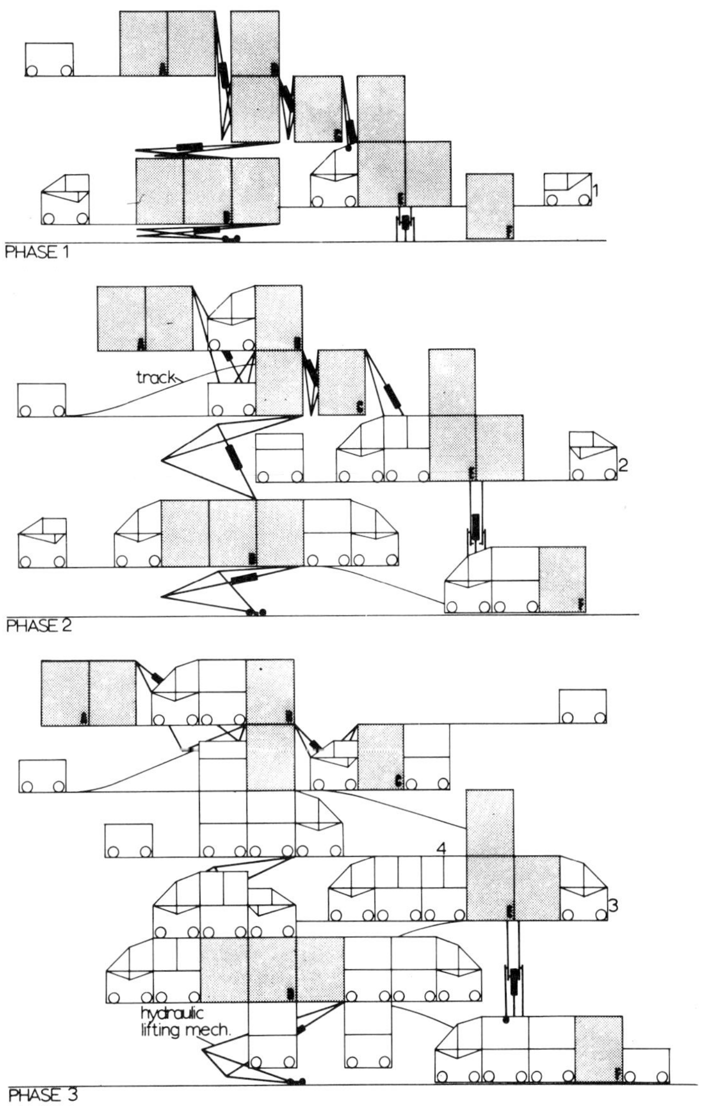

Drive-in housing

A proposition by Michael Webb and David Greene

An ability to dream up next year's architectura modes doesn't rely only on a knowledge o what next year's materials will do for you (plastic skins that dissolve in the sunlight to reform again when it gets cold, buildings tha can be brought to the site in a test tube and allowed to bud) but also on being able to see the meaning and significance behind such shrines of our mechanized society as drive-in cinemas, mobile homes, gadgetry, cars tha can turn themselves into caravans or boats supermarket doors that open as you walk up to them, U-haul trailers, etc. If you take the car, it can be a status-symbol, male-virility object and what-have-you means of getting about that's fun to own and drive, but it car also be a mobile room which can plug itsel into a drive-in bank and become extra floo area of that bank.

Trad versions of drive-in architectures can be broken down into two major parts: the service unit, where space is at a premium, stuffed to the lid with the mechanics of the kitchen, the chancel, office or cinema, serving ham burgers, God, money or films. A lavishly plan ned and styled up consumer space, a restau rant, nave, banking hall or auditorium. But thi consumer space is, of course, made up of series of mobile human containers – cars.

Applying this principle to the house: the kitchen, bathroom and dressing area, since they are essentially 'work' areas and contair bulky, heavy equipment like refrigerators baths, coolers, stoves, and w.c.s could be come fixed service units, and the living area be made up of parts which, by means of fold ing panels, could divide up to form mobil containers and be driven off.

This basic subdivision of function implie that living/sleeping space gadgetry such a TV, Hi-Fi, record player and shaver can slo back into the service unit and that such things as armchairs and tables be inflatable so that with varying air pressures they can be converted into car or seats.

In a drive-in home the volume at any moment is directly proportional to the number of people in it; when the family is away at the seaside the house consists only of folded-up storage units; during a party as many as thirty mobile containers might gather around a unit to form a big space.

The implications of this are that, when drive-in homes are grouped together, either horizontally or vertically, as in slab or tower blocks, the permanent, fixed service units will be at variable distances from each other depending on the number of mobile containers present, since it would be excessively wasteful to design for the maximum pressure condition, i.e. it's Saturday night and everyone's having a party.

Since most people will use their mobile containers to travel round the block, when someone throws a party – like the folks at number D – they are going to need a lot of space to accommodate all the containers. Thus, when these same folks are on vacation, there's going to be an awful lot of free, expensive space around their service/family heirloom box.

So the structure has been designed to get bigger or smaller, depending on the size of the container population present. When a driver enters the perimeter of the block, he dials for the part he wants to get to, and the hydraulic apparatus-cum-structure opens a parking space as shown in the three phases of the diagrams opposite. A-F are the service core units, 1-4 represent car/living units clustered around.

The containers in this scheme are four feet high, but when plugging into a service unit, fold out to make an eight feet high room.

When you start thinking about the pros and cons of this idea, you realize life isn't quite so cut and dried as all that: when travelling to and from the lump of stationary equipment you like to call home, it's nice to use equipment that normally is part of the service units, like telephone, radio, cocktail cabinet, and TV if you're a passenger.

Stage two in the development of the idea seems to be for the mobile container to take along with it some of the services it formerly plugged into 'at home'. Then, theoretically, you could make a home wherever you chose to park the container, since you would have with you all the equipment necessary for survival, high-standard-of-living style.

Americans have this already to a certain extent with their mobile homes – which are like caravans but bigger and longer – usually about eight feet wide and thirty feet long (two put side by side make a decent sized living room), but the floor area needed to serve them means that the overall container is an awkward and cumbersome object to lug around the country. If a microversion of the requisite service gadgetry could be devised, combined with a package structure that could reform itself to allow differing functions within the same basic space, the degree of mobility that mobile homes promise could be realized while retaining the space and aids to luxury living that conventional ground-based homes offer.

At this point some sceptic – which means nearly everyone – will ask, 'Why all this mobility kick anyway, why lug your house around with you?' And the answer is because we find it a solution to some of the inefficiencies present in the way our environment is organized; inefficiencies which will only be aggravated as Europe swings into the Space Age.

For example, the idea of the two-house family is spreading – a flat in the city in which people spend their working week and a weekend house by the sea or in the mountains, whose accommodation and equipment must necessarily duplicate that of the town flat. And, again, the car that carries you from city to seaside contains yet another set of identical equipment – usually the most luxurious of the three: hi-fi radio, Ford T-bird style tape recorder, heater, cooler, telephone, cocktail cabinet, naugahyde seats.

Going all basic and back to first principles you reach stage three: the only real difference between a house and the clothing you wear is one of size – your clothes form a one-man skin and your house will allow any number of people in it. Both are subject to changes of fashion and both cover up to differing extents one's indecencies – but it's interesting to compare how the skins that form the enclosure of a house are traditionally permanent while the clothing skins are removable/replaceable to suit any whim of climate, sexual fetish or what-have-you. But in principle an overcoat is a house/is a car when a motor's clipped on.

So a package structure has been designed to be deformable into a clothing skin.

The parts of the structure are:

The basic clothing skin that can be inflated to make a chaise-longue or further inflated to make a room. It consists of two layers, an opaque, thermal insulating skin and a transparent/part translucent external cover which, used separately or in conjunction with each other, offer varying degrees of protection against excessive heat, cold, damp, etc.

A short range bodyless vehicle, consisting of a tubular frame chassis floating on an air cushion. The owner's body becomes the body

Drive-In Housing 1964–66
Michael Webb

below left Drive-In Housing diagram 1 to show component system

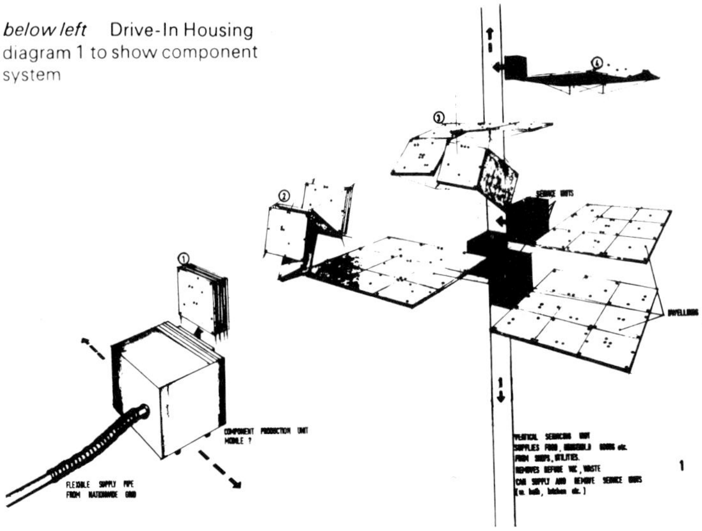

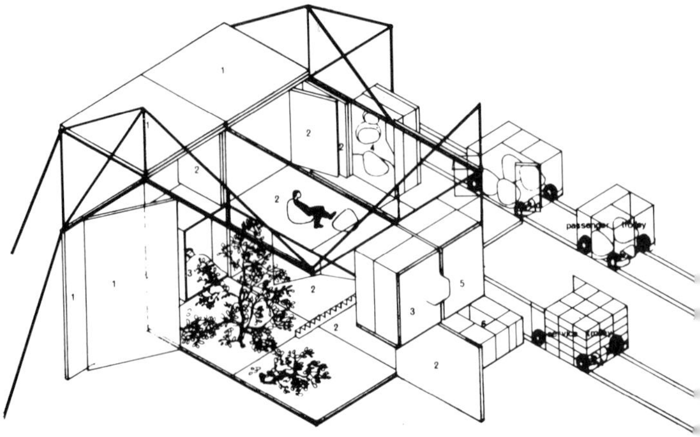

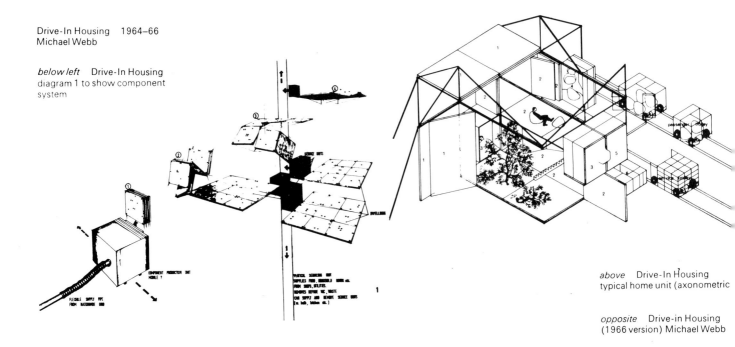

above Drive-In Housing typical home unit (axonometric

opposite Drive-in Housing (1966 version) Michael Webb

of the vehicle. Hence its rather Wellsian name, Cushicle (p. 64).

The third part is in two sections: first a hotted-up service core node dispensing food, movies, medicine, shows – in short, approximating to a city type and arranged on a country-wide grid pattern; and second, a high-speed continuous moving belt system which would link together these nodal cores and to which the Cushicles would attach themselves, just like the piggyback idea on American railroads.

Drive-in housing Mike Webb

The project is a preliminary study in the design of automated constructional, servicing and dismantling techniques applied to a large building development.

The building has been designed large enough to include its own component production units. These manufacture moulded reinforced plastic panels, which are conveyed, folded up, to their position in the structure and then open out to form usable floor space (diagrams 1, 2, 3, 4).

Plastics have been chosen in preference to steel as a constructional medium because the full advantages of on-site component production can be taken. In the case of plastics, transport consists of raw materials arriving at one of the ports and being, ideally, pumped through pipelines to the site production units.

In the case of steel, each member must be completed in the factory, which may be a great distance from the site.

Diagram 1
This diagram shows the automatic casting plant on the left, with the finished units being conveyed to their position.

It is assumed at this stage that there will be three basic types of casting plant:
Plant I producing components of a main supporting structure, possibly a structure based on Buckminster Fuller's 'Aspersion Tensegrity', whereby a standard tensegrity structure will erect itself in the air by tensioning its outer edges. This structure would form a transparent, weather-resistant skin to the interior spaces of the building.
Plant II producing components for floor space.
Plant III producing servicing units – see diagrams 2, 3 and 4.

Diagrams 2, 3 and 4 (page 58)
These diagrams show the folded units in diagram 1 opened out to form a dwelling unit on one level and measuring 400 sq ft.
The area can be increased/decreased by the addition/subtraction of extra units, e.g. if mother-in-law descends on the family for a month, extra panels can be ordered from stock.
Around the edge are placed service units which can be moved or renewed – kitchen, bathroom, cloaks, wardrobe, study deck, etc.
The dwelling unit is subdivided into rooms by means of panels four inches wide, forty inches long and one hundred inches high, which can pivot at both ends, thus becoming a door as well as a space divider.

Why is there the apparent wast age of space in the traditiona house? The bedrooms ofte occupy a greater area than th living and dining rooms, and i the daytime the bedrooms li empty and at night-time th living room is empty. The parti tioning of daytime usage room in the traditional home allows n adaptation for party giving, quie study, etc., because:
many people consider it un healthy to sleep in the same roor as you have been living in, but d not know about our changes double beds fill the room leavin a useless 'U' shape;
small articles peculiar to bed rooms are left lying around owin to antiquated storage systems.

This dwelling unit space can b created to fit round the intende activity merely by swingin panels into prearranged pattern Beds can be either folded up int a panel or situated under a floo panel. The space can be voi with panels stacked around th outside (diagram 3) or arrange in varying ways to form roor (diagrams 2 and 4).

The dwelling unit may use th Plant I main structure for it cladding (with openable glas panels placed in the tensio network).

B
C
A
D
A
C
E
E
A
K
A
D
A
A
C
G
B
B
A
J
Chevrolet

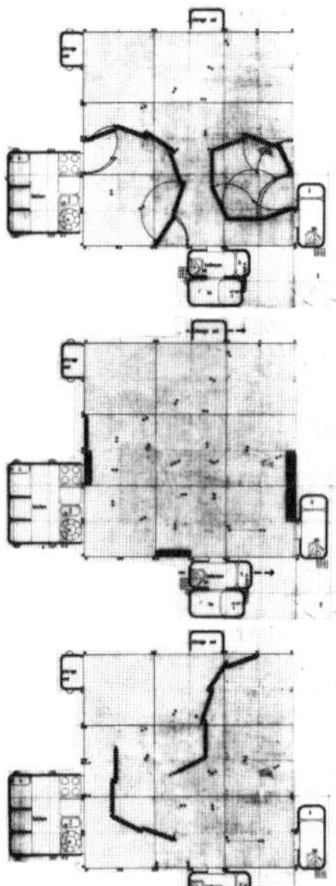

left (diagrams 2, 3, 4) Auto-Environment Alternative Plans

right Air Hab Village 1967 Ron Herron and Barry Snowden: collage showing village grouping, Air Hab unit, and interior of unit

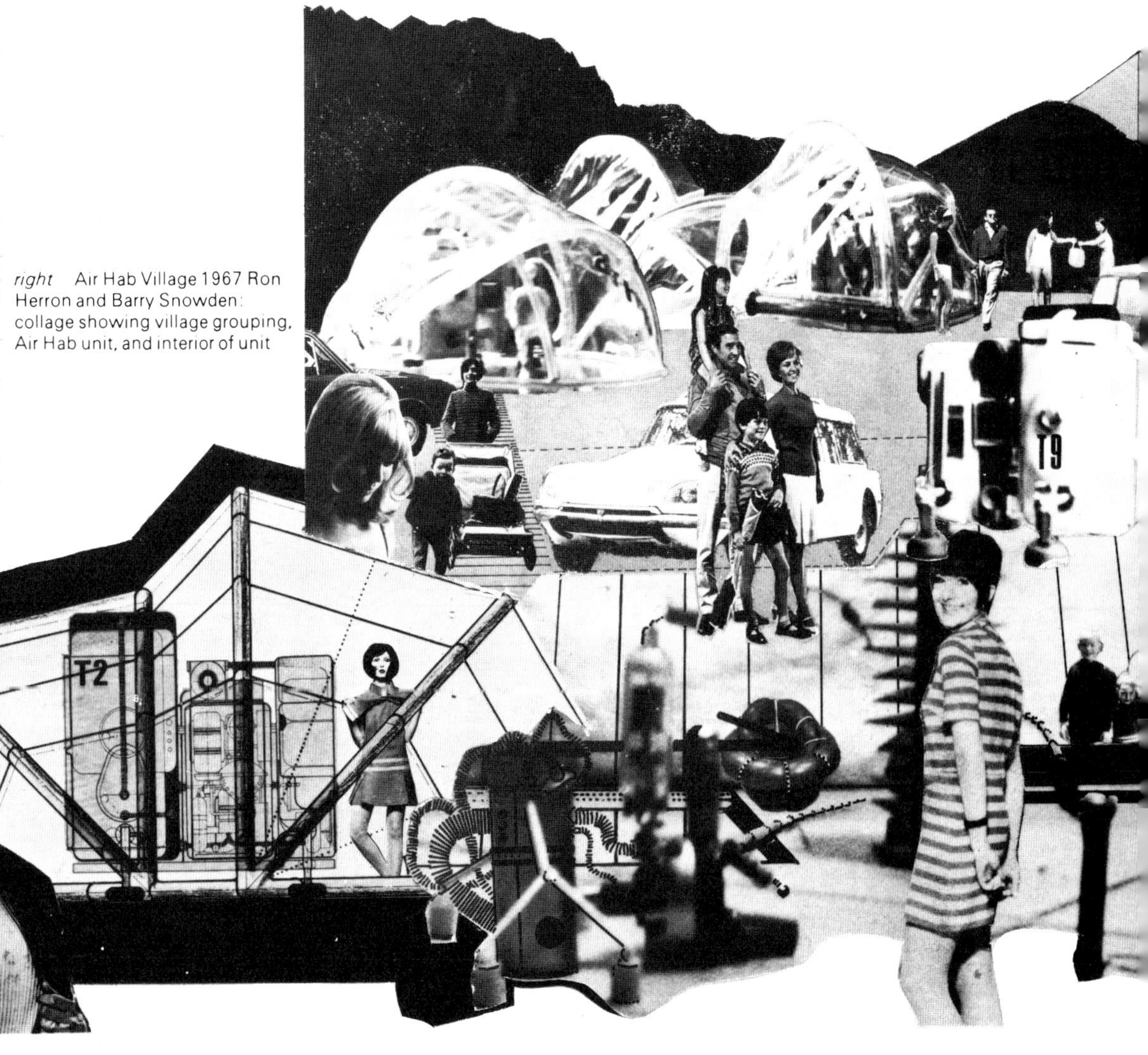

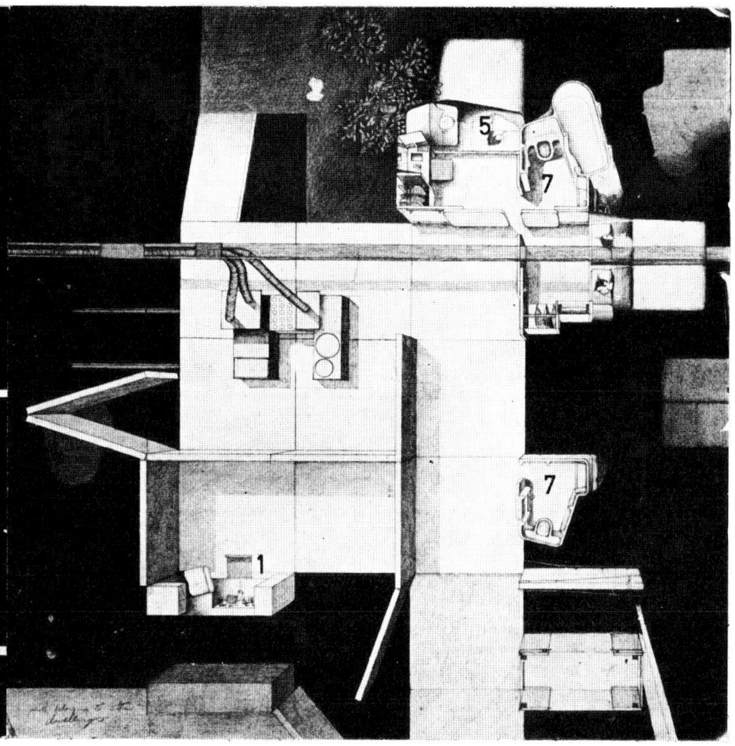

bove left and centre Drive-In Housing 1964 version
ichael Webb model

bove right Drive-In Housing: layout 1965

ght Free time node 1966 Ron Herron and Barry Snowden
lan and elevation

elow Free time node:
railer Cage 1967

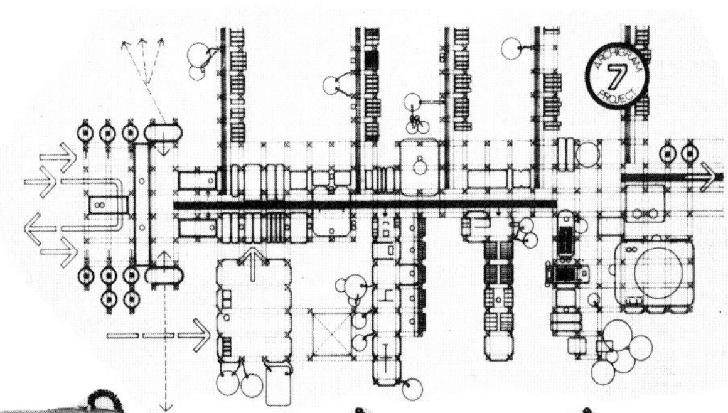

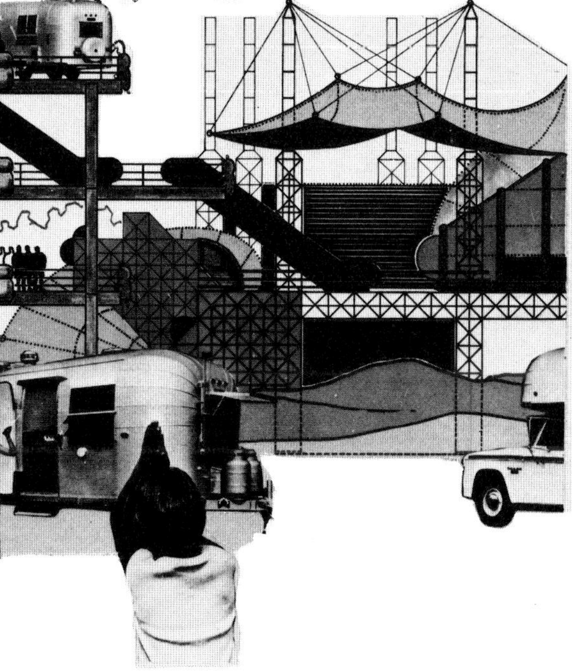

Stage 1: The hovercraft is in motion
Items: 1 The main mast folded up. 2 Air inflation unit. 3 Appliance units stacked. 4 Machine and control cabins stacked. 5 Home screens stacked. 6 Main engine room of craft. 7 Inflated toe of craft.

Stage 2: The village is beginning to blow-out
Items: 1 Main mast erect. 2 Dwelling components opening out. 3 Home screens upright. 4 Sub-mast erect. 5 Supports opening. 6 Machine and control cabins stacked. 7 Control cabin at 'crows' nest' position during erection. 8 Air inflation starting. 9 Ground spreaded locators digging-in.

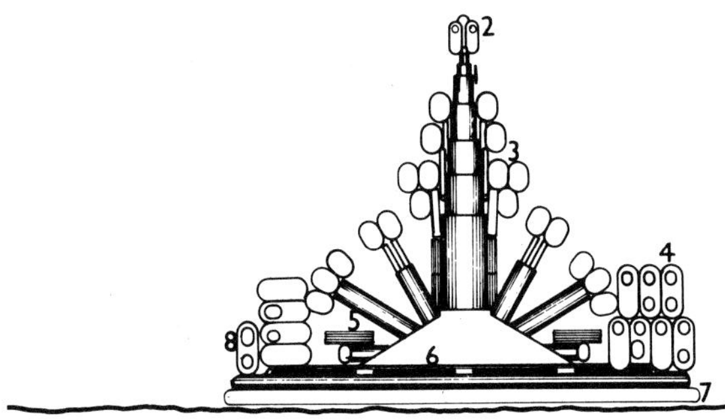

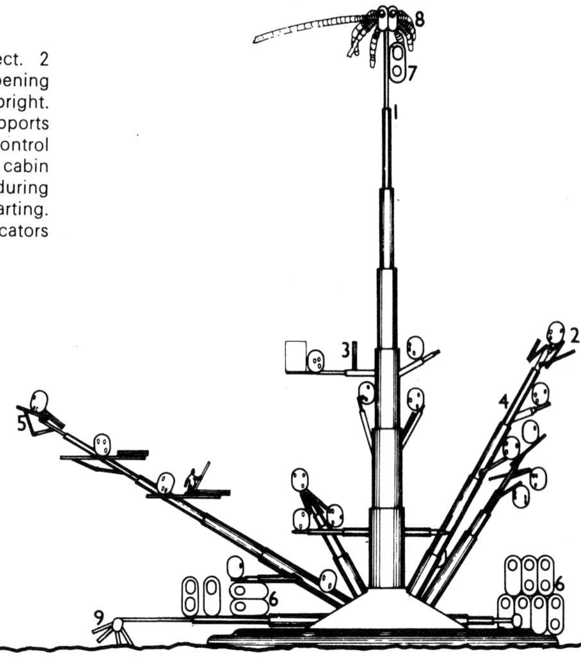

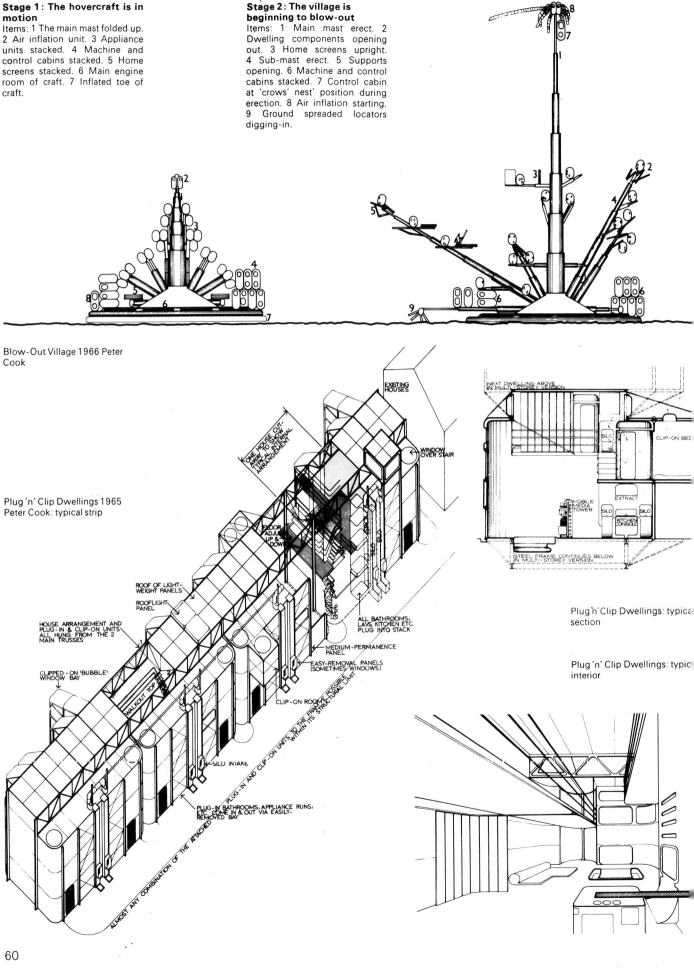

Blow-Out Village 1966 Peter Cook

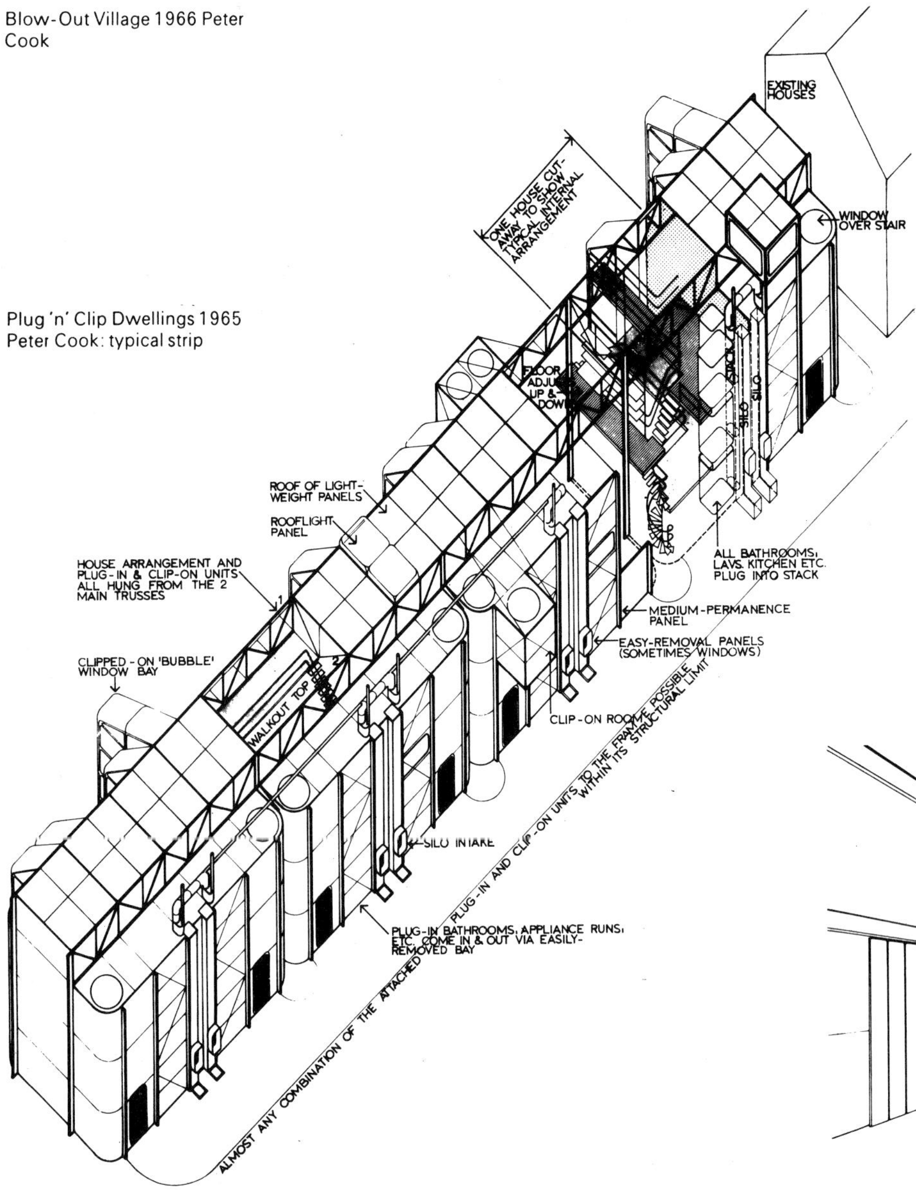

Plug 'n' Clip Dwellings 1965 Peter Cook: typical strip

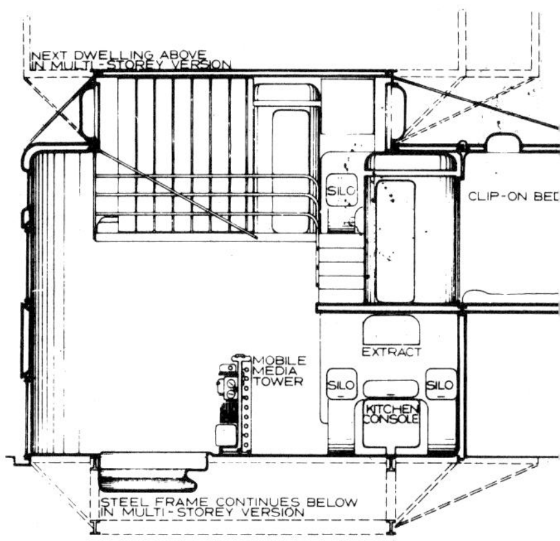

Plug 'n' Clip Dwellings: typica section

Plug 'n' Clip Dwellings: typic interior

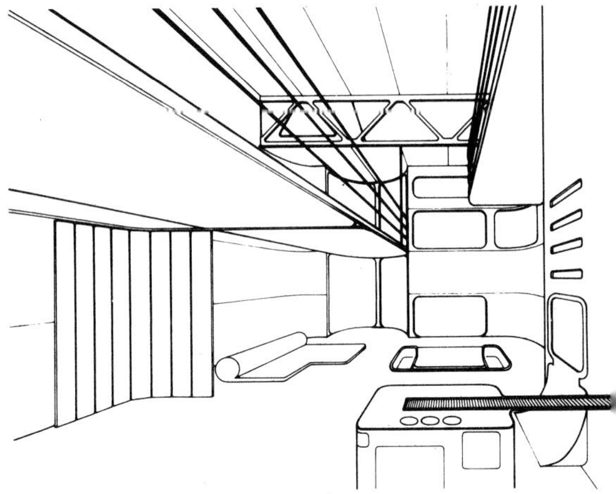

Stage 3: The village in use
tems: 1 Main mast. 2 Dwelling appliance unit. 3 Dwellings have screens for privacy. 4 Sub-mast. 5 Access ways (folded steel structure). 6 Machine cabin. 7 Air-inflated rib to controlling dome. 8 Areas of the dome can be customized. 9 Entry point. 10 Movie projection on to dome. 11 Engine room and hydraulics unit. 12 Free-standing dance floor.

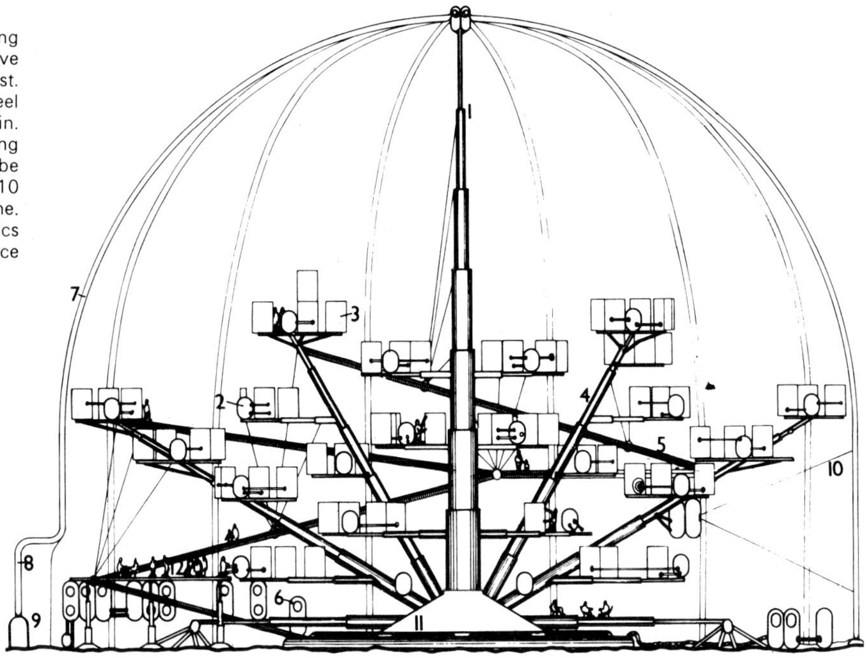

Blow-out village

Peter Cook

Mobile villages can be used everywhere to rehouse people hit by disaster, for workmen in remote areas, and as fun resorts sited permanently or seasonally at the seaside and near festivals. When not in use the village is quarter size. This is done by drawing off the hydraulic fluid from the main mast and the arms; the village then contracts. It is moved on to a site by a hovercraft motor and anchored by the two feet seen in the diagram. The main mast is raised hydraulically to the chosen height. Air-inflated ribs fall from the top of the main mast supporting a weatherproof transparent plastics cover over the whole village.

amily Dwelling (cage structure) 966 Peter Cook View of interior. This is an intermediate development of the notion of the structural cage with flexible interior parts and relates to the earlier Plug 'n' Clip series and the Hornsey Cages (page 47) and to the later 1990 Dwelling (page 62)

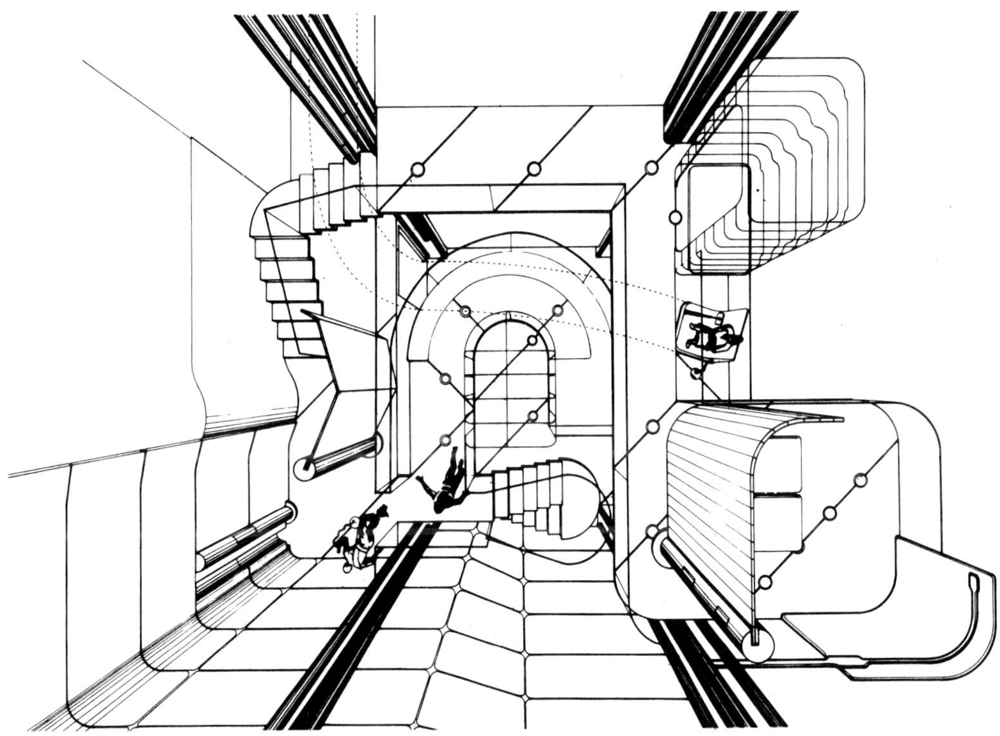

Living 1990 1967 Whole Group Project – commissioned by the *Weekend Telegraph* magazine – erected at Messrs Harrods of Knightsbridge

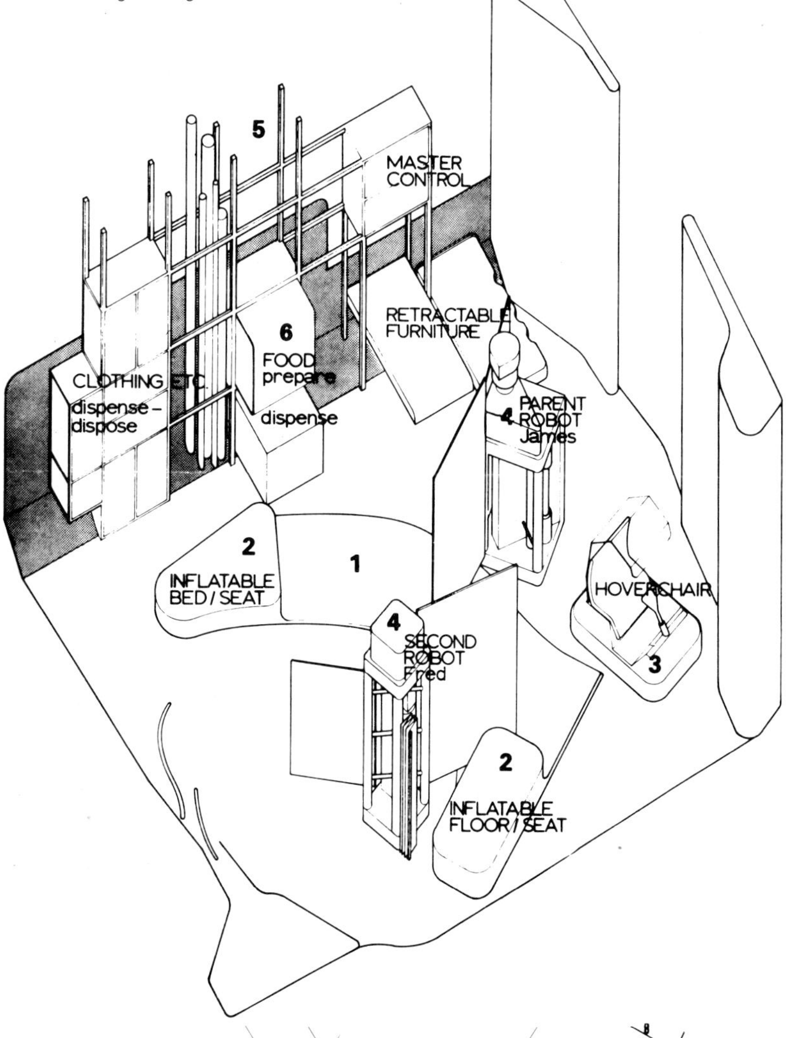

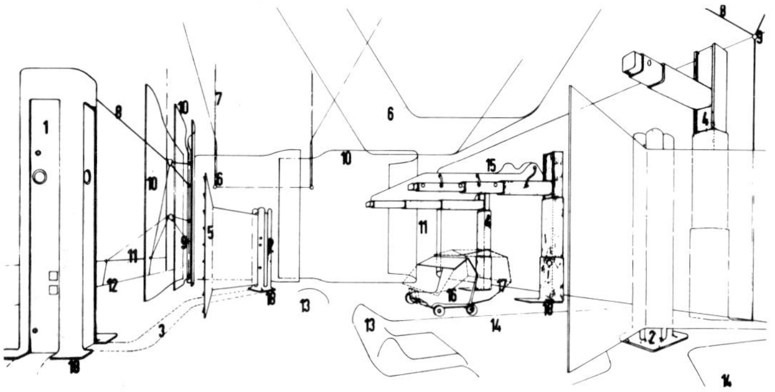

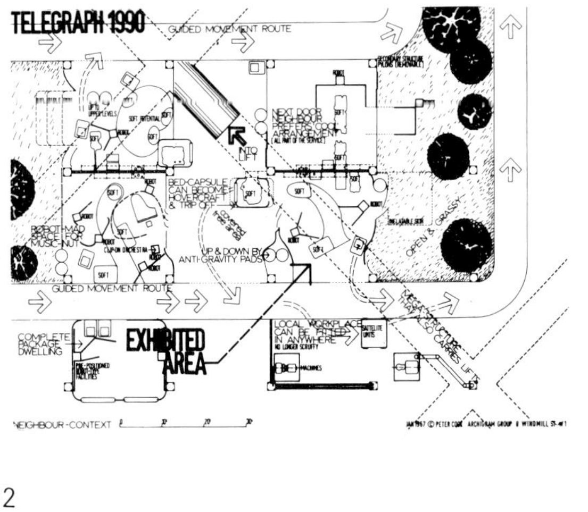

Living 1990

The Archigram Group was commissioned in 1967 by the *Weekend Telegraph* to design a 'house for the year 1990'. Naturally the definitions of function imply a fixed and permanent location. In essence the exhibited area illustrates the main part of the lower floor of a dwelling cage, with a situation and structure similar to the examples on pages 60, 61. The 'Robots' are a development in the direct lineage of the media trolley (in the Plug'n Clip house, p. 60) and the movable services, walls and machines that serve the occupants in Mike Webb's projects.

Walls, ceilings, floors – in this living area – are wall, ceiling and floor conditions, which adjust according to your needs. The enclosures of the living area are no longer rigid, but adjustable, programmed to move up and down, in and out. The floor state, too, is variable. At particular points the floor can be made hard enough to dance on or soft enough to sit on.

Seating and sleeping arrangements are inflatable, and details such as weight of bedcovers and number of cushioned elements are controlled by the user. The old concept of a movable chair has become a travelling chair-car. The model in the living area is designed on the hovercraft principle, and can also be used outside for driving around the megastructure city. The bed-capsule (not included in this display) can also change to a hovercraft and run outside. The robots can shoot out screens which enclose a required area of space. The ceiling lowers at this point, and whoever requires it has a private area. The robots are movable. Refreshments can be drawn from them. They contain a compressor for blowing up the inflatable furniture. They also have an element for extracting dust from the living area. The robots also incorporate radio and television – including favourite movie and education programmes, which can be switched on when you want them. The television is, at the present stage of development seen on wide screens, and can be programmed so that viewers are surrounded by realistic sound, colour and scent effects. The service wall connects with a vast service stack, shared with the megastructure city, which is one of the key facilities of the structure.

Each living area is fitted with ultrasonic cooking equipment for cleanest, quickest cooking, but otherwise arrangements will depend on the interest of the cook. The design of the living area goes some way towards allaying the widely-held fears that the future points inevitably to standardization and conformity of living accommodation.

top Living 1990: axonometric showing components

centre Living 1990: early version perspective

below The 1990 Dwelling in a neighbourly context

elow Typical Day
Sequence

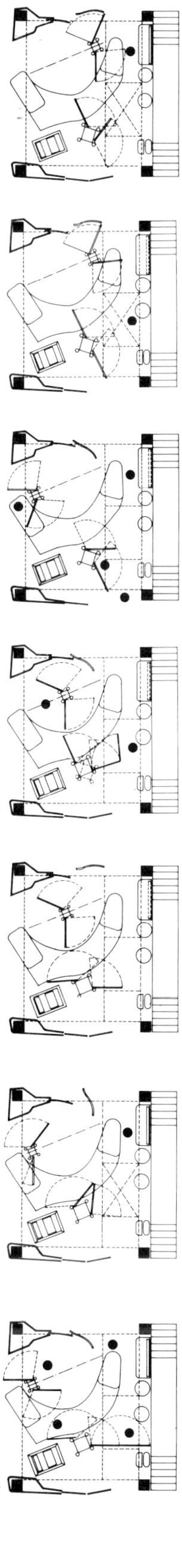

-7·30am
ep

am-9am
kfast

-4pm
idual
ities

n-6·30pm
ren
TV

m-8pm
s/adults
ities

-10pm

-3am

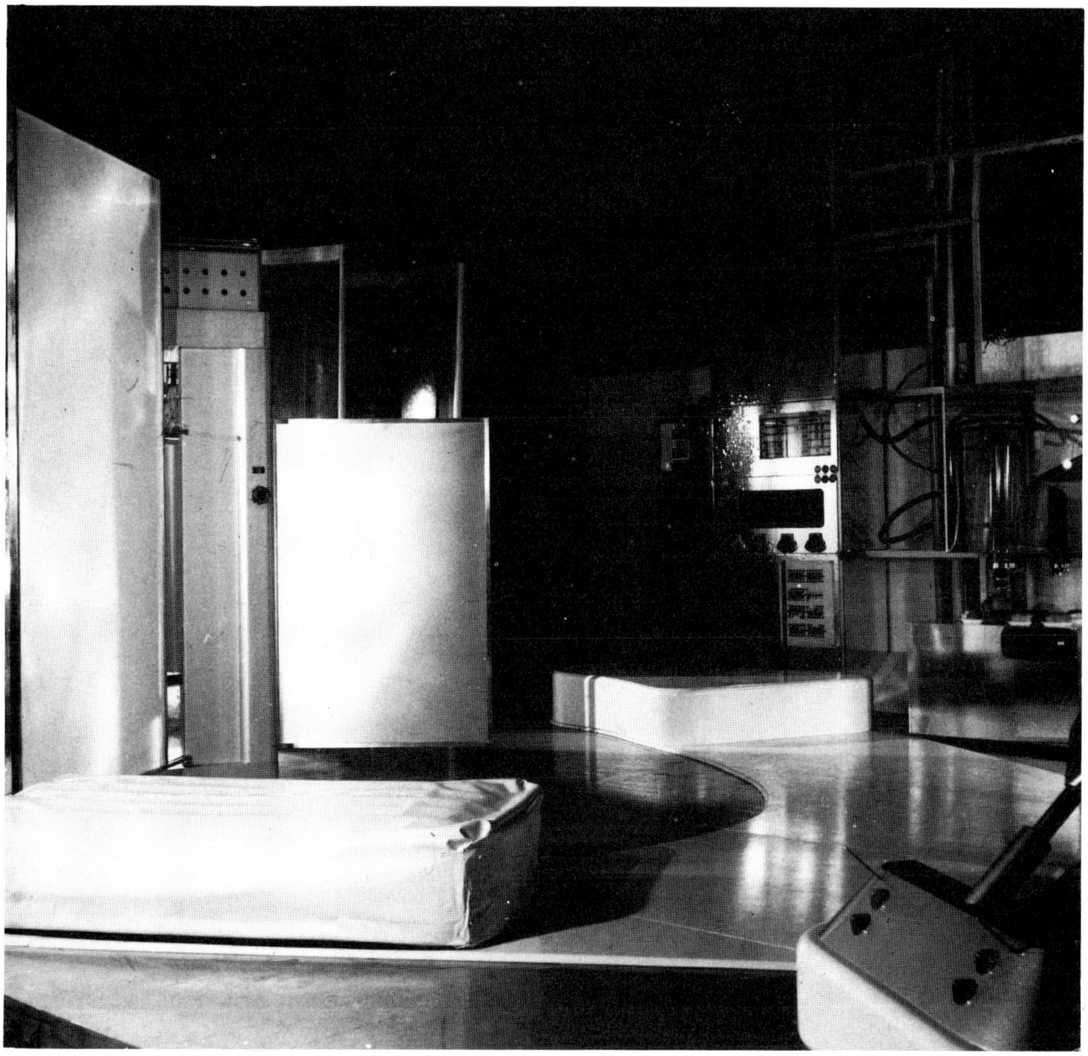

Living 1990: general view of exhibition version

Robots

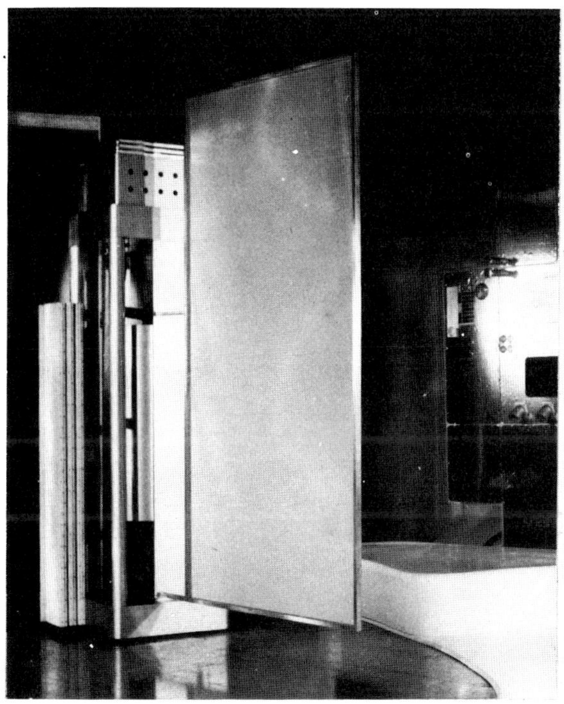

Vehicle

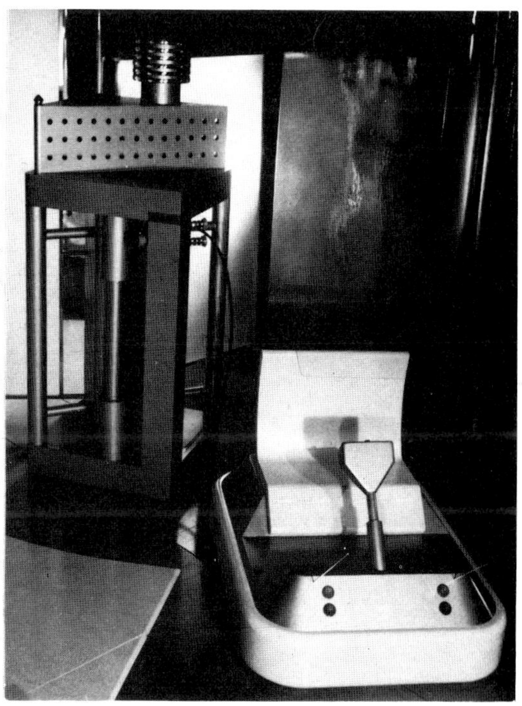

The Cushicle

Mike Webb

The Cushicle is an invention that enables a man to carry a complete environment on his back. It inflates-out when needed. It is a complete nomadic unit – and it is fully serviced.

It enables an explorer, wanderer or other itinerant to have a high standard of comfort with a minimum effort.

The illustrations show the two main parts of the Cushicle unit as they expand out from their unpacked state to the domestic condition. One constituent part is the 'armature' or 'spinal' system. This forms the chassis and support for the appliances and other apparatus. The other major element is the enclosure part which is basically an inflated envelope with extra skins as viewing screens. Both systems open out consecutively or can be used independently.

The Cushicle carries food, water supply, radio, miniature projection television and heating apparatus. The radio, TV, etc., are contained in the helmet and the food and water supply are carried in pod attachments.

With the establishment of service nodes and additional optional apparatus, the autonomous Cushicle unit could develop to become part of a more widespread urban system of personalized enclosures.

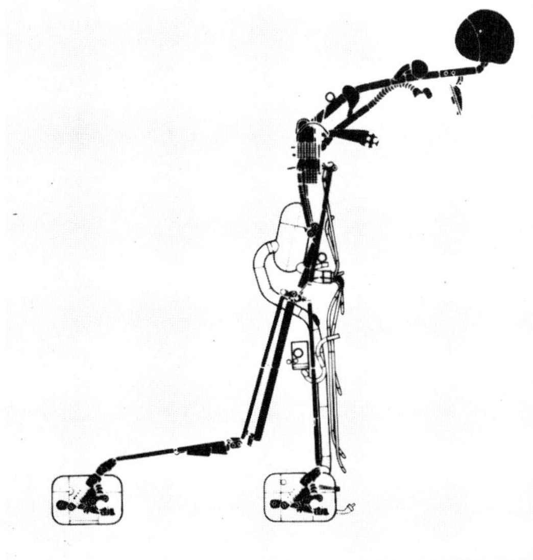

Stage 1:
chassis unopened

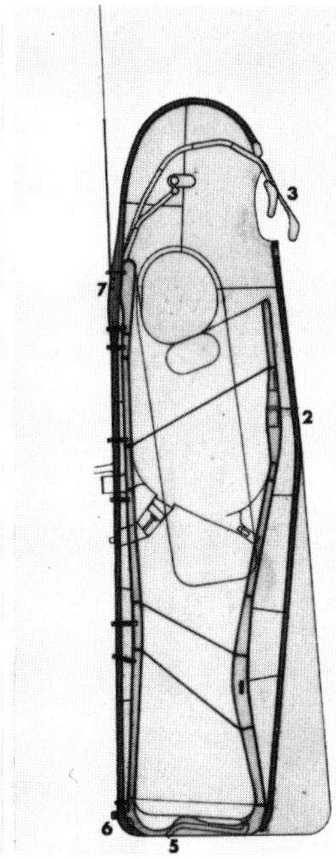

Stage 2:
suit unopened

Cushicle 1966–7 Michael Webb

Stage 5:
combination opening out further

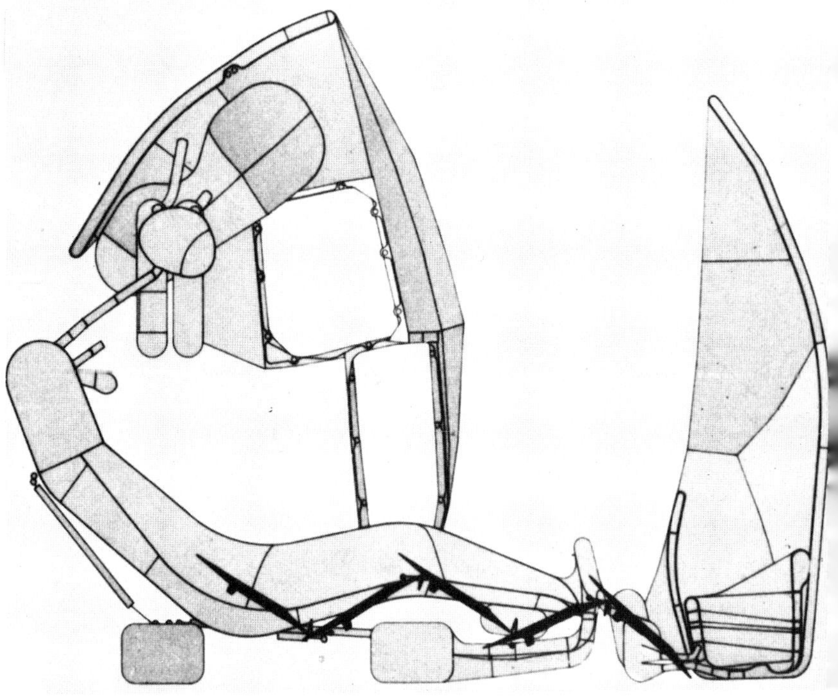

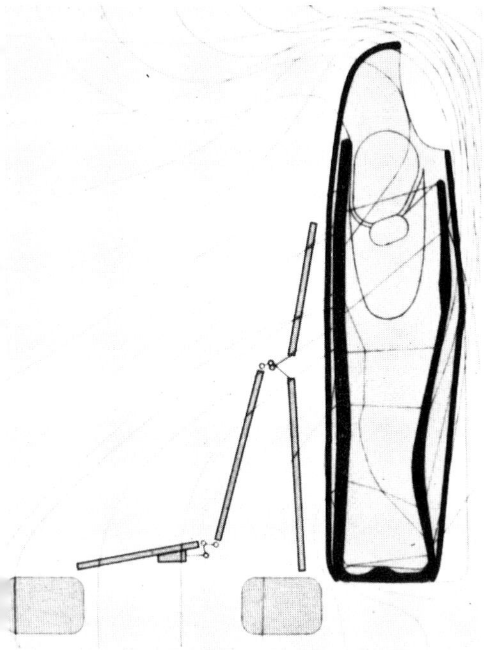

tage 3:
uit and chassis combining

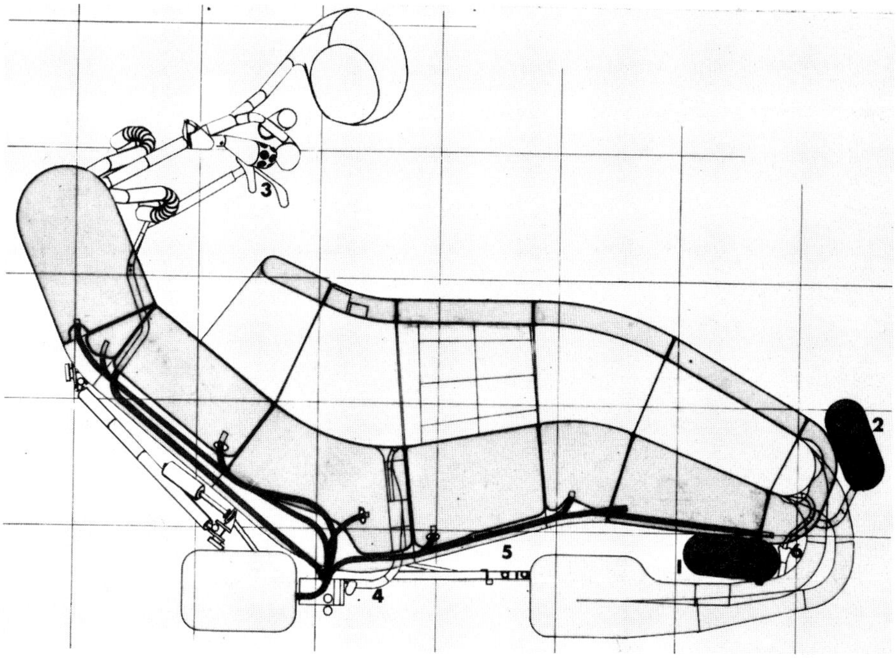

Stage 4:
combined suit, chassis opening out

tage 6:
otal Cushicle fully opened out and in use

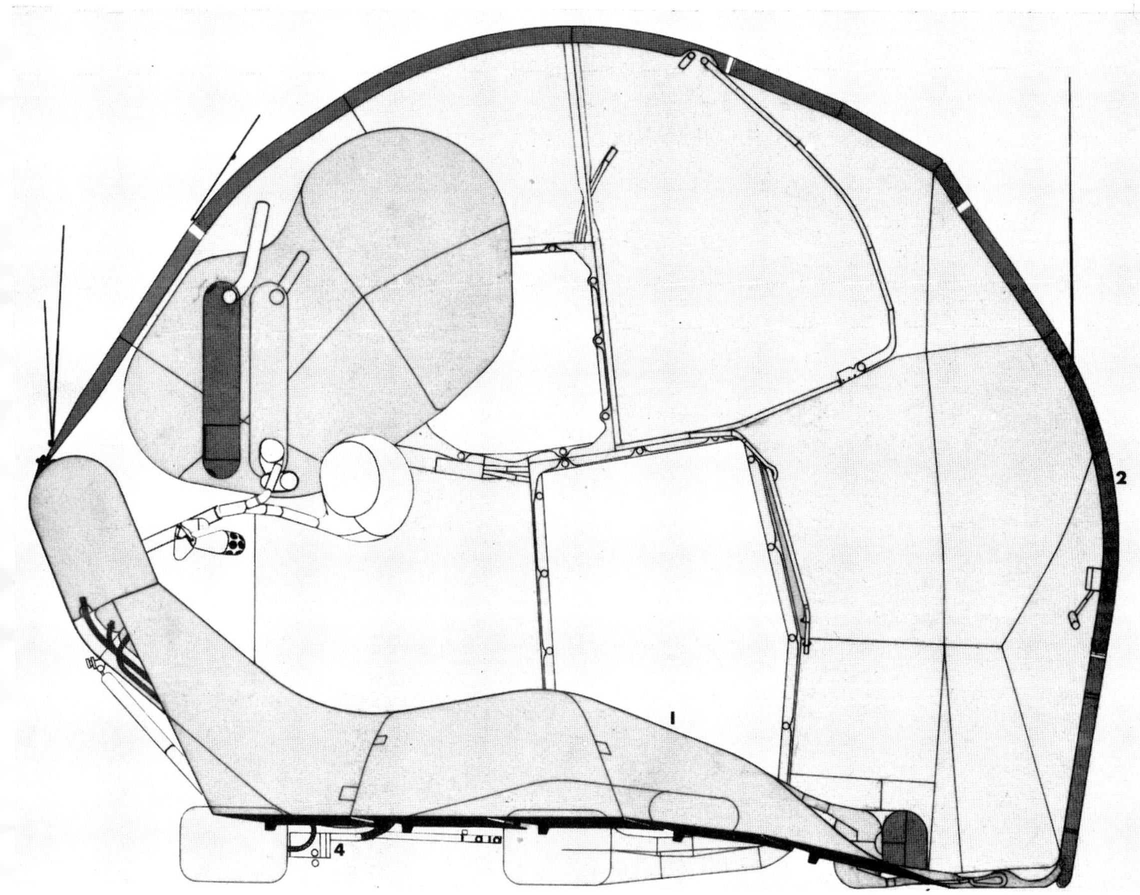

Rent-a-Wall 1966 Michael Webb

you'll appreciate Rent-a-Wall's
good looks and versatility....
says president Fred X. Shooman
jun.,III
ARCHIGRAM
BLACKSBUGRAM
7
TEAR OUT
AND SAVE
THIS VALUABLE
UNITED FILM CLUB, INC.
FILM
MAILER
our latest idea :
hire-a-spraygun
hydraulic arm
H
interior showing panels
opening to form enclosure
these are samples of some of our popular types
CD
L
EE
JA
LH
L
D
CD
Lady Guinevere's Drea
live in the twentieth ce
serenity of the Taj Ma
transparent
- opaque

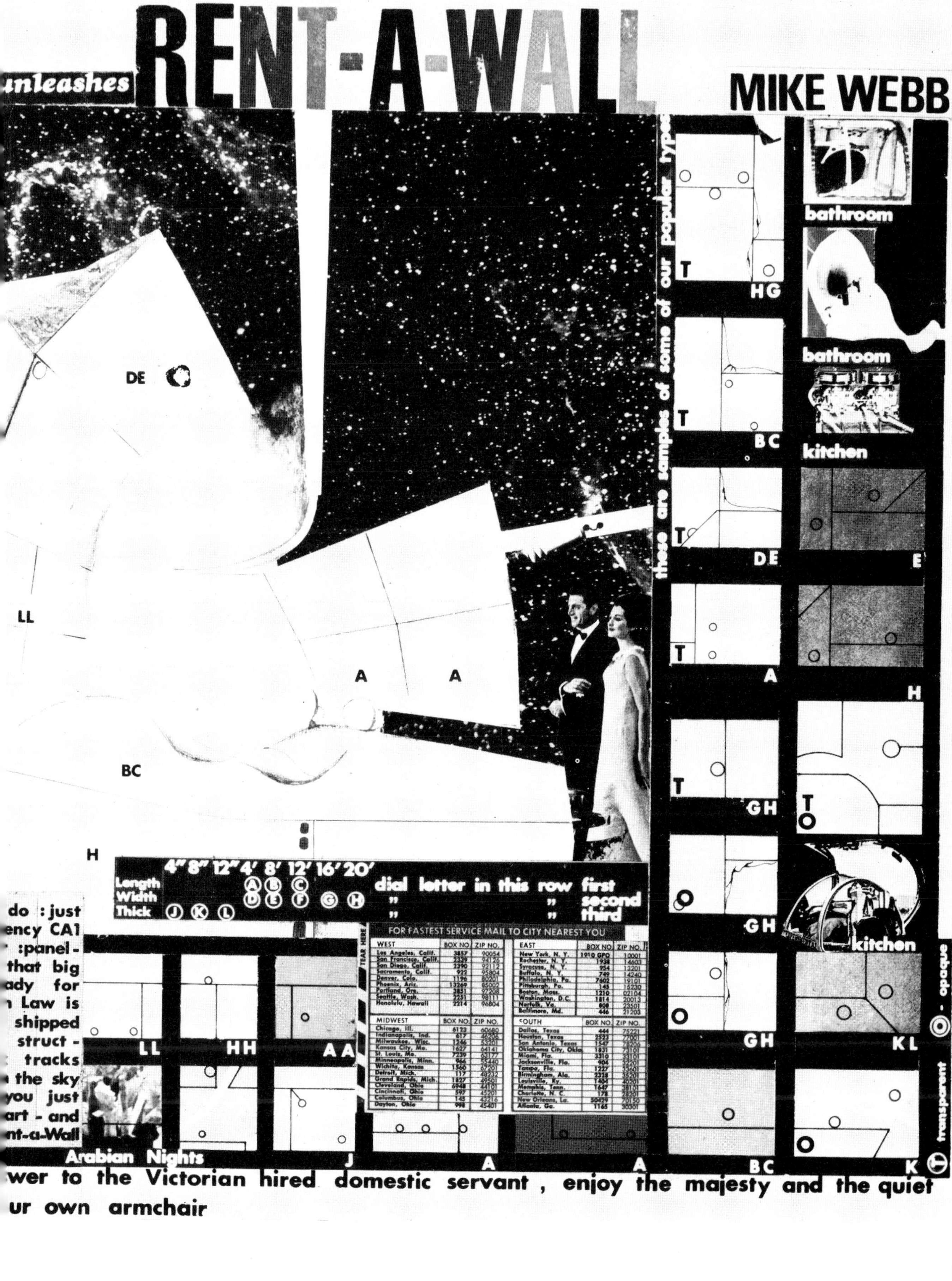

unleashes
RENT-A-WALL
MIKE WEBB
these are samples of some of our popular types
bathroom
bathroom
kitchen
kitchen
T
HG
BC
DE
E
A
H
GH
T
GH
GH
KL
BC
K
opaque
transparent
DE
LL
A
A
BC
H
Length
Width
Thick
4" 8" 12" 4' 8' 12' 16' 20'
dial letter in this row first
" " second
" " third
FOR FASTEST SERVICE MAIL TO CITY NEAREST YOU
WEST
EAST
MIDWEST
SOUTH
TEAR HERE
do : just
ency CA1
: panel -
that big
ady for
n Law is
shipped
struct -
tracks
the sky
you just
art - and
nt-a-Wall
LL
HH
AA
Arabian Nights
J
A
A
wer to the Victorian hired domestic servant , enjoy the majesty and the quiet
ur own armchair

8 Control and choice

The determination of your environment need no longer be left in the hands of the designer of the building: it can be turned over to you yourself. You turn the switches and choose the conditions to sustain you at that point in time. The 'building' is reduced to the role of carcass – or less.

Such conclusions built up gradually by the drift of argument that lay behind successive Archigram projects. The Auto-Environment and its developments suggested that the domain is at once mobile (car) and locational (pad); elemental (made up from identifiable components, and able to realize identifiable 'places') and elastic (since the components could be changed around and the places re-defined). The dwelling-cages formulated the notion of reserving spaces for an event (and then only for a limited time) and letting these reservations lie fallow if necessary before the event or when it becomes obsolete. Inevitably this led to some loosening up of ideas about the significance of otherwise useful labels like 'city' or 'unit'. The 1990 House was a first attempt to build an example of the transient pad. It was served by machines and facilities that responded to an immediate and passing whim of a single person and the passing moment's assembly became the environment. But the final stage of the cycle was the Cushicle, the home-on-your-back: at last a disintegration of 'house' and the inevitable end of 'tied' location.

Paradoxes were obvious and the first 'Control or Choice' conversation took the form of a deliberately hybrid document (page 69). Fixed diagrams of an architectural organization seemed increasingly inadequate, yet this could also be said of the verbal dissertation about something that was, after all, about response to space and objects. When Archigram was asked to send an exhibit to the 1967 Paris Biennale des Jeunesses the 'Control or Choice' conversation was extended very naturally into a project which was given the same name. In the cartoon (opposite) the word 'metamorphosis' is a summary of the whole discussion and the new set of parts that might make the project physically possible.

Inevitably, the assembly as drawn has to be a conglomeration of systems, organizations and technical apparatus that permit the choice of *one* response out of a number of alternatives and exploit the different natures of (say) the physical limitation of a piece of hardware against the unlimited atmospheric power of an ephemeral medium (such as projected pictures). Now, in the days when these two had quite separate architectural forms and defined roles within the environment, we could all adjust, and the architecture could be made to fit. The super cinema ceased to have particular significance as interior design whilst the film was being shown. In a place where the hardware, software and ephemera are all intermixed (and interdependent at any one time) there has to be a much looser hierarchy of parts. It becomes almost impossible to draw. It becomes necessary to try to summarize a time-space-atmospheric sequence that may never take up a finite configuration. The diagrams here must be read in this context. They are merely typical; they are a momentarily frozen summary of parts that can be drawn. The model of the project (page 68) comes a little nearer to the mood of the place. As shown, the living space is for a four person family. It is pitched at around 1978 but the majority of the parts exist in the common technology of today.

Control and Choice. Housing Study 1967 Peter Cook, Dennis Crompton and Ron Herron. Graphics by Warren Chalk. Model built with the help of David Harrison, David Martin, Simon Connolly, Johnnie Devas.

right Control and Choice project: model. This project was chosen to represent Great Britain at the Paris Biennale of 1967

far right Control or Choice. Hypothesis 1966 Peter Cook (produced for *Control* magazine) Control and Choice project: 'Metamorphosis' cartoon explaining the interface between a typical family and a possible robotised home.

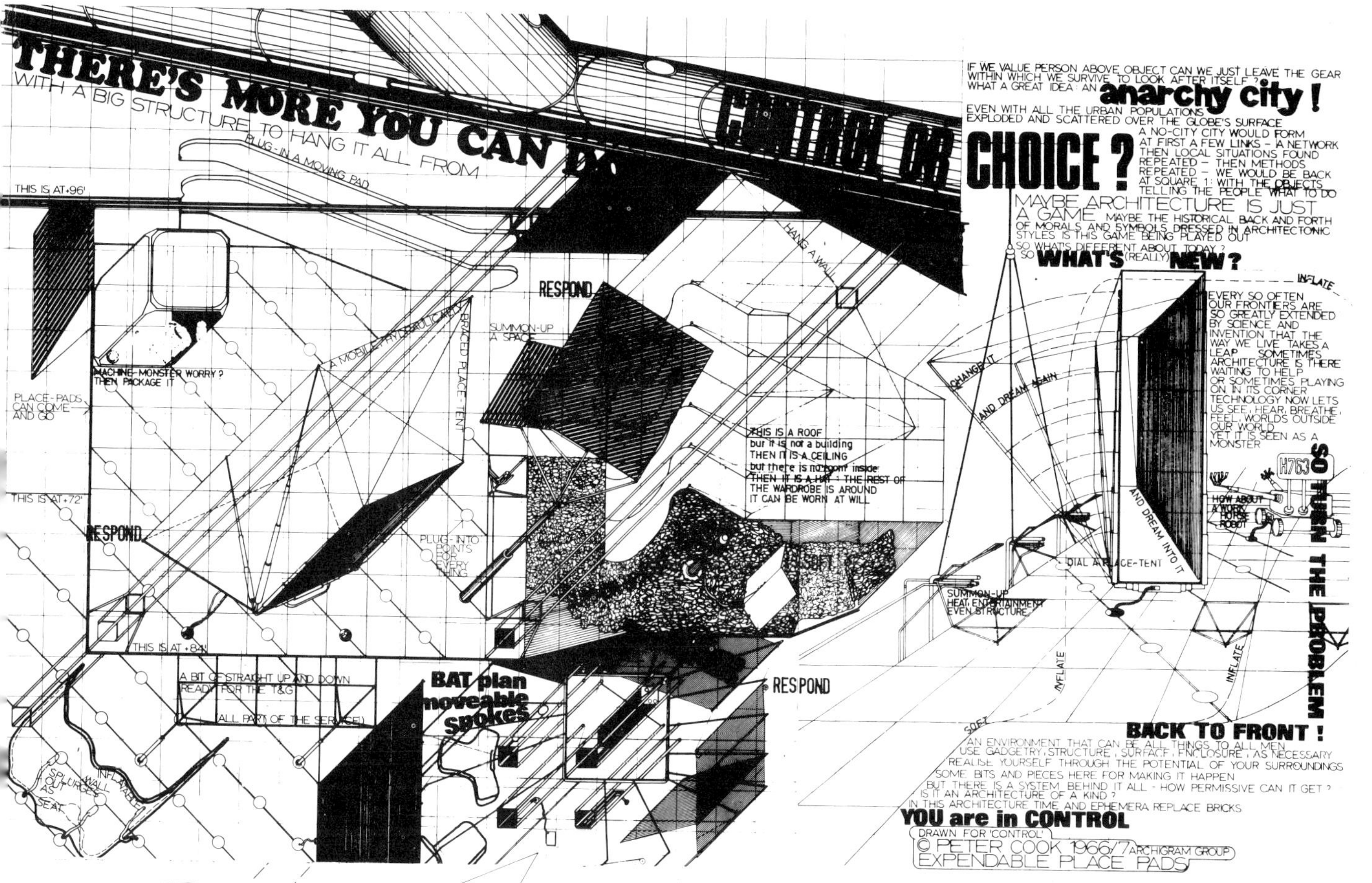
THERE'S MORE YOU CAN DO
WITH A BIG STRUCTURE TO HANG IT ALL FROM
PLUG-IN A MOVING PAD
CONTROL OR CHOICE ?
IF WE VALUE PERSON ABOVE OBJECT CAN WE JUST LEAVE THE GEAR WITHIN WHICH WE SURVIVE TO LOOK AFTER ITSELF ? WHAT A GREAT IDEA : AN anarchy city !
EVEN WITH ALL THE URBAN POPULATIONS EXPLODED AND SCATTERED OVER THE GLOBE'S SURFACE
A NO-CITY CITY WOULD FORM AT FIRST A FEW LINKS – A NETWORK THEN LOCAL SITUATIONS FOUND REPEATED – THEN METHODS REPEATED – WE WOULD BE BACK AT SQUARE 1: WITH THE OBJECTS TELLING THE PEOPLE WHAT TO DO
MAYBE ARCHITECTURE IS JUST A GAME MAYBE THE HISTORICAL BACK AND FORTH OF MORALS AND SYMBOLS DRESSED IN ARCHITECTONIC STYLES IS THIS GAME BEING PLAYED OUT
SO WHAT'S DIFFERENT ABOUT TODAY ?
SO WHAT'S (REALLY) NEW ?
INFLATE
EVERY SO OFTEN OUR FRONTIERS ARE SO GREATLY EXTENDED BY SCIENCE AND INVENTION THAT THE WAY WE LIVE TAKES A LEAP SOMETIMES ARCHITECTURE IS THERE WAITING TO HELP OR SOMETIMES PLAYING ON IN ITS CORNER TECHNOLOGY NOW LETS US SEE, HEAR, BREATHE, FEEL, WORLDS OUTSIDE OUR WORLD YET IT IS SEEN AS A MONSTER
THIS IS AT +96'
HANG A WALL
RESPOND
SUMMON-UP A SPACE
MACHINE-MONSTER WORRY ? THEN PACKAGE IT
PLACE-PADS CAN COME AND GO
CHANGE IT
AND DREAM AGAIN
THIS IS A ROOF but it is not a building THEN IT IS A CEILING but there is no room inside THEN IT IS A HAT : THE REST OF THE WARDROBE IS AROUND IT CAN BE WORN AT WILL
H763
HOW ABOUT A WORK HORSE ROBOT
SO TURN THE PROBLEM
THIS IS AT +72'
RESPOND
PLUG-INTO POINTS FOR EVERY THING
SOFT
AND DREAM INTO IT
DIAL A PLACE-TENT
SUMMON-UP HEAT, ENTERTAINMENT EVEN STRUCTURE
THIS IS AT +84'
A BIT OF STRAIGHT UP AND DOWN READY FOR THE T&G
ALL PART OF THE SERVICE
BAT plan moveable spokes
RESPOND
INFLATE
INFLATE
SPLURGE AS SEAT
INFLATABLE WALL
SOFT
BACK TO FRONT !
AN ENVIRONMENT THAT CAN BE ALL THINGS TO ALL MEN
USE GADGETRY, STRUCTURE, SURFACE, ENCLOSURE, AS NECESSARY
REALISE YOURSELF THROUGH THE POTENTIAL OF YOUR SURROUNDINGS
SOME BITS AND PIECES HERE FOR MAKING IT HAPPEN
BUT THERE IS A SYSTEM BEHIND IT ALL – HOW PERMISSIVE CAN IT GET ?
IS IT AN ARCHITECTURE OF A KIND ?
IN THIS ARCHITECTURE TIME AND EPHEMERA REPLACE BRICKS
YOU are in CONTROL
DRAWN FOR 'CONTROL'
© PETER COOK 1966/7 ARCHIGRAM GROUP
EXPENDABLE PLACE PADS

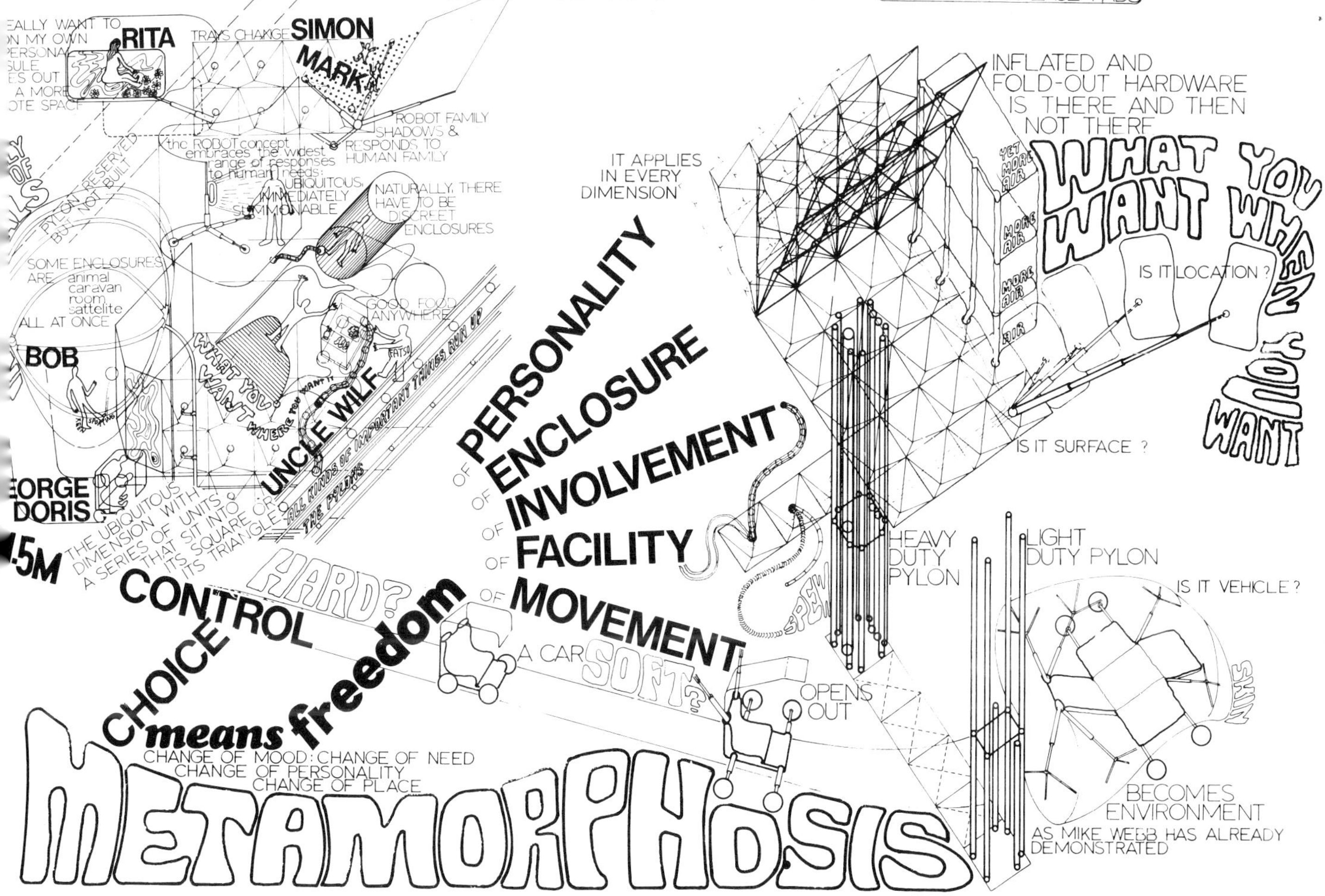
EALLY WANT TO
ON MY OWN
PERSONA
SULE
ES OUT
A MORE
OTE SPACE
RITA
TRAYS CHANGE
SIMON
MARK
ROBOT FAMILY SHADOWS & RESPONDS TO HUMAN FAMILY
the ROBOT concept embraces the widest range of responses to human needs: UBIQUITOUS IMMEDIATELY SUMMONABLE
PYLON RESERVED BUT NOT BUILT
NATURALLY THERE HAVE TO BE DISCREET ENCLOSURES
SOME ENCLOSURES ARE: animal caravan room sattelite ALL AT ONCE
GOOD FOOD ANYWHERE
BOB
WHAT YOU WANT
WHERE YOU WANT IT
UNCLE WILF
ALL KINDS OF IMPORTANT THINGS RUN UP THE PYLONS
EORGE
DORIS
1.5M
THE UBIQUITOUS DIMENSION WITH A SERIES OF UNITS THAT SIT INTO ITS SQUARE OR ITS TRIANGLE
IT APPLIES IN EVERY DIMENSION
OF PERSONALITY
OF ENCLOSURE
OF INVOLVEMENT
OF FACILITY
OF MOVEMENT
INFLATED AND FOLD-OUT HARDWARE IS THERE AND THEN NOT THERE
YET MORE AIR
MORE AIR
MORE AIR
AIR
WHAT YOU WANT WHEN YOU WANT
IS IT LOCATION ?
IS IT SURFACE ?
HEAVY DUTY PYLON
LIGHT DUTY PYLON
IS IT VEHICLE ?
SKIN
SPEW
CONTROL
HARD?
CHOICE
A CAR
SOFT?
OPENS OUT
means freedom
CHANGE OF MOOD: CHANGE OF NEED
CHANGE OF PERSONALITY
CHANGE OF PLACE
METAMORPHOSIS
BECOMES ENVIRONMENT
AS MIKE WEBB HAS ALREADY DEMONSTRATED

top Control and Choice project: section showing several strips of dwelling spaces

below Control and Choice: plans of typical dwelling space

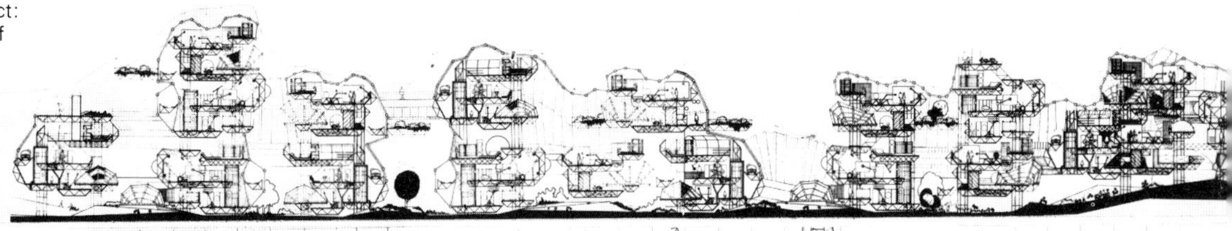

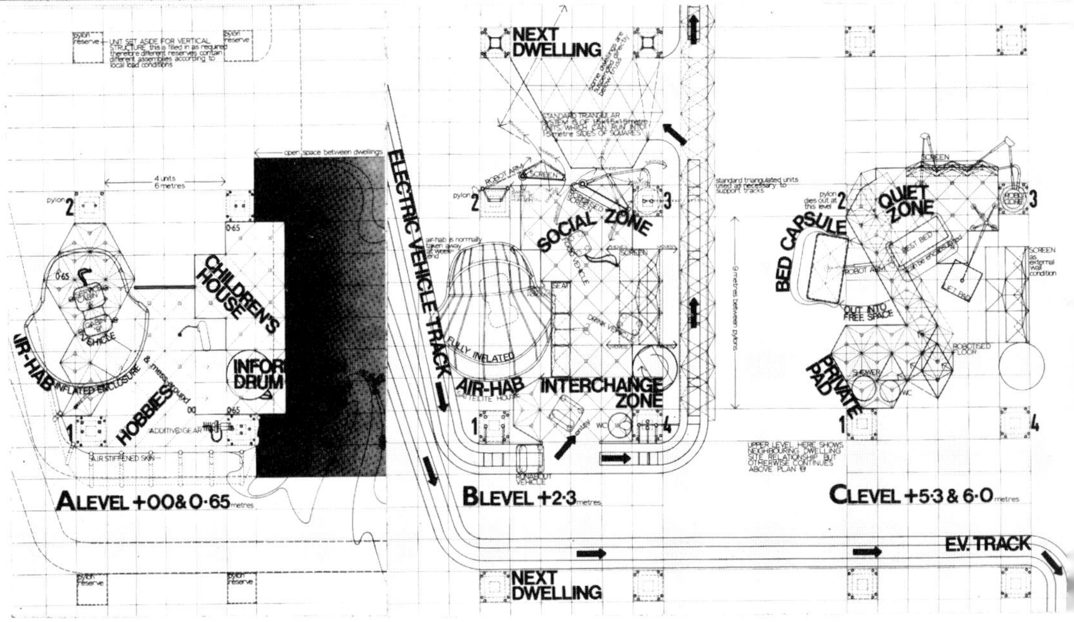

There is a natural fear in most of us that suspects the power of the machine and its takeover of human responsibility. This familiar bogey of the first machine age becomes even more terrifying with the dependence upon the *unseen* potential of electronic systems (they have even greater power of control than the obvious, symbolic and almost humanoid presence of a machine). The dependence upon such things for an emancipatory life is one of our paradoxes. The problem of exploitation of systems and machines and the continued recognition of 'friendly' and even 'passive' objects at the same time naturally leads to a hybrid assembly of parts.

Much of the project is still concerned with structure, mechanics and is of a defined mathematical order. It is necessary to postulate a system that can integrate with existing cities or imperfect sub-countryside.

The network proposed for accommodatin dwellings, entertainment facilities, industry c practically any other urban infill is here base on a $1\frac{1}{2}$ metre square grid. This interacts wher necessary with a system of $1\frac{1}{2}$ metre (equi lateral) triangles. Most parts of the syster that are structural, or have to be manufac tured in quantity, refer to this grid. The large scale of organization uses multiples of th $1\frac{1}{2}$ metre. There are optimum positions fc horizontal and vertical structure; but thes can be 'tuned' by greater or lesser infilling c pieces – or left out altogether. Naturall there are likely optima for the location c many things that we might find in a dwellin the need for several persons to congregate i one kind of place, the need for utmost privac in another kind of place are obvious but nee not lead to a complete and fixed hierarch that is the result of most architectur discipline.

opposite top Control and Choice: detail section

opposite below Control and Choice: model photographs

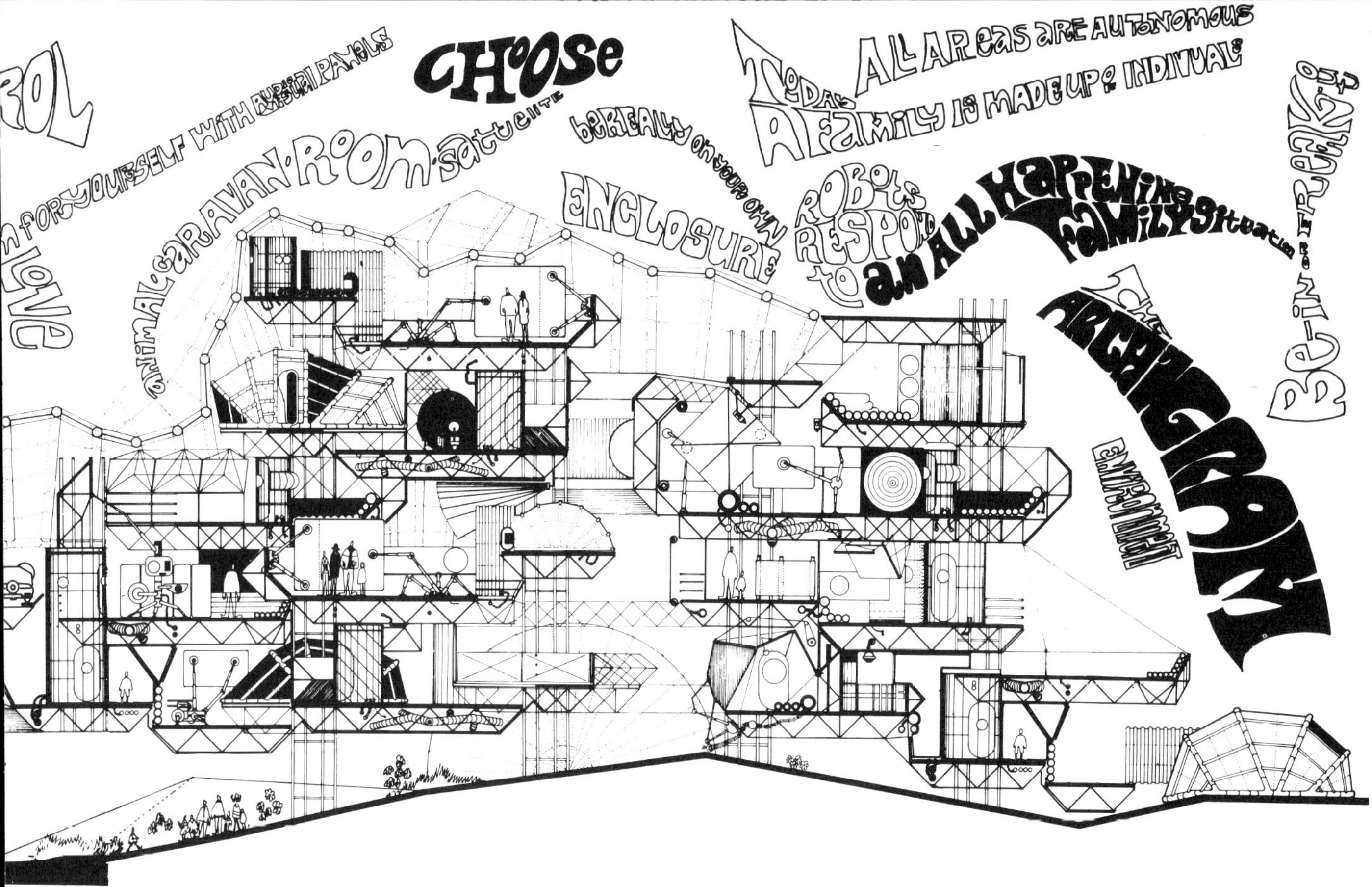

The hardware exists on a sliding scale that contains a parallel between size, permanence and rigidity of position. Starting at the largest, most permanent, most definitive, it runs as follows:

1 Structure/organization path with 'pylons'. The electric vehicle routes and the definition of one family's reserve as against another's tends to shadow this as well.

2 Typical floor/wall/truss/substructure kit (of $1\frac{1}{2}$ metre units). The intermixing of triangular and square elements is able to take up most locations. The pyramidal frame usually has a service outlet at its centre, so that any run of floor can be assumed to provide a facility for electricity, pressurized air, water, electronic circuitry, piped sound, information, and so on, at $1\frac{1}{2}$ metre centres.

3 'Robotized' elements. These are a development from the 1990 House robots. Now they are less humanoid, less a complete servant object, more a notion about facility that crystallizes around an armature. They can be thought of as analogous to a hi-fi unit, with more or less attachments added to provide better facilities. A small-scale plug-in system in each. These robotized elements include screens that carry the ephemeral end of the environment: screened happenings, television, colour, light. Food and drink trolleys are also robotized.

4 'Satellites'. There is really no dividing line between the 'hard' elements that stay in the same place most of the time and the 'soft' which are hardly there at all: for instance, the travelling units such as the electric cars which can become a 'room' in their own right. The most elaborate vehicle, with cooking and lavatory facilities, has an inflatable holiday house that grows out of it. As shown, it sits in the lowest level of the dwelling when at home.

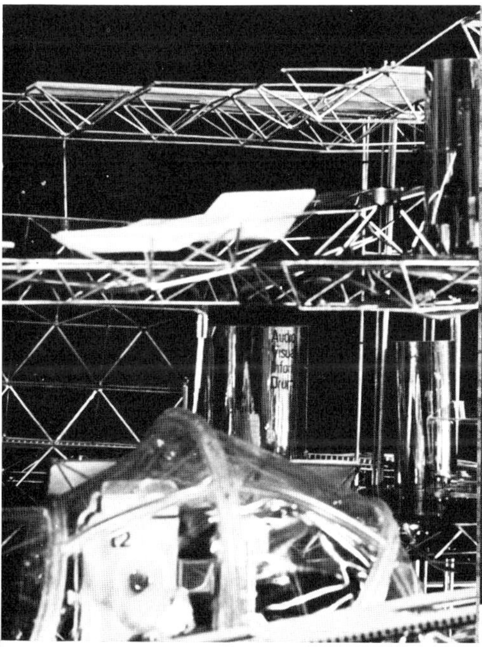

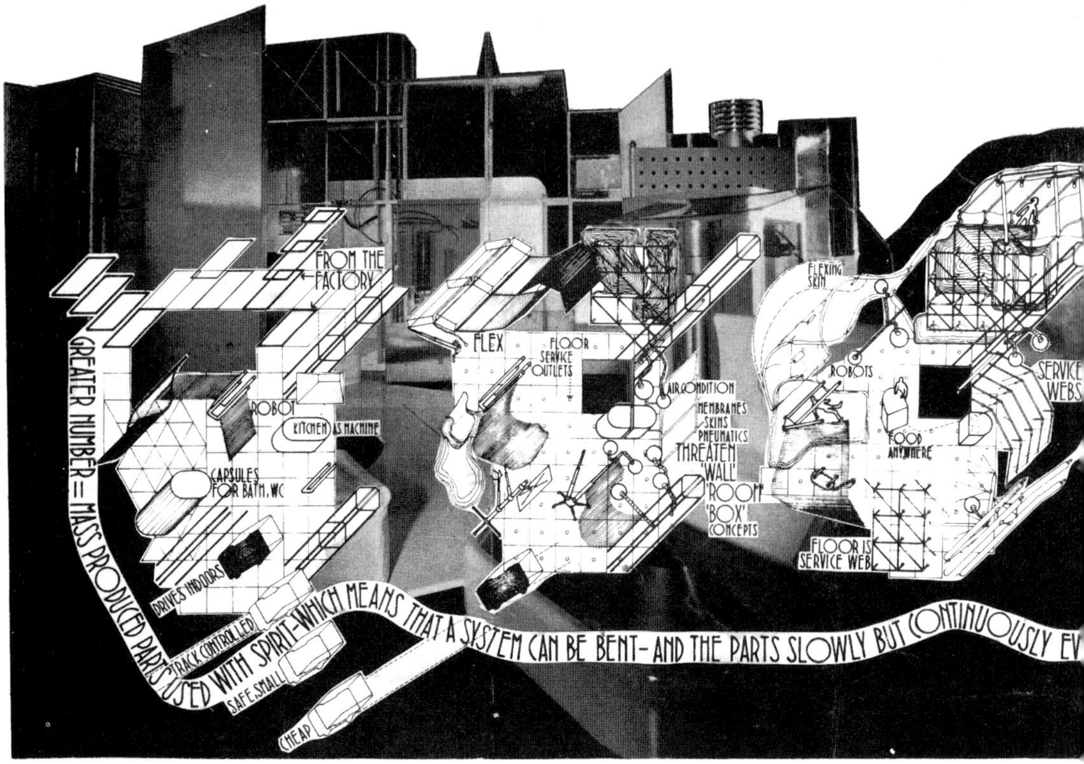

top 'Metamorphosis' sequence 1968 Peter Cook Some prognostications on how a Control and Choice situation might evolve

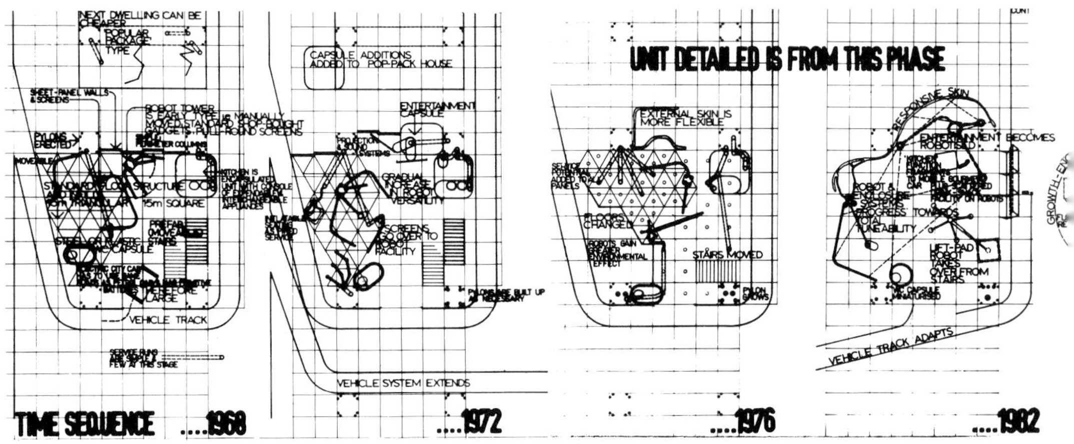

below 'Metamorphosis': plans related to Control and Choice dwelling

The forties
From *Archigram 6*
Warren Chalk

. . . apart from all that, the first half of the forties saw a great inventive leap made out of necessity for survival, advancing technology and mass-production techniques and demonstrating man's ingenuity, courage, effort and investment under the stress and pressure of war. Out of this period came too a strange social idealism. The idealism was to fade but not the technology: the laminated timber or geodesic framework of an aircraft, the welded tubular construction of a bridge, and the air-structure of a barrage balloon.

During the final stages of World War II several prefabricated house types emerged as part of the 'clip-on'/'plug-in' heritage. Given the official blessing of Winston Churchill, they were produced in quantity for the temporary housing programme.

However, soon the market was flooded with prefabricated systems, destroying the very basis of mass-production, and this, together with public prejudice and the social stigma attached to the word 'Prefab' proved fatal.

Compared with today, to the forties, pop-culture remained obscure, but it was there to be had in the shape of Jane Russell, and the original 'pin-up' girl, Betty Grable. 'Crooners' were still 'in' and Sinatra was king. Pop music was sticky – 'They Can't Black Out the Moon' by Ambrose, but Be-bop addicts tuned into AFN to hear snatches of Bird or Tadd Dameron, in between Miller and Kenton.

On the fine art scene there was little true pop: the romantic literary Englishness of John Piper and Edward Bawden held sway, and there was Trog. The Ad-man was still the art man. For pop reading there were the *Tropics* by Henry Miller, the original beat, and of course *Lilliput* and *Picture Post*.

Meanwhile the straight-up-and-down architectural situation had seen an end to the 'white boxes' of the thirties and the Modern Movement had become acceptable to all but the most reactionary. The standard of architecture was poor and only Lubetkin struggled manfully on. The social idealist camp looked

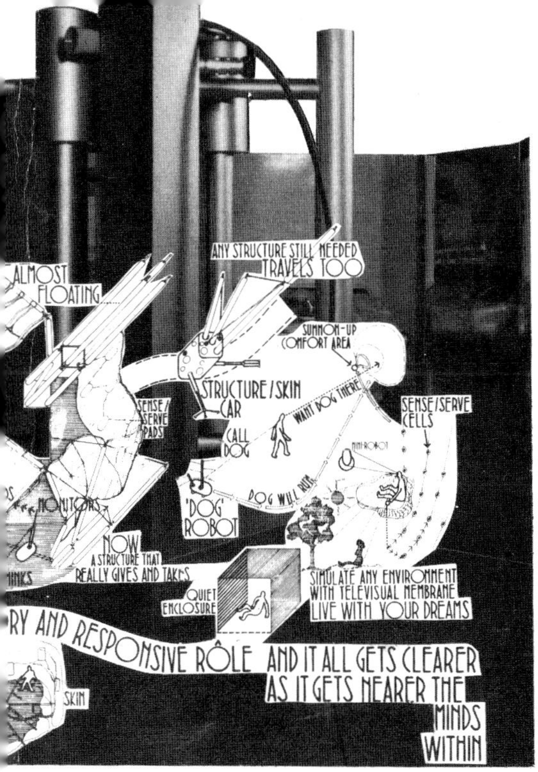

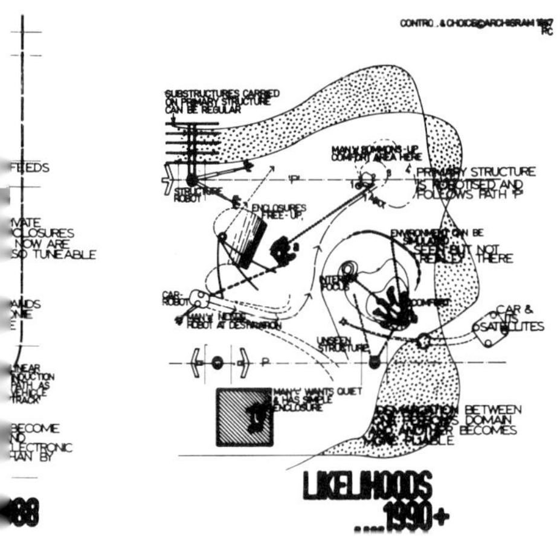

ɔwards Sweden and the copper clad mono-
itch was born, and a Mies type factory
Frankel) went up quietly in Wales.

ossibly only the Hertfordshire achievement
naped up to the promise of the forties, the
velter of proposals for the bomb-battered
ɔwns and cities certainly did not.

uring the war fashion design played a
ouble game, on the one hand squared
noulders, military looking hats, shoulder strap
andbags and clumpy shoes getting close to
e Services uniforms and on the other, the
ɔsolute antithesis, with silly little hats, silk
ockings and 'frocks'. In the austerity peace
at followed the most shattering events
ere of course the 'wasp-waist' and the 'New
ɔok', skirts dropping their hemlines to the
nkles. Paradoxically, the atom bomb inspired
nother fashion revolution in the form of the
ikini'. War surplus found its way on to the
ɔnsumer market and everything, from jeeps
duffle coats, has influenced us since.

Archigram 6 1967 front and back covers
Designed by Jeff Reeve

Typical strip illustrating 1940s scene

9 Open ends

Editorial from *Archigram 8*

The notions that have been running through our heads since the phase of the 1990 House and other experiments are much less easily frozen. As it is more irrelevant to contain an experiment in a single 'idea' such as a capsule house – where the image of capsule can replace the earlier image of cottage – or even a complex assembly like the Plug-in City can be read against a walled city of ancient times – it is now less a question of replacement ideas. It is less a question of total idea and total consistency. Yet there is a consistency somewhere: perhaps in the generics of the work now being done by Archigram which all, in some way, springs from the earlier outbreaks. Without setting-up too introspective a discussion, it is interesting for any one of the Archigram groups to trace the step-by-stepness of the new work.

There then emerges a stage where the notions themselves can be taken outside the description of a single design or proposition, and read against several. They can be detected in some ideas, and come through fiercely in others. We have eight notions that are still unanswered by any complete set of experiments though we have begun the series. They are dreams because we keep returning to them. They are dreams because they may never be completely satisfied by what a designer or a strategist or any operator can do. They are open-ended, and, whatever we are doing by the time that you are reading this, may in some way have sprung out of a dream or two.

Metamorphosis

Metamorphosis
Oxford Dictionary definition: 'Change of form (by natural development, etc.). Changed form, change of character, condition, etc.'
Archigram usage: 'Continuous evolution from one state (or arrangement of forms, values incidences or whatever) to another. Always alive but never the same. Always complete but always in metamorphic transience.'

Most cultured designers have been bred to regard one state of organization against another in terms of preference. Even non-formally, there are arrangements that are 'good' and 'bad'. Religion, formula, ideal, thesis, antithesis – all force one towards stating a fixed preference: a stated state. If we really believe in change, it will be a change in what we believe in, rather than a change in the means towards a different ideal. Growth itself has a dynamic and becomes a useful objective because it is the natural analogue of change. Now the analogy must be widened so that all parts are in an evolutionary state.

This business of widening range has taken us through some weird territory; it means that most of the projects we make are hybrid in content as well as notion, They themselves are in a constant change of state, assembly, and value. This last is the most difficult: and may be what metamorphosis is all about. Therefore there seem to be two levels of metamorphosis: the simple one by which an object has to change to keep going (the F-III has to swing its wing to perform usefully), and the more complex metamorphosis of our own regard for phenomena at all. So-called 'values' are the shorthand for this regard; so watch out for fixing too hard these value-judgements.

Nomad

Oxford Dictionary definition: 'Roaming from place to place . . . wandering.'
Archigram usage: includes the related notions of the satellite and the complete operation not necessarily tied to a locative system.

The nomad as man, as hunter, as freethinker . . . the total location possibility? . . . The nomad on land, sea, air. . . . Everybody is a satellite. . . . Choice of unseen attachment or seen attachment to an organization or system. . . . Trailers . . . Hovercraft. . . . Tents. . . . Pack-on-back. . . . Under water . . . Moon probe. . . . Suit environment. . . . Disappearing of for a smoke. . . . 'Don't bug me, Mac'. . . . 'See you.' . . .

This could be the most upsetting idea since it is close to the instincts of many people who like to be thought of as steady guys: those who rely upon being able to plug into a known network, who demand of life a continuity. It is these who are nearest the edge of escaping from it all. The car is useful for the game of freedom. The implication that the whole surface of the world can give equal service is possibly pointing to the time when we can all be nomads if we wish. At the same time the network of support (even if 'soft' like radio) is still there to be escaped from.

At the moment the situation is open-ended. This is the attraction of the car-as-satellite-on the-pad. Next the car becomes its own pad. Next the pad itself takes on the role of car. It divides and regroups. So too could large combinations of environment. The status of the family and its direct connotation with a preferred, static house, cannot last. What about the evidence of the Teenybopper family-within-the-family? Multiplication and proliferation (and a dynamic use of mass availables) could lead to breakaway and regroup as naturally as the traditional strict hierarchies. Time is a factor. Coming together and independence are compatible if we use time.

The effect of hybrid assemblies that are at once mass-produced and private world already exist. If developed, the extension of personality might become the central reason for environment. The interface of one man with one enclosure is a raw example. The moment-village is a project suggested by this development out of Nomadism. Its group-regroup-shift implication suggests that its ultimate might be an anarchy-city or that the concept of 'place' exists only in the mind.

top Moment-Village: plan

centre Moment-Village: sequence

below Camping Scene

The Moment-Village takes the hypothesis that anything beyond a wink or a nod from a person in one car to a person in another constitutes a communal act and from any point beyond this the village is created. The sequence shows the coming together of cars and support facilities which forms a casual community.

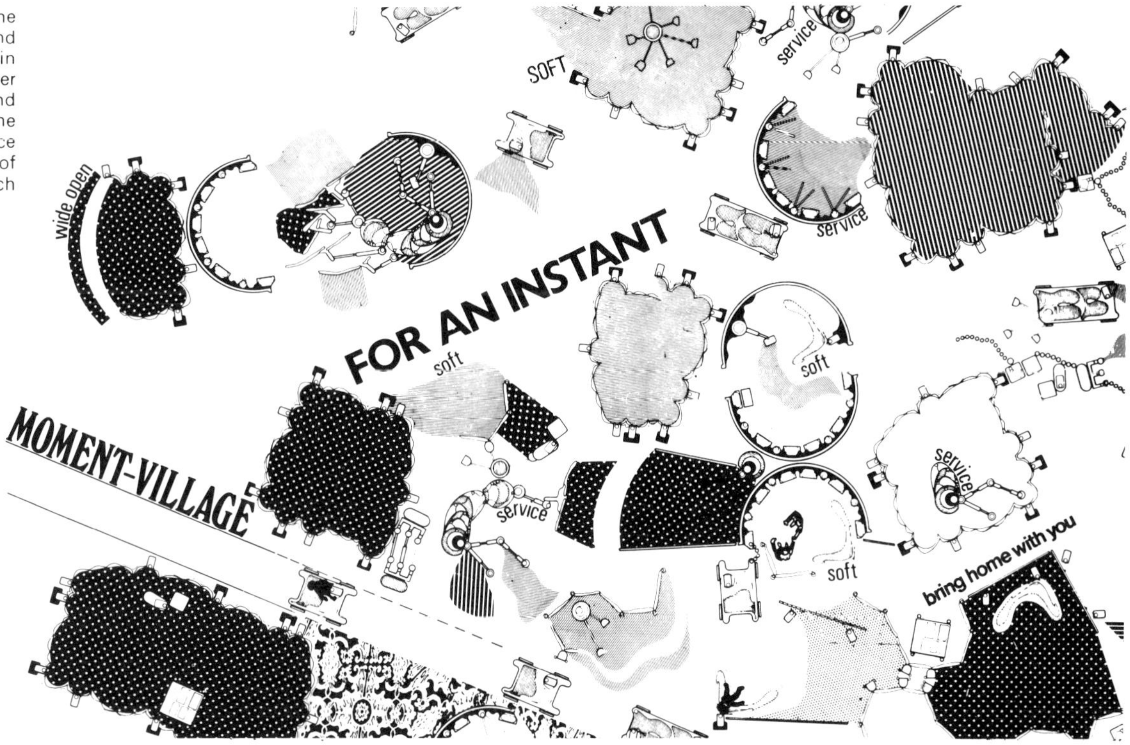

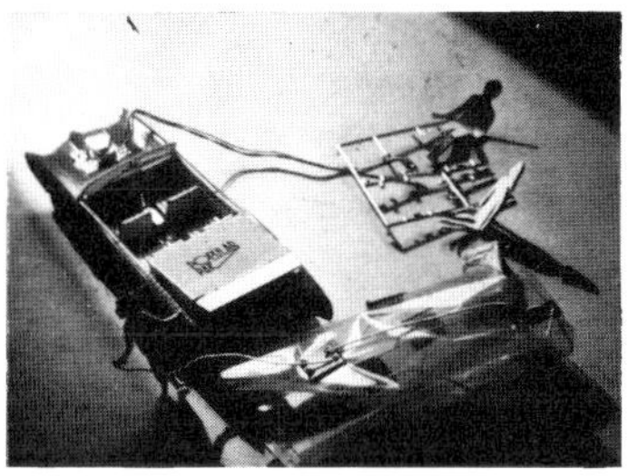

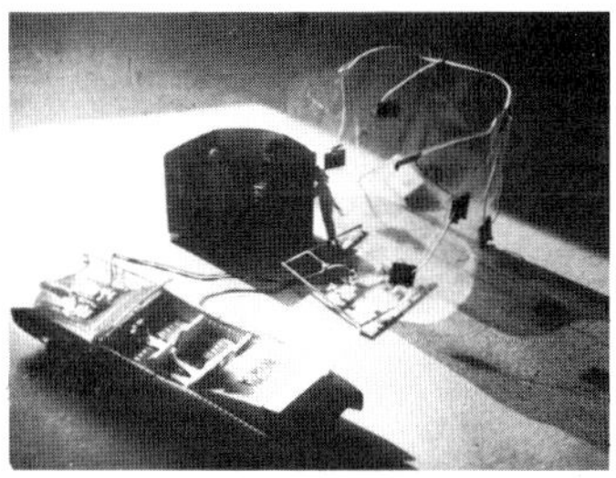

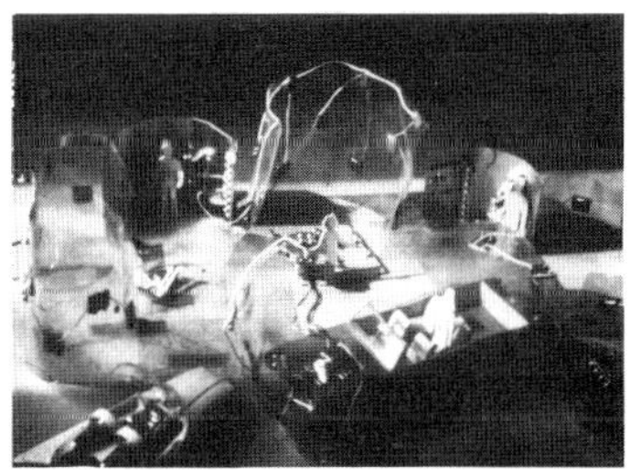

We offer ten pre-selected sets
David Greene

We offer ten pre-selected sets – or you can choose from forty-three individual fixtures and custom design your own set to suit your tastes. Part 4 – or in spite of the fact there is no sign of the Evinrude Aquanaut and skim-twin all-weathered carpeted multipurpose boat this picture tells you how it is – which also happens to be part 2 of a consideration of the completely friendly and satisfying environment and how to recognize it.

The passing cluster of equipment.
The transient space.
The backyard that happens as three magic tail-gates lower and the twin barrel V8s stop feeding horses through Synchro-smooth drive trains.
Slip off the hi-way.
Cut out automatic pilot control and cruisomatic.
Select down.
Super diamond lustre finish feeding back bent images of sky and trees.
Sports tach fliskers dead and supa wide ovals sink into the meadow.

Just unload the gear and live. Move on maybe. It's all different tomorrow anyway the backyard has become a party or kitchen and three days gunning down the Pan-American hi-way and you're stepping out of that feature foam cushioned bucket and setting up your luxurious and convenient equipment in the jungle and there still isn't a crease in your shirt.

See the picture, it's all there, at least until it's all in your pocket, or embedded in your nervous system or we don't need to go because we can re-create it all in Bradford or on the Central Line.

Comfort
Oxford Dictionary definition: 'Relief in affliction . . . cause of satisfaction, conscious well-being . . . possession of things that make life easy.'
Archigram usage: The broad instinct for well-being. Perhaps the greatest justification for environment – or any man-made effort – is well-being. Or is this moralizing?

Comfort

'Comfort' in its current English usage an old, rather 'hairy' (and therefore suspect) word but it is interesting that the most impressive modern architecture is most often accused (by lay people) of being 'uncomfortable'. This is at the level of the most literal interpretation of the word, but it serves as a warning that if we are not careful we shall end up by providing a commodity that by its inhumanity is just aesthetic fetish.

Returning to the fundamental comfort-instinct, it is reasonable to check designed situations against their probable 'plus' or 'minus' in terms of whether they make people feel safe or unsafe, propped-up or isolated, happy or unhappy.

Goodies. Enjoyment. Security. 'System' of structure, facilities, service, etc. is a comfort giving thing as much as ice-cream is a comfort giving goody.

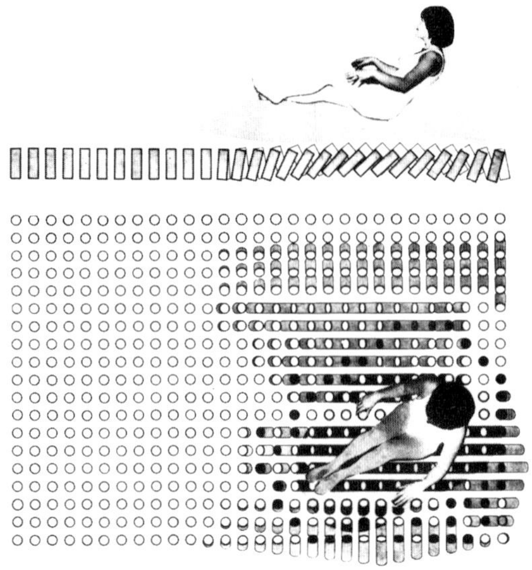

The hovercraft principle in reverse. Tubes blow air at varying pressures to maintain the body in a prone position or to raise it through sitting to the vertical. The tubes can pivot to maintain the body in a static position or to rock it; they can also eject gases for a static or moving enclosure.

Hard-soft
This refers to the 'hardware-software' relationship found in systems analysis, cybernetics, and the terms come from computer jargon. They are not yet in the Oxford Dictionary.

'Hard', e.g. monument, New York, wall, machine, hard architecture, metal, plastic, etc. Against **'Soft'**, e.g. programme, wire, message, instruction, graphic synopsis, equation, mood, abstract, informed machine, electronic music, light-show, computers, information feedback, information motivators.

Hard-Soft

In systems planning we are reaching a point where the 'software' – the unseen relationship – is sufficient to determine the control and positioning of elements with which we live. The environment can now be determined by a systems analysis of our requirements and the 'seen' world could become servant to the 'unseen' motivation. Now, naturally, we are all excited about this. At last we can escape from the hangup on hardware that has beset architecture throughout history; we need not bother about preference even. This over-simplification has the rhetoric that is necessary at this moment in history. In many ways it parallels the great excitement of the discovery of the machine for the Futurists fifty years ago. Hardware has limiattions, and the symbolism of bits and pieces can be a bore for a rational attitude to planning or performance specification. Software is at this moment being pitched against it in order to explode this seeming irrationality.

But once again, we are falling into this black versus white trap. Systems are not a panacea. They have a necessary place in the evolution of intelligence. They will take short cuts towards solving problems. The Plug-in City needed the Computer City as its shadow, otherwise it could not function. The Control-and-Choice discussion revolved around the potential of the unseen microswitches and sensors, but more than this: these devices would need the intelligence of a computed relay of information so that they came into your service at the moment when you needed them.

We shall really get somewhere when it has all cooled off a little, and hard and soft become relative to each other rather than in opposition.

Fluid and Air-Wall 1968 Michael Webb

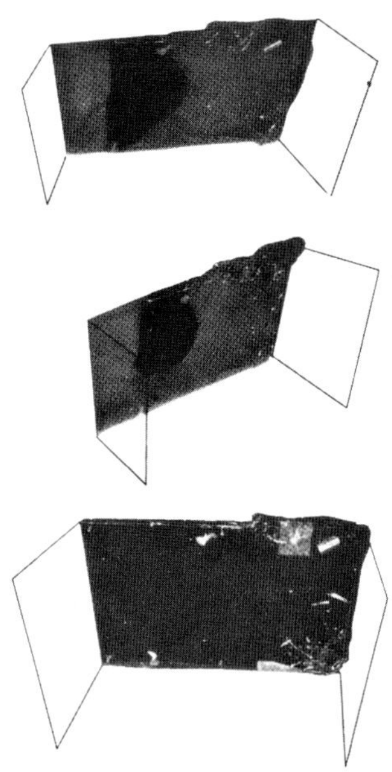

A cavity wall which changes its visual, thermal and insulative properties by means of fluids, gases and silver crystals. Above are three views of the wall showing the cavity empty with a curtain simulation fluid spreading and with the fluid fully spread.

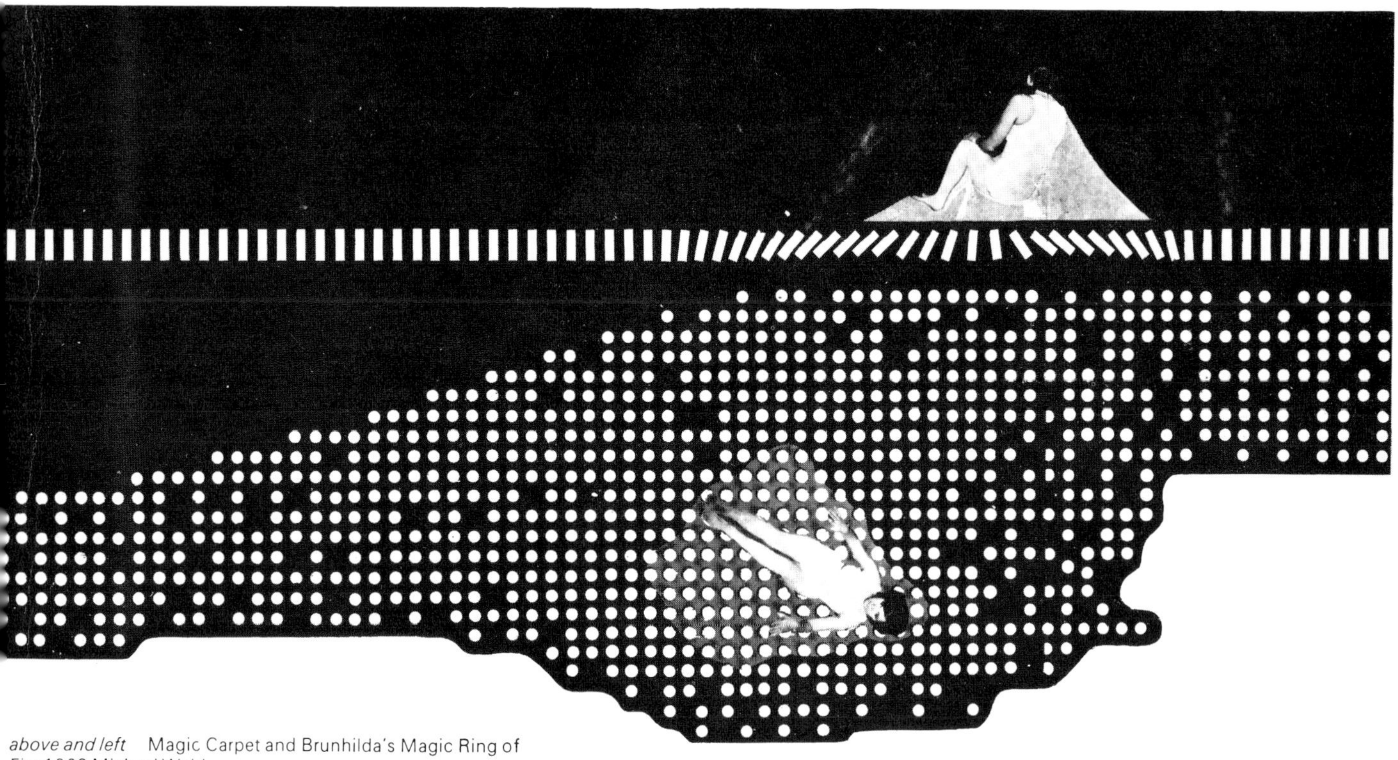

above and left Magic Carpet and Brunhilda's Magic Ring of Fire 1968 Michael Webb

Cushicle Mark II 1967 Michael Webb: model

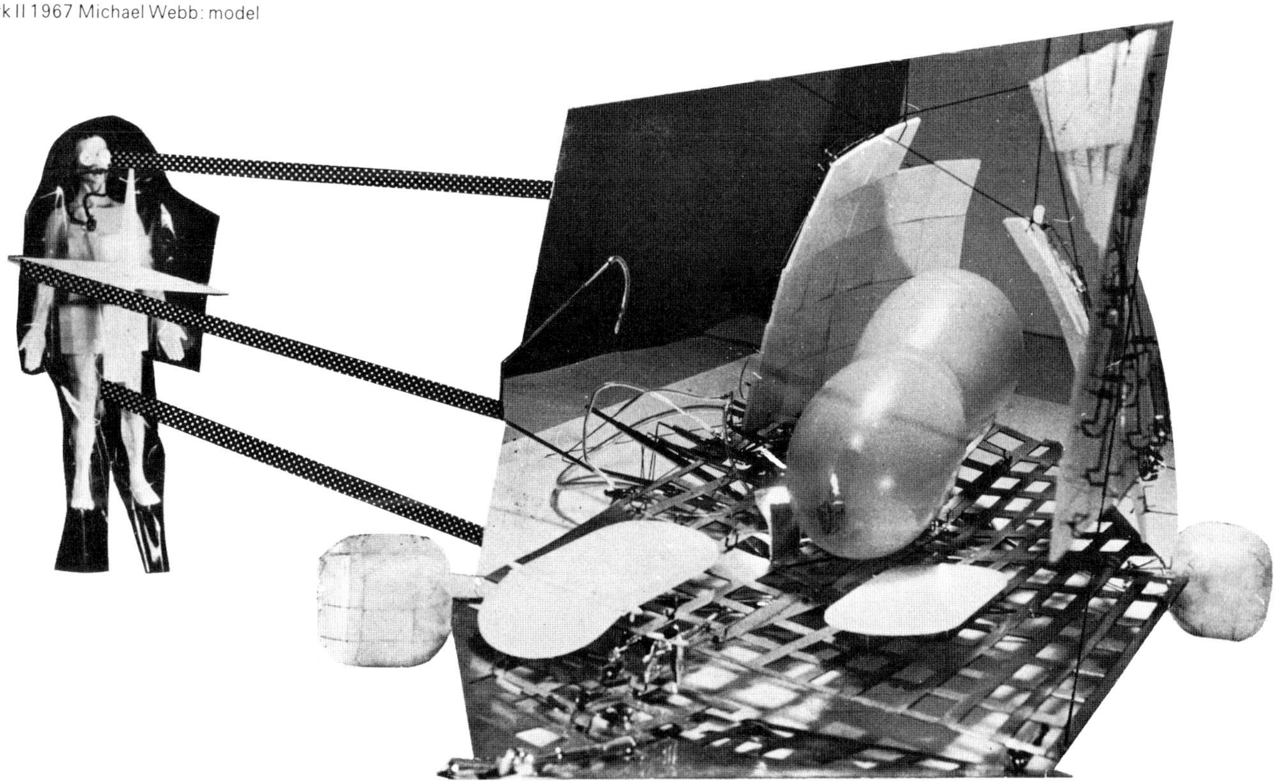

Tuned Suburb 1968 Ron Herron

Living Pods on high rise structure 1966 David Greene

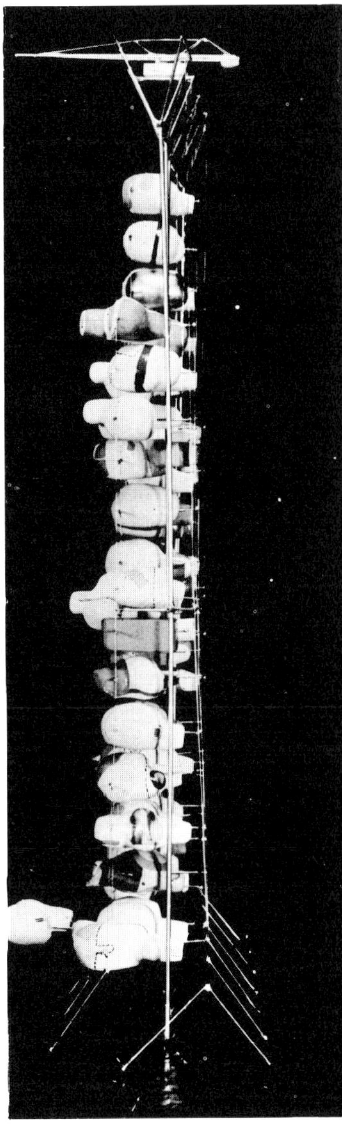

Emancipation
Oxford Dictionary definition: setting free, especially from slavery . . . from intellectual or moral fetters.

Archigram usage: directly follows this with particular reference to people's use of buildings.

Emancipation
- Goodies: more obvious fruits of high living standard plus obvious mass-production.
- Fruits of success/fruits of choice. The power to choose.
- Customizing the mass-produced object. Art customizing.
- The individual's effect upon his environment.
- Water/underwater as sport/fun/ English 'playing about in boats'.
- Choice of wardrobe.
- Switch-on fun. In-the-brain fun. Hobbies.
- Airplanes. Moon probe.
- Personality. Oddballs. Simulated individualism.
- Pastiche styling as fun.

Emancipation

The history of the last 100 years has been one of continued emancipation, irrevocably moving forwards despite the immense obvious setbacks of war and poverty, and the more hidden ones sustained by facets of culture and tradition that seek to preserve as much as possible in the face of social change. We are nearing the time when we can all realize our aspirations. It is too simple to see this merely as the amassing of objects, but they represent pretty accurately the directions outwards that our mental environment can reach: to the furthest *imaginable* limits. This is the crux of the matter: in the past the indulgence of the mind and intellect (as applied to artefacts) was the privilege of the rich.

If architecture laid claims to human sustenance, it should surely have responded as human experience expanded. For architects the question is: do buildings help towards emancipation of the people within? Or do they hinder because they solidify the way of life preferred by the architect? It is now reasonable to treat buildings as consumer products, and the real justification of consumer products is that they are the direct expression of a freedom to choose. So we are back again to the other notions of determinacy and indeterminacy and change and choice. We may reach a stage where this whole discussion seems academic because we shall all be much more relaxed about the choices we have and actually want a bit of abrasion in the way of bad buildings, but we are nowhere near that yet.

elow Oasis1968 Ron Herron This relates to the Free ime Node (page 59) and contrasts this notion with the eterminism of the familiar city buildings

Exchange
Oxford Dictionary definition: 'Give, receive, in place of another, for another; can be received as equivalent for.'

Archigram usage: 'Interaction of one event against another, directly analogous to interaction (and indeterminacy, in many cases) of one facility against another.'

Response
Oxford Dictionary definition: 'Answer given in word or act . . . feeling elicited by stimulus or influence.'

Archigram usage: 'Effective reply by situation or design or artefact to a need, stimulus or an idea.'

Exchange and response

Even the broad march of history that measures the action and reaction of one movement against another – and at every scale downwards – capitalizes upon interaction. At a purely functional level, the exchange of facility between one object and another is the basis of most design. It seems to us strange that architecture is expected to support a single value-system when today there is exchange between different fields of operation that can increase the possible means of our survival.

The other attractive aspect of 'exchange' as a fundamental is its implication of 'revision'. This has strong links with our concern with the necessity of building as an exchangeable commodity: extendable, expendable and under constant scrutiny.

All effort is responding to something. An active architecture – and this is really what we are about – attempts to sharpen to the maximum its power of response and ability to respond to as many reasonable potentials as possible. If only we could get to an architecture that really responded to human wish as it occurred then we would be getting somewhere.

Deliberate confrontation of forces so that one *responds* to the other: robot-serves-person; machine-serves-facility; machine-interacts-with-other-machine; person 'summons' facility; appliance serves food, person responds to scene. Objects: robots, enclosures, facility-machines. Man/machine interface. Information feedback results in environment change.

Suitaloon — Michael Webb

Clothing for living in – or if it wasn't for my Suitaloon I would have to buy a house.

The space suit could be identified as a minimal house. In the previous Cushicle, the environment for the rider was provided by the Cushicle – a mechanism like a car. In this project the suit itself provides all the necessary services, the Cushicle being the source of (a) movement, (b) a larger envelope than the suit can provide, (c) power. Each suit has a plug serving a similar function to the key to your front door. You can plug into your friend and you will both be in one envelope, or you can plug into any envelope, stepping out of your suit which is left clipped on to the outside ready to step into when you leave. The plug also serves as a means of connecting envelopes together to form larger spaces.

The Cushicle shown is for one rider only. Various models of Cushicle envelope and suit would of course be available ranging from super sports to family models.

1

2

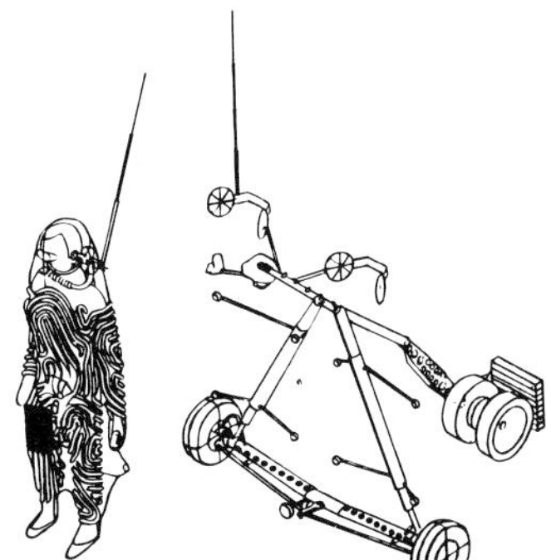

7

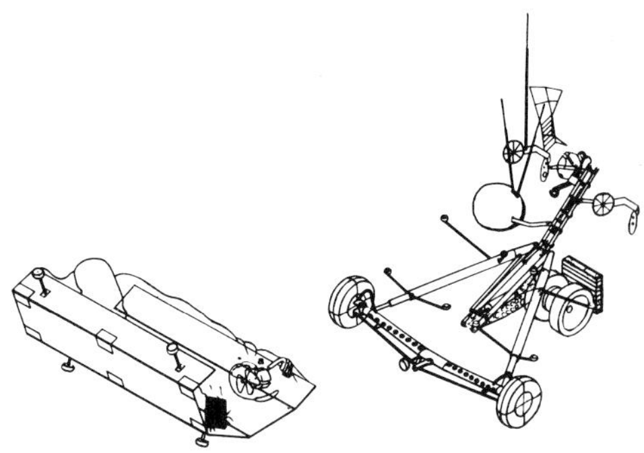

12

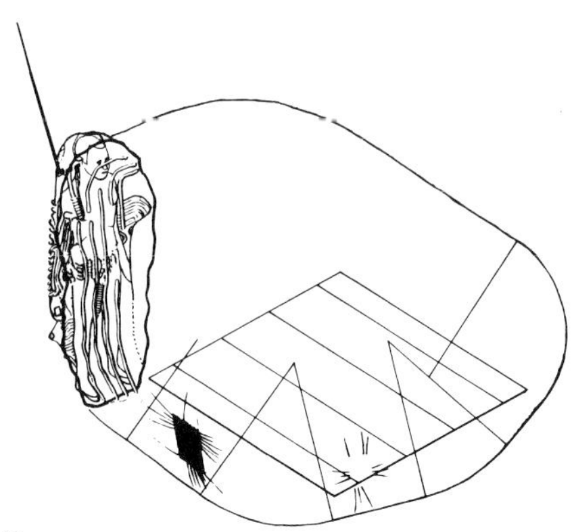

16

3

4

5

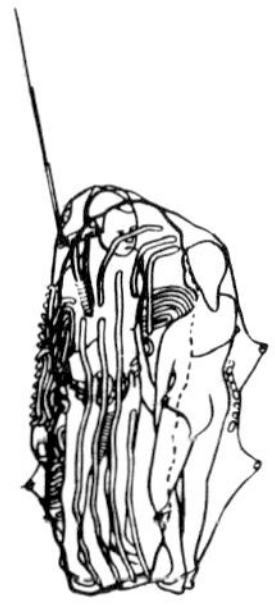

6

8

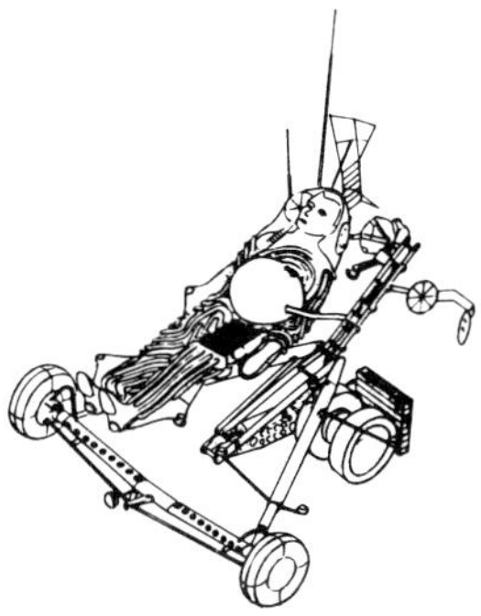

9

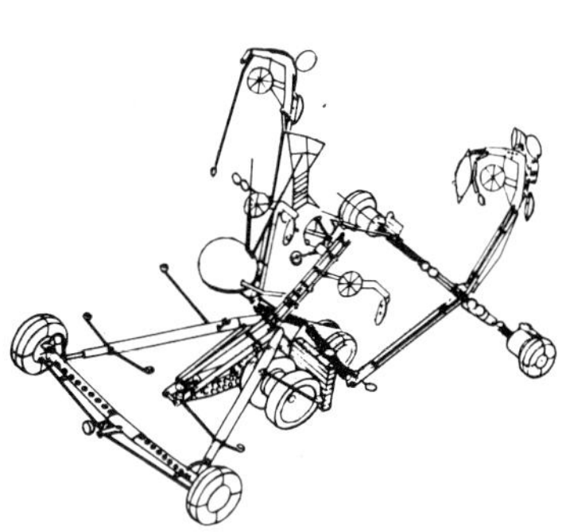

10

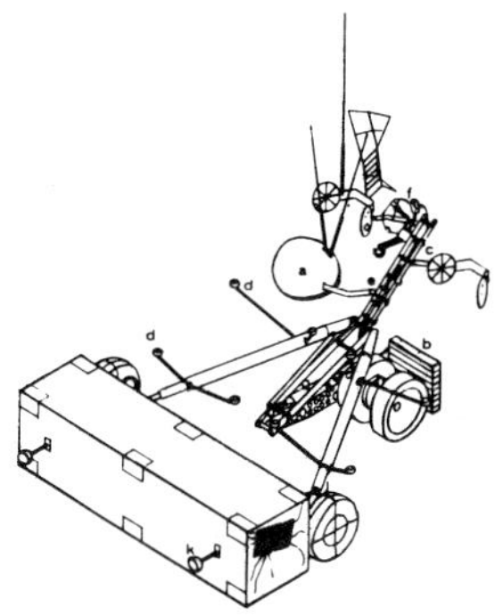

11

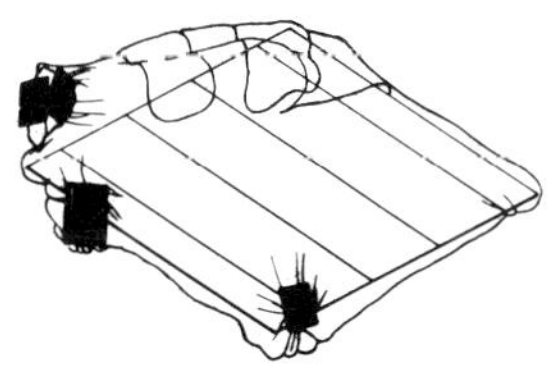

13

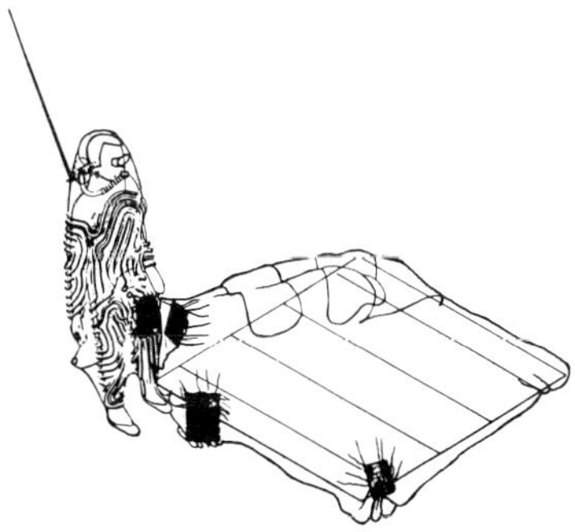

14

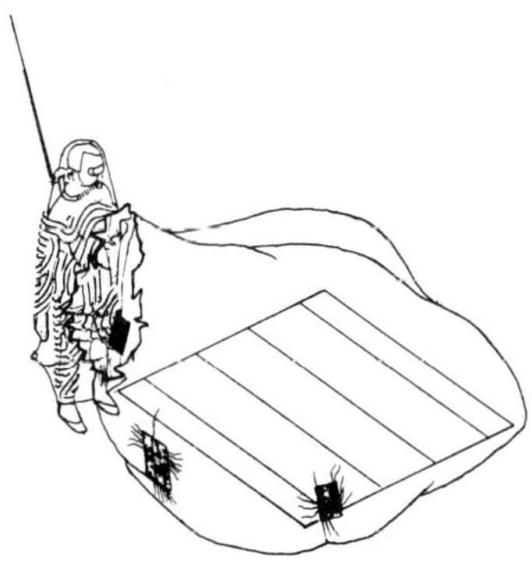

15

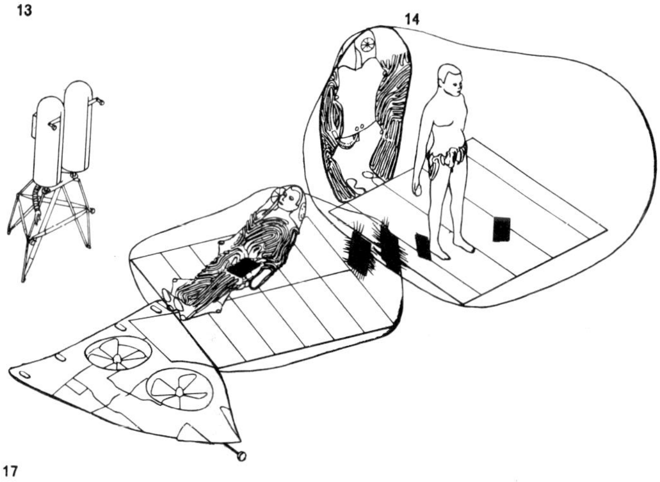

17

Archigram Exhibition at the Milan Triennale 1968 Whole Group Project

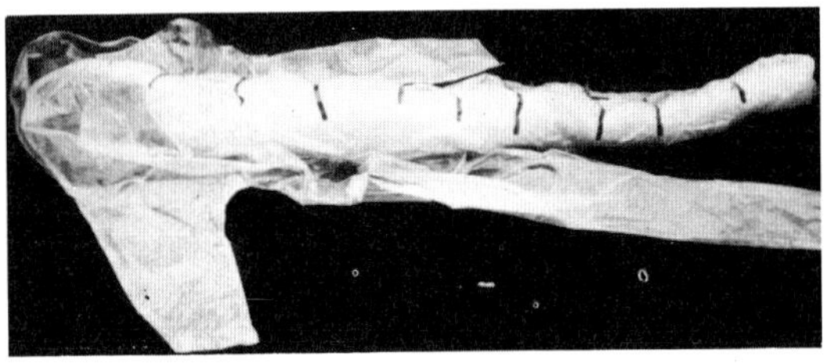

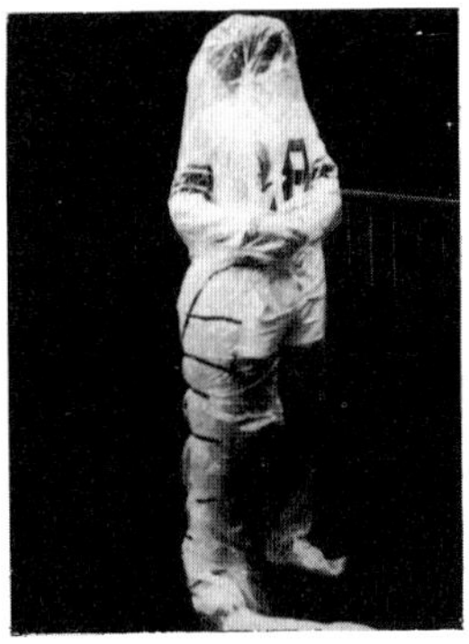

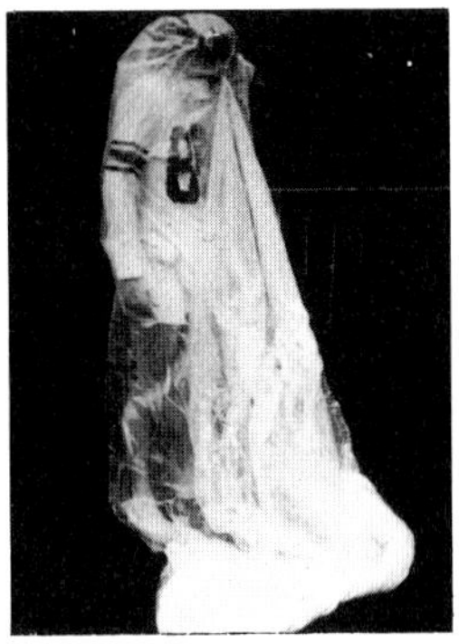

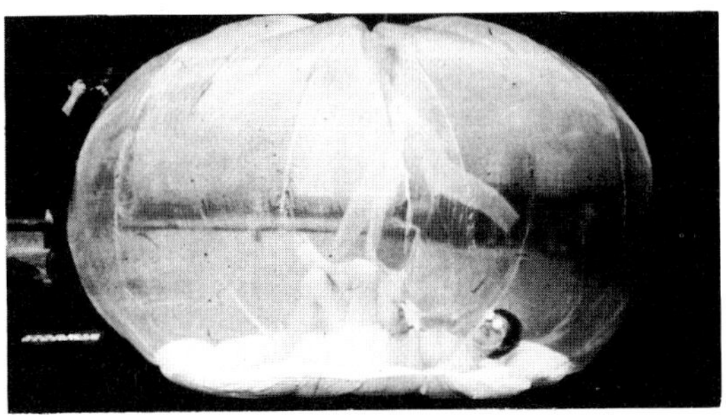

above Inflatable Suit-Home 1968 David Greene (suit made by Pat Haines), sequence: suit package, suit being worn, suit inflating out, suit as 'home'

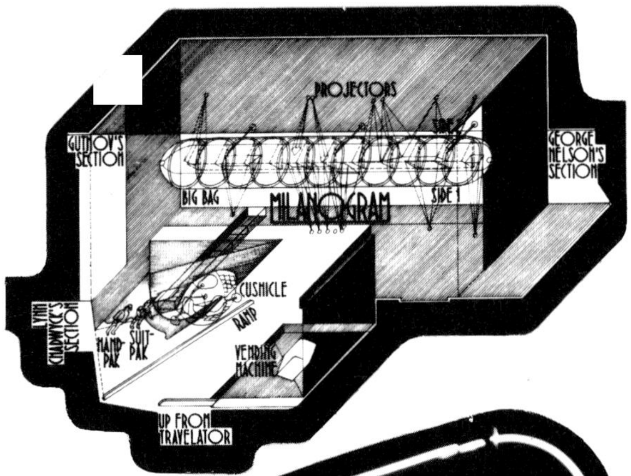

top Milanogram layout

centre Milanogram slogan

below Milanogram components

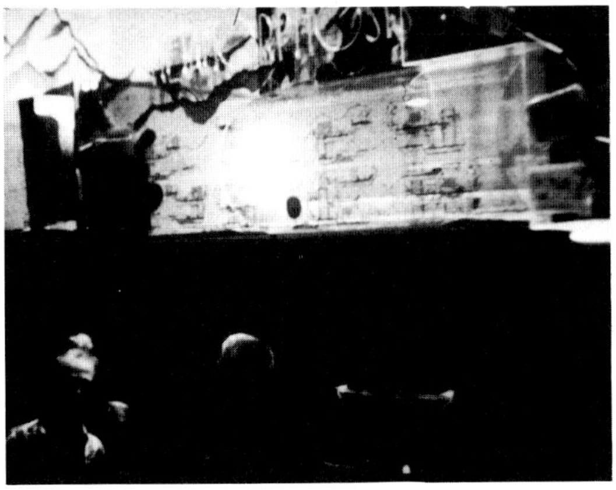

right Layout of the Milanogram Bag

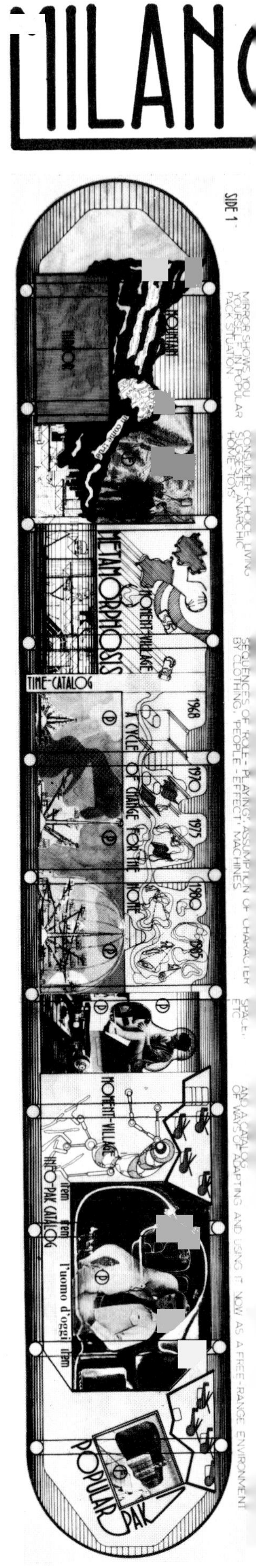

GRAM

Milan Triennale

The Archigram Group called their exhibit at the Milan Triennale 'Milanogram'. Conceived somewhat in the way of a magazine issue of *Archigram:* a synthesis of inventions, projects, theories, comment and designs wrapped together, an *Archigram* that can use time (a 12-minute cycle), and space and overlays of 2, 3, and 4-dimensional evidence.

The problem of 'greater number' is seen as the central issue of man's survival as an individual in the face of pressures of history, technology and tolerance. Being basically optimistic, the group have turned the problem back on itself. Greater number tends to mean repetition, noise, boredom, optimization: but it need not. It can also mean service, exchange, consumer-range, the breaking down of barriers. It is this paradox that is intriguing as a design problem. We can (as individuals) choose between the mass items and reach a range and excitement far beyond the possibilities of previous environments. We can take advantage of techniques like market research, high-stress technology, consumer-assembly but make sure that the context for them breaks out of the limited barriers of taste, town planning and the various mystiques invented by so-called 'experts'.

Several themes crop up in the exhibition that recurrently interest the Archigram Group. These themes are all to do with the personal choice that one can have over one's environment and the ways in which new combinations of parts can catalyse that choice.

The ability of objects and assemblies to metamorphose over a period of time so that we are no longer stuck with monuments of a forgotten day . . . the ability to use the world's surface and mobility to achieve personal freedom: the nomadic instinct and the nomadic potential of cars and car-based enclosures . . . the relinquishing of old hangups about determinism and the purity of hierarchies and preferred values . . . the interplay now possible between hardware: the manifestation of place, object and things seen, and software . . . the system, the computerized logic that is unseen . . . the realization that although we are beginning to be emancipated socially, economically and through a consumer society, building has not caught up with this range . . . that we all have an instinct for reassurance and support: the idea of comfort at a psychological and physical level . . . the interplay of man and machine to develop this responsive environment and the free-ranging exchange of all as and when needed . . . the notion of the 'popular-pak' as a presentation for the bits and pieces, that is the way that environmental ideas should now be: for the consumer . . .

The main exhibit is the 'Big Bag': an air inflated transparent plastic tube, 18 metres long and 2.9 metres in diameter, suspended just above head height. Inside, a series of surfaces with drawings of Archigram projects, models and hybrids overlaid with each other. On to these are projected film and slide programmes that illustrate the response to the 'greater number' problem.

The piped environment
Dennis Crompton

The environment business is all tied up with the extension of man's experience, and once extended things are never quite the same again. At first it is all a struggle against adverse conditions whether it is at McMurdo Sound, Ealing or LA, but once man gets the upper hand he starts to extend into and out of his personal world, the world of the Golden Fleece and 007. This world is a product of current events and experiences and is constantly developing and progressing as aspirations become reality and new wish dreams take their place. If we want to take a serious part in this environment business as something more than a participant then we have got to become fluent dream makers and not turn a blind eye towards what is around.

1 They are people
2 extending their experience
3 but it has very little to do with physical structures
4 although plugging-in, turning-on, dropping-out demand facilities.

It seems to have all started with Bell, Baird, Faraday, and the rest, although I doubt if they had thought of it in this way. What they did was to discover the facilities which have led to the Piped Environment. The immediacy of electrical response gave independence from the sun for light and heat and freed up many other situations in which the time lag of reaction had become an embarrassing restriction. Then the transmission of sound for communication made for an infinite expansion of the available information and exchange services.

Radio gave the first real mass transmission of the Piped Environment which started with our mums and dads transposing themselves to the Palm Court of Grand Hotel. It is curious to note that amongst the few serious environmentalists actually to harness this energy we see most notoriously the production lines of the factory and the broiler house, not to mention Musak, which is a world of its own. As a slight deviation there is an interesting cycle of development in the technique of audio environment. The radio and the telephone were originally highly personalized, for technical reasons playback was through headphones giving an extended individual environment which did not impose itself on others who were not plugged-in. As loud speakers and amplifiers developed, this individual quality declined until we were all involved in the hi-fi nut's world of 100 watt Vortexions and Tannoy drive units, whether or not this was the form of extension of our experience we were after. The earphone (cans) returned with the pocket transistor radio and the astronaut cult so that the hi-fi man can now sit in oblivion extending himself in full frequency stereo sound without including the block in his experience. The drawback of the audio-induced environment is that the visual content is by implication, you have to close your eyes and think pink. In its way this works fine, you can have a highly coloured audio experience, but having had this form of extension the situation changes and you are ready to move on. Cinema and TV drop into this visual void along with more recent image projection systems and the Piped Environment takes on a higher degree of reality. The limiting factor here has been the frame which contains the image and the individual has had to move into this frame in order to become part of the transmitted experience. This was helped by the darkness of the cinema and the intimacy of the TV set at the end of the sofa, but again once this has happened we are never the same again and are eager for a more sophisticated form of extension of our experience.

With multiple image technique the frame problem can be avoided and a more total, three-dimensional, situation occurs which envelops the participant. The factor about this condition which is very different and is its main characteristic, is that it is subject to constant and immediate change. On the face of it this puts it out of court for the serious environmentalists because they are dedicated to the creation of static objects, but this is an accidental position. If the environmental business is concerned with the extension of man's experience then the means of achieving this is by pushing current technology.

Letter to David Greene: 'Ghosts' (with reference to Albert Ayler) 1966
Warren Chalk

Architecture is probably a hoax, a fantasy world brought about through a desire to locate, absorb and integrate into an overall obsession a self-interpretation of the everyday world around us. An impossible attempt to rationalize the irrational. It is difficult to be exact about influences, but those influences that enter our unconscious consciousness are what I call ghosts.

Our lives exist within a complex web of these influences; which we either accept or reject; those we find acceptable are turned to advantage; they become our preoccupations, prejudices or preconceptions. Systematic analysis is such a preconception.

Ghosts help to reinforce and establish attitudes, build a very personal language, a complex labyrinth of ideals, constraints, theories, half-remembered rules, symbols, words that, ultimately digested, affect our concepts. It is unpopular, but essential, that existing attitudes come in for constant and rigorous renewal or reappraisal. We are confronted with a dynamic shifting pattern of events at both popular and intellectual levels, both simulating and confusing. In this ever-changing climate, old ghosts may be cast out and replaced by new; it is right that influences should last only as long as they are useful to us, and our architecture should reflect this. At a general level it is becoming increasingly apparent that due to historical circumstances the more tangible ghosts of the past – those grim, humourless, static, literary or visual images – will succumb to the onslaught of the invisible media, the psychedelic vision; the insight accompanying a joke; the phantoms of the future.

'Ghosts' – 'Phantoms'
The hangups and fears of one's past and future cultures 1966
Warren Chalk

The Instant City Programme and its attendant research has been made possible by an award from the Graham Foundation for Advanced Studies in the Arts, Chicago.

A PROJECT BY THE ARCHIGRAM GROUP - LONDON

INSTANT CITY

SUPPORTED BY THE GRAHAM FOUNDATION - CHICAGO

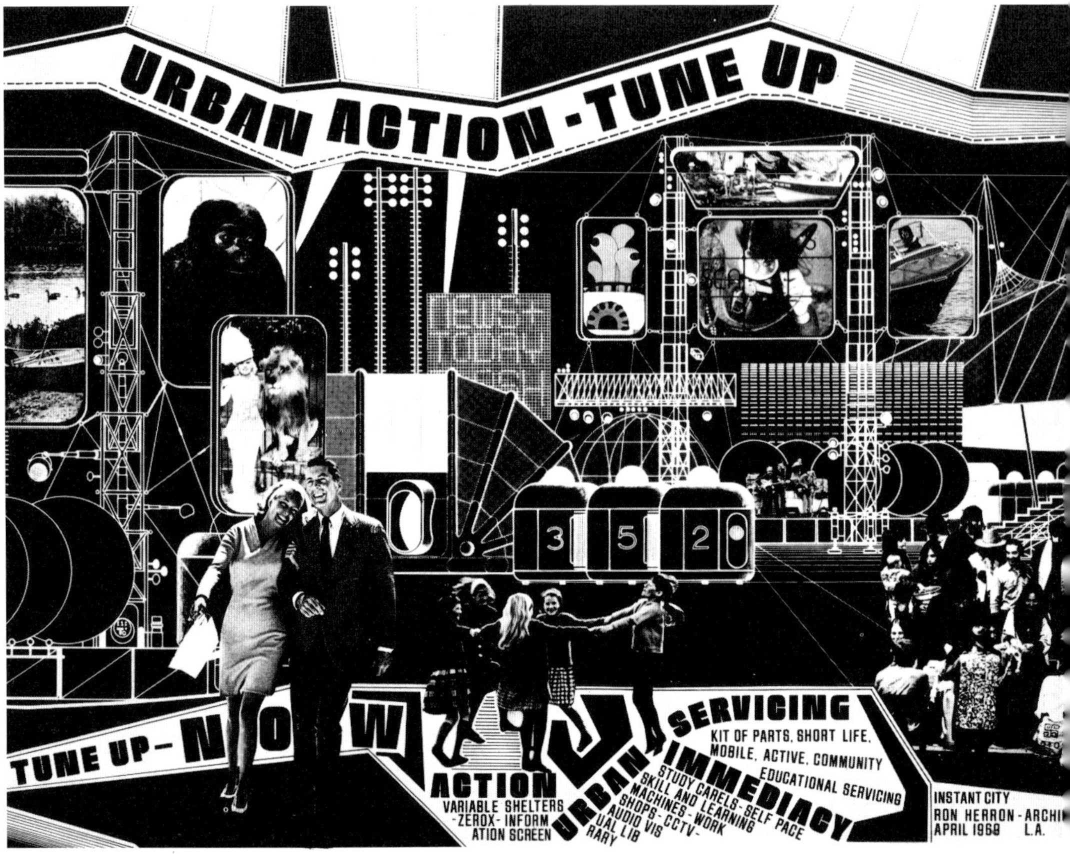

Instant City: Urban Action Tune-Up: the components in operation 1969 Ron Herron

The notion

In most civilized countries, localities and their local cultures remain slow moving, often undernourished and sometimes resentful of the more favoured metropolitan regions (such as New York, the West Coast of the United States, London and Paris). Whilst much is spoken about cultural links and about the effect of television as a window on the world (and the inevitable global village) people still feel frustrated. Younger people even have a suspicion that they are missing out on things that could widen their horizons. They would like to be involved in aspects of life where their own experiences can be seen as part of what is happening.

Against this is the reaction to the physical nature of the metropolis: and somehow there is this paradox – if only we could enjoy it but stay where we are.

The Instant City project reacts to this with the idea of a 'travelling metropolis', a package that comes to a community, giving it a taste of the metropolitan dynamic – which is temporarily grafted on to the local centre – and whilst the community is still recovering from the shock uses this catalyst as the first stage of a national hook-up. A network of information – education – entertainment – 'play-and-know yourself' facilities.

In England the feeling of being left out o things has for a long time affected the psychology of the provinces, so that people become either over-protective about local things, o carry in their minds a ridiculous inferiority complex about the metropolis. But we are nearing a time when the leisure period of the day is becoming really significant; and with the effect of television and better education people are realizing that they could do thing and know things, they could express themselves (or enjoy themselves in a freer way) and they are becoming dissatisfied with the television set, the youth club or the pub.

A background from Archigram work

The old Plug-in City programme of 196- pulled together a series of seemingly disconnected notions and small projects (throwaway unit here, an automatic sho there, or even an idea about a megastructure)

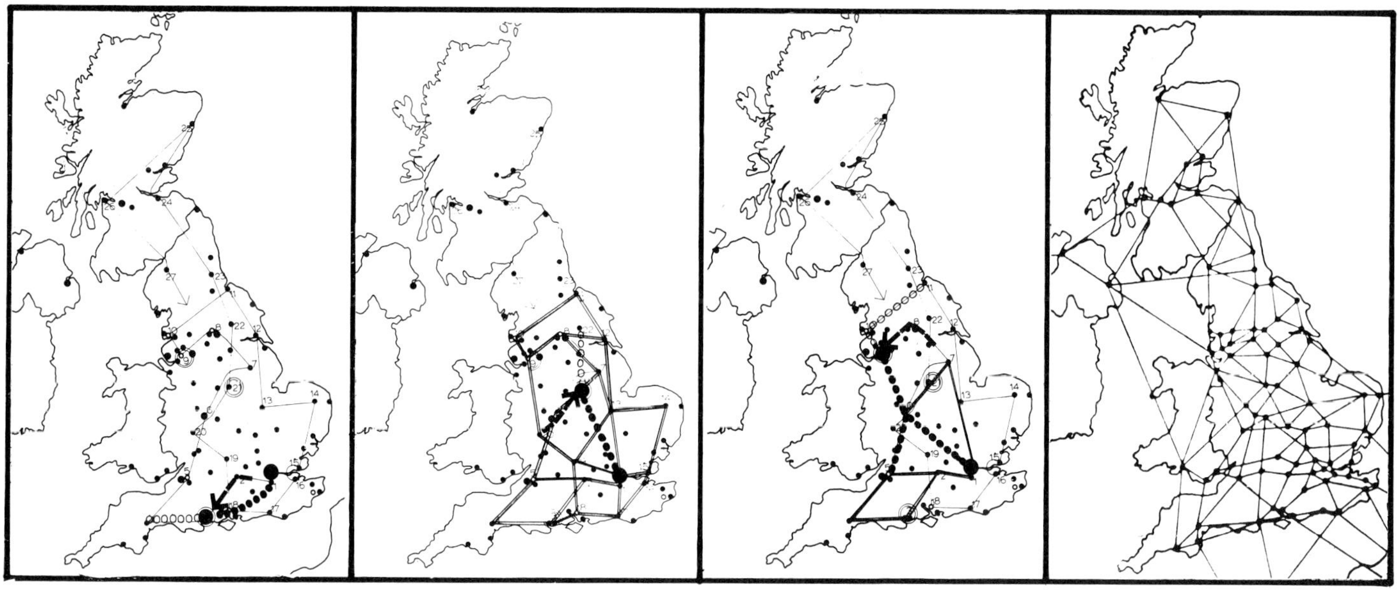

Great Britain: Instant City
progression

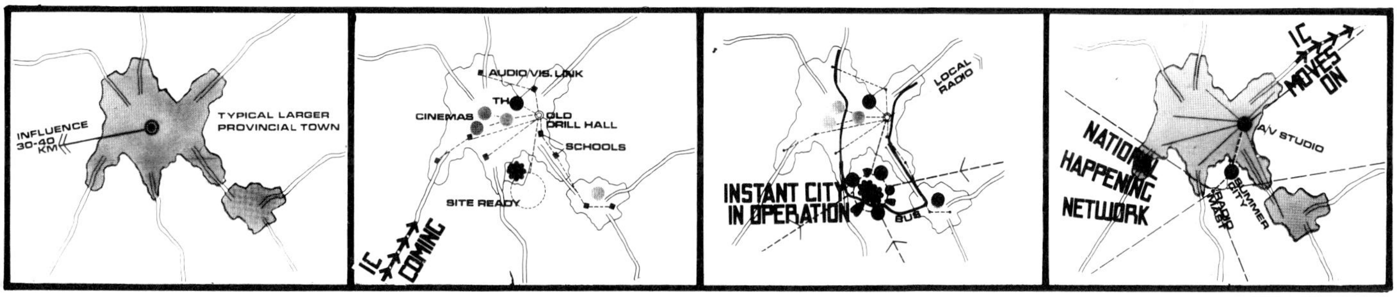

top, left to right
Visit No. 3 Bournemouth
Entirely fed by landline from London plus Instant City on-site provision with Local in-put
Exeter link being prepared

Visit No. 21 Nottingham Input from London less necessary as backlog network is building up

Visit No. 9 St Helen's
Main feeds from London, Birmingham, Bristol, Manchester
Backlog network being established (visits 1–6)

The ultimate: Britain City
The network has taken over

centre, left to right
Town before Instant City

Preparation stage

Catalyst stage

Aftermath

reinforcing and qualifying the theme and eventually suggesting a total project – a portmanteau for the rest. Later on, the work that Archigram had done with the Hornsey Light-Sound Workshop and on several exhibitions (with the actual techniques of audience participation and control of a responsive audio-visual system) began to form a working laboratory for the techniques of Instant City.

The Instant City is both collective and coercive: by definition there is no perfect set of components. On the drawings which have been made over a period of two years there are often quotes from other pieces of work (for instance, Oslo Soft Scene Monitor as the parent of Audio-Visual Juke Box). In such a machine people tune in to their environment by choosing and making from a range of audio-visual programmes; the Oslo machine is its progenitor but it really implies something where the participant plays a completely open-ended creative game. Around 1966, at an exhibition on Brighton pier, we made an experiment of putting a man in a circular drum, spinning him round and then bombarding him (two feet from his face) with wild coloured slides, and bombarding him (one foot from his ears) with wild sounds. A typical instance of a first-stage experiment, unsubtle and without feedback, unable to provide the man inside with a button to press to say 'stop'. Later, the Oslo machine moved on from this and the limit of choice was one of cost rather than of concept.

With our notion of the robot (the symbol of the responsive machine that collects many services in one appliance), we begin to play with the notion that the environment could be conditioned not only by the set piece assembly but by infinite variables determined by your wish, and the robot reappears in the Instant City in several of the assemblies.

The Instant City has planning implications the force of which have emerged more and more strongly as the project has developed, so that by the time we are making the sequence describing 'the airship's effect upon the sleeping town' (pp. 98, 99) it is the infiltrationary dynamic of the town itself that is as fascinating as the technical dynamic of the airship. Again we have to reflect on the

Instant City: a typical night time scene 1968 Peter Cook

psychology of a country such as England where there is a historical suggestion that vast upheaval is unlikely. We are likely to capitalize on existing institutions and existing facilities whilst complaining about their inefficiency – but a country such as England must now live by its wits or perish, and for its wits it needs its culture.

A programme background

The likely components are audio-visual display systems, projection television, trailered units, pneumatic and lightweight structures and entertainments facilities, exhibits, gantries and electric lights.

This involves the theoretical territory between the 'hardware' (or the design of buildings and places) and 'software' (or the effect of information and programmation of the environment). Theoretically it also involves the notions of urban dispersal and the territory between entertainment and learning. The Instant City could be made a practical reality since at every stage it is based upon existing techniques and their application to real situations. There is a combination of several different artefacts and systems which have hitherto remained as separate machines, enclosures or experiments. The programme involved gathering information about an itinerary of communities and the available utilities that exist

left to right Instant City arrives in an open field and sets up Location: St Helen's, Lancashire (model) 1969 Dennis Crompton

clubs, local radio, universities, etc.) so that he 'City' package is always complementary ather than alien. We then tested this pro-)osition against particular samples.

'he first stage programme consisted of as- emblies carried by approximately twenty 'ehicles, operable in most weathers and arrying a complete programme. These were pplied to localities in England and in the Los Angeles area of California. Later, having be- ome interested in the versatility of the air- hip, we came to propose this as another neans of transporting the Instant City assembly a great and silent bringer of the whole onglomeration).

ater we applied the method of the Instant City to proposals for servicing the Documenta xhibition at Kassel in Germany. By this time lso there had developed a feedback of ideas nd techniques between this project and our Monte Carlo entertainments facility.

Instant City: self-destruct
Environ-Pole 1969 Ron Herron

typical sequence of operations truck-borne version)

The components of the 'City' are loaded n to the trucks and trailers at base.

A series of 'tent' units are floated from alloons which are towed to the destination y aircraft.

Prior to the visit of the 'City' a team of urveyors, electricians, etc. have converted disused building in the chosen community nto a collection, information and relay station. andline links have been made to local schools nd to one or more major (permanent) cities.

The 'City' arrives. It is assembled accord- ng to site and local characteristics. Not all omponents will necessarily be used. It may nfiltrate into local buildings and streets, it ay fragment.

Events, displays and educational pro- rammes are partly supplied by the local com- unity and partly by the 'City' agency. In ddition major use is made of local fringe ele- ents: fares, festivals, markets, societies, with ailers, stalls, displays and personnel ac- umulating often on an *ad hoc* basis. The vent of the Instant City might be a bringing gether of events that would otherwise occur eparately in the district.

The overhead tent, inflatable windbreaks and other shelters are erected. Many units of the 'City' have their own tailored enclosure.

7 The 'City' stays for a limited period.

8 It then moves on to the next location.

9 After a number of places have been visited the local relay stations are linked to- gether by landline. Community (1) is now feeding part of the programme to be enjoyed by Community (20).

10 Eventually by this combination of physi- cal and electronic, perceptual and program- matic events and the establishment of local display centres, a 'City' of communication might exist, the metropolis of the national network.

11 Almost certainly, travelling elements would modify over a period of time. It is even likely that after two to three years they would phase out and let the network take over.

Instant City in a field: typical set-up 1969 Peter Cook

top Elevation

centre Plan (left to right) audio-visual vision, audio-visual museum. Study/Think/Info Play Centre, nightclub, lightsound, responsive tent, arena, music dome, car parking

below Instant City at Los Angeles 1969 Typical configuration Santa Monica and San Diego Freeway Intersection

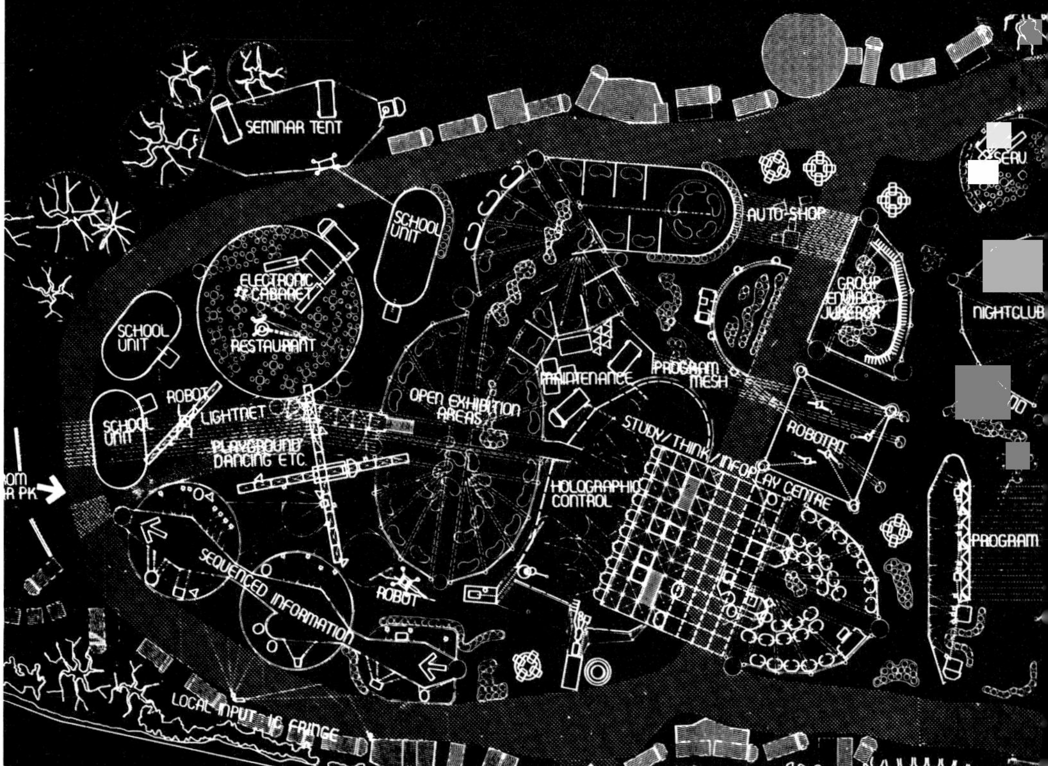

ht Santa Monica and San
ego Freeway Intersection

Instant City at Bournemouth 1969 Peter Cook The pier and cliffs would act as part of the activity zone with use made of local boats, jetties

Instant City components
below Stage element in operation and standard component catalogue

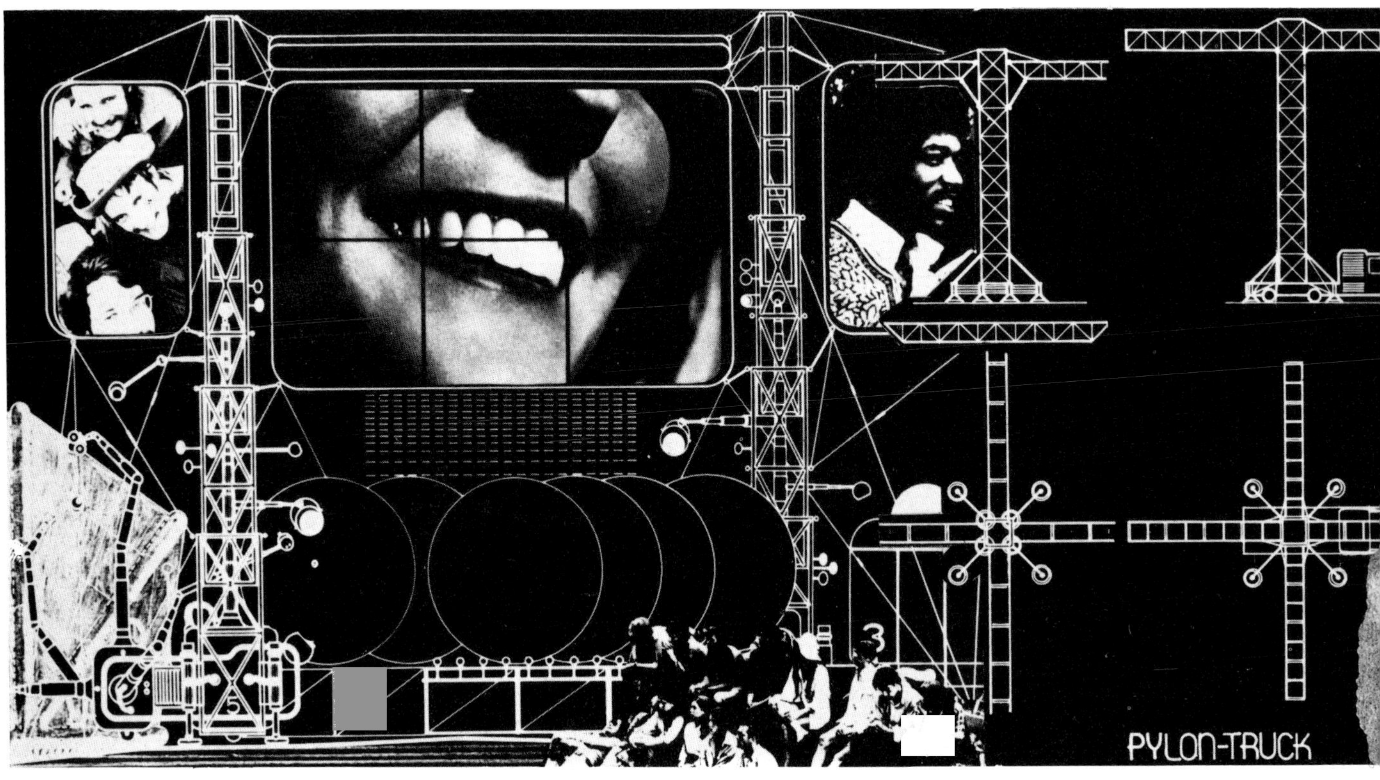

ıstant City: holographic scene-setter 1970 Ron Herron
ne creation of a simulated three-dimensional environment

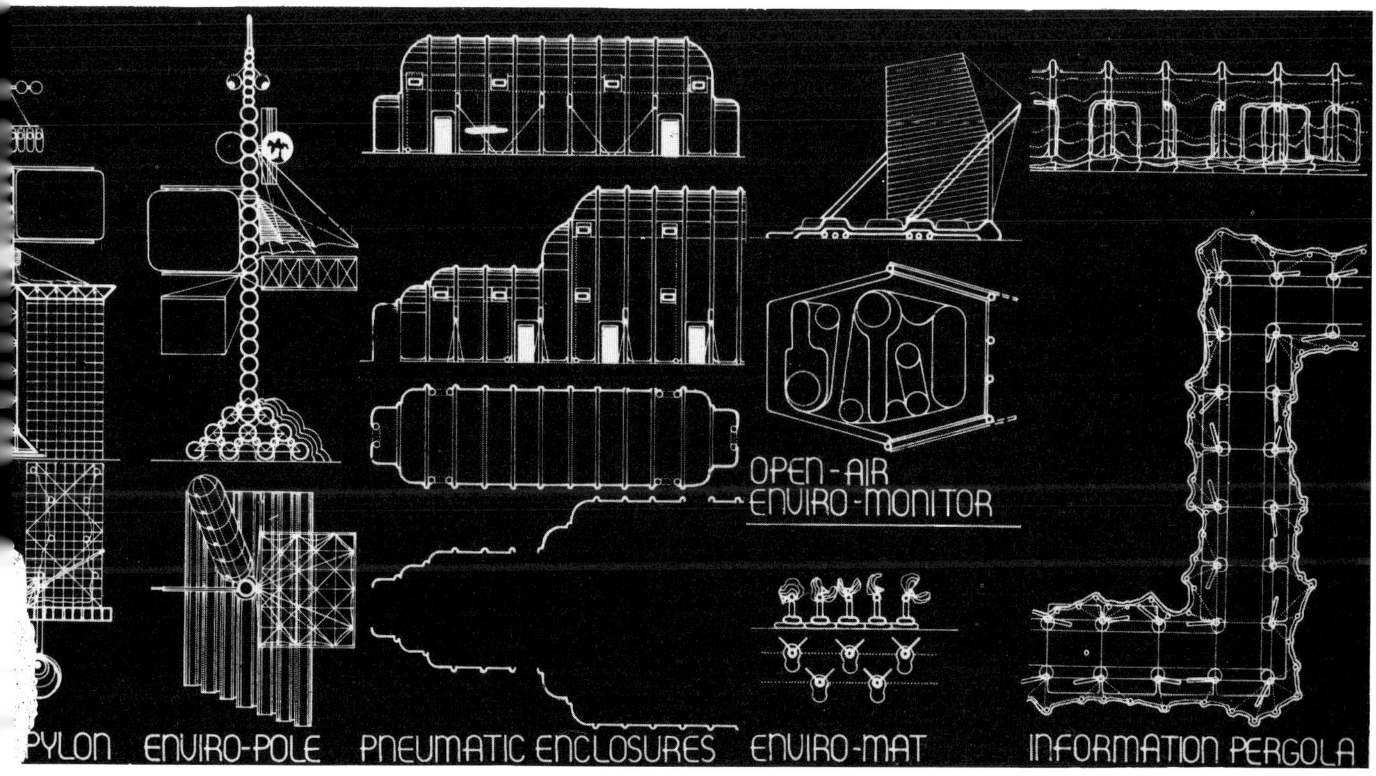

Instant City in the desert 1969
Ron Herron

below left Kassel components: *top row left to right:* balloon as information sign, media truck, screen wall; *middle row left to right:* pylon, fold-out acoustic stage, composite balloon as sign; *bottom row left to right:* pylon and tent, electric wall

below right Soft Scene Monitor Oslo 1969 Peter Cook, Dennis Crompton General view of machine

As the Instant City study developed, certain items emerged in particular. First, the idea of a 'soft-scene monitor' – a combination of teaching-machine, audio-visual juke box, environmental simulator, and from a theoretical point of view, a realization of the 'Hardware/Software' debate (which is still going on in our Monte Carlo work, as the notion of an electronically-aided responsive environment. Next, the dissolve of the original large, trucked, circus-like show into a smaller and very mobile element backed by a wonderful, magical dream descending from the skies. The model of the small unit suggests two trucks and a helicopter as the carriage, with quick-folding arenas and apparatus that can quickly be fitted into the village hall. Another stimulus was the invitation to design the 'event-structure' for the 1972 Kassel Documenta – an elaborate art/event/theatre scene requiring a high level of servicing but a minimum of interference with the 'open-air creative act'. The Kassel-Kit' of apparatus can therefore be considered as a direct extension of the original IC Kit.

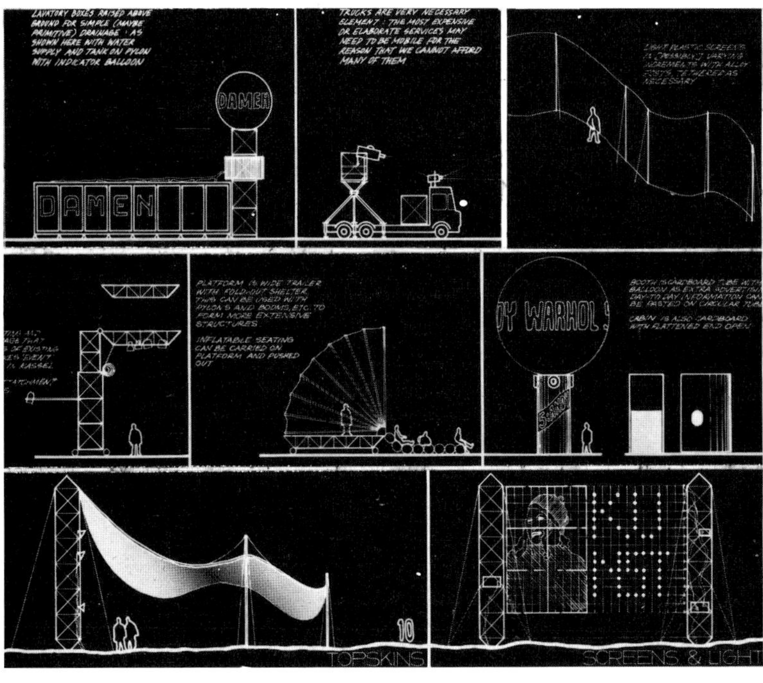

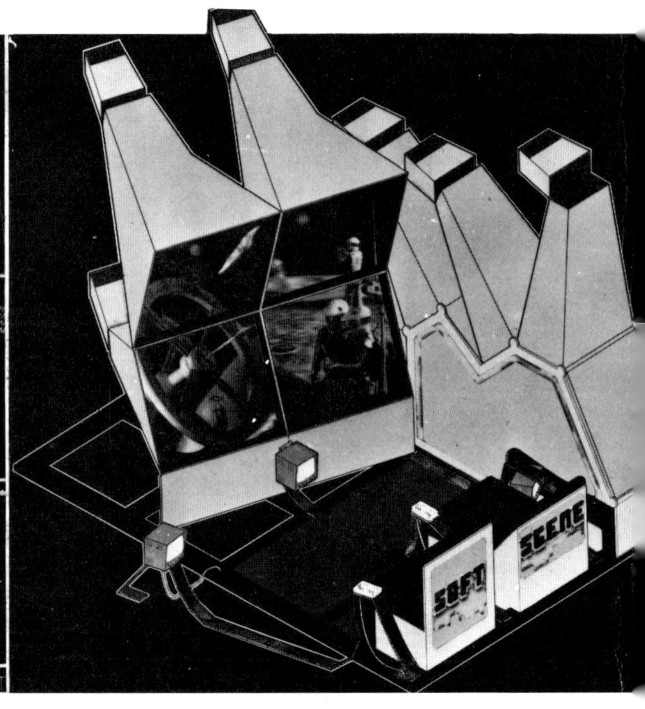

ssel Documenta project:
entstructures 1970
n Herron and Peter Cook

p General view

ntre Quick space for
ncert and minimal art exhibit
tant City/Kassel components

ow
Instant City: Audio-Visual
kebox
ht Soft Scene Monitor
o: in use

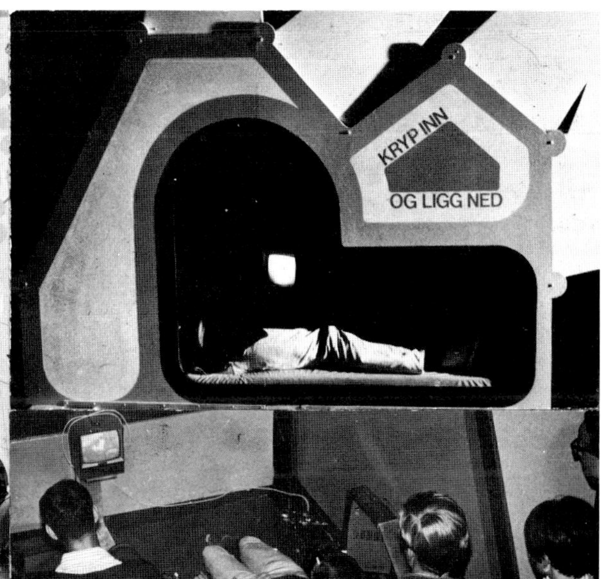

Are we back to heroics then, with a giant, pretty and evocative object? The Blimp: the airship: beauty, disaster and history. On the one hand we were designing a totally unseen and *underground* building at Monte Carlo, and on the other hand flirting with the airborne will-o-the-wisp. The Instant City as a series of trucks rushing round like ants might be practical and immediate, but we could not escape the loveliness of the idea of Instant City appearing from nowhere, and after the 'event' stage, lifting up its skirts and vanishing. In fact, the primary interest was spontaneity, and the remaining aim to knit into any locale as *effectively* as possible. For Archigram, the airship is a device: a giant skyhook.

Operationally, there were two possibilities. A simple airship with apparatus carried in the belly and able to drop down as required. Otherwise, a more sophisticated notion of a 'megastructure of the skies'. Ron Herron's drawings (p. 97) suggest that the 'ship' can fragment, and the audio/visual elements are scattered around a patch of sky. Once again, the project work of the group has picked u a dream of its own past – the 'Story of Thing' (pp. 22, 23) made (almost) real.

We then built a model, which could hang ou its entrails in a number of ways (pp. 98, 99) This was the simpler 'ship' which reads wit the scenario of a small town transformatior In the drawing with airship 'Rupert' (p. 100), major shift in Instant City was first articulated the increasing feeling for change-by-infiltra tion. The 'city' is creeping into half-finishe buildings, using the local draper's store, ga showrooms and kerbside, as well as the mor sophisticated setup. And there is a mysteriou creeping animal: the 'leech' truck, which i able to climb up any structure and servic from it: with the resulting possibility c 'bugging' the whole town as necessary. Gentl then, the project dissolves from the simpl mechanics or hierarchies of 'structuring' an like-objects. Just as did the Plug-in City: sowed the seeds of its own fragmentation int investigations of a gentler, more subtle en vironmental tuning.

Instant City components

below Instant City: Village Scale Kit: view of model

bottom left Audio-Visual Jukebox Tent 1969

bottom right Soft Scene Monitor for Expo '70 Osaka, Japan

opposite Instant City-Airships: elevation and plan 1970
Ron Herron

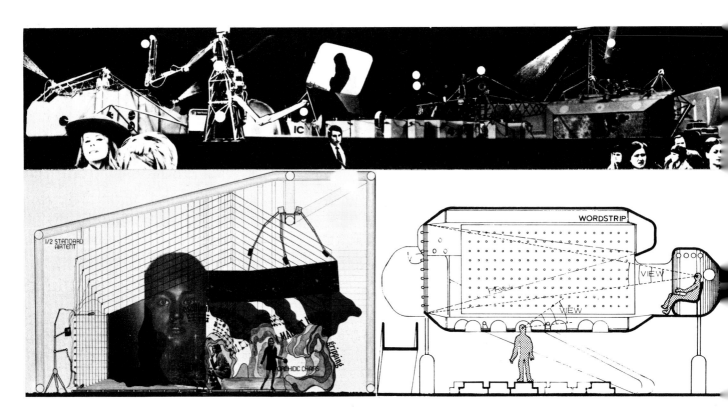

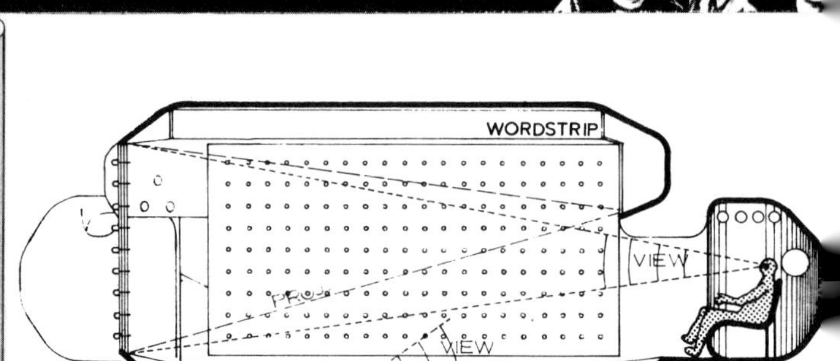

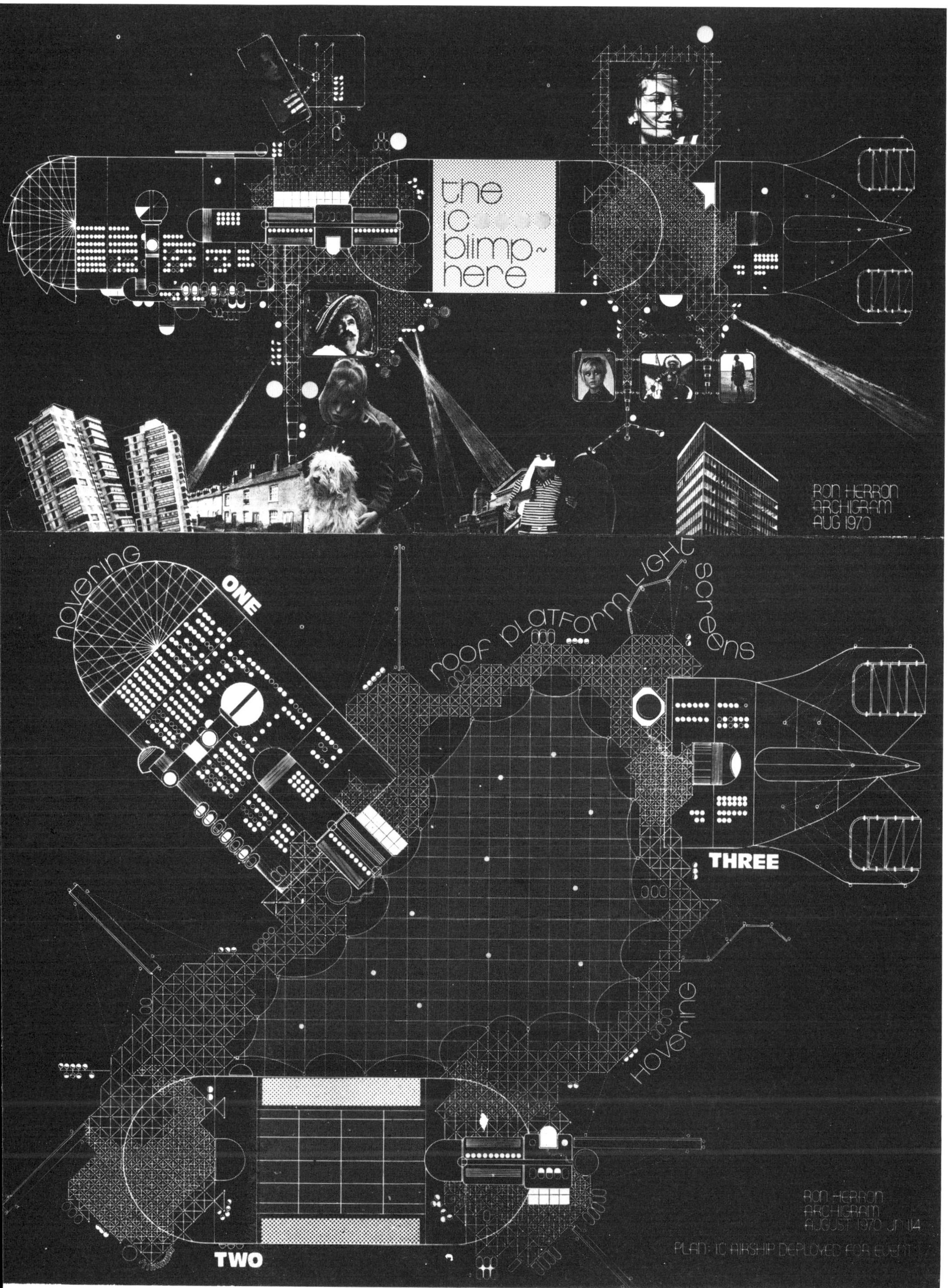
the
ic
blimp~
here
RON HERRON
ARCHIGRAM
AUG 1970
hovering
ONE
roof platform light screens
THREE
hovering
TWO
RON HERRON
ARCHIGRAM
AUGUST 1970 JN 14
PLAN: IC AIRSHIP DEPLOYED FOR EVENT

top right Instant City Airships: model/collage The Airship in Lancashire 1970 Peter Cook

below 'Instant Country' (cartoon) 1971 Peter Cook

below right Instant City Airships: sequence of effect on a typical English town 1970 Peter Cook

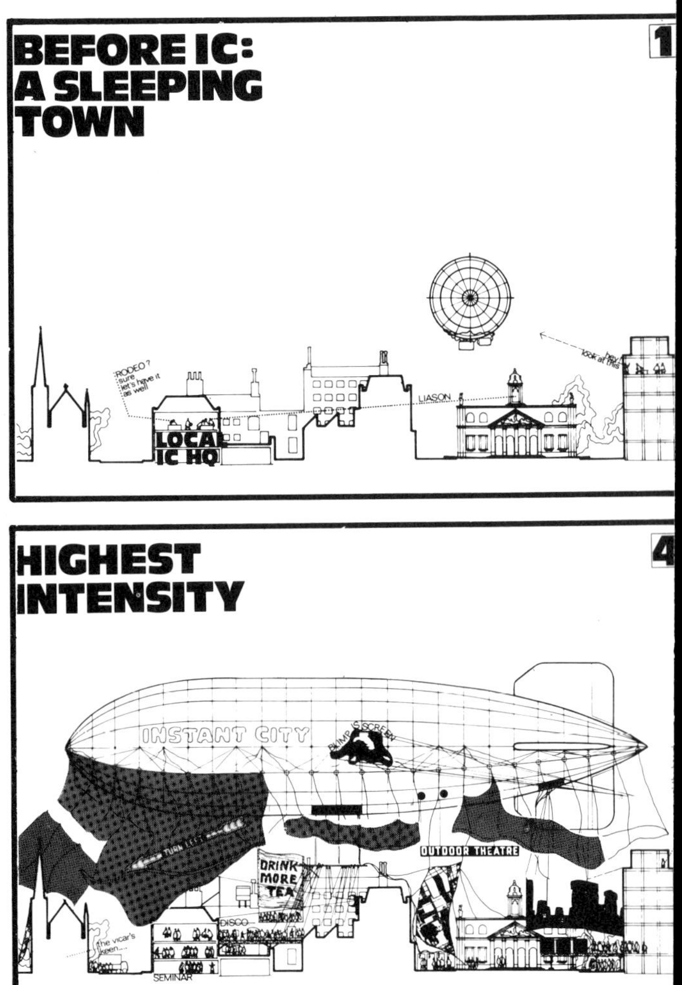

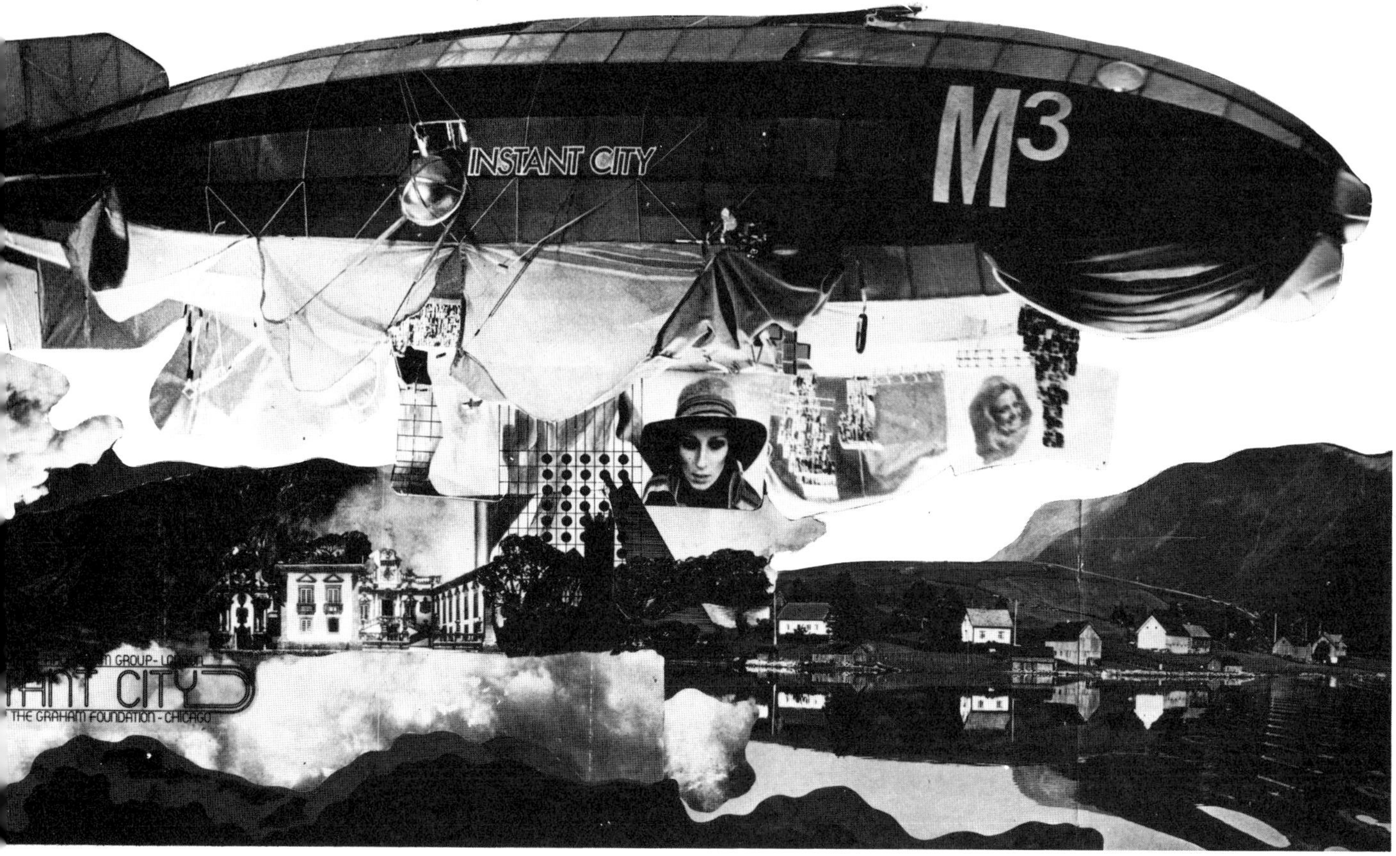
INSTANT CITY
M3
THE GRAHAM FOUNDATION - CHICAGO

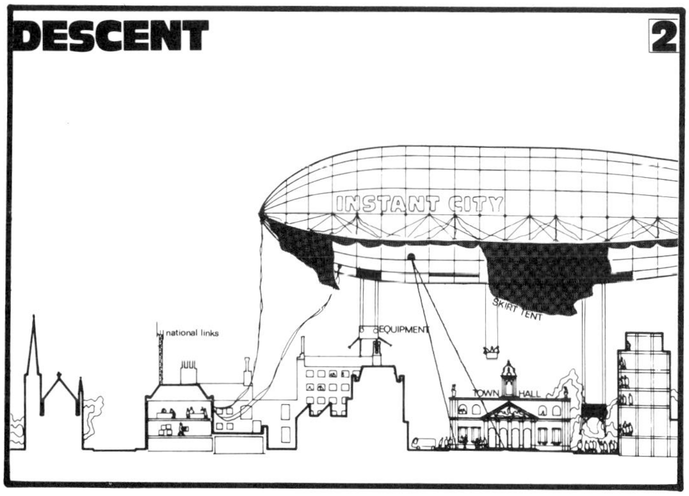
DESCENT
2
INSTANT CITY
national links
EQUIPMENT
SKIRT TENT
TOWN HALL

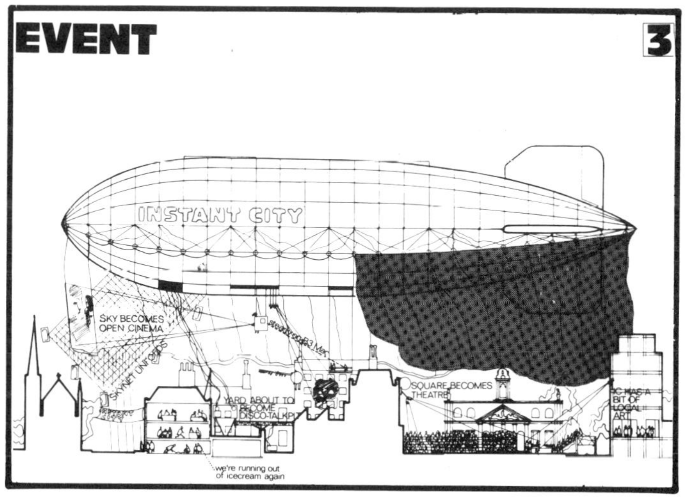
EVENT
3
INSTANT CITY
SKY BECOMES OPEN CINEMA
YARD ABOUT TO BECOME
SQUARE BECOMES THEATRE
IC HAS A BIT OF LOCAL ART
we're running out of icecream again

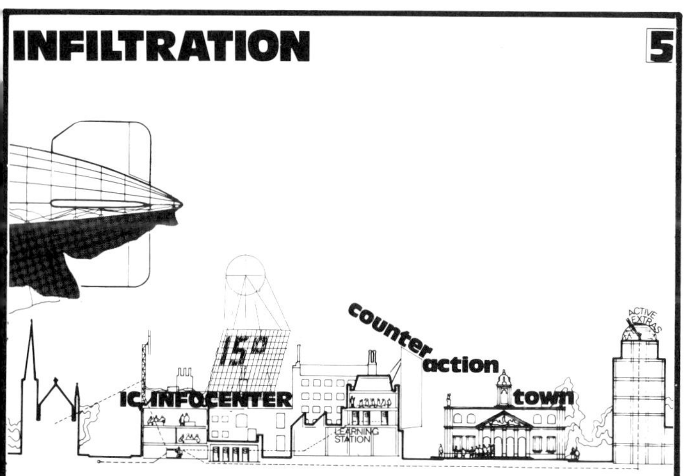
INFILTRATION
5
15p
counter action town
IC INFOCENTER
LEARNING STATION
ACTIVE EXTRAS

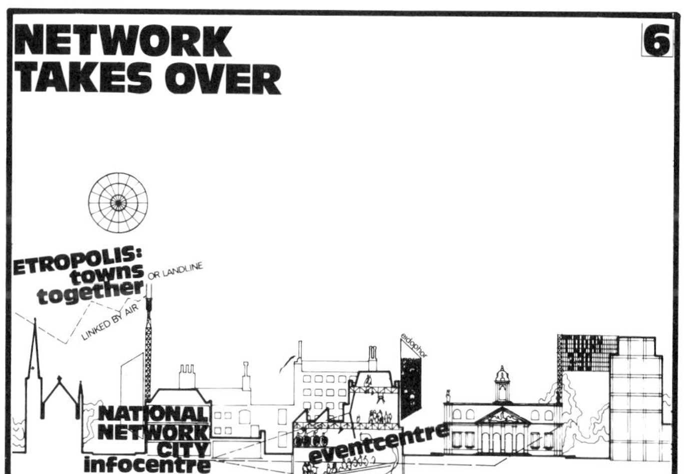
NETWORK TAKES OVER
6
ETROPOLIS: towns together
OR LANDLINE
LINKED BY AIR
NATIONAL NETWORK CITY infocentre
eventcentre

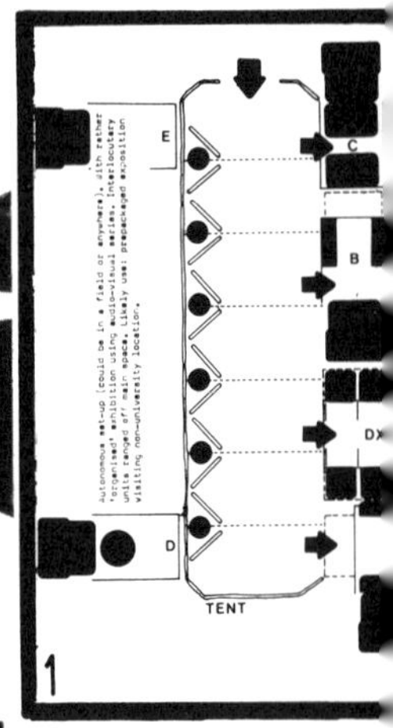

above Instant City Airships: visit to a small town 1970
Peter Cook

right Info Gonks (educational TV glasses and headgear) 1968
Peter Cook
Use of the 1½-in. television as a built-up pair of spectacles, with stereo-headphones all wired to headgear receiver: everyman his own on-the-eye and in-the-ear environment.

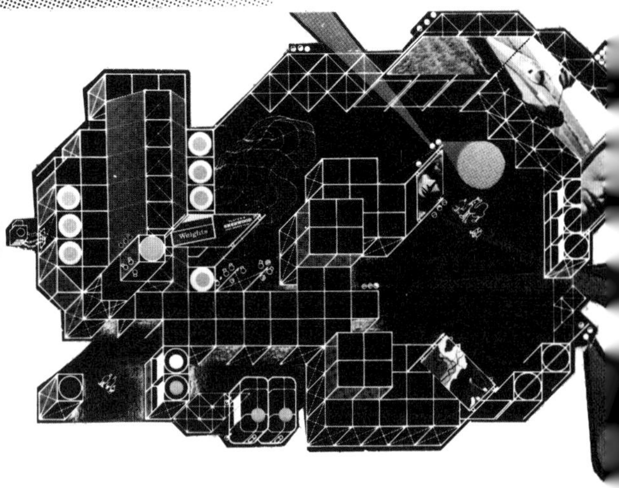

far right Promotional Event Kit 1970–1 Ron Herron and Barry Snowden. A small scale development of Instant City and other caravan concepts

Ideas circus

The notion of the Ideas circus came after the experience of several Archigram lectures and seminars where common characteristics of college and exhibition facilities could be experienced.

There is little interchange of ideas between one institution and the next, and display or documentation facilities have to be erected from scratch.

Scheme

To institute a standard package of five or six vehicles that contain all the equipment necessary to set up a seminar, conference, exhibition, teach-in or display. The package can be attached to an existing building, plugging-into such facilities as are there and using the shelter of existing rooms for Circus equipment. The Circus can also be completely autonomous: set up in a field, if necessary. The idea would be to circulate between major provincial centres, tapping local universities, bleeding-off from them personalities, documentation and such things as film of laboratory experiments; then carrying on to the next town. Weekend visits to smaller places could be made. Some vehicles could hive off for an afternoon teach-in at the local Women's Institute. The Circus would b programmed with basic film an slide material. The feedbac facility is most important: ver batim documentation of semi nars, documents, films, etc would be printed-off and le behind. Static educational facili ties need topping-up. Mobil educational facilities could s easily be a nine-day wonder. Th Ideas Circus is offered as a to for the interim phase: until w have a really working all-wa information network.

In the four weeks, the Circus first programmed from Londc with tapes, filmstrips, etc., on th tour subject. These are prepare

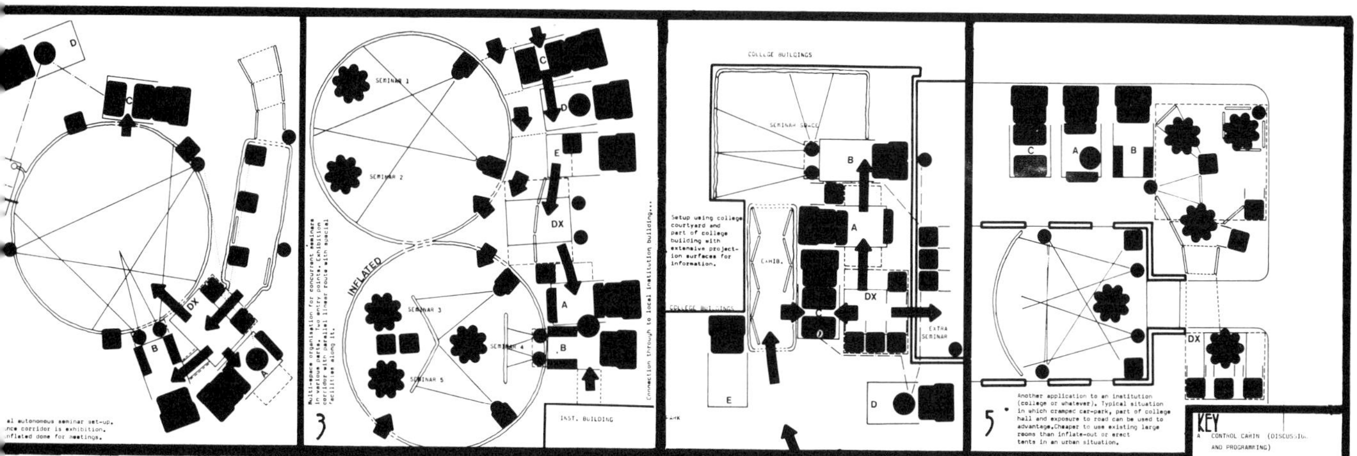

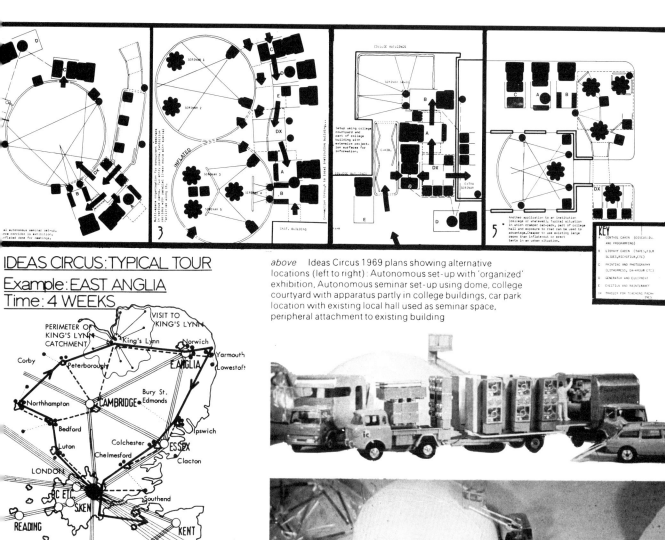

IDEAS CIRCUS: TYPICAL TOUR
Example: EAST ANGLIA
Time: 4 WEEKS

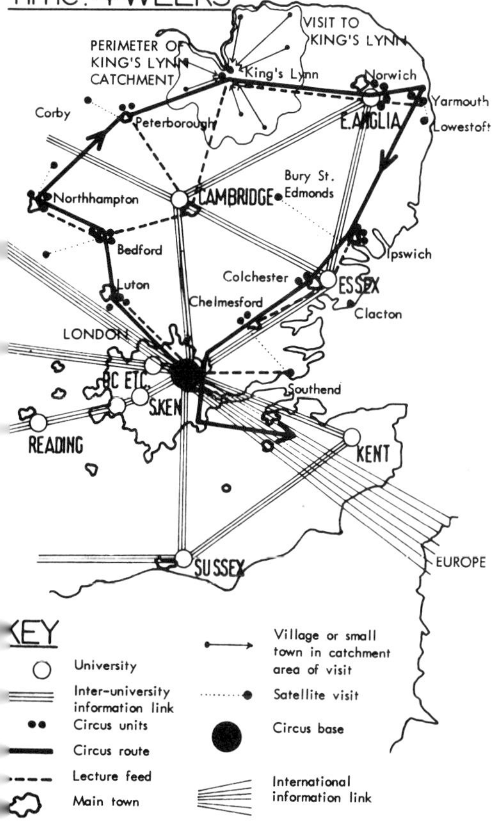

above Ideas Circus 1969 plans showing alternative locations (left to right): Autonomous set-up with 'organized' exhibition, Autonomous seminar set-up using dome, college courtyard with apparatus partly in college buildings, car park location with existing local hall used as seminar space, peripheral attachment to existing building

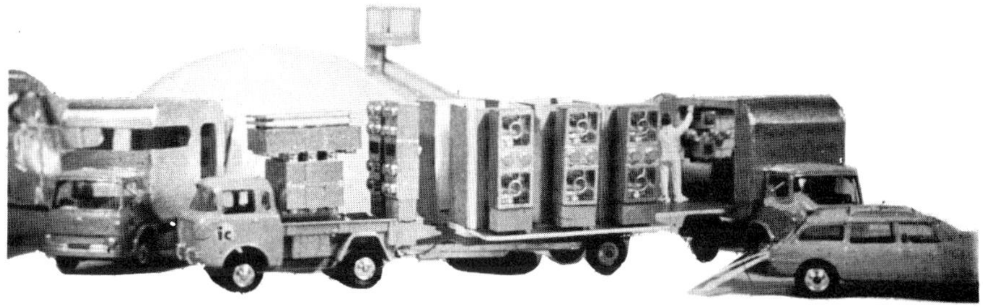

with help from institutions available.

The centres visited are geographically fairly close so that little time is spent actually on the road. In the multi-vehicle version there can be a programmed echeloning of the constituent parts so as to make best use of time and resources. In this version a single unit (vehicle simplified programme) can be sent to small towns nearby for a one-night stand or 'appetiser' demonstration. The instigation of a national information network such as that shown here between universities is important but not absolutely essential. Special 'personal boost' lectures are suggested and these plus the landlined information instance a meshing of the Circus network with any other available network.

The Circus is here shown as involved with an 'academic' tour such as 'Microbiology for All', 'New Maths', 'Modern Architecture', or whatever.

It could equally well cover similar territory with a commercial promotion or other non-academic tour.

above left Instant City: East Anglia tour (typical 4-week run)

above right Ideas Circus: views of model 1969

FEATURES: MONTE CARLO

Original project was awarded 1st prize in competition 1970
Competition project team: Ken Allinson, Peter Cook, Dennis Crompton, Colin Fournier, David Greene, Tony Rickaby.
Working stages: Peter Cook, Dennis Crompton, Colin Fournier, Ron Herron

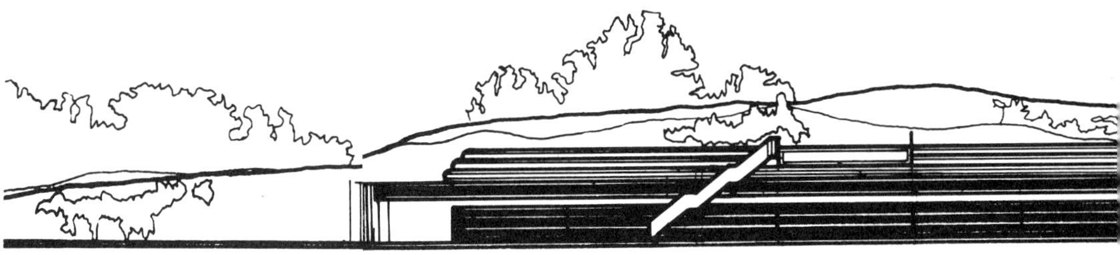

Section through development with typical event-scenes within 1970–1

11 Features: Monte Carlo

The project

We were invited by the Ministre d'Etat of Monaco to take part in a limited competition for an entertainments building on the reclaimed foreshore of Monte Carlo. The winning project is to be built.

The scene at Monte

The name Monte Carlo conjures up Glamour, Money, Indolence and the Exotic – unreality as real-life – Marienbad-in-California – cream suits and the white Rolls Royces – and, at last, a place in the sun for Archigram.

What is there is a quiet, wistful place. Unsure of its role and committed to its myth. Even with our heavy seaside background we wer not prepared for an empty promenade and th almost total absence of limousines.

Our site is well to the east of the Palace an the yacht harbour, and to the east also of th Casino. It was reclaimed from the sea. Im mediately alongside is another piece of re clamation that forms the new beach: thre concrete breakwaters holding bays of shingl that will encourage the drifting-in of sand. A night the beach is deserted apart from couple with dogs to walk or a few kids round th juke box, but in daytime it is the big Sun bathing Scene. Impeccable birds in regulatio bronze from most parts of Europe and th States provide the typical vignette: two sister are perched on a wall by the bookstall, ente

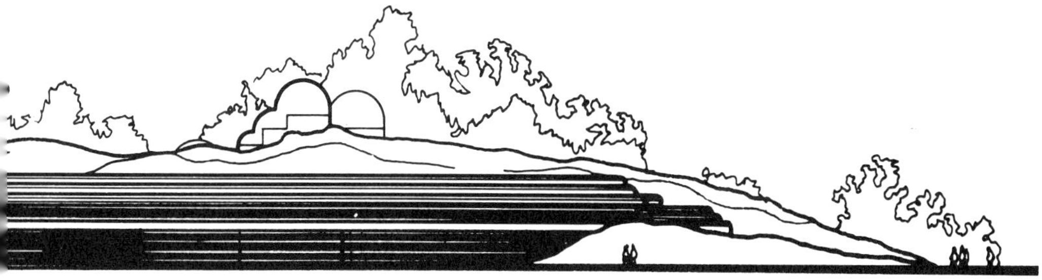

top left Site after development

top right Explanatory section 1971

centre Elevation to Avenue Princess Grace 1971 version

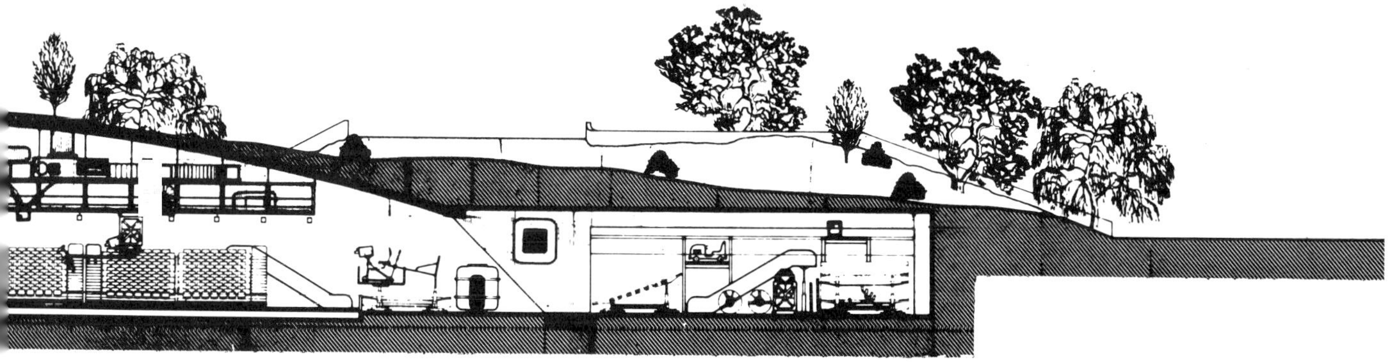

Franco-Italian Alain Delon type, proceeding well, when equally impeccable and ostensibly-35-year-old mother appears from frosted and carefully detailed beach-shower: she has seen it all before, instant and impressive dissolve by Delon. The actual place is a mixture of South Bank '51-type architecture and high level servicing: choice of ice-cream parlours, restaurants, shops, choice of ramps, stairs, steps. The use of the facilities is suitably well-mannered.

Our site looks over this, and is depressingly underused. It contains trees in abundance and a children's playground, and a promenade which lacks the vitality and business of those with which we are familiar. One can, however, appreciate its inadequacy and lack of appeal without wishing to implant a monument. We watched the coachloads of American tourists do the Casino, and were taken to an inevitably impeccable (and recently-built) marble gallery in which are hung architects' perspectives and models of every new building project for the Principality. The future is impressive: having diverted the railway under the Alps, the track is now a bypass. Behind our site and the beach is the Avenue Princesse Grace: a freeway that carries only two or three cars a minute, soon to be connected with elaborate intersections to more new roads. High-rise high-rent apartments are spreading eastwards: the significance of the project begins to emerge.

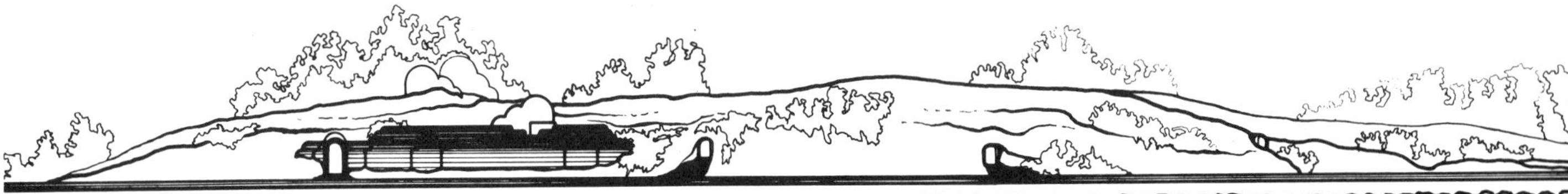

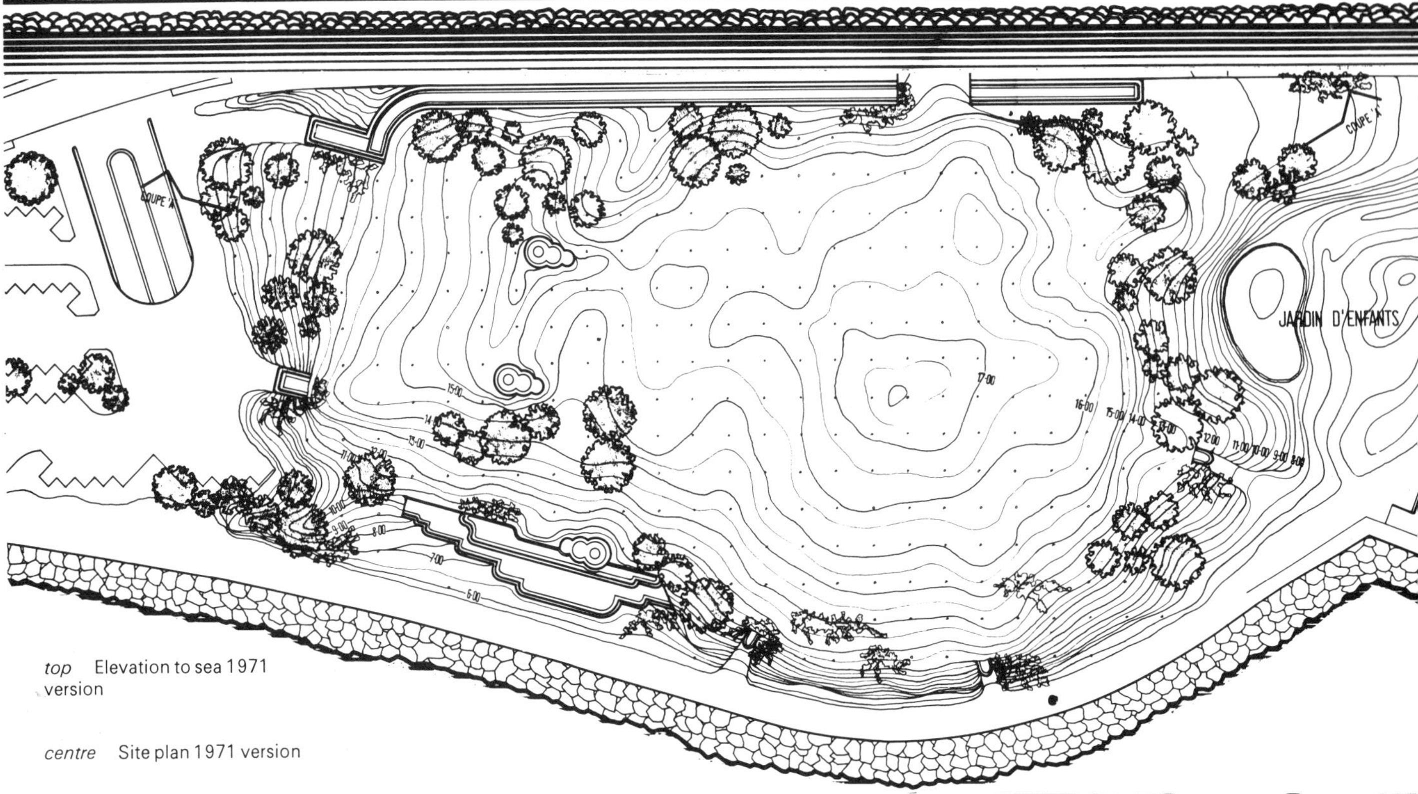

top Elevation to sea 1971 version

centre Site plan 1971 version

below Model at Competition stage 1970

Features as an idea

The brief required facilities for a large banquet, variety shows, a circus and public events. Everyone we spoke to wanted an ice rink, the idea of 'le sport' always being approved. There seemed also to be a taste for cultural events; a remnant perhaps of the great days of Diaghilev? The town tries to entice the holidaying French (though it is too expensive for most of them) but it does have a potential catchment from the whole of the linear city spread along the French and Italian coasts.

Nowhere else in Monaco is there a park th[a] you can use (the Jardin Exotique is remo[te] and steep). Here could be a place, next to th[e] beach, that extends its services but is com[-] plementary in atmosphere and experienc[e]. David Greene's Rokplug/Logplug provide[s] a clue: a grassy bank with trees (in th[e] 'English Tradition', etc.), with service outle[ts] at 6 metre intervals. How about a telephone[-] parasol-airbed-fan-TV appliance (a stick [or] pack) that you hire and plug in? Call f[or] drinks. Keep cool. No rok or log needed th[is] time, just a neat hole in the ground like

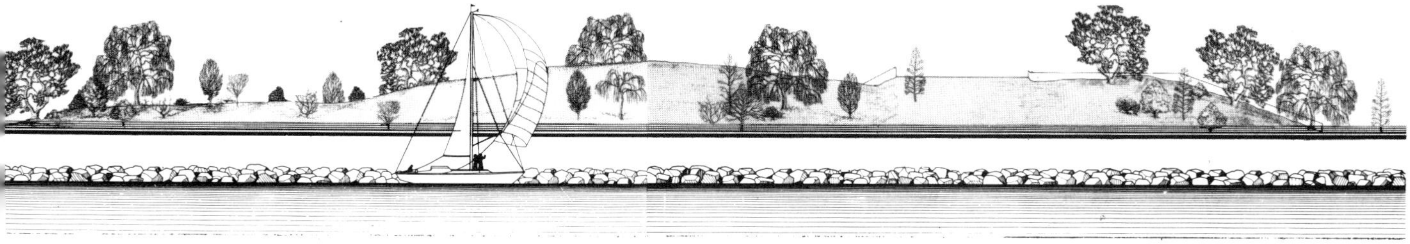

Elevation to sea 1970 version

View on surface and enviro-plug 1970

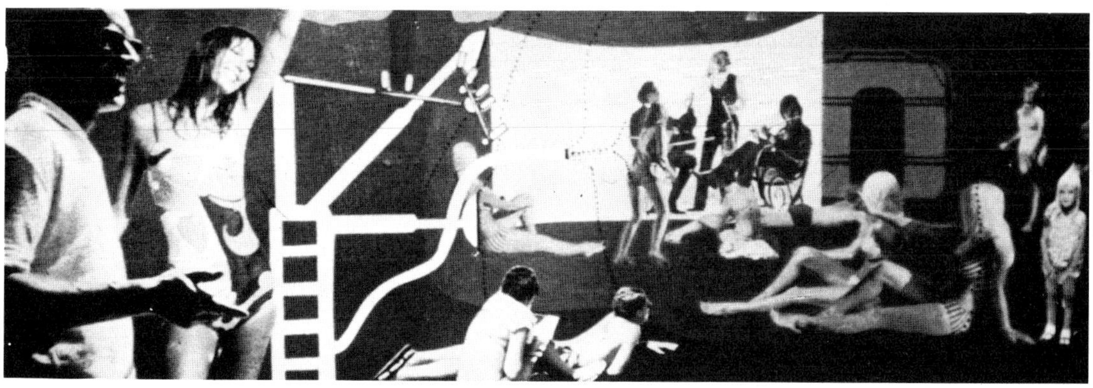

General ambience on surface

golf-hole. And the hot features? The events? They are inside.

A space large enough to take the banquet, elephants or go-karts. Ways of adapting from chamber music to ice hockey. An architecture that is made of the event rather than the envelope. So why not forget the envelope? The Features-space is buried. There are six entrances: deliberately more than necessary: each show makes its own environment – makes its own organization and its own circulation pattern.

Inside, the area needs optimizing: in the floor are service outlets, once more at 6 metre intervals. The ceiling is a gantry, similarly served. We found that the optimum space and structure suggested a circle that was covered by a concrete dome. Not our favourite shape: but such taste was an old formal hangup; the envelope is never seen. The total shape even is never seen as there is always something dropped down or hung or compartmented off – the whole thing is a stage.

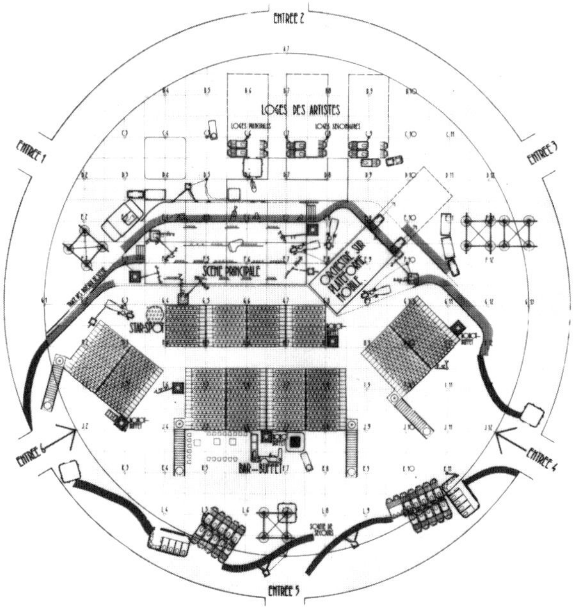

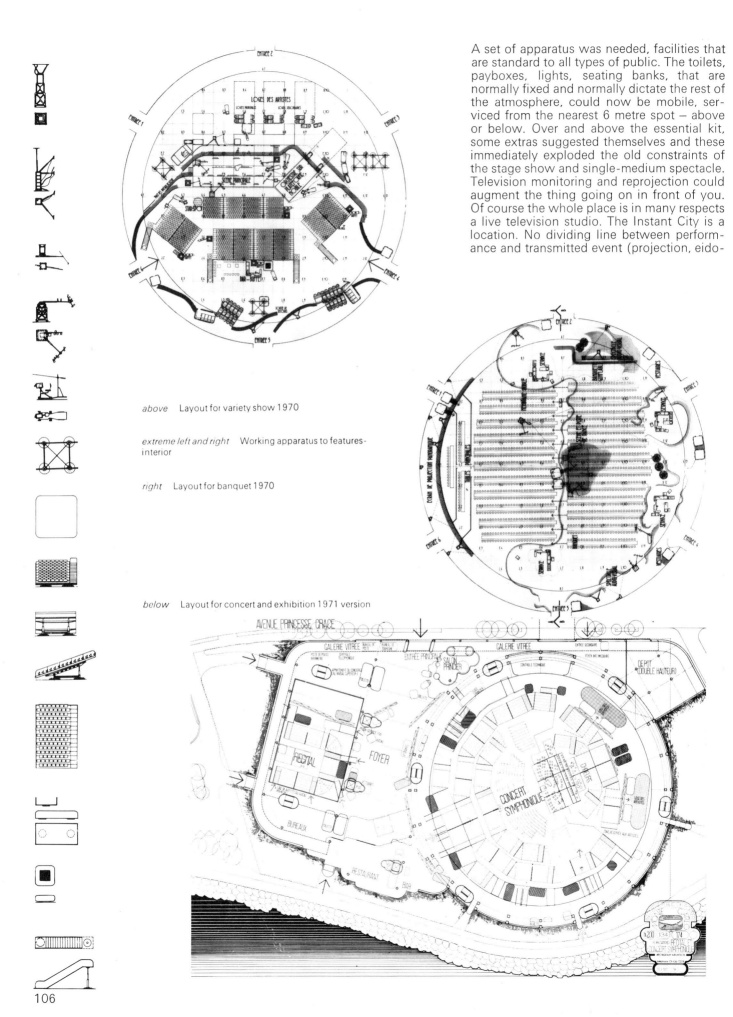

A set of apparatus was needed, facilities that are standard to all types of public. The toilets, payboxes, lights, seating banks, that are normally fixed and normally dictate the rest of the atmosphere, could now be mobile, serviced from the nearest 6 metre spot – above or below. Over and above the essential kit, some extras suggested themselves and these immediately exploded the old constraints of the stage show and single-medium spectacle. Television monitoring and reprojection could augment the thing going on in front of you. Of course the whole place is in many respects a live television studio. The Instant City is a location. No dividing line between performance and transmitted event (projection, eido-

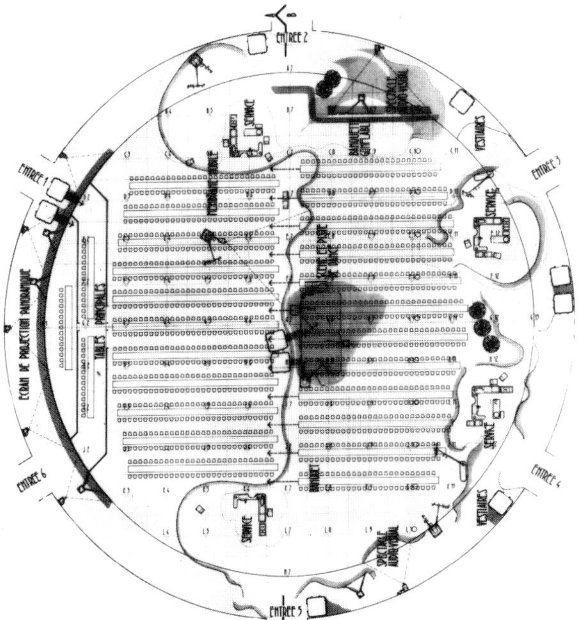

above Layout for variety show 1970

extreme left and right Working apparatus to features-interior

right Layout for banquet 1970

below Layout for concert and exhibition 1971 version

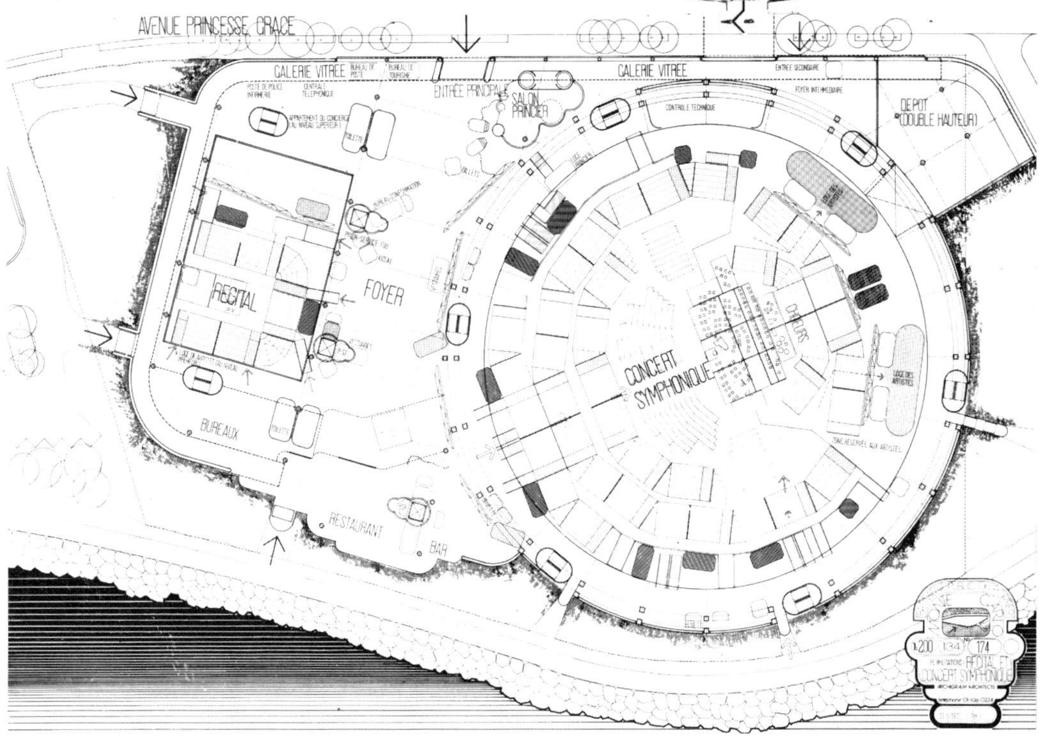

ohor, overlay of media); no dividing line between this space and the unknown (dissolving screens, sliding, lifting, multi-direction) Hopefully a visitor might need several visits to the place to even guess its colour or sonic distance, since it would on each occasion be the place of that day or that day's producer.

A note for architects

n designing the scheme we were subjected o an unusual situation for an Archigram project: not since Euston days had there been such a large unitary project with obligations of scale, type of drawings and the rest of the imitations that are implied in a competition.

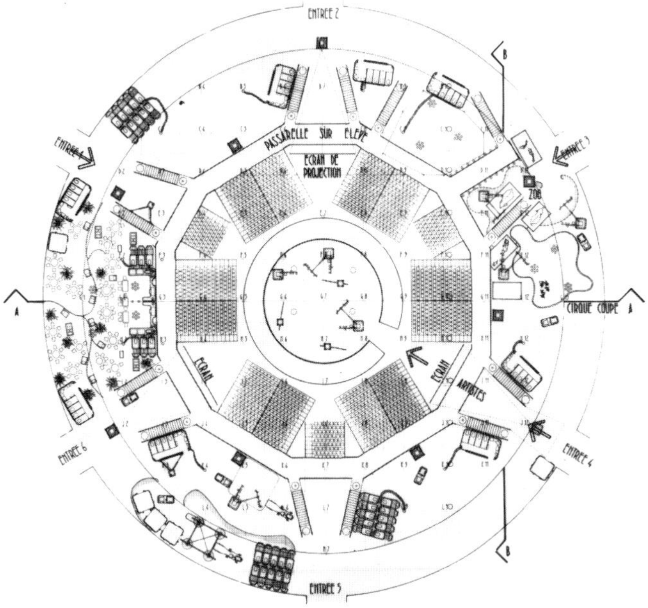

above Layout for circus 1970

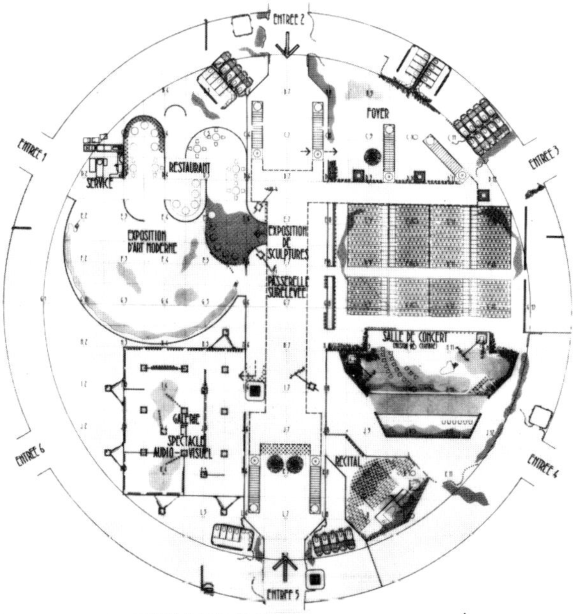

left Layout for arts events 1970

below Layout for indoor sports 1971 version

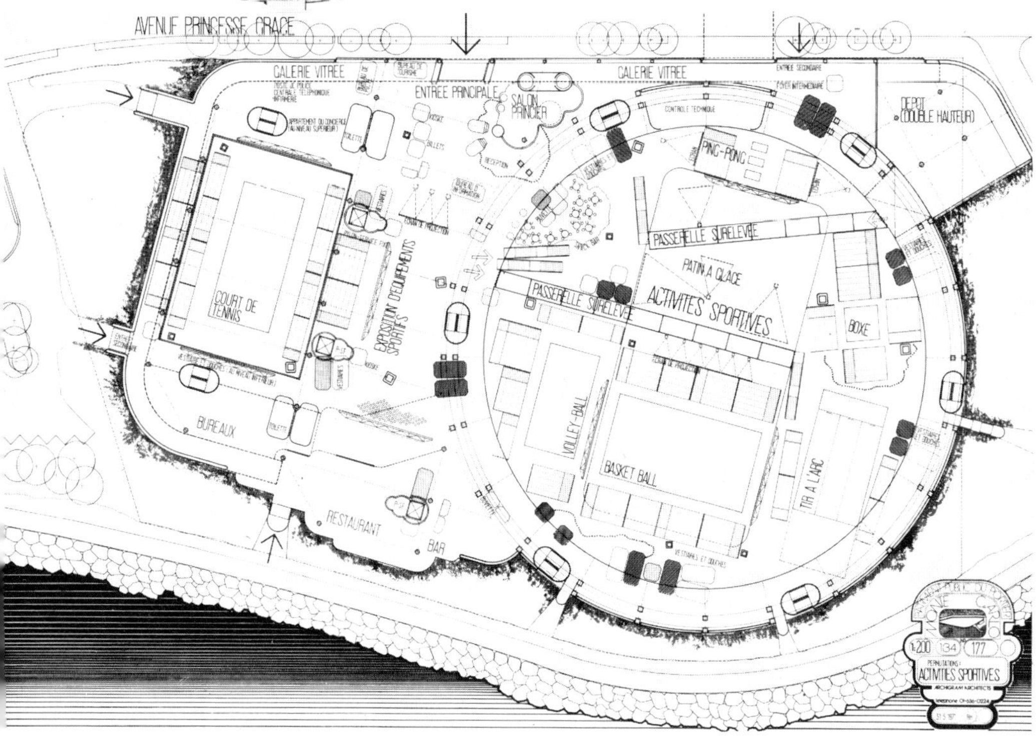

Interior ambiences: circus 1970

General section through project: study of rectilinear structure illustrating relationship of apparatus, insulation, etc. to general structure 1971

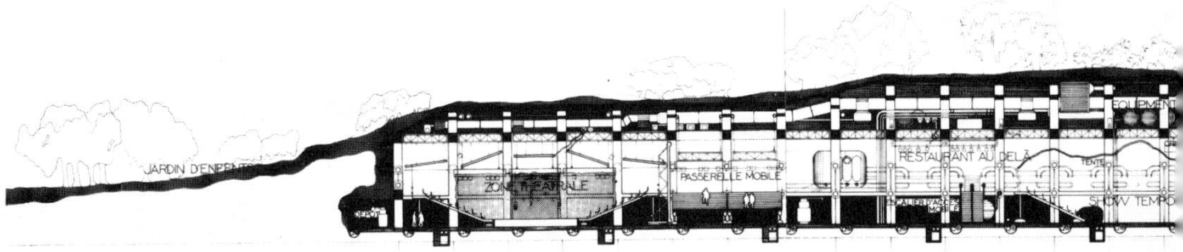

One proposed method of organization was far more expressionist and elemental than the final scheme: with the ice rink and auditorium tied to a servicing strip which held a 'Robot-Railway'. At one stage it seemed as if the park above would sprout pretty toys or glass domes and robotry. This idea was replaced by an 'exposed land-pier' in which the Robot-Railway was the only structure, the rest appearing and disappearing out of 'submarin pens'. There was a constant debate as t whether or not it could be rolled out of a she somewhere. But, clearly, this place is nc 'anywhere' in the way that it could be in a Instant-City Kit. The scheme presented i bloody-minded about blandness and opti mum conditions for the shed and the service bloody-minded about the open space on top

Internal ambiences: sports event 19

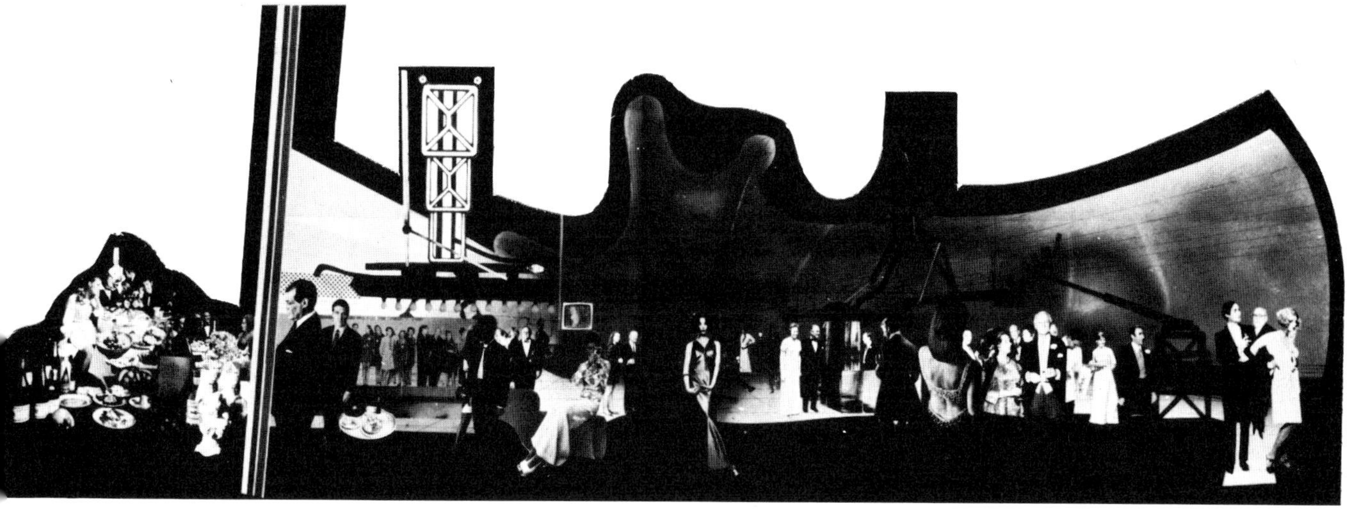

Interior ambiences: banquet 1970

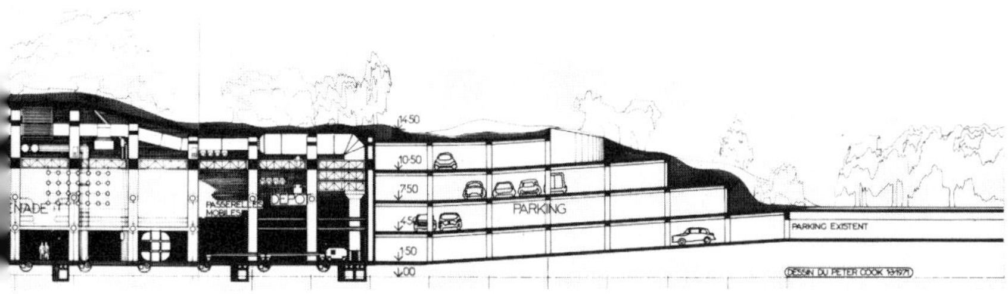

he decision to present so much of it by way f the Events themselves, one-by-one, came : the point of establishing the project.

 a way, this already seems to be one of our oolest and most theoretical productions. It ephemeral by necessity.

s it proceeds, Monte Carlo is now acquiring some parts that are less definitely of either the containing 'box' or the servicing 'kit', and is simultaneously softening into areas that are at once 'service', 'circulation' or 'event space', depending upon your attitude to definition. It is still a hidden thing, and still a total instrument without a preferred tune for it to play, but it is beginning to flex its muscles.

ncept of flexible foyer space and pylons 1971

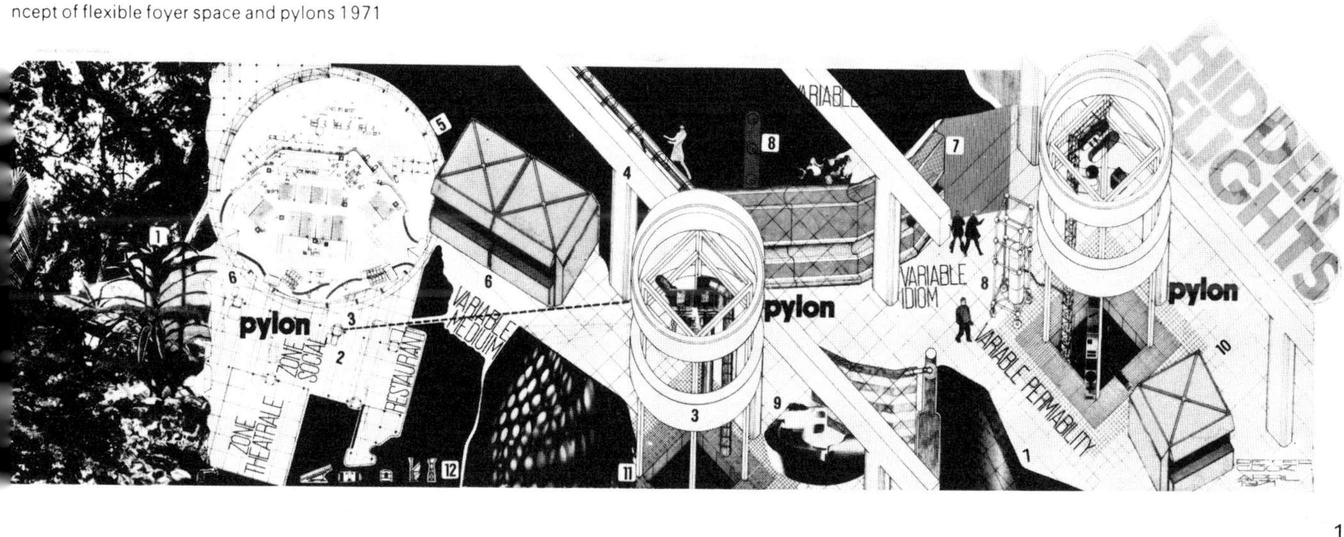

12 Gardener's notebook

David Greene

"I'm sorry but Sir Geoffrey is in his bath"

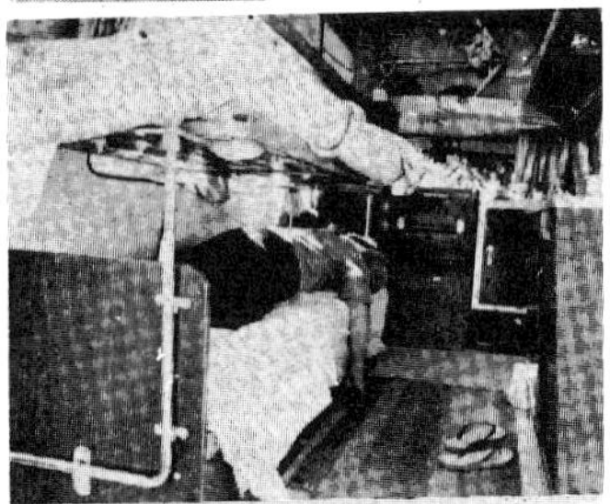

Available: Deluxe
Hunting Lodge
...when and where you want it.

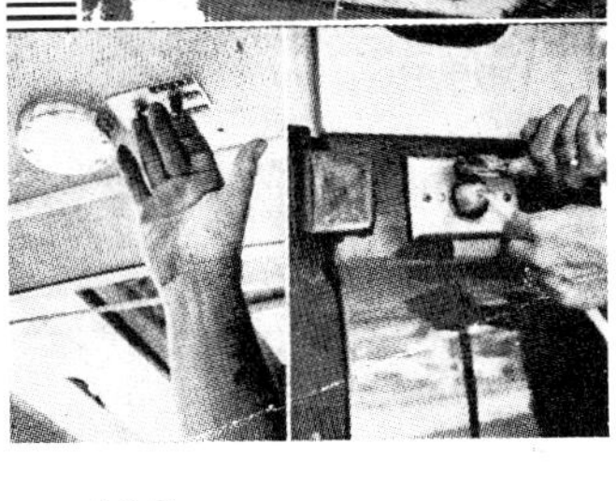

Here we present a Primer and sources, and some of the parts available so that you can go out now and make your own instant village. Don't hang about for all that architect-designed hardware. Also introduced here is Rokplug and Lokplug, a new kit for the node owner to supply the needs of non- or partially-autonomous unit visitors, that blend into the landscape and foliage, not forgetting the invitation to dream at the end. All the following pieces of living gear constitute hardware purchaseable now to make instant villages, towns, etc. (camping scene not included). All right – it's still a hard network.

We all know now that a car is a self-powered mobile room, with limited support systems (air-conditioning, communications).

We also know that a traffic jam is a collection of rooms, so is a car-park – they are really instantly formed and constantly changing communities. A drive-in restaurant ceases to exist when the cars are gone (except for cooking hardware). A motorized environment is a collection of service points.

The house car is a self-powered container adapted for living inside. Generating any gathering of living units. The forests of the world are your suburb – so long as there's a gas station somewhere.

The pickup camper is a container, purpose-designed to clip on to a pickup truck, a sort of hybrid between a caravan and a house car. Its main advantage is that the prime mover can be separated (unlike a house car). All towing problems (with the caravan) and legal use of living quarters whilst underway are eliminated.

The trailer home is a movable container used for living in for extended periods. It requires a high-powered prime mover. These containers are frequently adapted for other purposes, bloodmobile, artmobile, bankmobile, etc. Extensive style ranges are available, purchasable ready for living. Hook up on the site of your choice.

Villages of trailer homes like this are relatively immobile and their major concern, usually, is to imitate straight suburbia as closely as possible. This is achieved by a comprehensive inventory of purchasable stick-on extras to make the trailer look like a 'real' house.

The main problem for mobile living support systems is, of course, the energy source. Until an effective system is devised short-term energy will be taken from batteries or gas cylinders. For stopovers a plug will be required to draw off main power as in the photograph. This need will be satisfied by the ranges of Rokplug and Logplug. Read on.

This is an instant cluster of two campers next to three Rokplugs. Since it is difficult to recognize these outlets from nature's own products, they are equipped with a homing signal that locates each one within a radius of one mile. In your vehicle a dashboard for monitoring.

Rokplug and Logplug locations are indicated in the usual manner on hard routing systems. These signs will also inform the correct dial setting for Plugfind devices.

Opposite are photos of typical communities. Can you spot the Rokplugs and Logplugs? Notice the collapsible hardware that makes outdoor rooms in the grass. Plugs will increase the service to these communities and they will be work places, schools, universities, libraries, theatres, unencumbered by buildings, they build themselves conveniently where they are wished for. The whole of London or New York will be available in the world's leafy hollows, deserts and flowered meadows.

For the present we have to wait, until the steel and concrete mausoleums of our cities, villages, towns, etc., decay and the suburbs bloom and flourish. They in turn will die and the world will perhaps again be a garden. And that perhaps is the dream, and we should all be busy persuading ourselves not to build but to prepare for the invisible networks in the air there . . . Read a bit of this incredible poem – it's all watched over by Machines of Loving Grace

I like to think
  (right now please!)
of a cybernetic forest
filled with pines and electronica
where deer stroll peacefully
past computers
as if they were flowers
with spinning blossoms

The Reali

left Some of the influences and items related to Rokplug and Logplug

right Rokplug and Logplug 1968 David Greene
Rokplug, Logplug and beginning to find L.A.W.U.N. 1968 David Greene (first published in *Architectural Design* 1968)

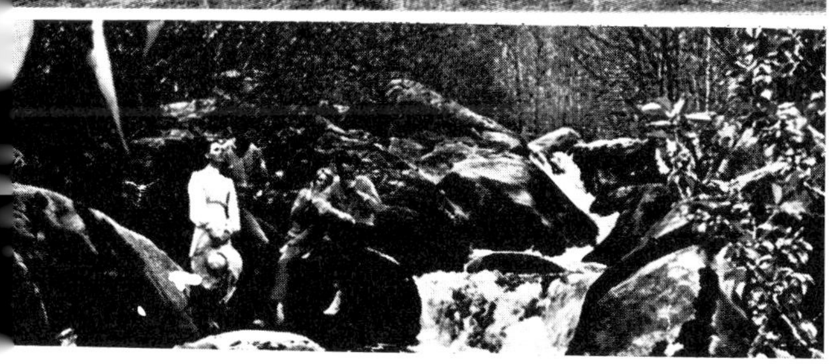

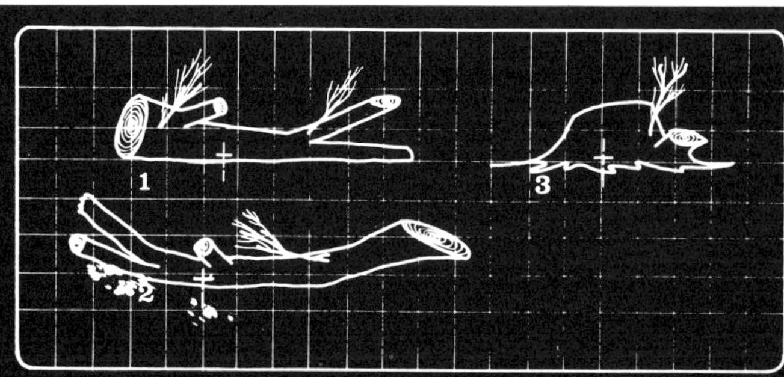

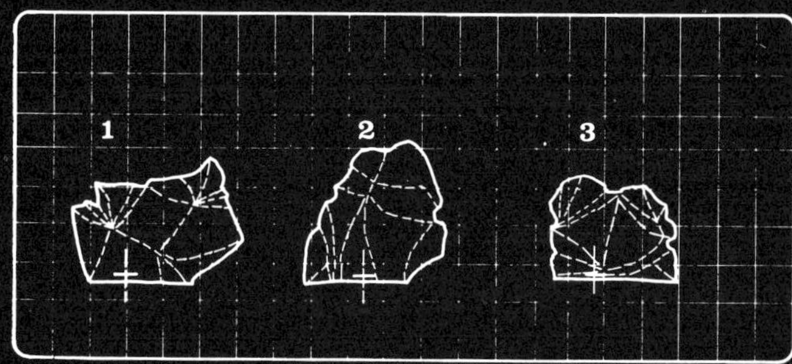

The ranges of **Logplug** and **Rokplug** shown above are selected grp simulations of real logs and rocks. They serve to conceal service outlets for semi- or non-autonomous mobile living containers. They would be unrecognizable from the real thing and would thus bring into any setting a high degree of support without detracting from natural beauty (this means that when no hardware is plugged in the village ceases to exist). All ranges are supplied with an embedded spore finish, to suit any locality, which will promote rapid moss, lichen or fungii covering

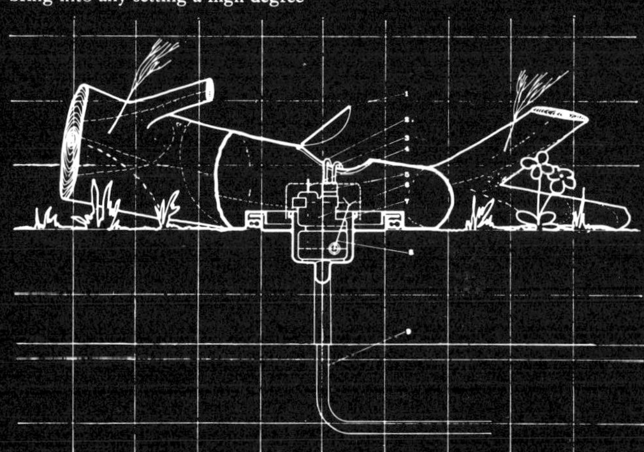

This diagram explains the workings of a typical simulation log. The fixing gasket for both **roks** and **logs** is standard and interchangeable

1 Access lid
2 Cold water service
3 Cable line delivering:
   A/C and D/C current
   Telephone
   International information hook-up
   Educational hook-up
4 Operating credit and slot
5 Plug connection
6 Service metering and control
7 Removable cover
8 Plug find original source
9 Supply cable

Operational procedure to use **Logplug** and **Rokplug**.
Raise access lid 1. Insert standard plug from mobile unit into female connection 5. Secure locking device. Place credit card in slot 4. Select service required on dial next to slot. Throw opening switch. All charges will be made onto your own credit number, these charges are displayed on your log-find device by pressing the yellow button

It is assumed all waste is handled electrostatically and the ash either thrown to the wind or deposited in bags inside the **logs** or **roks**

L.A.W.U.N. Project No. 1
An Experimental Bottery 1969
David Greene

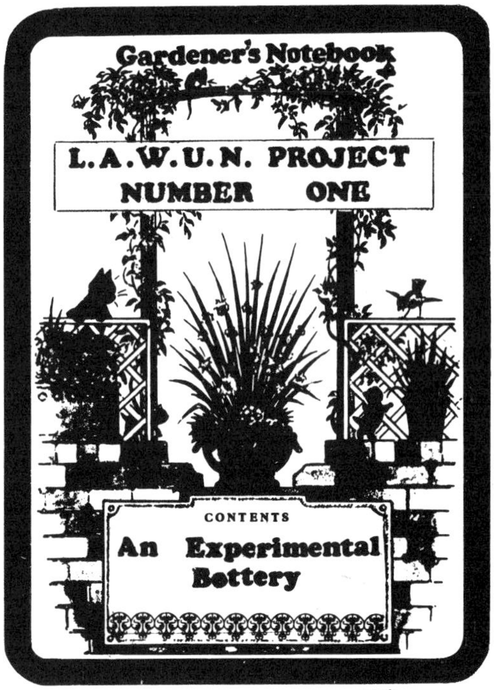

THE BOT.

MACHINE TRANSIENT IN THE LANDSCAPE.

World's last hardware event
and
gardening series

Definition A Bottery is a fully-serviced natural landscape

Contents examine 1 (an architecture of) Time 2 Planet earth Spacegarden 3 Some existing hardware 4 Some new hardware 5 The idea of the invisible

The Bot
Machine transient in the landscape

The picture of this man by the river collects together most of the images and influences that produced this project. The transient non-specialized environment is made possible by the development of sophisticated portable hardware.

Here he is sitting with his TV, ice box, car behind him, all neat, got his own scene going for him and yet it can all be taken away, and when it's gone there's nothing to show that it was there at all, except a small amount of crushed grass and perhaps a tyre track, a footprint. So it's all invisible in a way. The temporary place, retained perhaps permanently in the memory. An architecture that exists only with reference to time.

It's funny that for some years now time has been an important influence in the 'arts', that is, except in architecture. (Apart from nominal and superficial concessions to 'movement' and 'communications'.) Perhaps architects knew all along that if they came to grips with time they would be right out of a job.

I have a desire for
The built environment
To allow me to do
My own thing.

More and more people want to determine their own parameters of behaviour. They want to decide how they shall behave, whether it's playing, working, loving, etc. People are less and less prepared to accept imposed rules and patterns of behaviour. Doing your own thing is important.

. . . people are becoming more interested in people and reality, rather than in feeding mythical systems. Warron Chalk

Unfortunately, however, in terms of doing your own thing, architecture is clearly not working.

It is important to note that all the trends in society and technology are searching for flexibility and versatility. Specialization is dead. In the building world the idea of the multi-purpose shed pays lip-service to this observation, the idea of non-specialized systems and architecture begin to interact: the plane that jumps, the boat that walks, the tie that is a pen.

The idea of rooms for specific purposes is not viable any more, that's obvious, this is even before you ask whether rooms are viable any more. Everything is all mixed up, it's all fragmented.

That is, except for architects, who still seem to think that building types exist and that it's useful to give 'rooms' specific purposes on their drawings.

. . I have a desire for the environment to be nvisible in order that I may be free from the pornography known as buildings . . .

One of the most interesting observables 'or the architecture about some recent 'sculpture' (if it exists) is that it takes great care not o disturb the existing environment and in fact draws from its situation and feeds on all the on-going events and processes that any particular site contains.

. . using the untapped energy and information network of the day-to-day environment.

Jack Burnham

'he common threads that exist between the isherman and his Sony and the project above. Robert Smithson's 'Incidents of mirror travel n the Yucatan' are important.

Both involve the temporary placing of bits f hardware in the natural scene and their ltimate removal; about this project Smithson writes: 'It is the dimension of absence that is to be found.' So maybe you might say that ne development of portable hardware produces an architecture of absence. You've got) know about when it's not there as well as when it's there.

owboy international nomad-hero. It used) seem a nice idea to carry your environent around with you (spaceman, Cushicle, uitaloon, etc.), but it can be as much of a drag s having it stuck in one place. Cowboy was robably one of the most successful carriers f his own environment because his hardware eeds were low (mug, saddle, bedroll, atches and because his prime mover, orse, selected its own fuel and was a fairly ficient animal robot. The ranch was his asis, his base. Modern nomad sophisticated eeds servicing, Howard Johnson underands this; and in the Bottery this is achieved the technique of calling it up wherever you e, it's delivered by robots. It's anarchy – and s hardware – supported until it's under the in or in the mind.

arshall McLuhan has said that the planet rth can be understood now as a piece of ulpture in the galaxies.

e Bottery is part of the idea of the Spacerk Earth (write to Sierra Club Foundation, ill Tower, San Francisco, California 94104 r further information).

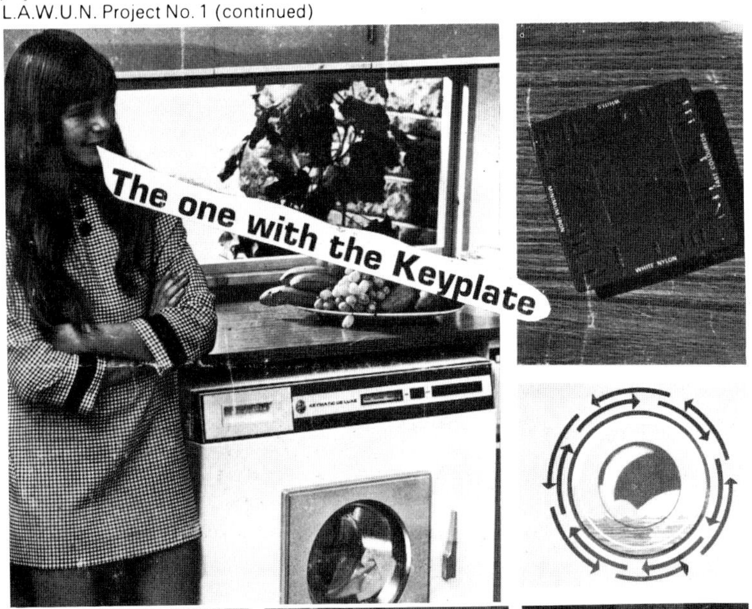

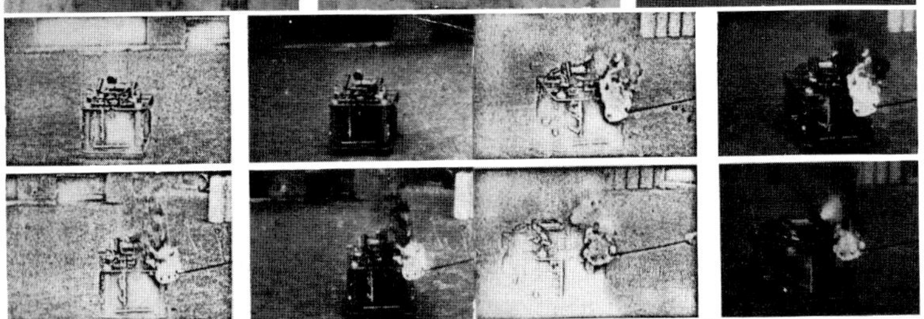

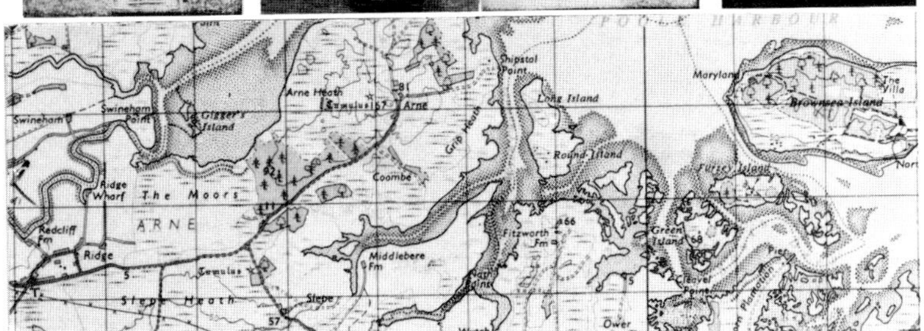

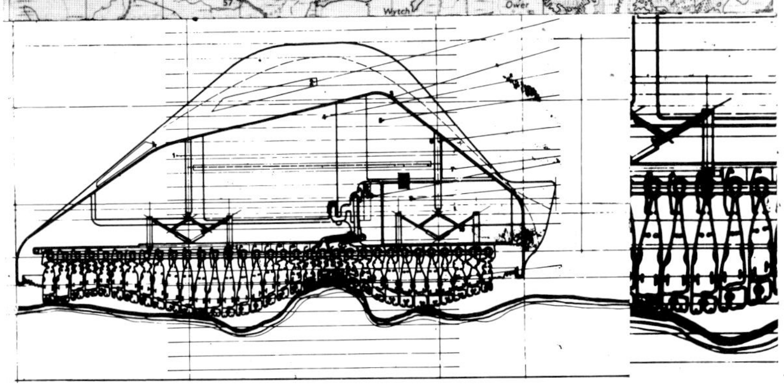

Keymatic (purchasable) is a familiar piece of hardware, part of a long line of crude domestic robots, dishwasher, mixer, central heating, etc. The thing about keymatic that's nice is the system of programming which is done by a plastic plate. It is interesting to compare the image of keymatic with much recent cooker design which has a jet-fighter cockpit aesthetic. The kitchen robot has become, in keymatic, not a vast piece of technical iconery, but an anonymous box and slot into which you place your programme. Every house now contains crude robots. Everybody wants a house full of robots but no one wants to look like a house full of robots. So why not forget about the house and have a garden, and a collection of robots?

Mowbot (purchasable), like keymatic, is easy, no sweat, set the grass cutting height on the dial and it will sense when the grass is needing a trim, you don't need to worry. And it's anonymous, and it's invisible, it's not a piece of permanent lawn furniture. It's still a fairly crude robot, however, because you will still need a hard network of wires embedded under the ground at the perimeter of its territory. It has to be a very short step from having just mowbot to having a shed full of bots and then all you would need would be a shed and a lawn.

Firebot is a piece of experimental hardware a heat sensitive bot, homing on to do its own thing. Developed by Professor Thring at Sheffield. (Who said sleepbot, the deliverer of slumberatic comforts to the needy body and mind, was an absurd idea?)

Bot call-up device. The type of service required is selected on a dial and the homing button pressed. Time to elapse before arrival displayed on the end. If more than one bot is required the multi-selection switch is activated. This is the only piece of hardware you need carry with you in a bottery.

For hardware lovers: a selection of available electric aids to natural growth to help the gardener in the world park. Also a diagram of a cross section of a skinbot. The basic bot consists of a primary frame, a power module and an exchange unit. On to this are clipped combinations of modules for various performance requirements. Compatibility is assured by the exchange unit which rejects any mismatched modules.

This is the diagram of L.A.W.U.N. This project is about calling it all up wherever you are. (Environmental anarchy.) A Bottery is robot-serviced landscape. This project is about the setting up of an experimental Bottery used solely by pedestrians for the purpose of (a) studying the nature and operation of the bot-man relationship (b) the development of reliable and efficient bot systems.

The selected area is situated in a UK area of heathland between the B3351 and Poo

Harbour. A little-used area of considerable natural beauty. Included in the Bottery are Arne Heath, Grep Heath, Slepe Heath, Wytch Heath, Rempstone Heath, Round Island, Newton Heath and Botham Plantation.

Picnic grove (dressed) somewhere in the world park. Skinbot (1) delivers 18 cu. metres of air-conditioned deformable space, enclosed by a Sunfilta gossamer membrane that can glow at night by voice command and whose opacity is infinitely variable to choice.

Combot (2) brings to your side out of the bluebells a way into your own secret mind, or selects out of the world's transmitted invisible pictures and sounds your own pattern of information and shows it on your shirt or on a screen. This is a brief community of people gathered together in the world park. They have called up their bots. The gathering s only related to time. Tomorrow, in half an hour, next week, it will all have changed, there'll be nothing remaining to indicate that t was there. The natural scene will remain unchanged. This small instant village will only exist in the memories of the people who were there and in the information memory of he robot. An invisible village. An architecture existing only in time.

This couple, still living in their nice house urn on with Combot in the evenings. However they are already wondering why they need any furniture and have their Combot networked into their office in town and don't need to commute any more. Maybe next year hey can move into a grass field somewhere. One of the questions often asked about this kind of project is 'How do you make it happen?' In this project, as well as the experimental landscape venture, it can be made to happen through the marketing of robots and heir gradual absorption into our everyday life. Just as frozen food has made a cooker in a way less necessary, less useful and yet even more desirable as a tool for creativity in the kitchen', so increasingly sophisticated and efficient domestic robots will make the permanent living base (or house) less useful and will open up new areas and meanings for the word 'home'.

.A.W.U.N. means the striving after basic objectives, doing your own thing without disturbing the events of the existing scene and in way which is invisible because it involves o formal statement, and because it is related to time, may or may not be there at any iven point in time.

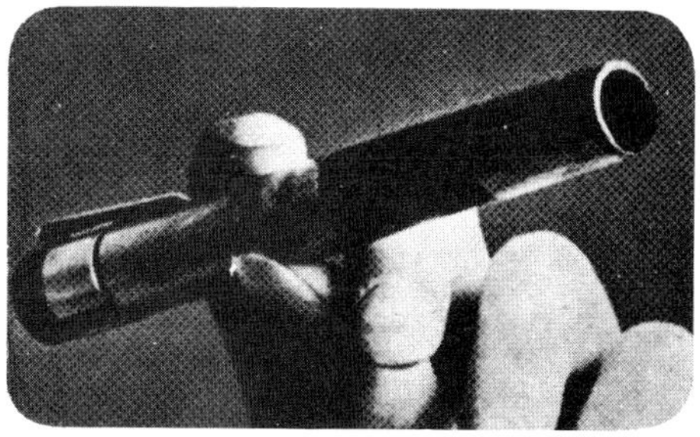

Imagining the Invisible University. Painting by Sally Hodgson

Imagining the Invisible University 1971 David Greene (first published *Architectural Design* April 1971)

Videoantics and Videotactics

The artist: Sally Hodgson
The artist's intention: Unknown to the author
The author's intention: To suggest to the reader that this picture contains information relevant to the architect, and to show to the reader this borrowed picture because it seems to have certain areas of correspondence to certain dreams of the author. The author's dreams that seemingly correspond to the artist's photograph can be described in quotation format. . . . 'I was looking at some photographs of the work of Richard Long – mowed marks in large areas of grass – and they appeared as works of architecture although I had previously been informed that they were intended to be read as works of art. I was interested as to why they seemed to be works of architecture.

I was similarly puzzled by the photograph. What are these lines? Are they the residue of some departed building, are they the plotted routes in space of a temperature gradient, are they the territorial limits (like the lines marking out a football pitch) of some environment yet to take place? What information exists within these lines, how far does it extend beyond them and in what direction and is it available for my use? I can see in my mind a picture of a nomad and within the pocket of his long-haired coat rests a television device, his life previously only interwoven with his natural environment is now also interwoven with the electronic environment, but both exist together, one does not replace the other, both together produce a new environment, an electric aborigine. Perhaps this long-hair-coated man understands these lines and also the marks of Richard Long. He has learned to weave his life almost chameleon-like into his environments.

Like the guerilla he makes a lot out of his minimal hardware. The development of electronics has allowed him to be a well-serviced primitive – a ridiculous thought maybe, but it is equally ridiculous to continually use electronics as a device for supporting industrial revolution lifestyles (and hence an 'architecture' to service these lifestyles).'

Man has always moved around the natural environment, the activity is not new; video mirrors increase our sense of psychological territory via a build-up of sensory fragments over a controllable time sequence.

Videoantics are videotactics.

The electric aborigine

One meaning of the phrase 'people are walking architecture' is disclosed when we carry our instrumentation around with us . . . eg. the astronaut, or his terrestrial counterpart, the infraneuralelectricaborigine, who carries knowledge sensors with him/her.

The more people who actively try being a social chameleon, the more chance they have of demonstrating the power of an alternative and weakening the power of a controlling system. To demonstrate the alternative means that if an alternative is recognized then it can be used as a lever, a tactic.

The Electric Aborigine 1971 David Greene, Mike Barnard

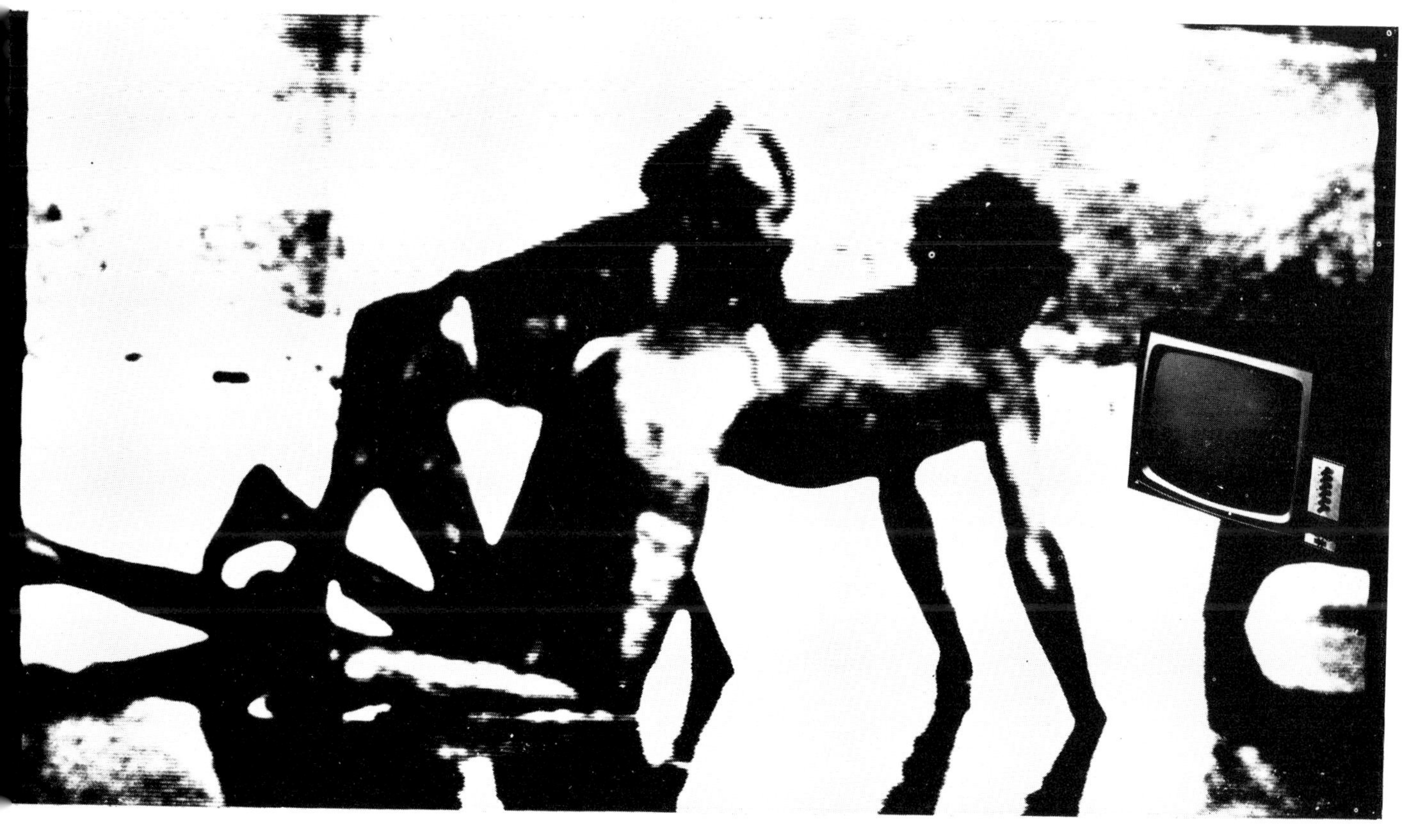

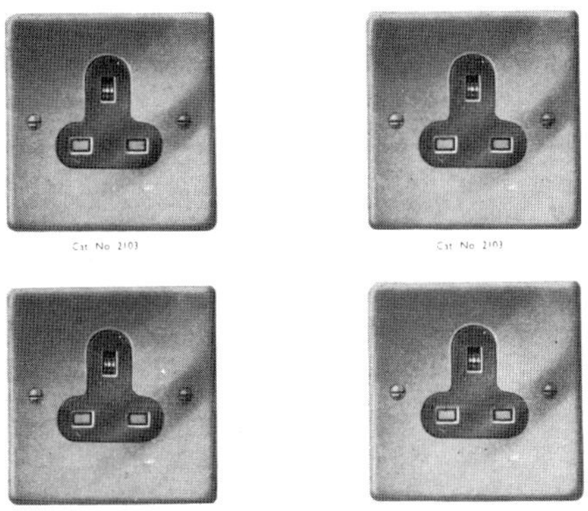

Collage 1972 David Greene

Video notebook

Bonnie Barrett, queen of the San Francisco Sports and Boat Show, and her pet, Ace, rode a one-ton floating rock in the Bay. The rock is powered by the New Chrysler 3.6 h.p. outboard 'Swinger', which can drive the big rock to speeds of up to $3\frac{1}{2}$ m.p.h.

There is no reality, only response, there is no morality, only situational ethics, nothing is absurd, the motorized floating rock, playing golf on the moon, typhoons in India, million dollar football players, continuous S. American revolution, all part of our total inability to comprehend who we are or what we are doing. Maybe architecture had some function as a gesture of faith, that in the violent situation that man has always found himself in we had to believe that there was some meaning to it all, so we invented systems of meaning, frameworks for action and belief. Is architecture such a framework?

Look at this picture. I feel it has something to do with architecture. Do you? It poses some questions (like Logplug) about reality. The basis of the modern movement is Judeo Christian in that it upholds truth and the search for it formally as an architectural medium. But we know truth to be relative to available information and prejudices. The guerilla camouflages himself and maximizes on available resources in a creative manner the American army is more of a monument to technology. It's the difference between a portable Videofax and the New York Public Library. Declare moratorium on buildings.

The infamous plug. Plugging-in is a term that has consistently been misused as a description of an architectural style. Plugging-in however, defines an attitude, not a style; a way of thinking that shows a shift in interest from the building to the device. A shift from aesthetics to the way portable hardware restructures our behaviour. The city is merely a giant socketry, and architecture has ceased to carry any symbolic value and has thus become irrelevant except maybe as a technology of containers of some sort. Declare moratorium on architecture.

Here is an aborigine, does she, like the guerilla have something to tell us about our situation Her technology was primitive but her lifestyle was complex, full of valuable myths and fantasies and she lived with her environment not parasitically upon it. Our architecture are the residue of a desire to secure ourselves to the surface of our planet, if only they were on wheels, or if some slippery substance could be injected under them, our anchor to the planet, like the aborigine's, should be software, like songs or dreams, or myths. Abandon hardware, earth's-surface anchor Electric aborigine makes for the moratorium on Buildings.

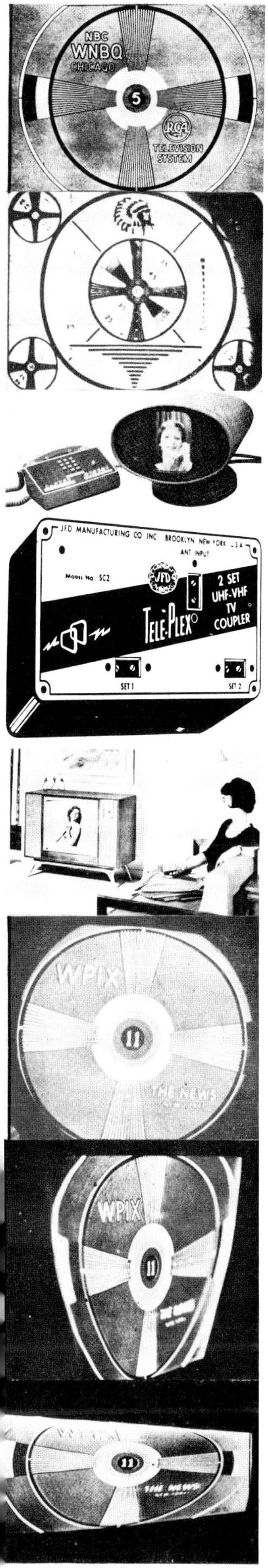

Video Notebook 1972 David Greene, Mike Barnard

WE ARE ENTERING PRIMITIVE HETEROGENEITY

Notes on 3 projects made in 1970–71
Michael Barnard and David Greene

THE SOFTWARE MOVEMENT

All 3 projects can be described as a search for the problems confronting architects.

THE INFRA-NEURAL CHAMELEON IS FACING A SOFTWARE BLOCKAGE

Our working base has been the proposition that there is 'a symbiotic relationship between human behaviour and architectural hardware'.

INFRA-NEURAL GUERILLA

The infra-neural network is the result of a symbiotic link between a body and portable hardware. It is the conceptual infrastructure developed out of this link.

SOCIAL SOFTWARE AND STONED STRATEGIES

Proceeding from this we have produced a series of speculations intended to question present-day conceptions of architecture. For instance, it is generally accepted that architects are concerned with the design of buildings and associated subsystems such as Town Planning.

PEOPLE ARE WALKING ARCHITECTURE

But for a variety of reasons, buildings become ineffective.

DISORGANIZE SITE-ATTACHMENT AND START WEAVING BEHAVIOUR

and the resulting problems are not solved by concentrated production of buildings of a bigger sort and in larger numbers . . .

WE MOVE FROM BODY TRIMMING TO MORATORIUM TACTICS

these types of solution ignore the sociological paradigm of the natural environment.

DISSOLVE THE MEMORY OF THE HOME AND PLABAX PORTABLE TYRANNY

Our speculations attempt to bypass the prejudices and lifestyles of straight architecture and capitalized upon by architects educationalists sociologists planners . . .

All three projects overlap and coverage around 2 points:

1 an interest in the possible influence of miniaturized electric hardware of lifestyles

VIDEO IS PORTABLE BODY MIRROR

2 an interest in the way decision making is becoming decentralized (as observed in fashion, dropout cultures, anarchy) and what this may mean in terms of new software.

THE ELECTRIC ABORIGINE IS A SOCIAL CHAMELEON

VIDEO GUERILLA HAS SPECIAL PSYCHIC DEMANDS

BAC-PAC PRIMER . . . looking at the world of the mail order catalogue, of Green Shield stamps and all the advertised networks that feed the soul of suburbia. Out of this we generated BAC-PAC MAN who carried Suburbia and the World's Universities in his PAC; who could also be free from the static physical restraints of these environments . . .

THE PRIMITIVE INFRA-NEURAL MIRROR TAPE . . .

INVISIBLE UNIVERSITY AND ALLOTMENTS are rich in SOFTWARE, because it is necessary in the allotment garden to operate and make useful the residue of the straight industrial society. A JUNK esthetic and ecological searchlight – in the middle of the city that can only at best be described as a monument to obsolete industrial hardware and economics.

ROCKANDROLL HARDWARE LEADS TO OTHER GRASS STRATEGIES

THE INFRA - NEURAL - ELECTRIC - ABORIGINE or people are walking architecture. A MYTHIC synthesis described in terms of the INAE . . . perhaps through technology we can achieve a highly developed ECO-SENSORY world like that of the aborigine. (The aborigine is considered a PRIMITIVE when he faces our concept of society. Aren't we in a parallel situation with regard to the potential of technology?) WHY doesn't your university know that it is the Xerox machine on the railway platform, or the anonymous handbag has more to do with learning than the local library?

SCREEN FIGHTING MAN
VIDEO GUERILLA

PRIMITIVE MIRRORS? THAT'S VIDEO GRASS

WE ARE ENTERING PRIMITIVE HETEROGENEITY

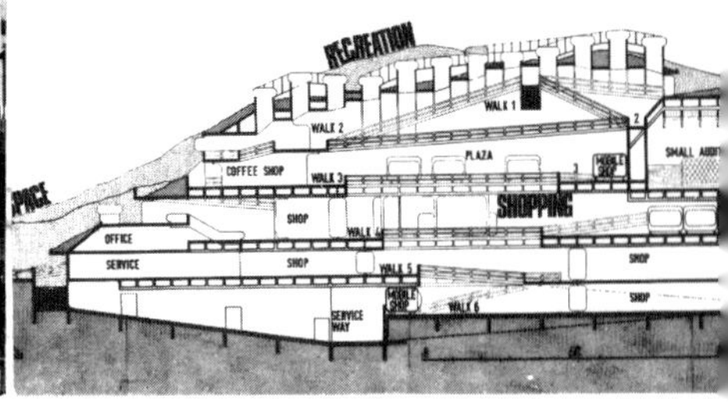

13 Mound, ground, and hidden delights

Since the early 1960s we have remained fascinated with the idea and the formation of the 'mound'. It has a myriad of conceptual links: to the idea of the 'city-as-a-single-building', to the aggregation of the unlike to the unlike in some amorphous, polyglot organism that is beyond single buildings, to the notion of place as ground and artefacts as transient plantings. Warren Chalk acknowledges the inspiration of the Mappin Terraces at London Zoo for the casual build-up of the South Bank Scheme. There followed a project in 1964 that placed Euston Station and its shopping centre under a mound of greenery and parkland. The outcrops of the Plug-in City were also, in their way, pile-ups of casually collected parts and quite deliberately mound-like in profile. The Features: Monte Carlo mound has therefore a lineage behind it: but in its interpretation it is a dogmatic disassociation of the aggregated bits-and-pieces from the groundwork itself (which is this time a gentle slope of real earth).

The Bournemouth Project carries on a dialogue with that of Monte Carlo: the culture of rich and well-heeled seaside with entertainments as a main function. A surrounding of cliffs or mountain with trees, gardens and rockeries and cream-painted hotels and villas, Bournemouth served as a blistering out of several expressionist games that we had purged from the Monte Carlo Scheme. It extends an already existing pattern of shopping arcades that network the centre of Bournemouth. Through the scheme these develop into piers and decks and into the sea-front scene. The seaside is traditionally the place where our notions of a flexible and 'responsive' environment are carried out: as the seasons and the weather change so do the functions and the architecture. The 'Steps' are formed by the piling-up of the shops and sheds and capsules that emanate from the arcades. The stepping is covered by undergrowth and extends the lawns and rockeries that are already there. The whole thing was designed very quickly, with several hands at work, and proved to be exhilarating, if somewhat undisciplined. It throws up a characteristic of Archigram: the need for exuberance and freewheel designing as well as the demonstration of a thesis. The Mound is in this instance more of a 'heap' – and this extension of the idea has to be pursued, becoming a casually collected *style* or mode of collection This last is the most difficult: in Bournemouth it ranged from quotations from Plug-in through Art Deco, intentional-nasty to intentional-refined. Inevitably, we stood back some months later and realized that the scheme was less important in its own right than as a hint of the next 'heap'.

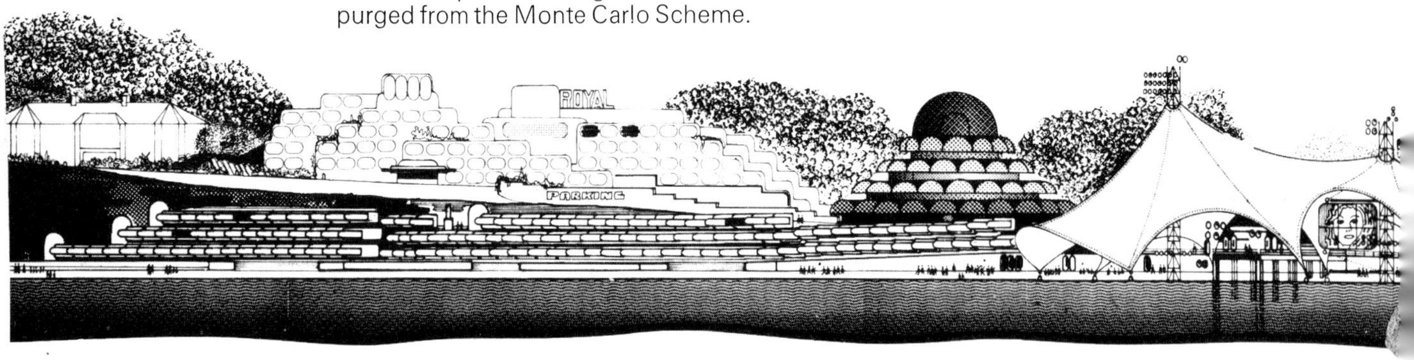

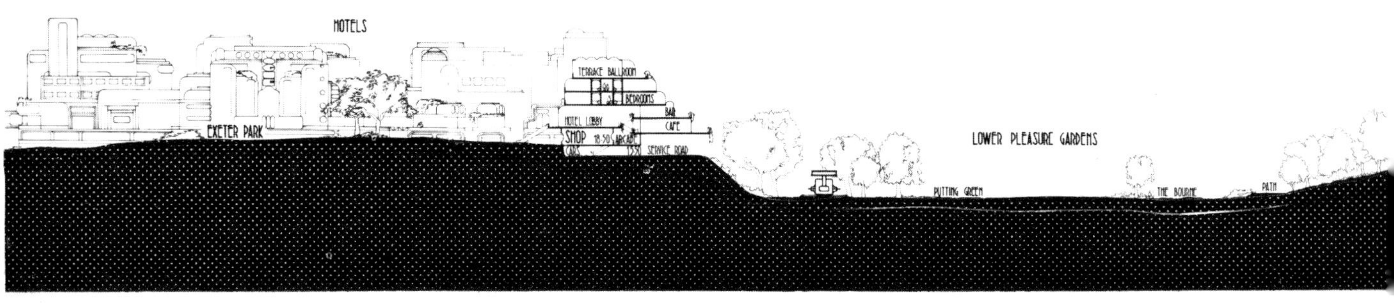

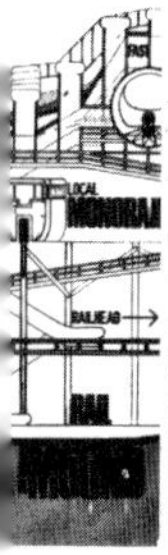

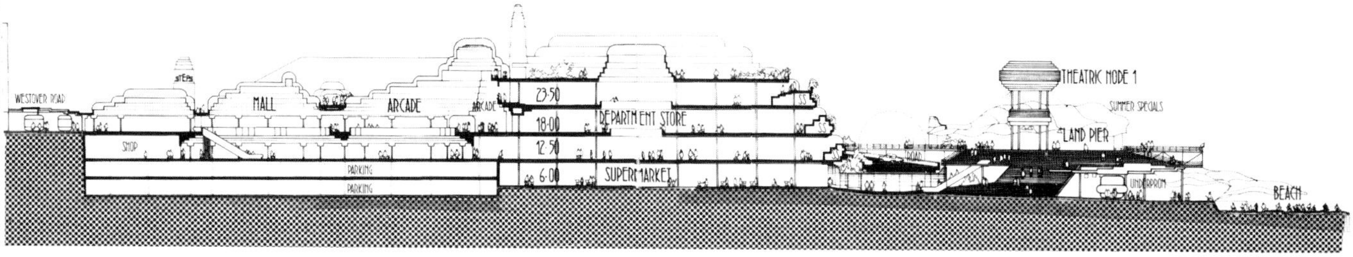

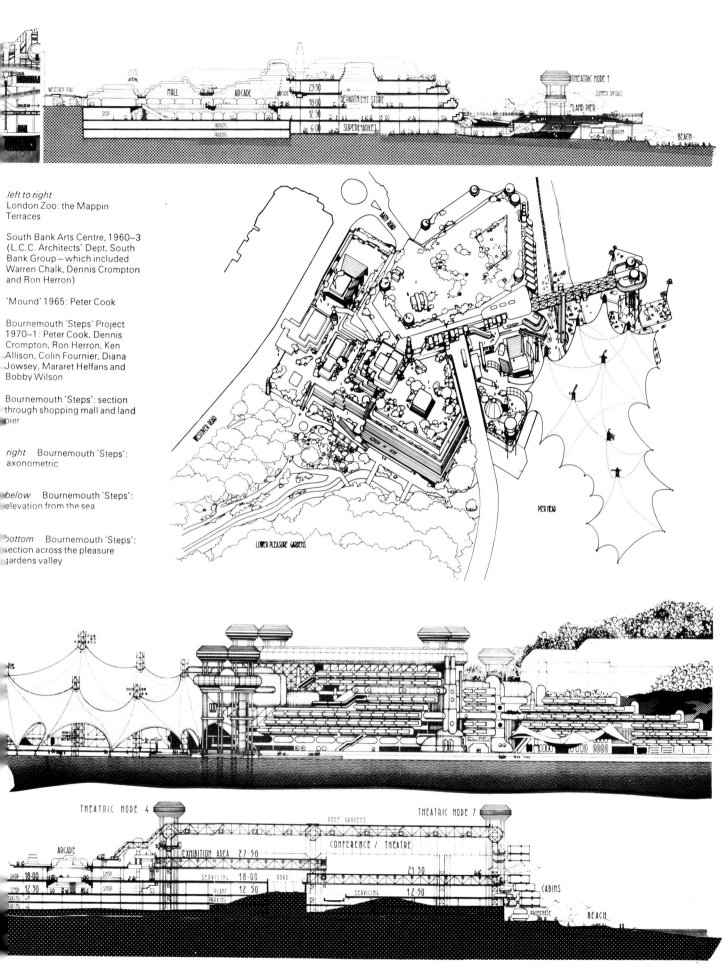

left to right
London Zoo: the Mappin Terraces

South Bank Arts Centre, 1960–3 (L.C.C. Architects' Dept, South Bank Group – which included Warren Chalk, Dennis Crompton and Ron Herron)

'Mound' 1965: Peter Cook

Bournemouth 'Steps' Project 1970–1: Peter Cook, Dennis Crompton, Ron Herron, Ken Allison, Colin Fournier, Diana Jowsey, Mararet Helfans and Bobby Wilson

Bournemouth 'Steps': section through shopping mall and land pier

right Bournemouth 'Steps': axonometric

below Bournemouth 'Steps': elevation from the sea

bottom Bournemouth 'Steps': section across the pleasure gardens valley

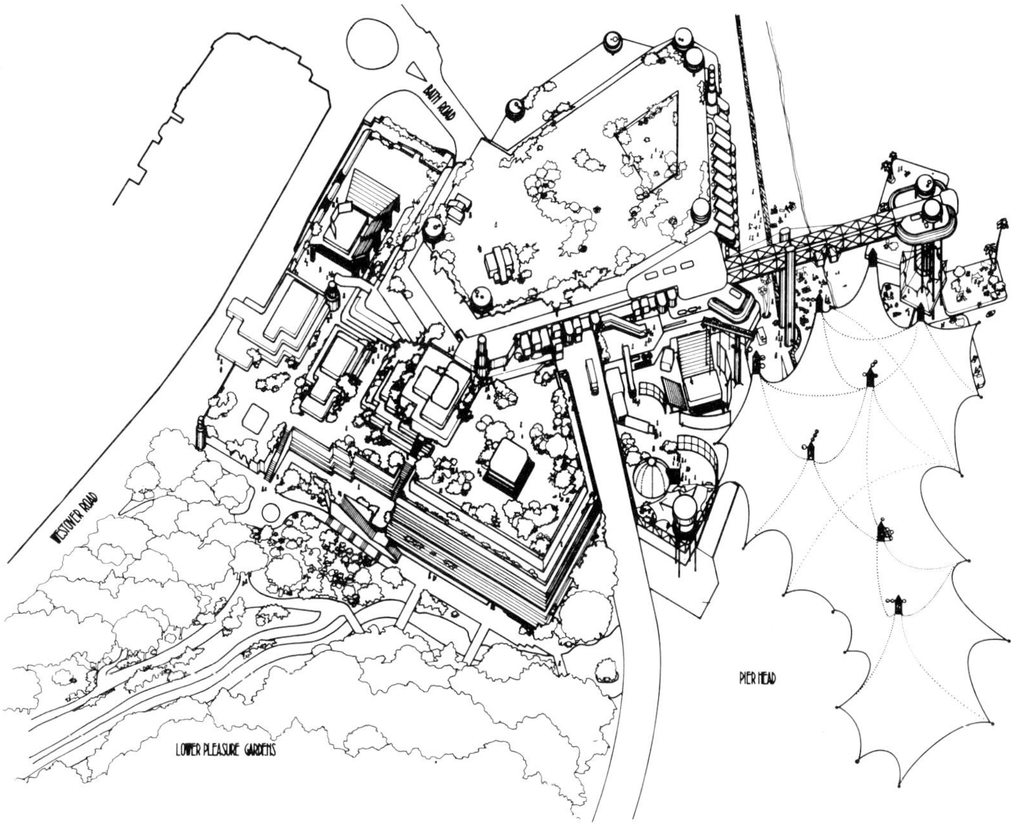

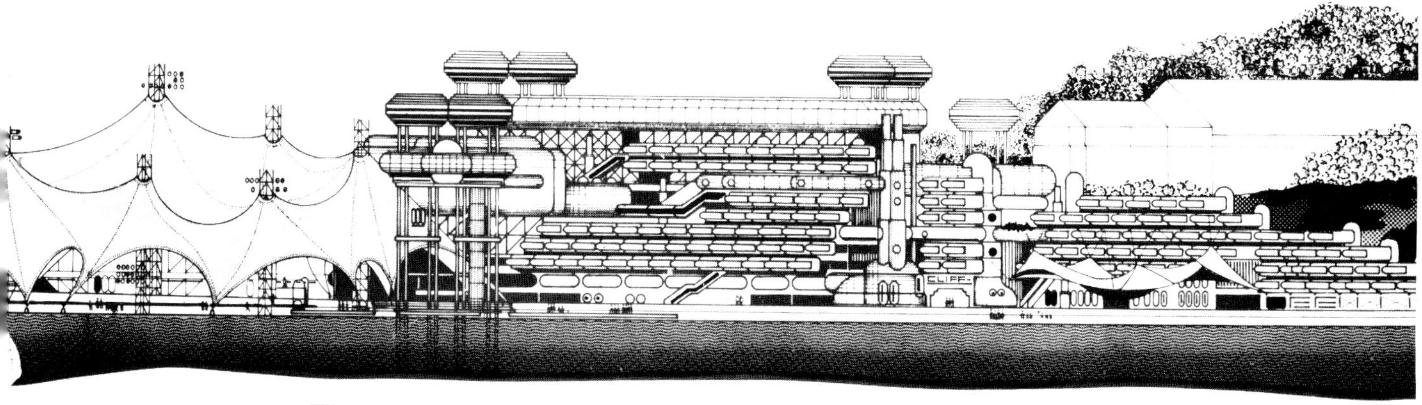

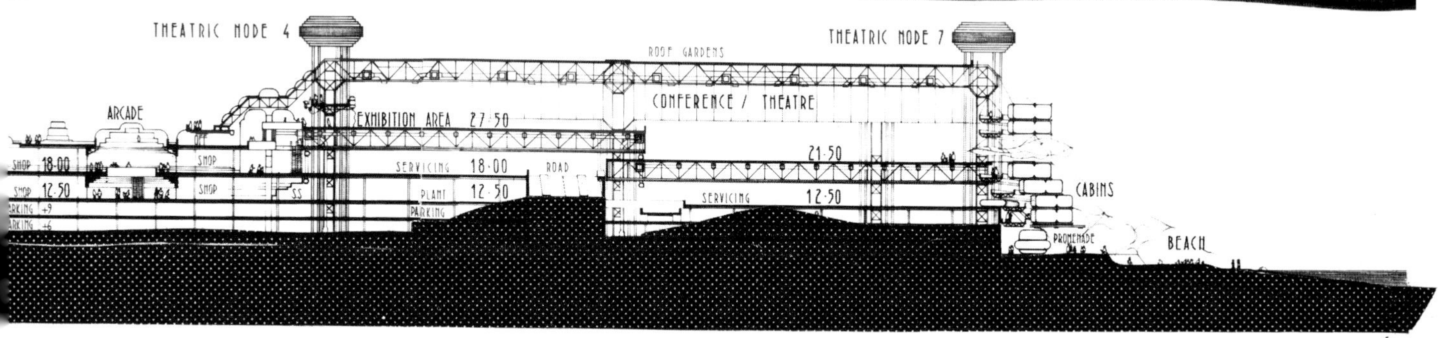

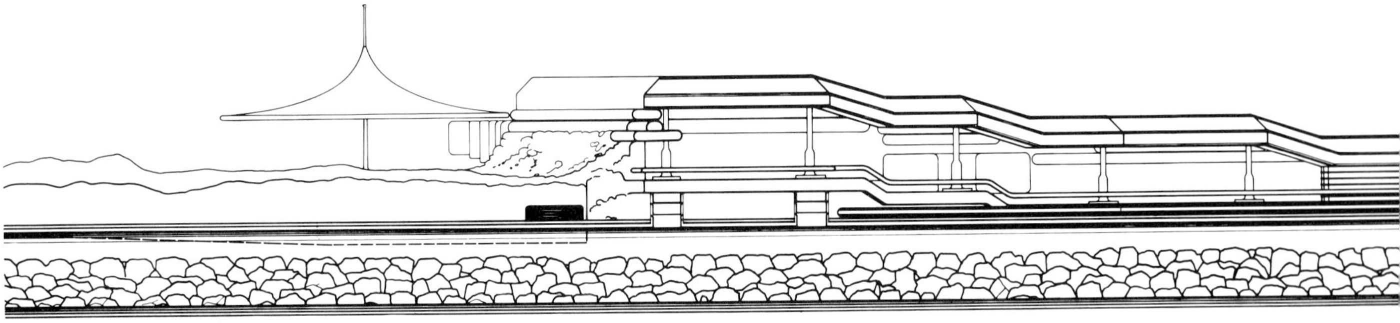

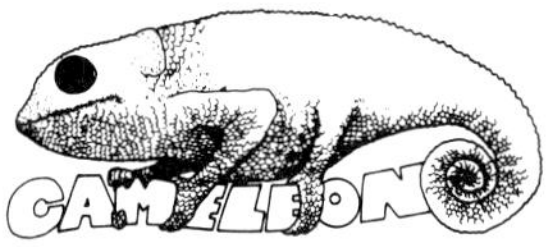

Monte Carlo Summer Casino: 'Cameleon' scheme 1971: Peter Cook, Diana Jowsey, Stuart Lever and Bernard Tschumi (above) elevation, (right) site plan

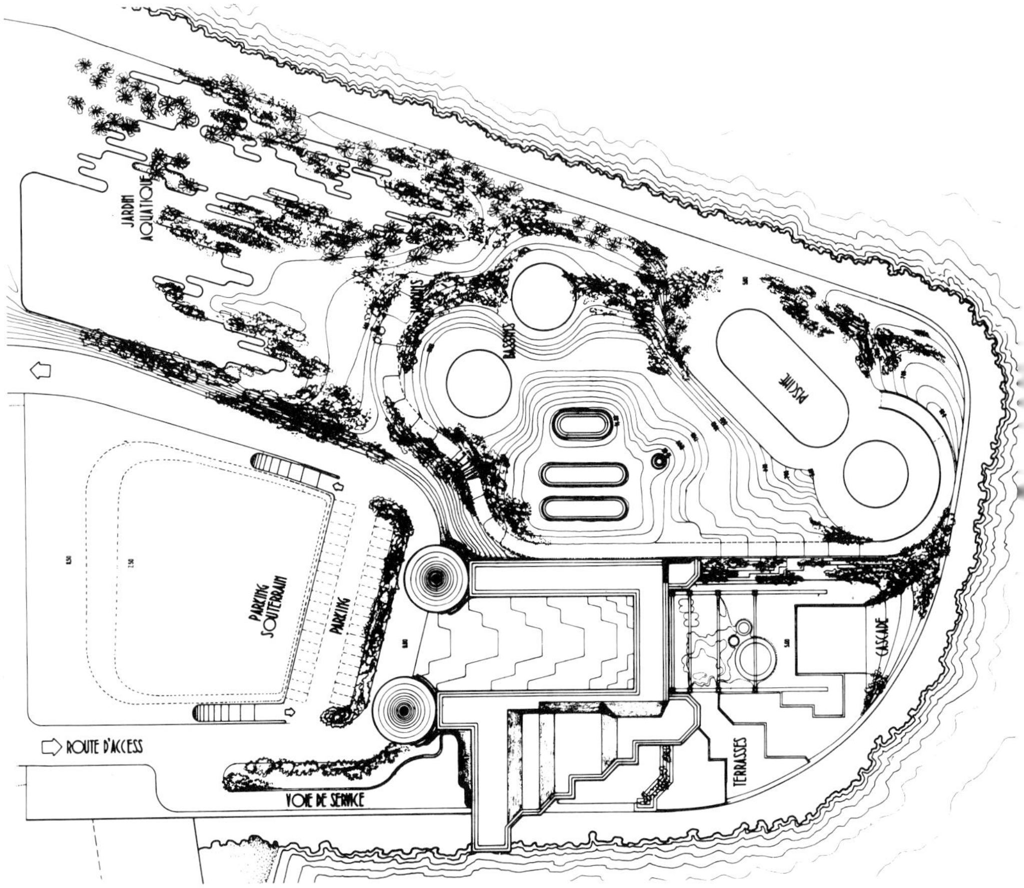

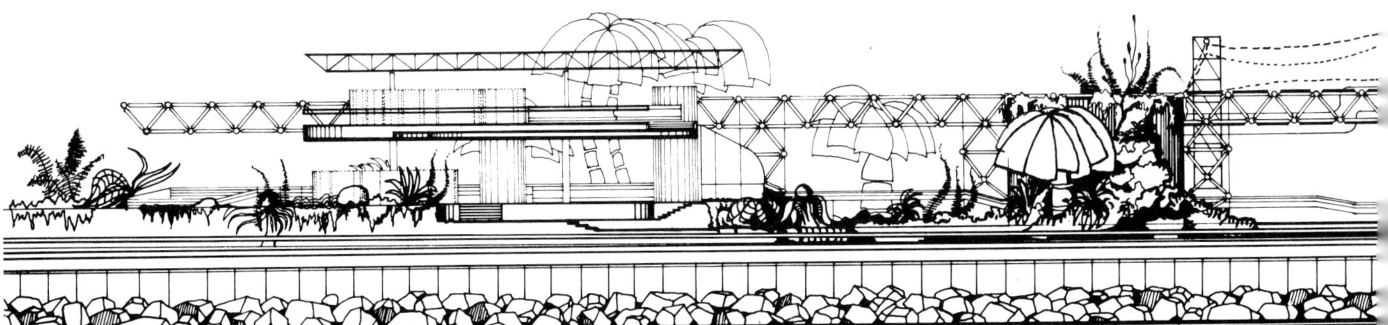

The Chameleon and the Palm Tree

Bournemouth Steps was a developer's competition and the Summer Casino projects were also designed in competition both external and internal. Archigram made two projects for this facility, which had to include gambling rooms, a night club, a restaurant and a events space known as the Gala Hall. Th present building contains such a space whic is really a trellis work able to absorb a quic change of surface styling and event. Th whole thing is very much open to the air an the sea.

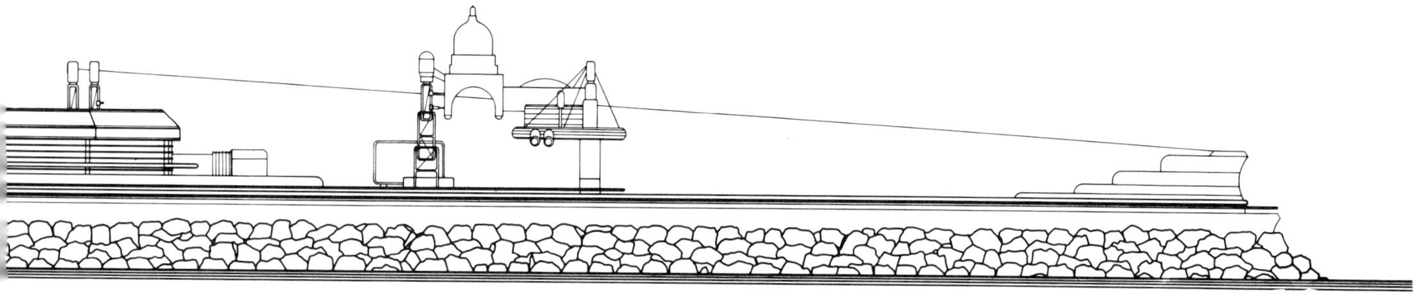

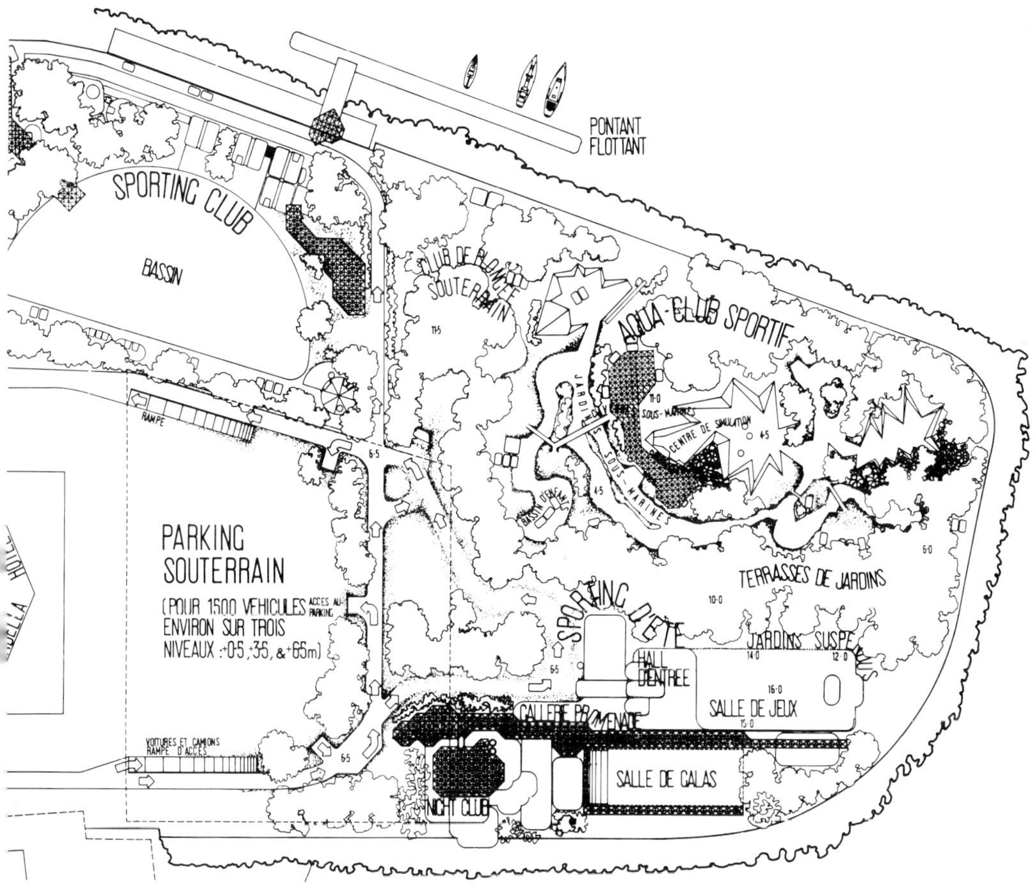

Monte Carlo 'Palm Tree' scheme 1971: Ron Herron, Ken Allinson, Colin Fournier (left) site plan, (below) elevation

Ve designed the two versions, one with the ymbol of the chameleon and one with the ymbol of the palm tree. The chameleon re- resenting the notion of frequent change of tmosphere and the palm tree calling atten- ion to the slightly unreal atmosphere of a elect club out on a flat promontory out in the Mediterranean. In both schemes the mounding and softening of natural landscape and designed elements and mechanized elements was at once obvious and – on second glance – ambiguous. These schemes represent a continuation of the Bournemouth Steps thinking but are perhaps simpler and more gentle.

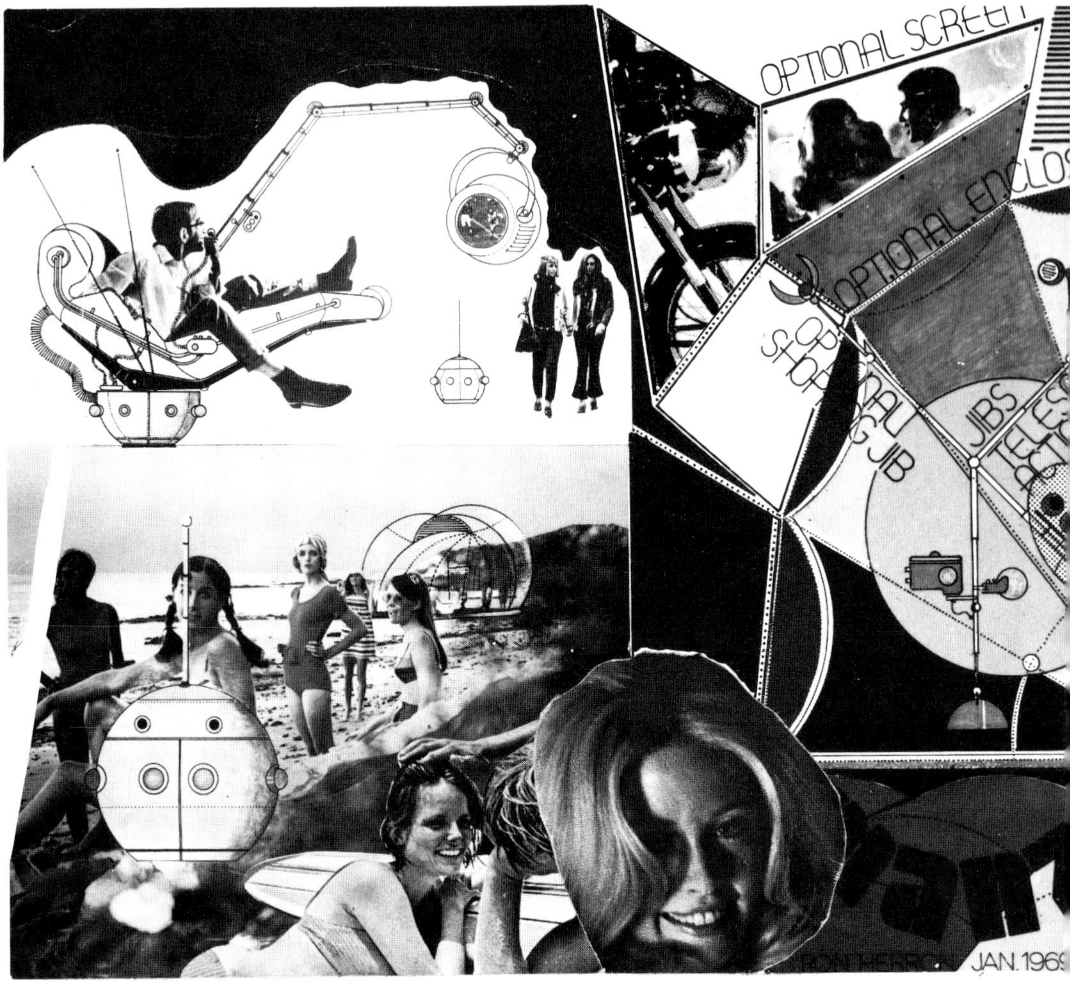

Manzak and Electronic Tomato

Ron Herron, Warren Chalk, David Greene

Tired of supermarket shopping? Is it becoming a nightmare – up and down narrow aisles between high walls of brand name uniformity, with the lights glaring down and canned music boring in, as you search desperately for one can of Cream of Mushroom where every label reads Tomato? Then you haven't heard of MANZAK or the ELECTRONIC TOMATO.

MANZAK is our latest idea for a radio-controlled, battery-powered electric automation. It has on board logic, optical range finder, TV camera, and magic eye bump detectors. All the sensory equipment you need for environmental information retrieval and for performing tasks.

Direct your business operations, do the shopping, hunt or fish, or just enjoy electronic instamatic voyeurism, from the comfort of your own home.

For the great indoors, get instant vegetable therapy, from the new ELECTRONIC TOMATO – a groove gizmo that connects to every nerve end to give you the wildest buzz.

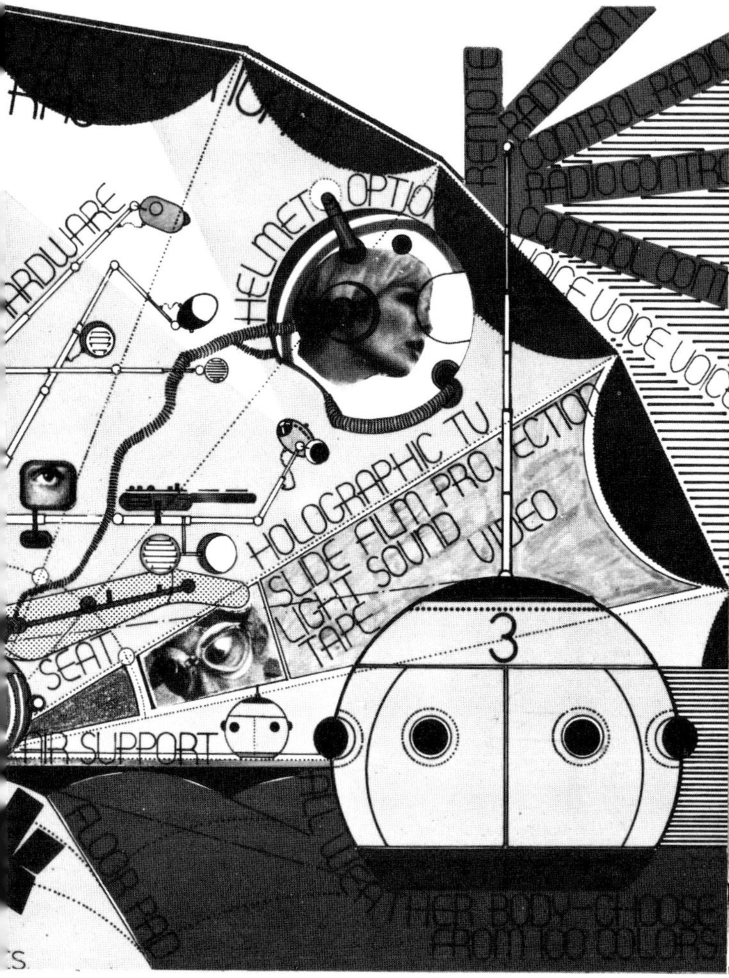

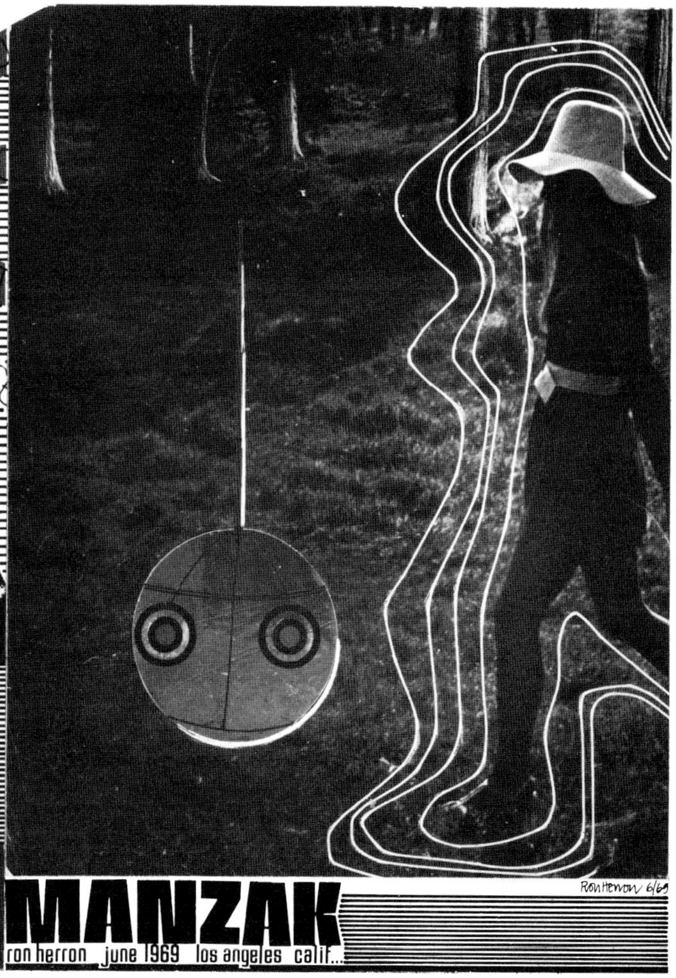

Manzak' Robot: Collage: 1969 Ron Herron

ight Bathamatic 1970 Warren Chalk

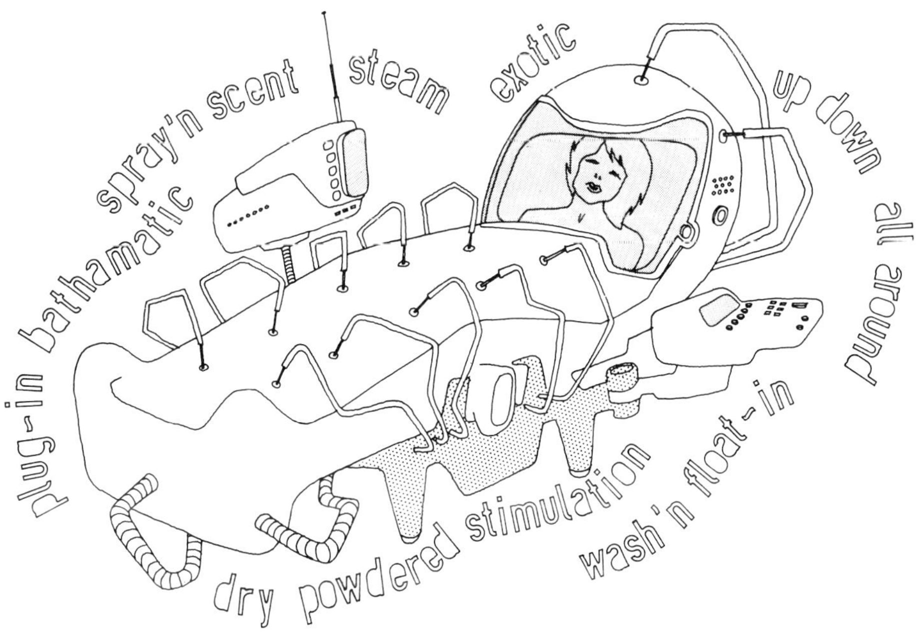

ft 'Electronic Tomato' 1969 Warren Chalk and avid Greene

The Metamorphosis of an English town 1970 Peter Cook

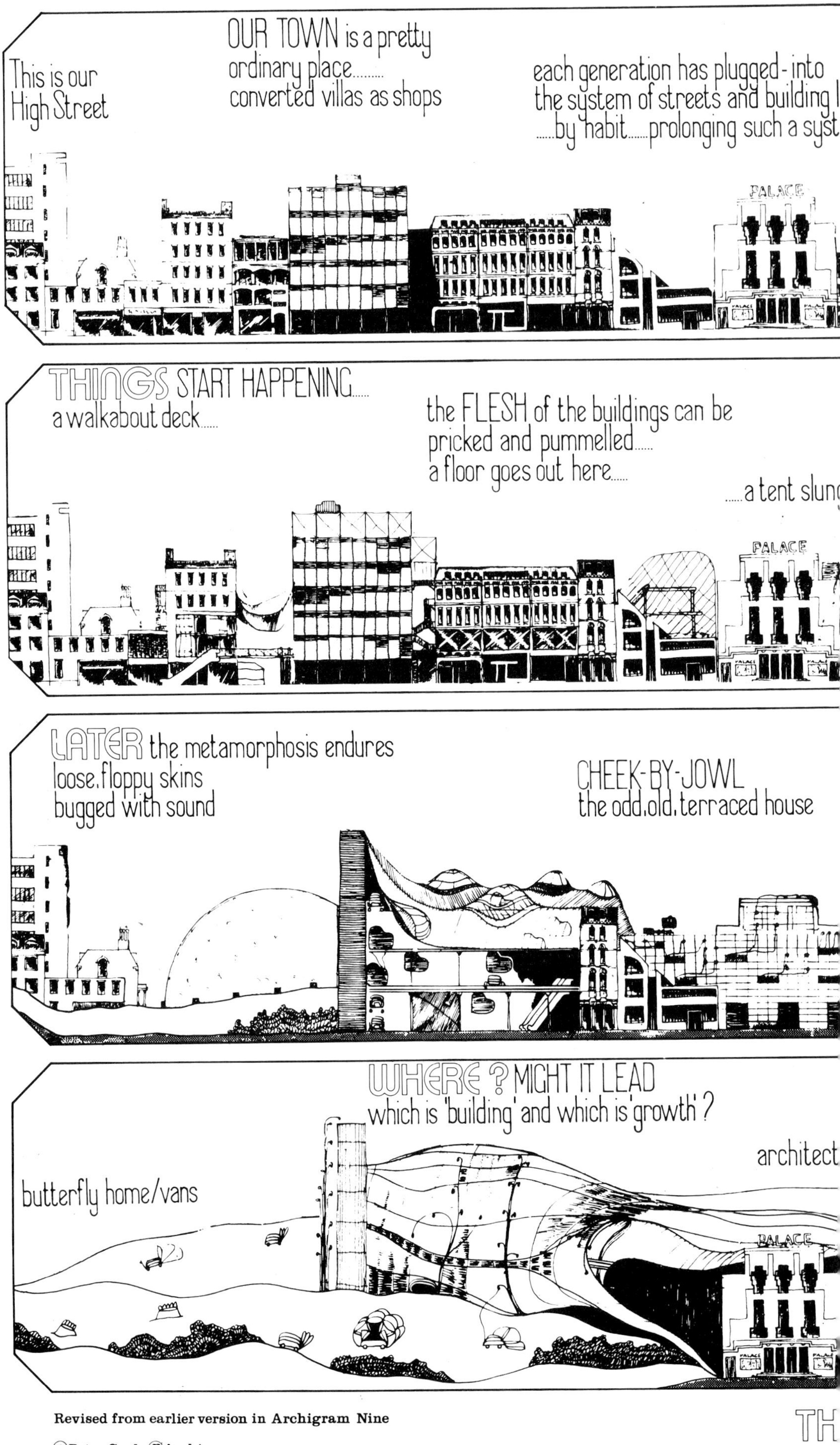

This is our High Street
OUR TOWN is a pretty ordinary place......... converted villas as shops
each generation has plugged-into the system of streets and building l ......by habit......prolonging such a syst
PALACE
THINGS START HAPPENING......
a walkabout deck......
the FLESH of the buildings can be pricked and pummelled...... a floor goes out here......
......a tent slun
PALACE
LATER the metamorphosis endures
loose,floppy skins bugged with sound
CHEEK-BY-JOWL the odd,old,terraced house
WHERE ? MIGHT IT LEAD
which is 'building' and which is 'growth' ?
architect
butterfly home/vans
PALACE
TH

Revised from earlier version in Archigram Nine

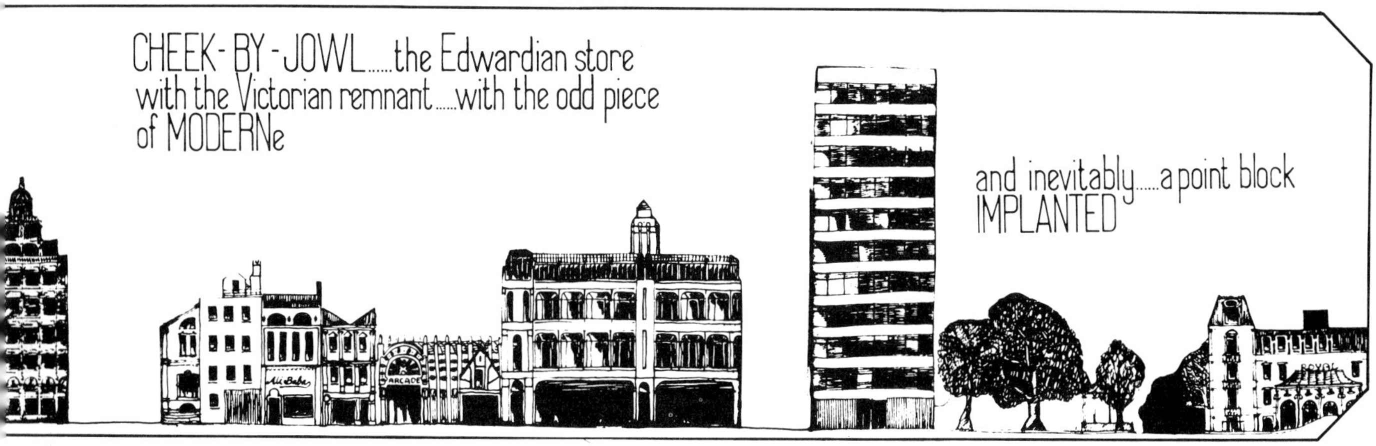

CHEEK-BY-JOWL......the Edwardian store
with the Victorian remnant......with the odd piece
of MODERNe
and inevitably......a point block
IMPLANTED

ARCHITECTURE AS AN OPTIONAL EXTRA
amongst many things......
the tower......now the perch for
the quaint......the individualist
space

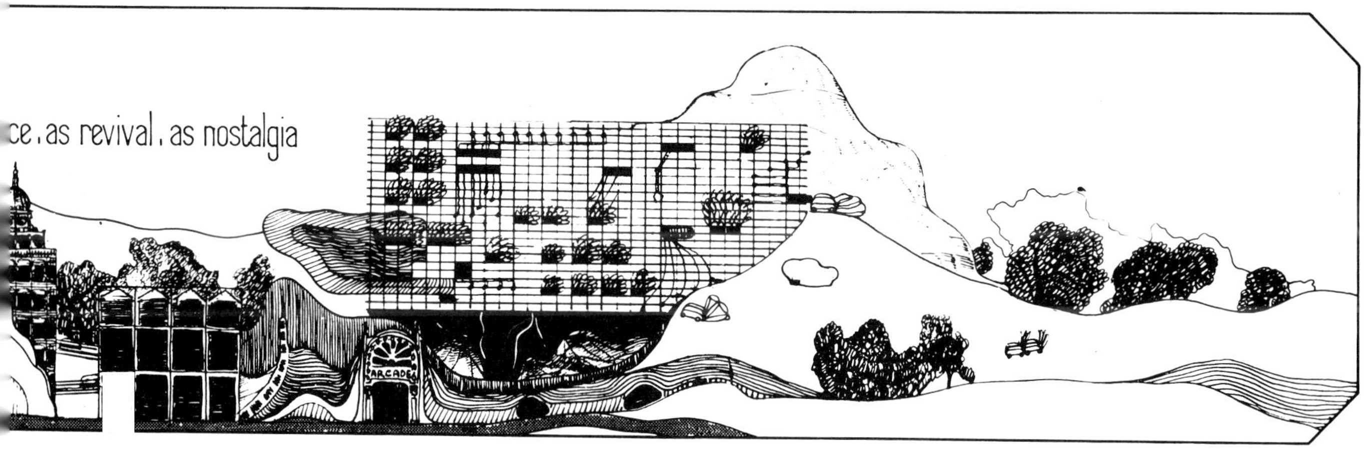

MORPHOSIS OF OUR TOWN .... IT HAPPENED CHEEK-BY-JOWL

Dreams Come True 1970 Mike Webb (left) Sample plate (right) fold out

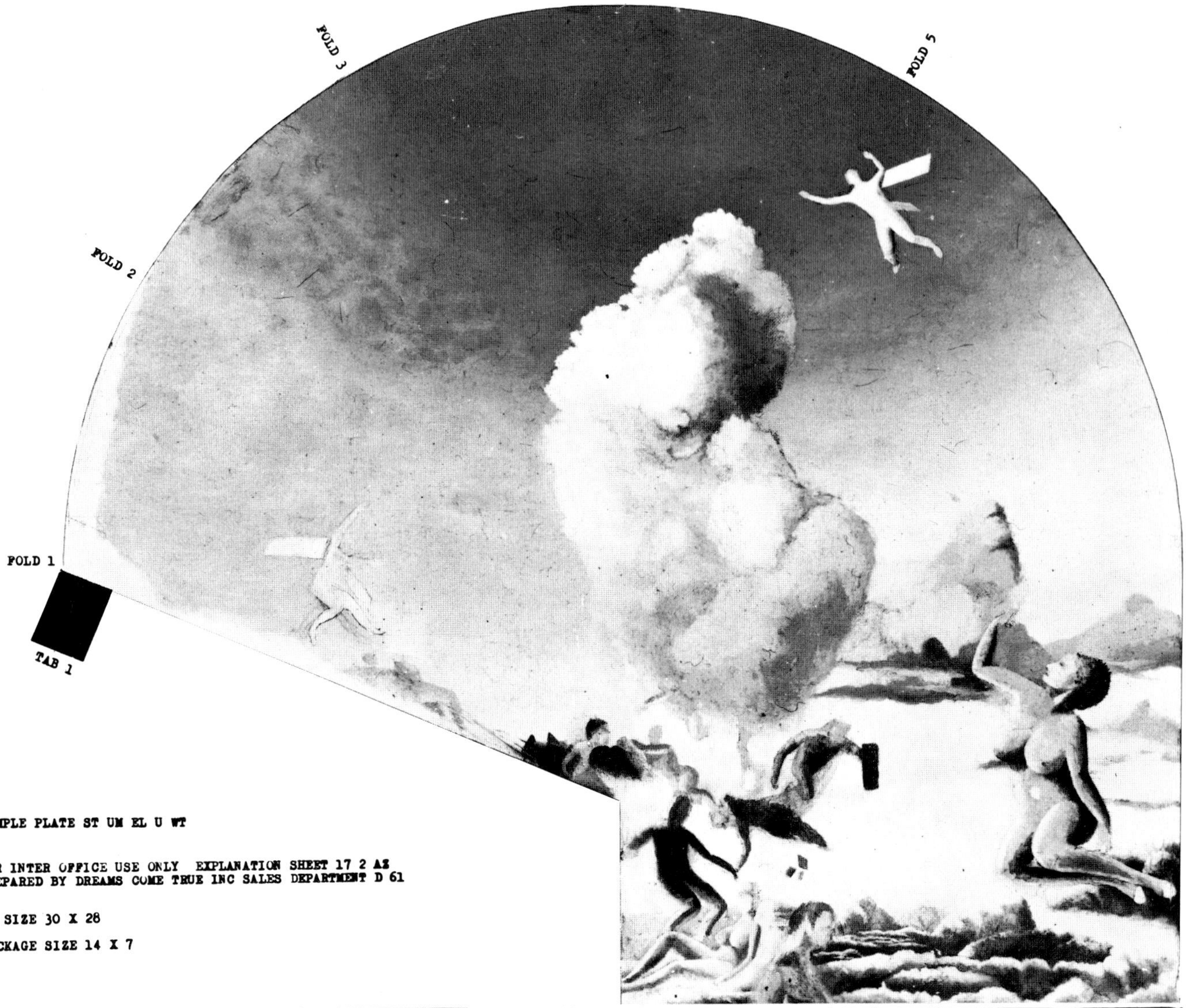

SAMPLE PLATE ST UM EL U WT

FOR INTER OFFICE USE ONLY EXPLANATION SHEET 17 2 AZ
PREPARED BY DREAMS COME TRUE INC SALES DEPARTMENT D 61

OA SIZE 30 X 28

PACKAGE SIZE 14 X 7

The Park
Norton.

Dear Sirs

I read with consumate interest your spell binding literature about changing lifestyles.

I have at the moment an old lifestyle which I would like to trade in for a new model it consists largely of a suburban ranch house + ideal family. Due to the long time that I have had this style I am pissed off and so is my wife who spends all morning screwing our epileptic postman.

Please forward under plain cover your Bum Pak with hippie-extras

I wait in anticipation,

D. Greene.

THE FOLLOWING IS A PRINT OUT OF THE OPTIONS CHOSEN BY RECIPIENT

		HARDWARE NEEDED	
WORK 70	OFFERS 12 MONTH CONTINUATIO OF PRES EMPLOYM THEN NON CENTRALISED MIN EMPLOY USE OF COMM CEN NETWORK	TRAD OPTIONS MOBILE ANTENNAED WORK UNIT + LINK OFFICE ORIFICE	MU 6 2X1
LEISURE 44	3 WEEKS IN THE BAHAMAS HOTEL STYLE ACCOMO	TRAD OPTIONS DAEANESCENT SUIT	DX 4
LEISURE 06	2 WEEKS CAMPING GAS PUMP TOTEM RECHARGE		
LEARNING D3	EDUCATION SYST RELATED TO WORK TYPE BI WEEKLY SEMINARS IN SEMBOX	MOBILE LEARNBOX	ML1
FOOD SUPPLY 4E	WISPACOPTER FOOD DELIV AND PREPARATION	LINK ORIFICE + CC TELEPHONE	ZZ3 XP 1
WASTE PROD 3F REMOVAL	WISPACOPTER CONTAINERISED WAST PROD REMOVAL	LINK ORIFICE + CC TELEPHONE	ZZ4 XP1
DWELLING Z5	NOSTALGIBOX DAMASK THICK RUGS AND BRIC-A BRAC	NOSTALGIBOX + LINK ORIFICE + LINK ORIFICE + LINK ORIFICE	NB2 ZZ3 ZZ4 ZX1
DWELLING 2N	MOBILE 3D CLOUD HOUSE WISPACOPTER ADAPTORS	CLOUD HOUSE + LINK ORIFICE	

DREAMS COME TRUE INC
EXPLANATORY SHEET D4 1

PREPARED BY DREAMS COME TRUE
SALES DEPARTMENT 29 A

SHEET 48 of 84 SHEETS
FOR INTER OFFICE USE ONLY

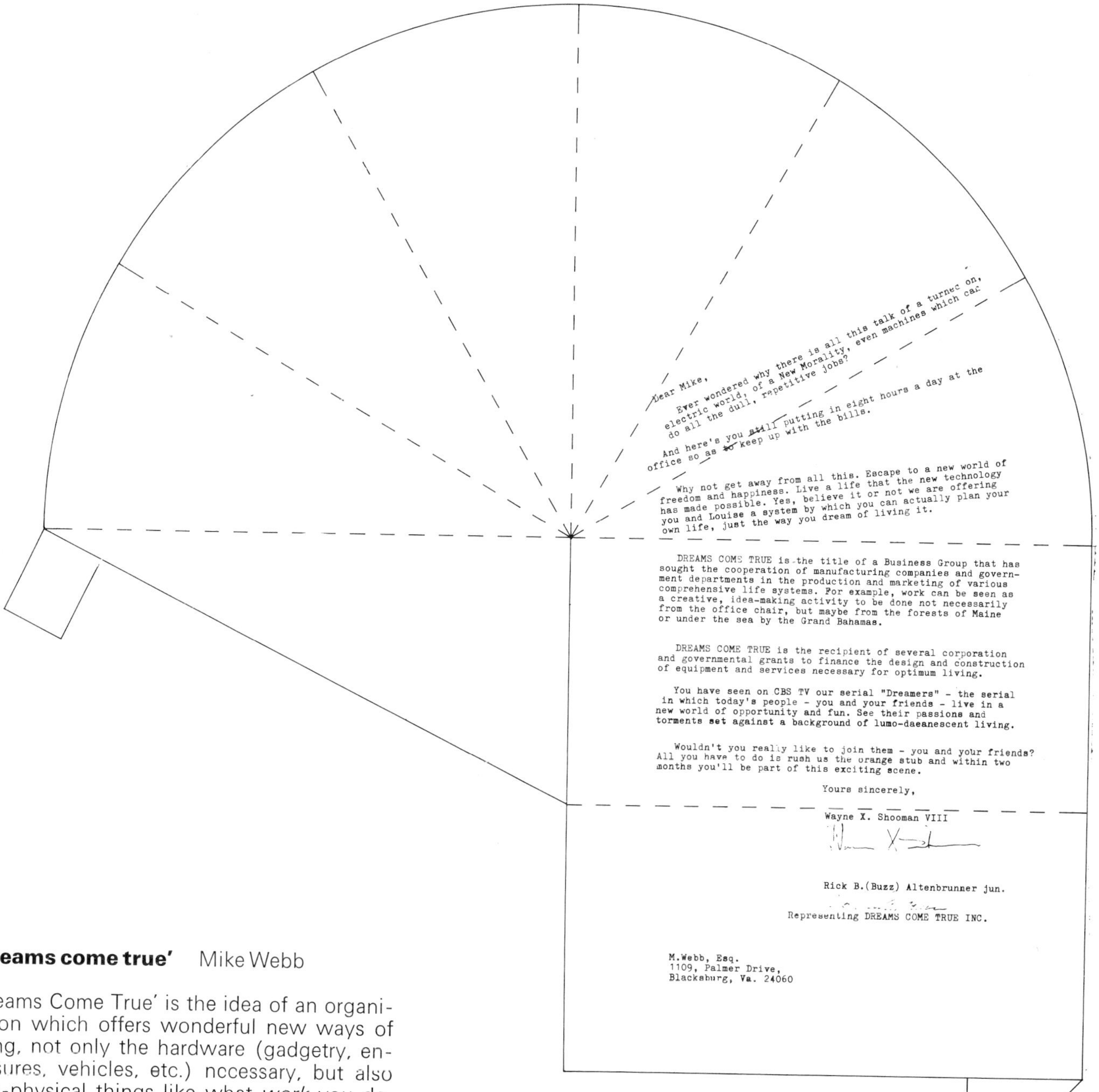

Dear Mike,

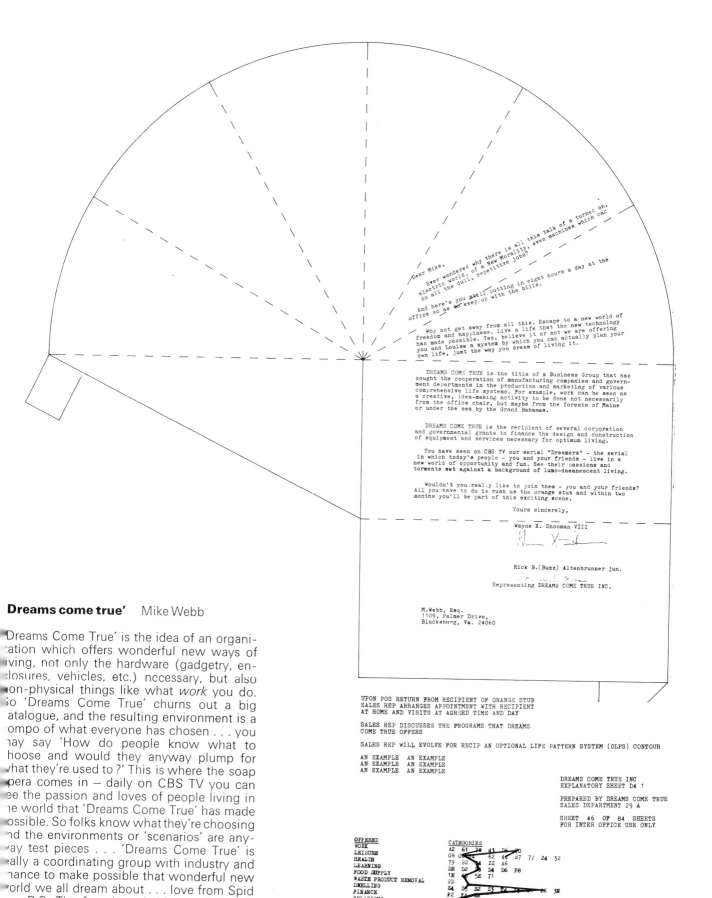

Ever wondered why there is all this talk of a turned on, electric world, of a New Morality, even machines which can do all the dull, repetitive jobs?

And here's you ~~still~~ putting in eight hours a day at the office so as ~~to~~ keep up with the bills.

Why not get away from all this. Escape to a new world of freedom and happiness. Live a life that the new technology has made possible. Yes, believe it or not we are offering you and Louise a system by which you can actually plan your own life, just the way you dream of living it.

DREAMS COME TRUE is the title of a Business Group that has sought the cooperation of manufacturing companies and government departments in the production and marketing of various comprehensive life systems. For example, work can be seen as a creative, idea-making activity to be done not necessarily from the office chair, but maybe from the forests of Maine or under the sea by the Grand Bahamas.

DREAMS COME TRUE is the recipient of several corporation and governmental grants to finance the design and construction of equipment and services necessary for optimum living.

You have seen on CBS TV our serial "Dreamers" - the serial in which today's people - you and your friends - live in a new world of opportunity and fun. See their passions and torments set against a background of lumo-daeanescent living.

Wouldn't you really like to join them - you and your friends? All you have to do is rush us the orange stub and within two months you'll be part of this exciting scene.

Yours sincerely,

Wayne X. Shooman VIII

Rick B.(Buzz) Altenbrunner jun.

Representing DREAMS COME TRUE INC.

M.Webb, Esq.
1109, Palmer Drive,
Blacksburg, Va. 24060

Dreams come true' Mike Webb

'Dreams Come True' is the idea of an organi-
ation which offers wonderful new ways of
ving, not only the hardware (gadgetry, en-
losures, vehicles, etc.) nccessary, but also
on-physical things like what *work* you do.
o 'Dreams Come True' churns out a big
atalogue, and the resulting environment is a
ompo of what everyone has chosen . . . you
ay say 'How do people know what to
hoose and would they anyway plump for
hat they're used to?' This is where the soap
pera comes in – daily on CBS TV you can
ee the passion and loves of people living in
e world that 'Dreams Come True' has made
ossible. So folks know what they're choosing
d the environments or 'scenarios' are any-
ay test pieces . . . 'Dreams Come True' is
ally a coordinating group with industry and
ance to make possible that wonderful new
orld we all dream about . . . love from Spid
. . P.S. The fan-shaped thing and the oil
ainting show what oerndaspeodic living
n be like . . . and are both sides of the send
t.

UPON POS RETURN FROM RECIPIENT OF ORANGE STUB
SALES REP ARRANGES APPOINTMENT WITH RECIPIENT
AT HOME AND VISITS AT AGREED TIME AND DAY

SALES REP DISCUSSES THE PROGRAMS THAT DREAMS
COME TRUE OFFERS

SALES REP WILL EVOLVE FOR RECIP AN OPTIONAL LIFE PATTERN SYSTEM (OLPS) CONTOUR

AN EXAMPLE AN EXAMPLE
AN EXAMPLE AN EXAMPLE
AN EXAMPLE AN EXAMPLE

DREAMS COME TRUE INC
EXPLANATORY SHEET D4 1

PREPARED BY DREAMS COME TRUE
SALES DEPARTMENT 29 A

SHEET 46 OF 84 SHEETS
FOR INTER OFFICE USE ONLY

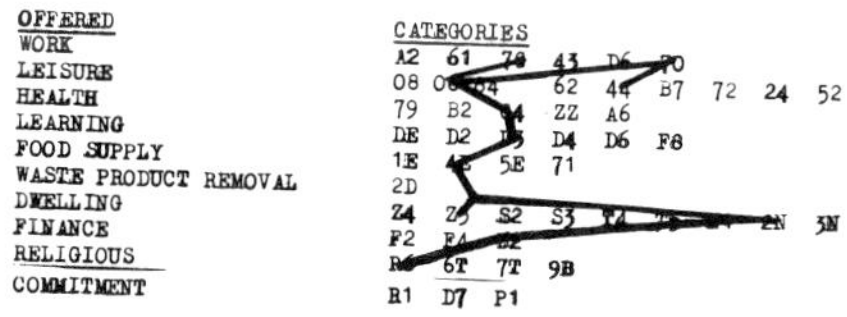

Enviro-Pill 1969 Ron Herron

Dream . . . Ron Herron

I had a holographic scene setter – a light space – switch on/walk around/3D/walk thro'/Hollywood Boulevard in my TV room/ Death Valley on my patio/Tahiti in my pad/ Laurel and Hardy in the morning/The 'Who' at night . . . change film – new environment/ switch on/off/there – not there . . . what's real/it's observable/it's real when it's there/is

Room of 1000 Delights 1970
Peter Cook

Holographic Scene-Setter 1969
Ron Herron

it a dream? – a ghost? – a turn-on? . . . Holographic ceiling – cloud – rainbow – cloud – people – John (pee on your shoes) – scenery – event – television . . . great . . . switch on the people/turn on the crowd/ bring in the whole scene . . . turn off the ceiling.

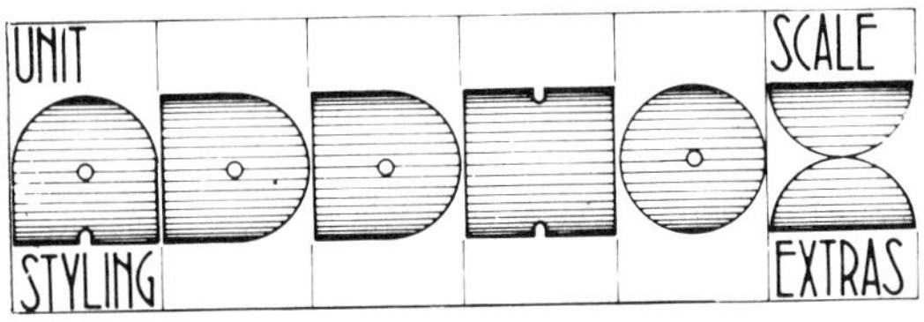

'Addhox' 1971 Peter Cook
right a suburban sequence
below and far bottom right typical 'Addhox' elements

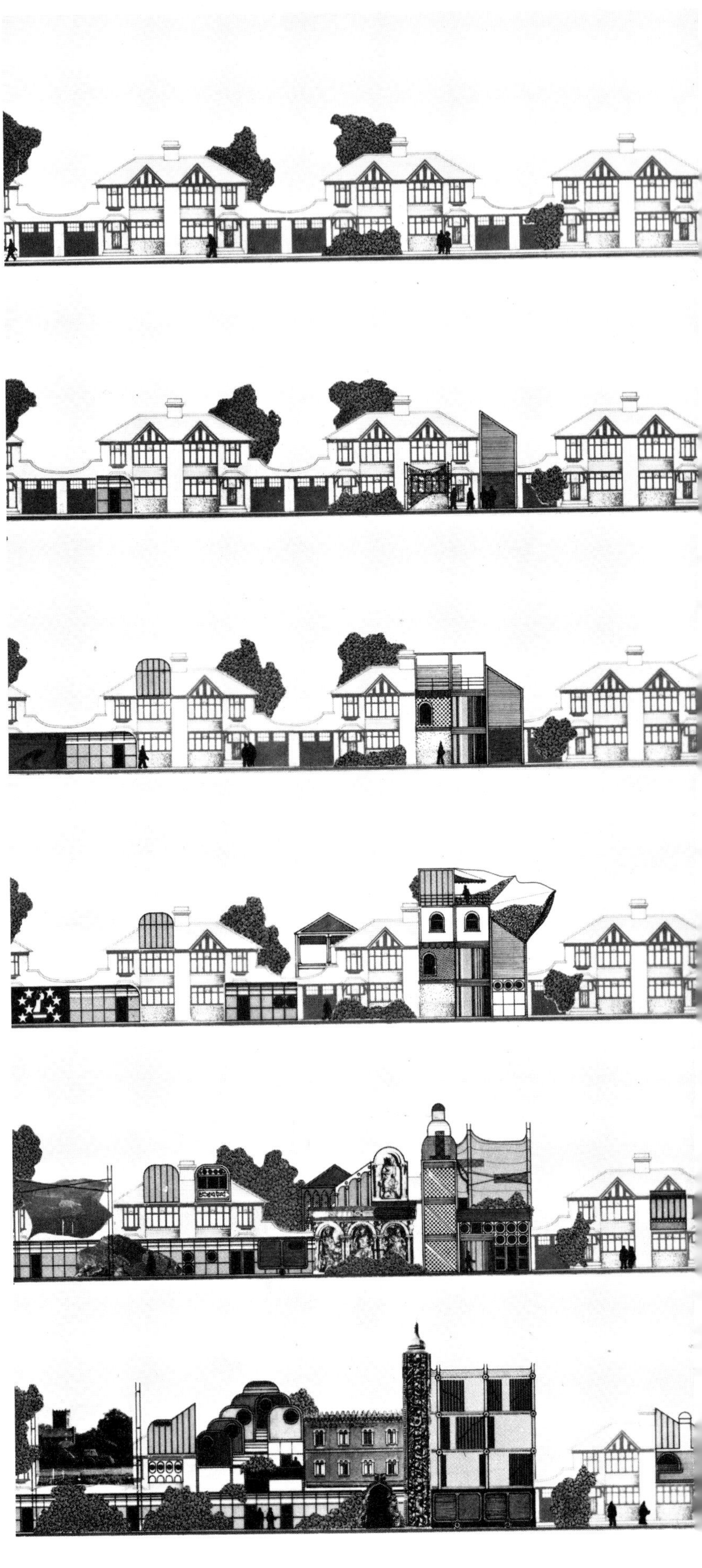

Addhox Peter Cook

The typical English suburban avenue could evolve into quite a different environment by the introduction of simple elements of a very wide range. They could be bought over the counter as components, and allow for a high degree of 'do-it-yourself' involvement. The styling is wide open: it can be bolted-in, and 'Gothic', 'Bauhaus', 'Pop-Art' – or off-the-cuff aesthetics are interchangeable.

The development is totally random, *ad-hoc,* and one option (as with the house second from the right) is to do nothing at all.

The kit suggested ranges from 'building' elements such as room-boxes that can replace a bay window, loose structuring of pylons that can be infilled with anything from canvas tenting to panels, to purely decorative screening that is hung out in the back garden: you can be looking at the Swiss Alps rather than Mrs Jone's washing. The caravan-as-satellite-as-room, the clip-on rooftop garden and a whole host of earlier Archigram ideas are here offered in a simple way.

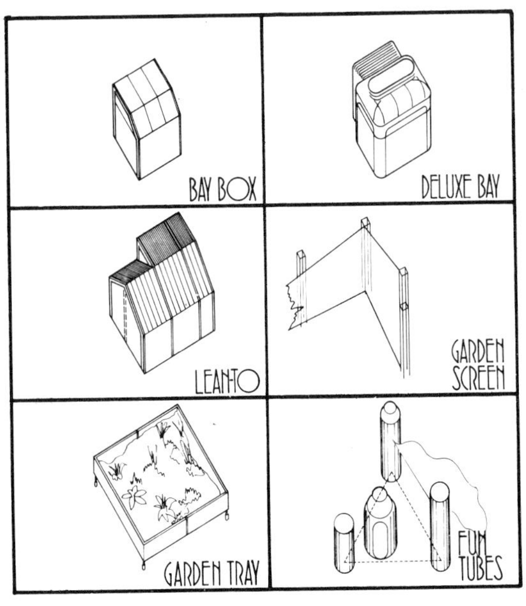

below 'Addhox' applied to Notting Hill: cheap development of a street-corner for an underprivileged situation

right 'Addhox' in the Hedgerow Village (see next page): 1972 Peter Cook

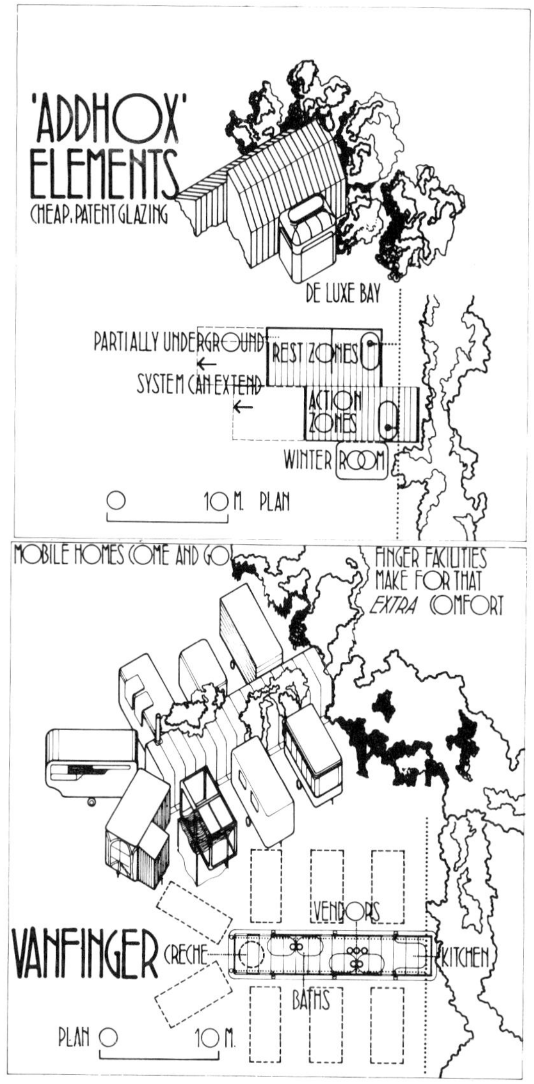

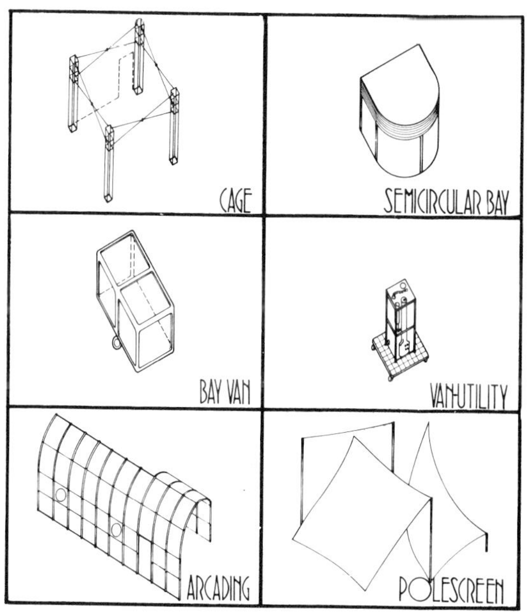

PEEPING FROM THE TREES. CONCEALED UNDERGROUND. OR EXPLICIT !
no dividing line between home in a paper sleeping bag and the sophistication of the Farnsworth House : between one night and ten years : give the edge of a field service lines....under discreet outlets....and let it happen

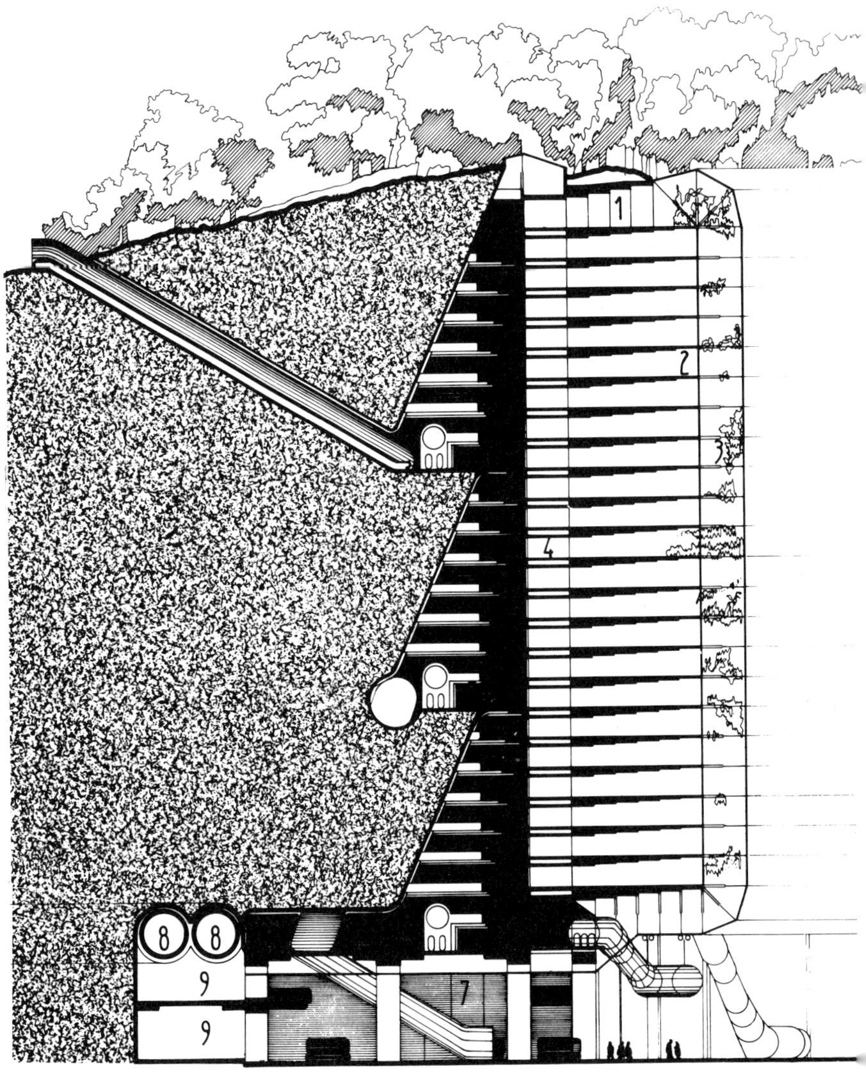

Crater city and hedgerow village

Peter Cook

The crater city and the hedgerow village are two parts of a strategy for the hinterland to the new Foulness Airport. Instead of building an 'airport city' we propose to provide either of two extreme suburb types. The 'crater city' would be virtually a hotel for 16,000 people, with carpeted corridors and a very high level of servicing, air-conditioned apartments. It would have an outer wall which is a conservatory so that in summer the apartment would become one third bigger and in winter the two skins that sandwich the conservatory would insulate the apartment. The 'crater city' looks inward on to a large impeccably mown lawn a third of a mile across. This whole city is a circular crater and the outside of the circle is earth-banked up like a prehistoric mound with a ring of trees planted on the top. Nothing would be seen except this hill with trees.

The hedgerow village, by contrast, is a surreptitious development which is progressively fed into narrow strips alongside large fields. Each village would be imperceptible from the country lane. Each village would permit the implanting of a very wide range of dwelling types from 'architected' houses to wayfarers with sleeping bags and spanning through lean-tos, inflatable tents, caravans, etc., a deliberately relaxed and ramshackle combination/conglomeration.

left Hedgerow village

below left Section through crater city

right Plan of crater city apartments

below Typical Essex countryside with hedgerow villages and craters

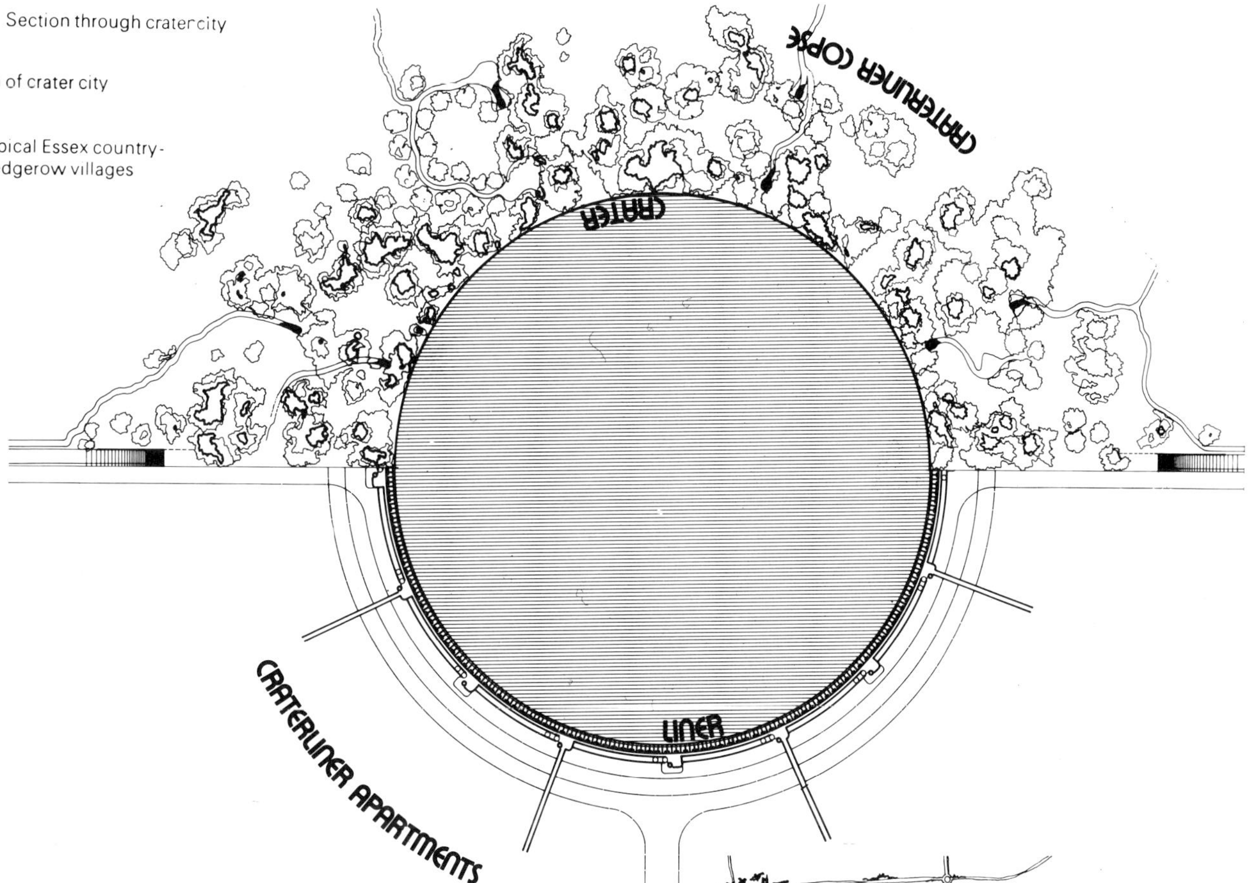

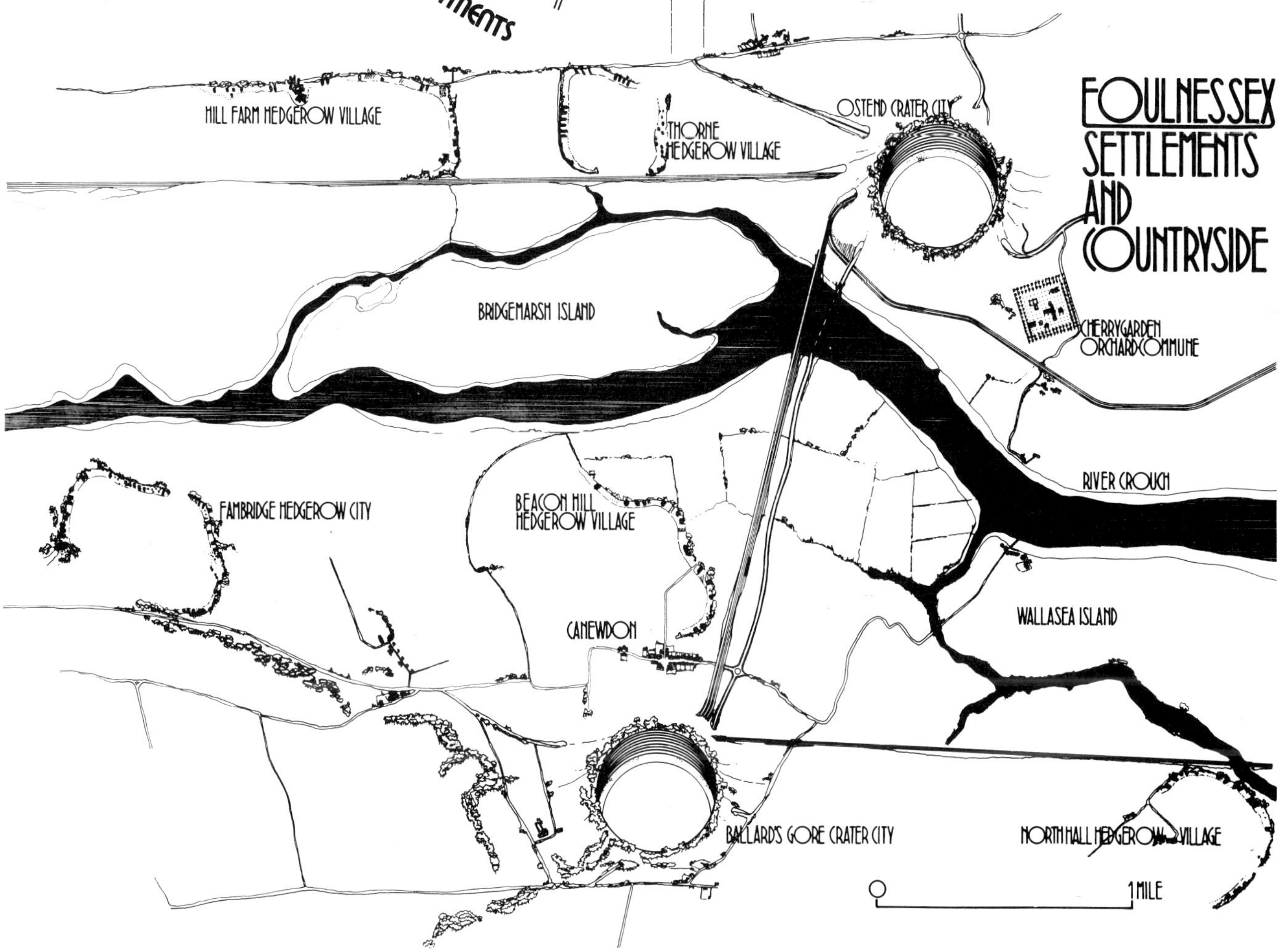

It's a......
1972 Ron Herron

It's a . . .

Shit – The Label's come off. The sign's down. What is it – it was a conference arena last May / a tuned for sound concert happened for three days in August/September it was full of guys and their birds cooking, eating, sleeping, fooling around, and generally living the good life / last week it was full of people, cars and the painful scream of stripduster, houndog and the Chrysler rail as they belted down the quarter mile straight-burn out for grabs / tomorrow it's a . . .

Let's leave the label off for Christsake – let the sheep back in – the grass needs cutting.

Hang on though – we don't want to upset the sheep – let's put the old label up – for today it's a meadow . . . what's in a label anyway? The action comes and goes. The servicing goes too, on your back, in your car, on your truck, in your trailer, in your minds. The architecture of the invisible. What's in a label anyway? It's a . . .

Take the label off a can of beans and what have you got – a can of beans. Take the label off a can of soup and put the beans label on it, and what have you got – a can of beans? No . . . A can of soup. Space and time and servicing condition use and activity – labels condition nothing but your mind.

"It's a poor sort of memory that only works backwards," the Queen remarked.' (*Through the Looking Glass.*)
The Failure of the Modern Movement to establish an architectural language for public buildings is a reflection of a much wider confusion of what public life is about.' (Quote from *RIBA Journal.*)

FLASH!
A select committee will be set up to study the potential architectural language for . . . public baths – public houses – public conveniences, etc., etc. . . . yeah, I'm widely confused – what is public life about anyway, and what's architectural language? . . . You can always put a label on a building . . . you can have a label so that when people arrive they know what they're in for, you could even better that, you could have a taped description – like they have in front of the cages in the zoo . . . but then the animals don't know what they're in for.

'The Metropolis today is a classroom; the ads are its teachers.'
The traditional classroom is an obsolete detention home, a feudal dungeon.' (Marshall McLuhan *Counterblast.*)

It's not a university – it can't be . . . show me, where's the building, where's the label? I have to sit in the comfort of my own home with the telly or radio on to be a part of it, with an occasional chat with my tutor in the local drill hall. That's not a university, a university is a lot of buildings and a lot of people milling around on bicycles . . . come on. The Open University asks that you are 21 (pity, why not 16?) or over and have the energy to fill in the application form. Of course there is a mandatory one week residential summer school session for the 25,000 undergraduates – surely this will take place in an enclosure of some description and give, for a week at least, some physical manifestation of university. But supposing some nut puts it under canvas, paper sleeping bags, pnu's or the like . . . it's a?

'By side-stepping the mammoth cost of establishing a residential program, the British have managed to hold the capital budget for Open U's first five years of operation to only $14.4 million – most of which will be devoted to the construction of the University Center in Buckinghamshire, 50 miles outside London.' (*Newsweek*, Jan. 25, 1971.)

There we go, I knew there would be some physical manifestation of university, a piece of architecture on to which we can hang the label – university. Hold on, though, it's an administrative centre – no students, no caps and gowns, no students union, no colleges and no halls of residence. We can't attach the label . . . and what about the architectural language what is an administrative centre in terms of the Open U, the invisible university . . . program / input / control / storage / processing / output . . . it's a?

People promote activity – activity conditions use – servicing responds to activity +use – time conditions all – there today gone tomorrow.

'On the *QE2* you can be totally inaccessible to the rest of the world. Or, if you prefer, the ship's telex, telephone, telegram and picture transmission service are at your disposal 24 hours a day. Lift the 'phone, and shorthand typists, dictaphones, conference rooms, recording facilities, film and slide projectors, screens, blackboards and printers, are all yours. Let us know and we'll even arrange simultaneous translation equipment for you.'

Is it an administrative centre? A university? Government centre? . . . A ship? . . . It's a?

'After work – or instead of it – *QE2* offers you a West End sized cinema, with three performances a day. Plus night clubs, the theatre bar, card rooms, libraries and four swimming pools. Not to mention sports decks, a turkish bath, sauna and gambling casino.'

Is it an entertainment centre? Soho? The Strip? . . . A ship? . . . it's a?

Sit and play cards – it's a cardroom? Call up a projector – it's a cinema? Drink with your friends – it's a bar? Sit at a typewriter – it's an office? Soak up information – it's education? . . . or wrap these up and it's an enclosure . . . label the monument and it's architecture?

Goodyear has put eye-popping colour and cartoons in the sky and they call it 'Super Skytacular' night sign Columbia – more than 7000 lights are mounted on the side of the company's airship, the *Columbia*. The lights spell out messages and animated cartoons in colour. The sign screen, on either side of the ship, is 105 feet long by 24.5 feet high. A typical six-minute tape consists of 40 million bits of 'on-off' information which, when run through electronic readers aboard the ship, control lamp and colour selection and the speed at which messages are run. It's an airship? It's an educational tool? It's entertaining – it's that, it's instant information . . . it's a?

Ron Herron

Touch not

Warren Chalk

Touch not the shoulder of the knight who passes. He would turn and it will be night, a night without stars, without arc or clouds. What then became of all that makes the sky, the moon in its passage and the sound of the sun? You would have to wait until a second knight as powerful as the first consented to pass. On such an expectancy rests a large part of the fantasy in science fiction. The coexistence of interlinked and separate notions, and the hazard, the improbable hazard of passing from one notion, from one set of ideas, to another and back again along the protracted time scale of the now.

To the silent awareness the skinny cat is all cat, the very essence of cat. Its sneaky feline motions are of a piece, speaking directly to the consciousness in soundless tones of all that cat means, of cat in past, present, future. The eternal cat. And even buildings, they have less to say than cats, but they communicate. They almost turn themselves inside out in their eagerness to share secrets. They tell of the men that made them, the beings that dwell in them. They portray a whole history of architecture, but without words, without discourse.

We seem to have found the art of suspended time. What we said ten years ago we are saying today, repeating the same recurrent episode, the same series of events as a stylus caught in the groove. What we must look for now is the linkage of the simultaneous and not the vista of the successive. A self scan display system reveals a discreet trauma, the glow on each side of the cathode transfers itself to the understanding that life systems are important, that they really matter. The seed packet in *Archigram 9* is available.* Great. The problem is discovering some fertile ground in which to plant these seeds. And beware of the creeping slugs. Apparently the path of events has been deflected from its original direction. We have discovered something – technological backlash. And bargain-hunters for tomorrow are reluctantly tuning down their electronic cycle environmental equipment of events. The electric last minute no longer thrills. But dare we face the source of our own negation? Could it be technocratic society? Everyone is too giddy to notice. Everyone? Well, not quite. The very sense men have of reality, the wisdom of insecurity, the search for the miraculous is still there.

Ecology – there, I've said that word – is a social problem. We have been told so by *Time*, *Life*, *Newsweek*, *Look* and the Nixon administration. Pollution is insidiously growing. Either the environment goes or we go. And you all know what will happen if the environment goes. We have produced a society with production for the sake of production. The city has become a market place, every human being a commodity. Nature is a resource. Human beings are a resource. Well. Our very survival depends on an ecological utopia, otherwise we will be destroyed.

This technological backlash we are experiencing must be fought with a more sophisticated technology, a more sophisticated science. Present beautiful chemistry has turned out as not so beautiful biology. But if we are to prevent eco-catastrophe it can only be done by more sophisticated environmental systems, not by dropping out. Nor the hippy type philosophy. Did you see Drop City in *Easy Rider*? Every man his own tree, an acre to till. Let's face it, total dispersal won't work economically any more than total centralization. Apart from being a head-in-the-sand attitude we need to fight technology, to produce David Greene's cybernetic forest. Too simplistic translations of technology average out people's lives. What we look for is technological play, so that individuals can create an even greater environmental stimulation. A person switched on to the Electronic Tomato, or the proud possessor of the personalized robot like Manzak, can extend an existing situation, and a new man/machine relationship be established getting people, through their extension with a machine, into action.

Experiments such as these could achieve a people-oriented technology of human liberation, directed towards pleasure, enjoyment, experimentation: a try-it-and-see attitude.

Synthetic environments are something different. Synthetic experience is not better or worse, just different, than that from the natural environment. But let's have it all. At Woodstock Music Festival you got both – a field turned on, a three-day city, half a million young people; the only hardware, mind-blowing amplification. Beautiful. On the brink of the seventies a whole new era can be seen to be opening up. Man has jumped up and down on the moon and in the streets. Students have laid down at Woodstock and Hyde Park and on campus. Some, unfortunately, for the last time. Among all the conflicting ideas, all these divergent opinions none seems more important at this time than creating a humane environment. Life systems, trees, plants, flowers, animals, birds and man himself, are fantastically responsive mechanisms. Mechanical systems, including the goop and ticky-tacky with which we construct the man-made environment, have always been less so; with little ability to respond. But our search for adaptive systems should have a prime objective, to produce an environment to which the ordinary individual at any level of intensity can reconcile himself without the intolerable effort and stress of his own mental and physical adaptation. We must continue to try to establish appropriate systems for a natural relationship between life systems and mechanical systems. Hopefully some environmental magic will then prevail and we will again think up the impossible in order to be realistic.

*A packet of seeds was inserted in each copy of *Archigram 9*

The Urban Mark – A Study of Disintegration And Metamorphosis 1972 Peter Cook

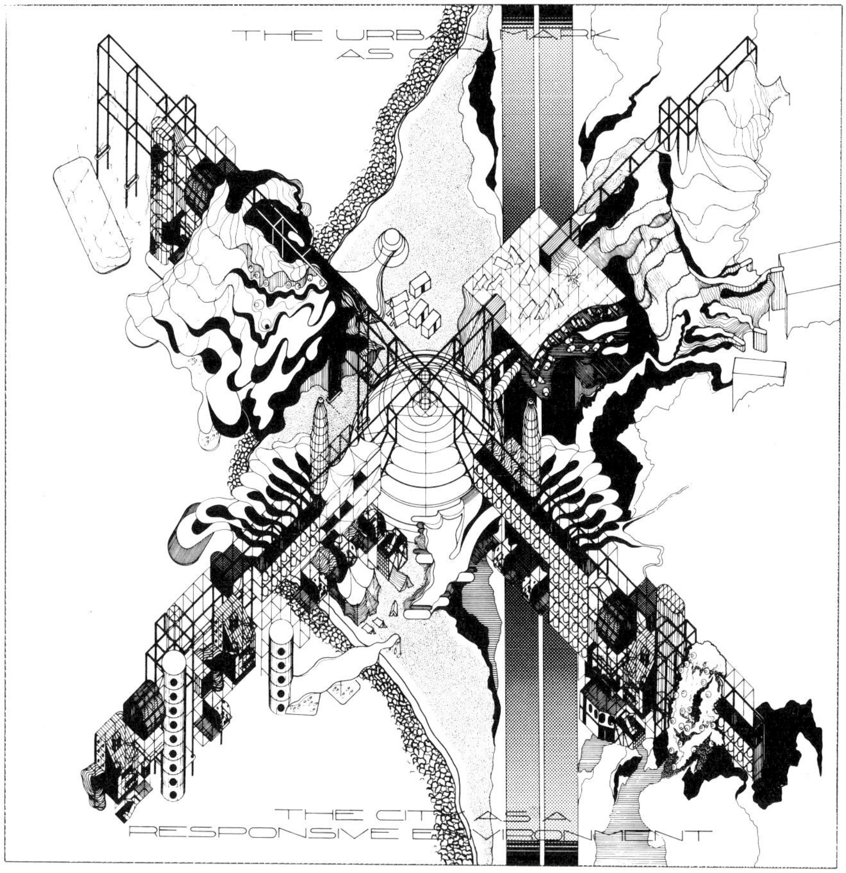

right 2nd stage from a set of nine stages

below 3rd stage
The banal and the sophisticated together changing

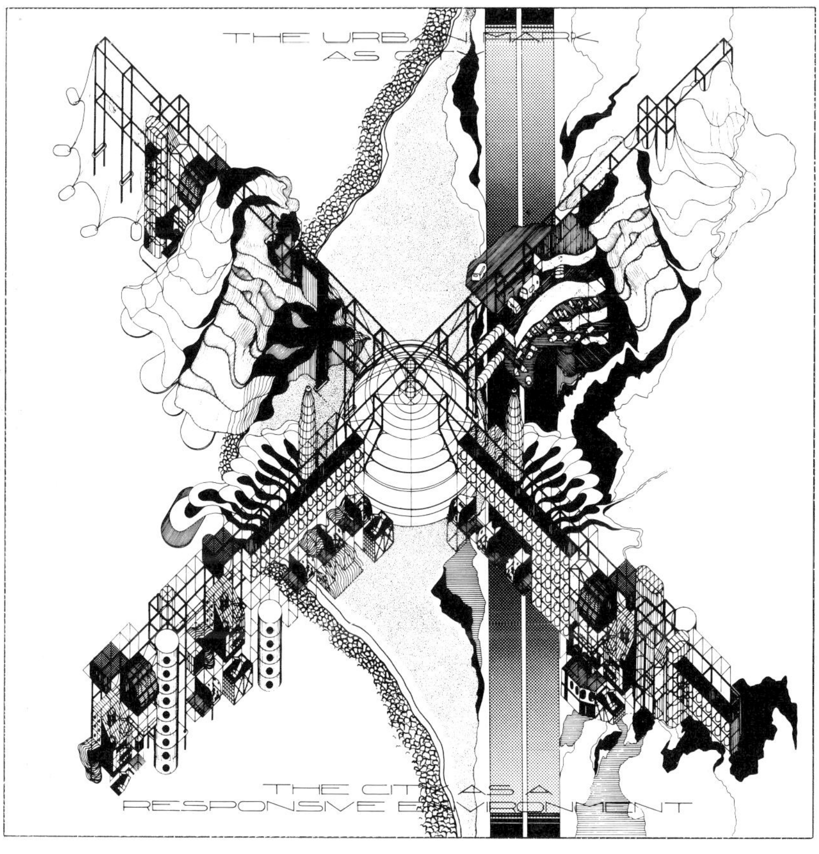

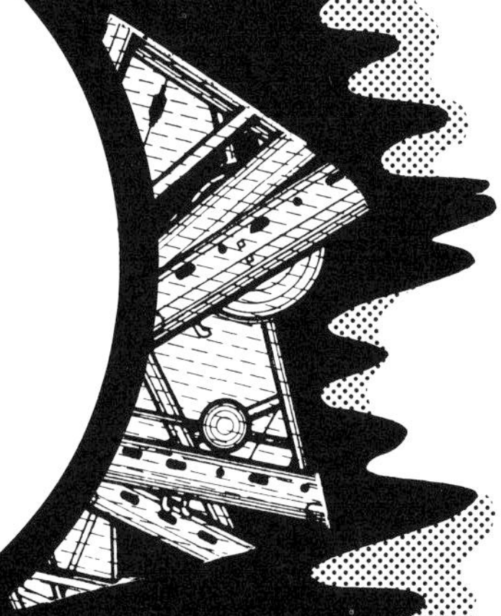

Warren Chalk

Born in London in 1927. During his early years at Manchester Art College, he was torn between painting and architecture. The most abrasive and critical of the Archigram Group, his doubts and dissatisfaction with the obvious and the banal have many times been justified by subsequent events. Writes frequently in *Architectural Design* on a variety of topics, often based upon a re-observation of the myths and curiosities of our culture, where this can give a clue to alternatives to the obvious and the banal.

Peter Cook

Born in Southend on Sea in 1936. The most talkative and 'public' member of the group. Enjoys inventing situations and very much enjoys forming analogies between the quirks and experiences of individual people and possibilities for the environment that are ambiguous and unexpected. Preoccupied by the idea of 'Metamorphosis'. Enjoys drawing illustrations of these analogies and metamorphoses rather than writing about them.

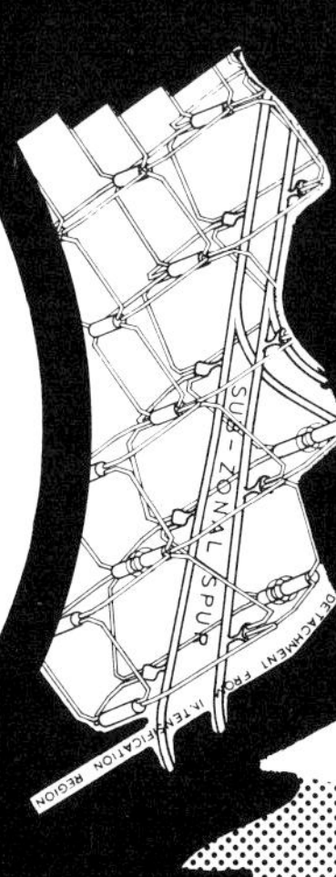

Dennis Crompton

Born in Blackpool in 1935. Conspicuously in charge of all the technical matters that form part of Archigram's output. The inventor of the 'things that go bang in the night'. An enthusiast on gadgets, machines, techniques and systems. The most practical member of the group who has nevertheless been known to flip completely when confronted with the opportunity to make a bigger and better and more bang-in-the-night apparatus.

David Greene

Born in Nottingham in 1937. The poet of the group. His enthusiasm (as in Chapter 12) for gardening and growths is no fashionable move, more a gradual extension of the mode of his thinking which goes right back to the 'Story of a Thing' in 1963. Sometimes contemplative, sometimes fatalist, he reacts to these moods in a positive way: writing or inventing something that often has reference to the existing world, contrived in an original way. Concerned with conceptual art and therefore with conceptual possibilities of architecture.

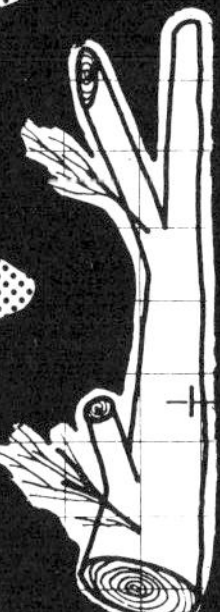

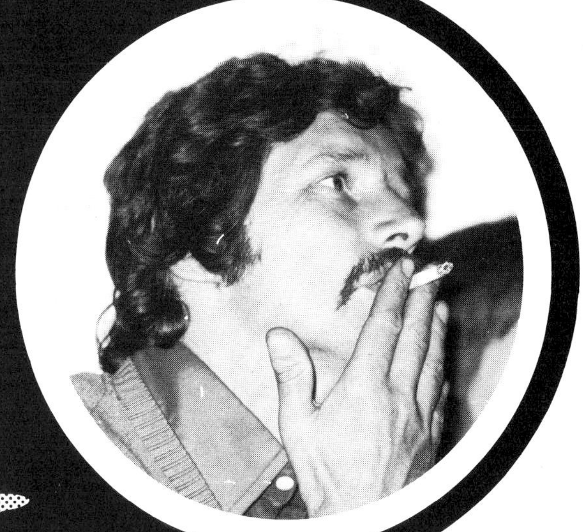

Ron Herron

Born in London in 1930. Draws like a dream . . . apparently effortlessly. Doesn't enjoy superfluous chat but does enjoy cheerful situations. Always sees good in people and situations. An optimist who cannot see why everyone makes such a hassel over everything. Observes quietly . . . and then synthesises it all through a project. Beyond this all, not as uncomplicated as he may seem, on the odd occasion when he does really dig his heels in on an issue, he is the toughest and least transigent of the lot.

Mike Webb

Born in Henley on Thames in 1937. Has for some considerable time been living in the United States of America, and so is in a sense a 'corresponding' member of the Group. Nevertheless, his airmail relationship (and occasional head-to-head sessions) with the London part of the group is a very necessary part of its thinking and the total effort. Always something of a loner, he too feels the pull and the necessity of the total Archigram effort.

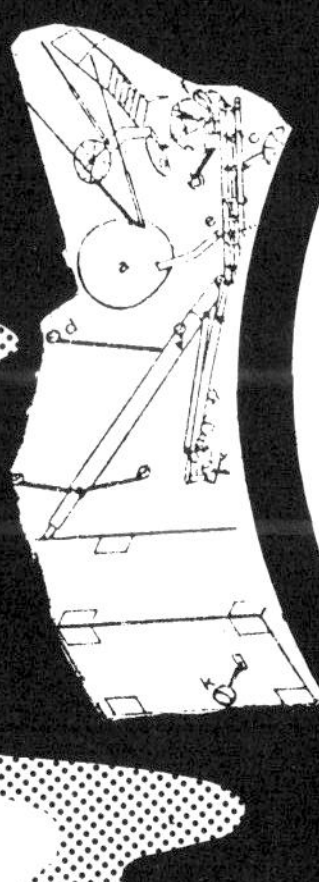

Chronology

Projects realized are indicated thus ***

Pre-1961 **Warren Chalk**
Shoreditch Secondary Modern School, London*** LCC 1956–7
(with Ron Herron) Paisley Technical College Competition (second prize) 1957
(with Ron Herron) Enfield Civic Centre Competition, 1958
Clapham County College for Girls, London*** LCC 1958
Hall of Residence and Fire Station, Chelsea, London*** LCC 1958
(with Ron Herron) Halesowen Housing Competition (second prize) 1959 **11**
(with Ron Herron) 'Sunday Times' National Gallery Extension Competition, 1959
Hertfordshire Primary School Competition, 1959
(with Ron Herron) BEA Office and Terminal, Manchester*** 1959
(with Ron Herron) BEA Office, Regent Street, London*** 1960
(with Ron Herron) BEA Office, Carlton Street, London*** 1960
(with Ron Herron) BEA Terminal, Guernsey*** 1961

Dennis Crompton
Liverpool Catholic Cathedral Competition Project, 1959

David Greene
Mosque, 1959 *Archigram 1* **9**

Ron Herron
Prospect County College for Girls, London*** 1954–7
Hall of Residence, Northampton College of Advanced Technology, London 1958
(with Alan Forrest) Hotel, South Bank, London, 1958
(with Alan Forrest) Television Centre and Offices, South Bank, London, 1958
Woolwich Polytechnic College, London*** 1959

Mike Webb
Furniture Manufacturers' Association Headquarters, High Wycombe, 1958 **10**

Group work, Events, etc.
(Warren Chalk, Dennis Crompton, Ron Herron) South Bank Arts Centre, London: Queen Elizabeth Hall, Hayward Art Gallery, Decks, etc.*** LCC with Norman Engleback and John Attenborough, 1960–2 **120**

1961 **Warren Chalk**
(with John Attenborough, Dennis Crompton, Ron Herron, Terry Kennedy, John Roberts, Alan Waterhouse) Lincoln Civic Centre Competition (mention)

Peter Cook
(with Gordon Sainsbury) Piccadilly Circus Competition Project (highly commended) **9**
(with David Greene) Lincoln Civic Centre Competition
Gas House Competition (first prize)

David Greene
Poems in *Archigram 1* **8**
Cliffside Entertainments Stalk **11**

Group work, Events, etc.
Archigram 1, May 1961 **8–9**

1962 **Warren Chalk**
(with Ron Herron) Liverpool University Halls of Residence Competition

Peter Cook
Metal Cabin Housing **10**
(with David Greene) Nottingham Shopping Viaduct **38**

David Greene
Spray Plastic House **11**
(with Peter Cook) Berkshire County Offices Competition
(with Peter Cook) Harlow Housing Competition

Mike Webb
Sin Centre, Leicester Square, London, 1959–62 **12**

Group work, Events, etc.
Archigram 2, April 1962
Euston Station Redevelopment, London (Taylor Woodrow Design Group, under Theo Crosby), 1962–5

1963 **Warren Chalk**
(with Ron Herron) Interchange transport node **22–3**
Liverpool Comprehensive Area Development Project

Peter Cook
Editorial, *Archigram 3* **16**
'City Within Existing Technology' **38**
'Europa' **38**
Housing for Charing Cross Road **38**
Come-Go Project
Ideal Home House Competition
Shopping Centre Project, Oxford Street, London

Dennis Crompton
City Synthesiser Project

David Greene
(with Mike Webb) 'Story of A Thing' **22–3**

Ron Herron
(with Warren Chalk) Shops, Old Street, London
(with Warren Chalk) Woolwich Ferry Dock Installations

Mike Webb
Ideal Home House Competition

Group work, Events, etc.
Archigram 3, August 1963 (cover by Peter Taylor) **14–16**
Living City Exhibition, June 1963: Institute of Contemporary Arts, London; Manchester City Art Gallery; Walker Art Gallery, Cambridge*** **18–23**
Fulham Study: Redevelopment of Twilight Areas in London
Exhibition of Fulham Study, RIBA, London (Taylor Woodrow Design Group, under Theo Crosby)

Publications
'Il Grattacielo', *Edilizia Moderna No. 80* (Milan)
'Il Novocento e l'Architettura', *Edilizia Moderna No. 81* (Milan)
Review and fifty-page catalogue of Living City Exhibition in *Living Arts Magazine No. 2* (London 1963)

1964 **Warren Chalk**
'Space Probe', *Archigram 4* **28**
Underwater City **32**
Plug-in capsule homes **44–5**
(with Peter Cook) Hull Development Competition

Peter Cook
Plug-in City 1964-6 **36-43**

Dennis Crompton
Plug-in City National Network **39**
Computer City **40**

David Greene
ICSB 63.4 – A mechanized Pod-House **31**

Ron Herron
Science fact/Science fiction assemblage for *Archigram 4* **30**
Walking City **48–9**
Walking City on the Ocean **32**
City of London Office Block Project
Stand for IBSAC Exhibition Project
Ulster Museum Competition, Ireland (second prize)

Mike Webb
Auto-Environment

Group work, Events, etc.
Archigram 4, May 1964 (cover by Warren Chalk)
Archigram 5, November 1964 (cover by Rae and Ben Fether)
(Warren Chalk, Peter Cook, Dennis Crompton) Kensington Housing Study

Publications
'Recherches', *L'Architecture D'Aujourd'hui June/July 1964* (Paris)
'Plug-in City Study', *Architectural Forum 8 September 1964* (New York)
'Plug-in City', *Sunday Times Colour Supplement 20 September 1964* (London)

1965 **Warren Chalk**
Ocean City Project
(with Ron Herron) Gasket Homes **46–7**

Peter Cook
Plug-in City at Paddington **40–1**
Plug-in University **42–3**
Hornsey Capsules and Family Cages 1965–6 **47, 61**
Plug'N Clip Dwellings **60**
(with Dennis Crompton) Plug'N Clip Unit*** (exhibition at Woolands, London)
Mound **120**
Project for locating the LSE at Euston
Plug-in Mews: first stage in transition from existing houses to Plug-in City

Dennis Crompton
(with Ron Herron) Industrialised Hospital Building: 500-bed maternity unit, Reading
FFG Machine

David Greene
Living Pod **51–4**

Ron Herron
Capsule Pier **46**
(with Dennis Crompton) Monorail Transportation Study and Exhibition***

Leisure Zone: Seaside Net
Airhouse Project, Cardiff Castle Exhibition

Group work, Events, etc.
Exhibition at the Salines Royales, Arc et Senans, Doubs, France***
Archigram 6, November 1965 (cover by Jeff Reeve)
(Peter Cook, Dennis Crompton, Ron Herron) Industrialised Housing Project for Southall Borough Council (for 800 families)
Archigram Exhibition, November 1965, Architectural Association, London***

Publications
Reyner Banham, 'A Clip-On Architecture', *Design Quarterly No. 63* (Minneapolis)
'Leaves from the Silver Book', *AD November 1965* (London). Most comprehensive magazine coverage to that date (including reprint of Reyner Banham's article 'A Clip-On Architecture')
'Pop-Arkitektur', *Aftonbladet 23 May 1965* (Stockholm)
'Town Planning', *A No. 2* (Helsinki)
'Architecture en Grande Bretagne', *L'Architecture D'Aujourd'hui No. 50* (Paris)
'Archigram: Magazine for New Ideas in Architecture', *Megascope No. 3, November 1965* (Bristol)
Peter Collins, 'Plug'N Clip', *Sunday Times Colour Supplement September 1965* (London)

1966 **Warren Chalk**
'Housing as a Consumer Product', *Arena March 1966* **18**
'Ghosts and Phantoms', *Archigram 7* **84–5**
Frost Book Jacket

Peter Cook
Blow-Out Village **60–1**
Bournemouth Nets Project
Local

David Greene
Living Pods: high-rise structure **80**
(with Mike Webb) Drive-in housing **54–5**

Ron Herron
(with Barry Snowden) Free Time Inflatable Dwelling***
Leisure Study: Inflatable Units for sea, land and air

Mike Webb
Drive-in Housing Units 1964–6 **56–9**
Auto-Environment **58–9**
Rent-A-Wall **66–7**

Group work, Events, etc.
Archigram 7, December 1966 (cover by James Meller)
International Dialogues in Experimental Architecture (IDEA): exhibition and conference at Folkestone, 30 June 1966***

Publications
Blow-Out Village and Cage Housing, *Woman's Mirror September 1966* (London)
Peter Cook, 'The Environment Must Fit our Needs', *Chicago Daily News 3 September 1966* (Chicago)
Article on IDEA exhibition at Folkestone, *BAU No. 3* (Vienna)
Warren Chalk, 'Architecture as a Consumer Product', *Arena March 1966* (London)
'Drive-in Housing', *AD November 1966* (London)
Mike Webb, 'Cushicle and Auto-Environment', *AD November 1966* (London)
Dennis Crompton and Ron Herron, 'Industrialised Hospital Building, Reading', *AD April 1966* (London)
David Greene, 'Living Pod', *AD November 1966* (London)
'Folkestone', *AD June 1966* (London)
Mike Webb, 'Mobile Unit', *Studies in Environmental Design Clip-Kit – AA* (London)

1967 **Warren Chalk**
'The 1940s', *Archigram 6* **73**

Peter Cook
Moment-Village **75**
(book) *Architecture: Action and Plan* (London, New York, Milan and Tokyo 1967)

Ron Herron
Free Time Node Trailer Cage **59**
(with Barry Snowden) Air Hab and Air Hab Village **58**
(with Barry Snowden) Free Time Node **59**

Mike Webb
Cushicle 1966–7 **64–5**

Group work, Events, etc.
Living 1990*** (project and exhibition at Harrods, London) **62–3**
Control and Choice: housing study and exhibit at the Paris Biennale*** 1967 **68–74**
Indesem: conference at Delft, Holland
'Current Archigram Preoccupations – Eight Non-Fictions' (Terry Hamilton Memorial Lecture), Institute of Contemporary Arts, London
Beyond Architecture: exhibition at the Museum of Modern Art, Oxford***
St Katherine's Dock Development

Publications
'Living 1990', *Weekend Telegraph* (London)
Peter Cook, 'Control or Choice', *Control* magazine (London)
Hogar y Arquitectura No. 72, September/October 1967 (Madrid): whole issue devoted to Archigram
Reyner Banham, 'The Archigram Vision', *Hogar y Arquitectura No. 72*
Peter Cook, 'Mirrors', *Arena May 1967* (London)
'The Pluralistic Situation' (seminar), *Arena September 1967* (London)
Warren Chalk, 'This City Now', *Habitat January/February 1967* (Montreal)
'Experiments and Utopia', 'Living Pod', *Bauen und Wohnen May 1967* (Zurich)
'Building in England', *Bauen und Wohnen December 1967* (Zurich)
'Control and Choice Living', *Bauwelt 46/47* (Berlin)
'House 1990', *AD March 1967* (London)
'Control and Choice', *AD October 1967* (London)
Peter Cook, 'Archigram, The Name and the Magazine', *Perspecta 11* (Yale)
'English Architects', *Kenchiku Bunka January 1967* (Tokyo)
'Metamorphosis', *L'Architecture D'Aujourd'hui December 1967* (Paris)
F. G. Quintana, 'Nueva Arquitectura', *Hogar y Arquitectura No. 72*
Mike Webb, 'Cushicle', *Domus December 1967* (Milan)

1968 **Warren Chalk**
(with Ron Herron) Housing Development, Santa Monica, California

Peter Cook
Sea Farming **32**
Instant City in a Field **90**
Instant City at Bournemouth **92**
Info Gonks **100**

Dennis Crompton
Instant City Model **88**
Media Experiments 1–4
(with Peter Cook) House for Today Competition

David Greene
Inflatable Suit-Home **82**
Rokplug and Logplug **110–11**

Ron Herron
Tuned Suburb **80–1**
Oasis **81**
Urban Action Tune-Up (Instant City) **86**
Self-Destruct Environ-Pole (Instant City) **89**
Instant City at Los Angeles **90–1**
Holographic Scene-Setter (Instant City) **93**
Instant City in the Desert **94**

Mike Webb
Suitaloon **76–7**
Fluid and Air Wall **78**
Magic Carpet and Brunhilda's Magic Ring of Fire **78**

Group work, Events, etc.
(Peter Cook, Dennis Crompton, Ron Herron) Instant City (funded from 1969–70 by the Graham Foundation of Chicago) 1968–71 **88**
Milanogram***, Archigram exhibit at the fourteenth Milan Triennale
Springhall Wharf Housing
Summer Collection Woburn
Archigram 8 (cover based on Instant Village Project)

Publications
'The Visionary Tradition in Architecture', *Metropolitan Museum of Art Bulletin April 1968* (New York)
Peter Cook, 'Conversations', *Arena June/July 1968* (London)
'Inflatable World', *Sunday Times 12 May 1968* (London)
'Control and Choice', *Domus 458* (Milan)
'Milanogram', *Domus 468* (Milan)
'Cushicle', 'Living Pod', 'Milanogram', *Bauwelt 10 June 1968* (Berlin)
Denise Scott-Brown, 'Little Magazines in Architecture and Urbanism', *Journal of the American Institute of Planners July 1968* (Baltimore)
'Tendances', *L'Architecture D'Aujourd'hui 139* (Paris)
'Ideas Circus', 'Milanogram', *Architects' Journal 29 May 1968* (London)
'Milanogram', *AD April 1968* (London)
Mike Webb, 'Drive-in Housing', 'Suitaloon', *AD June 1968* (London)
'Archigram at the Milan Triennale', *AD July 1968* (London)
'Oslogram', *Bilag Til Arkitektnytt No. 12 1968* (Oslo)
Mike Webb, 'Cushicle', *Summa 13 November 1968* (Buenos Aires)
'Warren Chalk and Ron Herron, English Architects', *Kenchiku Bunka March 1968* (Tokyo)

1969 **Warren Chalk**
(with David Greene) 'Electronic Tomato' **124–5**

Peter Cook
(with Ron Herron) Kassel Documenta Eventstructure **94–5**
(with Dennis Crompton) Soft Scene Monitor***: exhibit at Oslo **95–6**
(with Dennis Crompton) Ideas Circus **101**

David Greene
LAWUN (Locally Available World Unseen Networks) **112–3**
Bottery

Ron Herron
Manzak Robot **124–5**
Enviro-Pill **130–1**
Long Beach Entertainments Park, California

Group work, Events, etc
Exhibition at Kunsthalle, Lund, Sweden
Shop for Consortium, London
Archigram Exhibition, April 1969, Camden Arts Centre, London

Publications
'Instant City', *Domus No. 477* (Milan)
'Archigram's Exhibitions', *AAQ July 1969* (London)
Charles Jencks, 'Pop-Non Pop', *AAQ April 1969* (London)
'London – Centre of Tactility', *Esquire December 1969* (New York)
'Process and Imagination', *Design Quarterly 74/75* (Minneapolis)
Peter Wolf, 'The Structure of Motion in the City', *Art in America January 1969* (New York)
'Instant City and Rokplug and Logplug', *AD May 1969* (London)
Articles by Warren Chalk and David Greene in issue of *AD* entitled 'Despite Popular Demand' (London, September 1969)
'Archigram – Drug-in City', *AD November 1969* (London)
'Milanogram', *Toshi Jukatu January 1969* (Tokyo)
Articles in *Actualidades Tecnico Cientificas Arquitectura No. 1* (Havana)
J. K. Watkins, 'Ultimate Flexibility', *Architects' Journal, 1 October 1969* (London)
Astragal, 'Cooking the Books', *Architects' Journal, 29 October 1969* (London)
'Archigram Group: Instant City', *L'Architecture D'Aujourd'hui October/November 1969* (Paris)
'Instant City: The Archigram Group', *Werk November 1969* (Zurich)
Ron Herron, 'Arata Isozaki', *Lotus No. 2* (Milan)

1970 **Warren Chalk**
Bathamatic **125**

Peter Cook
Instant City Airships **98–9**
Metamorphosis of an English Town **126–7**
Room of 1000 Delights **130–1**
(book) *Experimental Architecture* (London and New York 1970)

Ron Herron
Instant City Airships **97–8**
(with Barry Snowden) Promotional Event Kit **100**
(with William L. Pereira Associates, Los Angeles) Ford Properties Development, Detroit
(with William L. Pereira Associates, Los Angeles) Pan American Air Terminal

Mike Webb
Dreams Come True **129–30**

Group work, Events, etc.
Interior of Archigram Capsule*** at Expo '70, Osaka, Japan **96–7**
Archigram 9 (cover by Tony Rickaby)
(Ken Allinson, Peter Cook, Dennis Crompton, Colin Fournier, David Greene, Tony Rickaby) Competition Project for Monte Carlo Entertainments Centre (also known as Features: Monte Carlo) (first prize) **102–9**
(Peter Cook, Dennis Crompton, Colin Fournier, Ron Herron, Diana Jowsey; engineer: Frank Newby) Working stages of Competition Project for Monte Carlo Entertainments Centre, 1971 onwards
(Ken Allinson, Peter Cook, Dennis Crompton, Colin Fournier, Margaret Helfand, Ron Herron, Diana Jowsey, Bobby Wilson) Bournemouth Steps **120–1**
(Ken Allinson, Peter Cook, Dennis Crompton, Ron Herron, Diana Jowsey) British Rail and British Industry exhibits***, for the Central Office of Information, at British Design Exhibition, Paris
Seminars and construction on Instant City Airship Model, International Institute of Design Summer Session, Bartlett School of Architecture, London

Publications
Comprehensive coverage of Archigram in *Kenchiku-Bunka No. 279* (Tokyo)
'La Ciudad Viviente', *Cuadernos Summa No. 10* (Buenos Aires)
'Monaco Underground', *Architects' Journal January 1970* (London)
'Archigram Competition – Monte Carlo', *AD September 1970* (London)
David Greene, 'LAWUN', *AD September 1970* (London)
Peter Cook and Ron Herron, 'Instant City in Progress', *AD November 1970* (London)
Peter Cook, 'Some Notes on the Archigram Syndrome'; Warren Chalk, 'Architecture as a Consumer Product', *Japan Architect July 1970* (Tokyo)
Peter Cook, 'The Many Sided Archigram', *AAQ Autumn 1970* (London)
David Greene, 'Living Pod', *Toshi-Jutaku July 1970* (Tokyo)
'Instant City', *Design Quarterly 1970* (Minneapolis)
'Monte Carlo', *L'Architecture D'Aujourd'hui November 1970* (Paris)

1971 **Peter Cook**
Instant Country **98**
Addhox **132–3**
Foulness Study
(with Diana Jowsey, Stuart Lever, Bernard Tschumi) 'Chameleon' Project for Monte Carlo Summer Casino **122–3**

David Greene
Imagining the Invisible University **116–7**
(with Mike Barnard) The Electric Aborigine **117**

Ron Herron
(with Ken Allinson, Colin Fournier) 'Palm Tree' Project for Monte Carlo Summer Casino **122–3**

Group work, Events, etc.
Foulness workshop and seminars, International Institute of Design Summer Session, Architectural Association, London
First showing of Archigram Opera (Roadshow subsequently shown extensively in England, United States and Europe), Summer Session, Architectural Association, London

Publications
'La Distruzione dell'Ogetto', *IN No. 2/3* (Milan)
Ron Herron, 'Walking City', *IN No. 2/1 January/February* (Milan)
Article on Archigram projects and similar projects from the USSR, *Architecture USSR 728* (Leningrad)
'Student Magazines', *AAQ July/September 1971* (London)
'A Letter from Peter Cook to Warren Chalk', *AD February 1971* (London)
'Archigram 1970–1' (major article) *AD August 1971* (London)
Peter Cook, '75 New Architects', *AD December 1971* (London)
'The New Architecture', *Newsweek 19 April 1971* (New York)
Warren Chalk, 'Bathamatic', *Deutsche Bauzeitung April 1971* (Stuttgart)

1972 **Peter Cook**
Foulness Settlements **134–5**
Hedgerow Village **134–5**
Crater City **134–5**
The Urban Mark (The City as a Responsive Environment) **139**
Orchard Place

David Greene
(with Mike Barnard) Video Notebook **118**

Ron Herron
It's A **136–7**
(with Diana Jowsey) Tuning London
(with Diana Jowsey) IID Graphics

Group work, Events, etc.
Adhocs Gallery***
(Peter Cook) Cheerful Chats sequence, International Institute of Design Summer Session, Institute of Contemporary Arts, London

Publications
'Utopia', *Du, January 1972* (Zurich)
'An Architect in Ambivalence', *A + U, January 1972* (Tokyo)
'The Corb that Might Have Been', *AD April 1972* (London)
Peter Cook, 'Towards a Quietly Technologized Folk-Suburbia'
Warren Chalk, 'Archigram Opera', *AD April 1972* (London)
'Map of London', *AD May 1972* (London)
Manhattan Workshop Book for Consolidated Edison, N.Y. (London, 1972)
Review of Experimental Architecture, *Bauwelt 21 February 1972* (Berlin)

In preparation at the time of publication
Archigram Exhibition: Institute of Contemporary Arts, London; Walker Art Center, Minneapolis; Architecture League, New York; Graham Foundation, Chicago; Kunsthalle Hamburg; Franz Hals Museum, Haarlem
Architectural Association 125th Anniversary Exhibition
Rod Stewart House
Children's Adventure Playground, Milton Keynes
Malaysia Exhibition, Commonwealth Institute, London